Honoring the Wise

Australian College of Theology Monograph Series

SERIES EDITOR GRAEME R. CHATFIELD

The ACT Monograph Series, generously supported by the Board of Directors of the Australian College of Theology, provides a forum for publishing quality research theses and studies by its graduates and affiliated college staff in the broad fields of Biblical Studies, Christian Thought and History, and Practical Theology with Wipf and Stock Publishers of Eugene, Oregon. The ACT selects the best of its doctoral and research masters theses as well as monographs that offer the academic community, scholars, church leaders and the wider community uniquely Australian and New Zealand perspectives on significant research topics and topics of current debate. The ACT also provides opportunity for contributors beyond its graduates and affiliated college staff to publish monographs which support the mission and values of the ACT.

Rev. Dr. Graeme Chatfield
Series Editor and Associate Dean

"Seldom do you read scholarship that explores so broadly around a single theme and then engages with remarkable relevancy the modern world. After investigating the complex portrayal of wisdom in the Old Testament, this book turns our attention to a diverse array of contemporary contexts and applications. A fitting tribute to a career built on wisdom."

—**Nathan Lovell**, George Whitefield College

"With exegetical care and pastoral sensibility, these articles are a fitting tribute to a man who has taught and shepherded students for thirty years. The contributors ably cover a wide range of texts in the Hebrew Bible, and their accessible insights will no doubt make their way into my classroom as I share them with students. Bravo to everyone involved, especially the honoree!"

—**Carmen Joy Imes**, Talbot School of Theology, Biola University

"A rich, informative, and enjoyable collection of essays exploring the biblical theme of wisdom. These varied and insightful contributions demonstrate well the need to read wisdom (and not just in the obvious places) as well as the need to read and teach wisely."

—**Tim Davy**, All Nations Christian College

"Lindsay Wilson's colleagues and past students have gifted him, and us, with a large and wide-ranging collection of essays whose focus is consistently biblical. Between them, they draw from across the Old Testament to demonstrate that biblical wisdom cannot be confined to biblical wisdom literature. Whatever their interests, students of the Bible will find something in this volume to stimulate, interest, and provoke them to think more deeply about wisdom."

—**Andrew Shead**, Moore Theological College

"I am delighted to commend this wide-ranging collection of essays to honor a good friend and fine scholar. The focus is on wisdom, but the scope is much broader than simply biblical wisdom literature. The international flavor is notable, with contributions from Europe, Africa, and Asia, as well as Australia."

—**David L. Baker**, All Nations Christian College

"The essays contained in *Honoring the Wise* bear the hallmarks of the Old Testament scholar they are written to honor: careful analysis of the biblical text, wise judgments, readings with a strong ethical flavor, and pertinent application to the current world. It is not common for there to be such a concord between what scholars spend their life studying and their own character and life, but this is true for Lindsay Wilson."

—**Gregory Goswell**, Christ College

"Like wisdom itself, this stimulating collection of essays is concerned with all of life: the pastoral and practical as much as the academic. There is much to think about, much to delight in, and much to put into practice. It will indeed be an honor for Dr. Wilson to receive."

—**Ros Clarke**, Associate Director, Church Society, England

"Very few academics combine the abilities of insightful scholar, compelling teacher, compassionate pastor, wise counselor, and advocate for those on the margins with the integrity of Lindsay Wilson. The chapters of this Festschrift confirm my experience of working with Lindsay within the setting of the Australian College of Theology over twenty years."

—**Graeme Chatfield**, Australian College of Theology

"This is a stimulating and varied collection. Diverse contributors explore different aspects of wisdom in the Bible, in life, and in Christian ministry with insight and understanding. Those who read it will gain much from it."

—**James Robson**, Ministry Director, Keswick Ministries

"As a member of the Ridley community for several years and a fellow member of Tyndale Fellowship, I offer my wholehearted endorsement of this work that celebrates a life committed to Old Testament research and teaching as well as ministry in the global church. Lindsay Wilson is a most worthy recipient of such a volume, with its prestigious contributors from around the world."

—**Brittany N. Melton**, Palm Beach Atlantic University

Honoring the Wise

Wisdom in Scripture, Ministry, and Life:
Celebrating Lindsay Wilson's Thirty Years at Ridley

Edited by
JILL FIRTH
and
PAUL A. BARKER

WIPF & STOCK · Eugene, Oregon

HONORING THE WISE
Wisdom in Scripture, Ministry, and Life: Celebrating Lindsay Wilson's Thirty Years at Ridley

Australian College of Theology Monograph Series

Copyright © 2022 Wipf and Stock Publishers. All rights reserved. Except for brief quotations in critical publications or reviews, no part of this book may be reproduced in any manner without prior written permission from the publisher. Write: Permissions, Wipf and Stock Publishers, 199 W. 8th Ave., Suite 3, Eugene, OR 97401.

Wipf & Stock
An Imprint of Wipf and Stock Publishers
199 W. 8th Ave., Suite 3
Eugene, OR 97401

www.wipfandstock.com

PAPERBACK ISBN: 978-1-6667-3647-2
HARDCOVER ISBN: 978-1-6667-9480-9
EBOOK ISBN: 978-1-6667-9481-6

04/05/22

Scripture quotations marked CSB are from the Christian Standard Bible®, copyright © 2017 by Holman Bible Publishers. Used by permission. Christian Standard Bible®, and CSB® are federally registered trademarks of Holman Bible Publishers, all rights reserved.

Scripture quotations marked ESV are from the Holy Bible, English Standard Version®, copyright © 2001 by Crossway, a publishing ministry of Good News Publishers. Used by permission. All rights reserved.

Scripture quotations marked HCSB are from the Holman Christian Standard Bible®, copyright © 1999, 2000, 2002, 2003, 2009 by Holman Bible Publishers. Used by permission. Holman Christian Standard Bible®, Holman CSB®, and HCSB® are federally registered trademarks of Holman Bible Publishers.

Scripture quotations marked KJV are taken from the 21st Century King James Version®, copyright © 1994. Used by permission of Deuel Enterprises, Inc., Gary, SD 57237. All rights reserved.

Scripture quotations marked NASB are from the New American Standard Bible®, copyright © 1960, 1971, 1977, 1995, 2020 by The Lockman Foundation. Used by permission. All rights reserved.

Scripture quotations marked NIV are taken from the Holy Bible, New International Version®, NIV®, copyright © 1973, 1978, 1984, 2011 by Biblica, Inc.™ Used by permission of Zondervan. All rights reserved.

Scripture quotations marked NRSV are from the New Revised Standard Version Bible, copyright © 1989 the Division of Christian Education of the National Council of the Churches of Christ in the United States of America. Used by permission. All rights reserved.

Scripture quotations marked RSV are from the Revised Standard Version Bible, copyright © 1946, 1952 and 1971 the Division of Christian Education of the National Council of the Churches of Christ in the United States of America. Used by permission. All rights reserved.

COVER ART

Anne G. Ellison, "Between the Serpent and the Cross"

This work shows man and woman, the first humans facing each other, representing the human race. In the background, the serpent and the cross represent the backdrop to the Old Testament, the period between the fall and redemption.

זָרַח בַּחֹשֶׁךְ אוֹר לַיְשָׁרִים
חַנּוּן וְרַחוּם וְצַדִּיק

They rise in the darkness as a light for the upright;
they are gracious, merciful, and righteous.
Psalm 112:4 (NRSV)

Contents

Contributors | xi

Preface | xvii
—Jill Firth and Paul A. Barker

Abbreviations | xix

Introduction | xxv
—Jill Firth and Paul A. Barker

Part I: Wisdom in Narrative

1 The Theological Purpose of Wisdom Elements in Exodus 1–2 | 3
   —Katherine Davis

2 Judges 19 as Wisdom: Sitting with the Wise in Ambivalence and Discontinuity | 15
   —Andrew Judd

3 Critical Views of Wisdom in Samuel's Revolt Narratives | 28
   —David G. Firth

4 Honoring the Wise King: The Solomonic Ideal in 1–2 Kings and Beyond | 39
   —Andrew T. Abernethy

Part II: Wisdom in Prophecy

5 Finding Relational Wisdom: Terror, Shame, and Retribution in the Book of Jeremiah | 53

—Jill Firth

6 The Gracious Absence of the Love of God in the Book of Ezekiel—A Missional Reading | 68

—Andrew Sloane

7 Knowledge and Rebellion, Judgment and Grace: An Examination of the Impact of the Portrayal of Yhwh in the Golden Calf Narrative on Joel and Jonah | 82

—Heather Reid

8 Habakkuk's Calling for a Faithful Response to a Faithful God | 97

—Lwin Thida

Part III: Wisdom in the Writings

9 Dusted Off and Polished to Fresh Luster: David's Crown in Psalm 132 | 111

—Charlie Fletcher

10 Jesus, Job, and the Suffering Image of God—An Exploration in Biblical Anthropology | 126

—Andrew R. Prideaux

11 A Study of the Relational Construct Behind the Discipline of the Lord (Proverbs 3:11–12) | 145

—David C. Ray

Part IV: Wisdom in Preaching and Teaching

12 Wise Preaching from Proverbs 10–29 | 161

—Paul A. Barker

13 Honoring a Wise Tanzanian Woman: Ufoo Kassa George's *Biblia Na Utajiri* (The Bible and Wealth) | 176

—Tamie Davis

14 "I Hear and Forget, I See and Remember, I Do and Understand": Helping People in Central Asia to Understand and Use the Old Testament | 191
    —Robin Payne

15 Worldly Wisdom in 1 Corinthians and Its Implications for Theological Education | 206
    —Brian S. Rosner

Part V: Wisdom in Life

16 Where Shall Wisdom Be Found? | 219
    —Peter Adam

17 Old Testament Calls to Thankfulness | 233
    —Andrew S. Malone

18 Waiting with Wisdom | 249
    —Michelle Brennan

19 Lindsay Wilson: A "Living Treasure" | 261
    —Ruth Weatherlake (Editor and Compiler)

Major Publications by Lindsay Wilson | 279
    —Ruth Weatherlake

Contributors

Andrew T. Abernethy

Andrew T. Abernethy is Associate Professor of Old Testament and Degree Coordinator for the MA in Biblical Exegesis at Wheaton College. His writings include *God's Messiah in the Old Testament* (Baker, 2020) with Gregory Goswell, *The Book of Isaiah and God's Kingdom* (IVP, 2016), and *Discovering Isaiah: Content, Interpretation, Reception* (SPCK, Eerdmans, 2021).

Peter Adam

Peter Adam trained for the ministry at Ridley College. He also studied at London and Durham Universities and lectured at St John's College, Durham. Peter became Vicar of St Jude's Carlton in 1982, where he served for twenty years. He was Principal of Ridley Melbourne from 2002 to 2012.

Paul A. Barker

Paul Barker is a bishop in the Anglican Diocese of Melbourne, and a former visiting lecturer and board member at Ridley College. His PhD on Deuteronomy was through the University of Bristol. For some years Paul was Langham Preaching and Scholars Coordinator for Asia and has taught and trained preachers with Lindsay Wilson in several Asian countries.

Michelle Brennan

Michelle Brennan is married to John, a Presbyterian minister. She taught Hebrew and tutored in New Testament Greek and Old Testament at Ridley (2000–2001). Since graduating from Ridley with her MTh on the topic of "Is the Concept of Resurrection Evident in the Pentateuch, Former Prophets or Psalter?," which was supervised by Lindsay Wilson, Michelle has ministered with John at Horsham, Sorrento-Rye, and currently at the Ballarat North Presbyterian Parish.

Katherine Davis

After completing a Master of Theology under the supervision of Lindsay Wilson at Ridley College, Katherine Davis completed her doctorate in 2018 through Trinity College, Bristol (University of Bristol) focusing on the rhetorical function of Leviticus within the Pentateuch. She is currently a Research Fellow at Sydney Missionary and Bible College and is writing the Exodus commentary for the Zondervan Exegetical Commentary of the Old Testament series.

Tamie Davis

Tamie Davis is a PhD Candidate with Sydney Missionary and Bible College researching the theology of prosperity among a group of Tanzanian women. She is an Associate Researcher of the Angelina Noble Centre, a gospel worker of CMS Australia and an Associate of Tanzania Fellowship of Evangelical Students. She has been living in Tanzania with her family since 2013.

David G. Firth

David Firth is Tutor in Old Testament and Academic Dean at Trinity College, Bristol. He and his wife served for a number of years with Global Interaction (the mission agency of Australian Baptists) before settling in the UK.

Jill Firth

Jill Firth is a lecturer in Hebrew and Old Testament at Ridley College, Melbourne. She holds a PhD in Old Testament and an MA in Spiritual Direction. She publishes on Jeremiah and Psalms and is writing a commentary on Jeremiah for Cascade's new series, *The Bible in God's World*. With Denise Cooper-Clarke, she recently edited *Grounded in the Body, in Time and Place, in Scripture: Papers by Australian Women Scholars in the Evangelical Tradition*.

Charlie Fletcher

Charlie Fletcher has worked in student ministry in Melbourne and Mexico City, in theological education at Ridley College, and in missionary training with CMS Australia. He now serves as Vicar of All Saints Anglican Church, Clayton. His research interests include the canonical approach to the Psalms and the translatability of Scripture.

Andrew Judd

Andrew Judd, an Anglican minister, joined the faculty at Ridley in 2018, teaching Old Testament and Hermeneutics. He is currently completing his doctorate on Hans-Georg Gadamer, genre theory, and biblical hermeneutics through Sydney University. He is married to Stephanie, also an Anglican minister, and they have two children.

Lwin Thida

Lwin Thida is an Old Testament lecturer at Holy Cross Theological College, Church of the Province of Myanmar. She completed her MTh thesis, "The Character of God and Human Response in the Book of Habakkuk," supervised by Lindsay Wilson at Ridley College. She is married to Mr. Charles Samuels.

Andrew S. Malone

Having arrived to study at Ridley College in 1995, Andrew has completed most subjects and levels offered by the college. Still there, he now teaches and writes in the field of biblical studies and serves as the Dean of Ridley Online.

Robin Payne

Robin Payne (DMin) is an Anglican minister. She taught Old Testament and Hebrew at Ridley, on the faculty and as a visiting lecturer, from 1984 to 1998. Having taught in high schools, parish, and theological colleges for over fifty years, she has spent the last fifteen years teaching with local colleagues in Central Asia.

Andrew R. Prideaux

After reading Classics (University of Melbourne), Andy studied at Ridley College. His MTh on Job was supervised by Lindsay Wilson. A regular contributor to The Gospel Coalition, Andy's work on Job has appeared in *RTR*. His commentary on Job is forthcoming (Aquila, 2022). Since 1999 Andy has served as an AFES Staff Worker at Monash, Melbourne University, and the Simeon Network. Andy and his wife Ness have four children.

David C. Ray

David C. Ray completed his PhD at Ridley College in 2021 under the supervision of Lindsay Wilson and Jill Firth. His thesis focused on conflict and enmity in the Asaph Psalms. Based in Darwin, David is the Diocesan Business Manager/Registrar of the Anglican Diocese of the Northern Territory. David hopes to utilize his skills in commerce, linguistics, and knowledge of the Hebrew Bible to preserve Australian Aboriginal languages.

Heather Reid

Following a move to Melbourne in 2005, Heather was Senior Staff Worker at RMIT University with Australian Fellowship of Evangelical Students and completed an MDiv at Ridley College. She is currently engaged in Old Testament doctoral studies. In 2016, Heather moved to Singapore with her husband, Andrew, and was appointed as a lecturer in Hebrew, Old Testament, and Ministry at the Evangelical Theological College of Asia (ETCAsia).

Brian S. Rosner

Brian Rosner (PhD, Cambridge) is the Principal of Ridley College, having formerly taught at Moore Theological College and the University of Aberdeen. Brian is the author or editor of more than a dozen books, including *The New Dictionary of Biblical Theology*, the Pillar commentary on *1 Corinthians* (co-author Roy E. Ciampa), *Greed as Idolatry*, *Paul and the Law*, and *Known by God*.

Andrew Sloane

Andrew is Lecturer in Old Testament and Christian Thought at Morling College (2002–). He teaches in the areas of OT exegesis and interpretation, integration of faith and work, philosophy of religion, and bioethics. Andrew practiced briefly as a doctor before going into Baptist ministry. He taught at

Ridley College in Melbourne (1996–2002). He has published in Old Testament and hermeneutics, ethics, philosophy, and theology. His most recent book is *Vulnerability and Care: Christian Reflections on the Philosophy of Medicine* (2016).

Ruth Weatherlake

Ruth has served as the College Librarian at Ridley College, Melbourne since 1992. She graduated from Ridley with a Bachelor of Theology.

Anne G. Ellison

Cover Art

Anne's academic background is interdisciplinary, including a PhD in Political Science, a PGradDip in Business Administration, and a Master of Divinity. Her professional career spans tertiary and specialist medical education. In 2015, she became a full-time artist exploring the interface between academia, art, and the Christian faith. Her website is https://www.annellisonart.com.

Lindsay and Clarissa Wilson on the old Ridley front lawn, 1995

Lindsay with Ronald Laldinsuah at Tyndale Old Testament Study Group, Cambridge, 2018

Preface

Lindsay Wilson has been a wise friend, colleague, mentor, and teacher to many at Ridley College and beyond, and we are delighted to present him with this volume in honor of his thirty years of teaching at Ridley. This book has been authored by past and present colleagues and research students of Lindsay, and co-edited by Jill Firth, who has been Lindsay's friend, student, and colleague for over twenty of those years, and Paul Barker, who has been a friend and colleague since Lindsay's first year at Ridley.

Lindsay is Senior Lecturer in Old Testament at Ridley College in Melbourne, a Senior Research Scholar in the Australian College of Theology, and former Ridley Academic Dean and Vice Principal. He has published commentaries, dictionary articles, and book chapters on Job and Proverbs, and a book chapter on Ecclesiastes, but his wide-ranging interests across the canon are reflected in his PhD on the intersection of wisdom and covenant in the Joseph narrative, and his publications on Genesis, Joshua, Isaiah, and Psalms, and his co-edited collection on wisdom that also examines the Song of Songs, Ruth, Psalms, and narrative texts. Lindsay is currently working on a book on wisdom and Old Testament ethics and is looking forward to further research on wisdom in non-wisdom books. A bibliography of his major publications can be found at the end of this volume, along with words of appreciation from colleagues and students.

In his thirty years at Ridley, Lindsay has delighted in teaching new courses, and in incorporating various approaches, including feminist readings, and cross-cultural concerns. As well as Wisdom Literature, Lindsay has taught courses including Hebrew, Genesis, Pentateuch, Former Prophets, Ezekiel, Old Testament Apocalyptic, Psalter, Megillot, Eighth Century

Prophets, Ethics, Biblical Theology, and Old Testament Preaching. He has taught graduate and postgraduate courses at SAIACS (South Asia Institute of Advanced Christian Studies, Bangalore, India); Zarephath Bible Institute (Rawalpindi, Pakistan); STM (Seminari Theoloji Malaysia, Seremban, Malaysia); MEGST (Myanmar Evangelical Graduate School of Theology, Yangon, Myanmar); Colombo Theological Seminary (Sri Lanka); and Lanka Bible College (Sri Lanka), among other places. Lindsay has led preaching training for Langham/Crosslinks in Yangon and Malaysia, and he attended the ICETE (International Council for Evangelical Theological Education) conference in Antalya, Turkey, in 2015. Since 1994, he has led many study tours to Israel, Greece, and Turkey, often with Paul Barker. His generous mentoring of students and staff, and commitment to appointing women, is greatly valued. He has contributed to student ministry, and has been a director of the Australian Institute of Archaeology, and on the editorial board of *Buried History* and *Colloquium*.

Lindsay has supervised doctorates and master's theses on hermeneutics, Hosea, Psalms, Lamentations, Resurrection, Job, and Habakkuk, including Michelle Brennan, "Is the Concept of Resurrection Evident in the Pentateuch, Former Prophets or Psalter?" MTh, 2003; Andrew R. Prideaux, "The Relationship between the Creator and the Creature in the Book of Job: An Exploration of the Theme of the Book of Job," MTh, 2006; Katherine M. Smith, "A Theology of God's Grace in the Psalter," MTh, 2010; Andrew Reid, "Evangelical Hermeneutics and Old Testament Preaching: A Critical Analysis of Graeme Goldsworthy's Theory and Practice," ThD, 2011; C. J. Fletcher, "The Return of the King: The Davidic Motif in Book V of the Psalter," MTh, 2012; Ronald Laldinsuah, "Responsibility, Chastisement and Restoration: Relational Justice in the Book of Hosea," ThD, 2014; Gillian Firth, "The Representation of David in Psalms 140–143," PhD, 2016; Lwin Thida, "The Character of God and Human Response in the Book of Habakkuk," MTh, 2017; David Ray, "Conflict and Enmity in the Asaph Psalms," PhD, 2020; and Heather Reid, "Reading Lamentations in the Light of Exodus 34:6–7 and Its Context Within the Narrative of the Golden Calf," PhD, forthcoming, 2022. Lindsay was also co-supervisor of Karl Deenick, "A Biblical Theology of Circumcision as a Sign of Righteousness by Faith," PhD, 2016.

Along with all the contributors, we congratulate Lindsay on his thirty years of service, so far.

Jill Firth
Paul Barker
Melbourne, August 2021

Abbreviations

AB	Anchor Bible
ABD	*Anchor Bible Dictionary*. Edited by David Noel Freedman. 6 vols. New York: Doubleday, 1992
ACT	Australian College of Theology
AFES	Australian Fellowship of Evangelical Students
AGJU	Arbeiten zur Geschichte des antiken Judentums und des Urchristentums
AIL	Ancient Israel and Its Literature
ANE	Ancient Near East
AOTC	Abingdon Old Testament Commentaries
ApOTC	Apollos Old Testament Commentary
AYB	Anchor Yale Bible Commentaries
BCOTWP	Baker Commentary on the Old Testament Wisdom and Psalms
BDB	Brown, Francis, S. R. Driver, and Charles A. Briggs. *A Hebrew and English Lexicon of the Old Testament*
BETL	Bibliotheca Ephemeridum Theologicarum Lovaniensium
BHT	Beiträge zur historischen Theologie

BN	*Biblische Notizen*
BSac	*Bibliotheca Sacra*
BST	The Bible Speaks Today
BZAW	Beihefte zur Zeitschrift für die alttestamentliche Wissenschaft
CBQ	*Catholic Biblical Quarterly*
CSB	Christian Standard Bible
DCH	*Dictionary of Classical Hebrew.* Edited by David J. A. Clines. 9 vols. Sheffield: Sheffield Phoenix, 1993–2014
DOTWPW	*Dictionary of the Old Testament: Wisdom, Poetry and Writings.* Edited by Tremper Longman III and Peter Enns. Downers Grove: IVP Academic, 2008
ECC	Eerdmans Critical Commentary
EEC	Evangelical Exegetical Commentary
ESV	English Standard Version
GKC	*Gesenius' Hebrew Grammar.* Edited by Emil Kautzsch. Translated by Arthur E. Cowley. 2nd ed. Oxford: Clarendon, 1910
HALOT	*The Hebrew and Aramaic Lexicon of the Old Testament.* Ludwig Koehler, Walter Baumgartner, and Johann J. Stamm. Translated and edited under the supervision of Mervyn E. J. Richardson. 4 vols. Leiden: Brill, 1994–1999
HB	Hebrew Bible
HBM	Hebrew Bible Monographs
HCOT	Historical Commentary on the Old Testament
HCSB	Holman Christian Standard Bible
IBC	Interpretation: A Bible Commentary for Teaching and Preaching
ICC	International Critical Commentary
IECOT	International Exegetical Commentary on the Old Testament
IFES	International Fellowship of Evangelical Students

ITC	International Theological Commentary
JAAR	*Journal of the American Academy of Religion*
JANER	*Journal of Ancient Near Eastern Religions*
JBL	*Journal of Biblical Literature*
JCE	*Journal of Christian Education*
JESOT	*Journal for the Evangelical Study of the Old Testament*
JPS	Jewish Publication Society
JSOT	*Journal for the Study of the Old Testament*
JSOTSup	Journal for the Study of the Old Testament Supplement Series
JTS	*Journal of Theological Studies*
KJV	King James Version
LCC	Library of Christian Classics
LEH	Lust, Johan, Erik Eynikel, and Katrin Hauspie, eds. *Greek-English Lexicon of the Septuagint*. Rev. ed. Stuttgart: Deutsche Bibelgesellschaft, 2003
LHBOTS	The Library of Hebrew Bible/Old Testament Studies
LUT84	*Die Bibel Nach Der Übersetzung Martin Luthers*. Stuttgart: Deutsche Bibelgesellschaft, 1984
LXX	Septuagint
MT	Masoretic Text
NAC	New American Commentary
NACSBT	New American Commentary Studies in Bible and Theology
NASB	New American Standard Bible
NCB	New Century Bible
NCBC	New Cambridge Bible Commentary
NDBT	*New Dictionary of Biblical Theology*. Edited by T. Desmond Alexander and Brian S. Rosner. Leicester: Inter-Varsity Press, 2000

NIB	*The New Interpreter's Bible.* Edited by Leander E. Keck. 12 vols. Nashville: Abingdon, 1994–2004
NIBC	New International Biblical Commentary
NICNT	New International Commentary on the New Testament
NICOT	New International Commentary on the Old Testament
NIDOTTE	*New International Dictionary of Old Testament Theology and Exegesis.* Edited by Willem A. VanGemeren. 5 vols. Grand Rapids: Zondervan, 1997
NIGTC	New International Greek Testament Commentary
NIV	New International Version
NIVAC	New International Version Application Commentary
NovTSup	Supplements to Novum Testamentum
NRSV	New Revised Standard Version
NSBT	New Studies in Biblical Theology
NTS	*New Testament Studies*
OTL	Old Testament Library
PBM	Paternoster Biblical Monographs
PNTC	Pillar New Testament Commentary
RBTS	Reading the Bible Today Series
ResQ	*Restoration Quarterly*
RSV	Revised Standard Version
RTR	*Reformed Theological Review*
SBL	Society of Biblical Literature
SBLDS	Society of Biblical Literature Dissertation Series
SHBC	Smyth & Helwys Bible Commentary
SNTSMS	Society for New Testament Studies Monograph Series
TAFES	Tanzania Fellowship of Evangelical Students

THOTC	The Two Horizons Old Testament Commentary
TOTC	Tyndale Old Testament Commentaries
TWOT	*Theological Wordbook of the Old Testament*. Edited by R. Laird Harris, Gleason L. Archer Jr., and Bruce K. Waltke. 2 vols. Chicago: Moody, 1980
TynBul	*Tyndale Bulletin*
VT	*Vetus Testamentum*
VTSup	Supplements to Vetus Testamentum
WBC	Word Biblical Commentary
WBT	Word Biblical Themes
WEC	Wycliffe Exegetical Commentary

Introduction

SINCE THE GARDEN OF Eden, a choice between true and false wisdom has confronted human beings, and the need for discernment is consistent throughout Scripture, as illustrated by the canny decisions of the Hebrew midwives, the moral chaos of the Judges era, dilemmas in the monarchy, and prophetic responses to the turmoil of the threat of empires. The chapters in this volume examine wisdom across the Old Testament, reflecting on texts from Exodus, Judges, 2 Samuel, 1 Kings, Jeremiah, Ezekiel, Joel, Jonah, Habakkuk, and Psalms, along with books which are traditionally considered to belong to a wisdom corpus, such as Job and Proverbs. Wise preaching and teaching are enriched by insights from Tanzania, Myanmar, and Central Asia, and wisdom in daily life is found in biblical practices and is centered on Christ. By such a varied array of approaches, past and present colleagues and research students honor Lindsay Wilson whose wide-ranging research interests include Old Testament ethics and wisdom in non-wisdom books.

The chapters are grouped into five sections: Wisdom in Narrative (chapters 1–4), Wisdom in Prophecy (chapters 5–8), Wisdom in the Writings (chapters 9–11), Wisdom in Preaching and Teaching (chapters 12–15), and Wisdom in Life (chapters 16–19).

1. Wisdom in Narrative (Chapters 1–4)

The first group of essays examines wisdom approaches in narratives in the Pentateuch and Former Prophets. In chapter 1, Katherine Davis takes a literary approach to explore the rhetorical function of wisdom elements within

Exodus 1–2, noting "strong continuity" with the Joseph narrative (Genesis 39–50) and with the book of Exodus as a whole. Davis draws a sharp contrast between wisdom and folly, highlighting the wise actions of the Hebrew midwives, Miriam, Jochebed, and Pharaoh's daughter, which help bring about God's kingdom purposes. In chapter 2, Andrew Judd approaches the horrific rape narrative of Judges 19 as a wisdom text. After noting wisdom elements in the text, Judd proposes a wisdom reading strategy, showing how key moments of ambivalence and discontinuity invite the reader to sit with the wise in the messiness of the story. David Firth undertakes a narrative-critical reading of revolt narratives in 2 Samuel 13–20 in chapter 3, demonstrating the use of wisdom to abuse others, or as an obstacle to Yahweh's purposes, as well as to advance Yahweh's purposes in David's life. Firth contrasts the wisdom of insiders Jonadab and Ahithophel with the wisdom of outsiders, such as the wise woman from Tekoa, Hushai the Archite, and the wise woman from Abel, noting the power dynamics of the text. In chapter 4, Andrew Abernethy challenges a negative reading of wisdom in 1 Kings 1–11. Abernethy distinguishes between Solomon's wisdom and his failed Torah obedience, then applies his findings to the royal ideal presented in 1–2 Kings and the prophets, and culminating in Jesus Christ.

2. Wisdom in Prophecy (Chapters 5–8)

A relational approach is taken to prophecy in the second group of essays, on wisdom in prophecy. In chapter 5, Jill Firth proposes insights for times of trauma and chaos. The book of Jeremiah proposes a wise approach in the midst of violence, warfare, and ridicule, inviting the prophet and the nation to trust God's love, righteousness, and justice in a season where the conventional aspirations of long life, family flourishing, and satisfying work may not be achievable. Andrew Sloane explores Ezekiel's surprising lack of references to God's love or compassion in present purposes or future acts on behalf of Israel in chapter 6. He proposes that the emphasis on God's name displaces Israel from the center of Israel's understanding of God and his purposes, revealing God's missional love for the whole world. In chapter 7, Heather Reid considers the significance of citations in Joel and Jonah of Exodus 32–34. She argues that these uses of the golden calf narrative and Yahweh's self-declaration in Exodus 34:6–7 reveal Yahweh as a God abounding in *hesed*, a revelation which will be overwhelmingly displayed in the cross of Jesus. Lwin Thida argues that Habakkuk offers a concrete way to live in crisis, rather than focusing on theodicy, in chapter

8. The book paints a picture of God's faithful character and invites a faithful response in this broken world.

3. Wisdom in the Writings (Chapters 9–11)

Davidic hope, theological anthropology, and wisdom vocabulary are explored in the section on Wisdom in the Writings. In chapter 9, Charlie Fletcher revisits Davidic kingship in Book V of the Psalter. Employing a canonical approach, he examines Psalm 132 in the context of the Songs of Ascents, Book V, the Psalter as a whole, and 2 Samuel 7. Fletcher sees David as a suffering, faithful servant and conquering king. Andrew Prideaux considers the ethical question of the value of the suffering human person in chapter 10. In conversation with Peter Singer, he examines the image of God in Job, Psalm 8, and Hebrews 2, and argues that suffering paradoxically anticipates human glory being made in the image of Christ. In chapter 11, David Ray offers a contextual analysis of the Hebrew term *musar*, often translated as "discipline" in Proverbs 3:11–12. Ray proposes that the term "discipline of the Lord" is a relational construct, reflecting a parent-child relationship. God's discipline is always linked to his wisdom and love.

4. Wisdom in Preaching and Teaching (Chapters 12–15)

Wise preaching of Proverbs and wisdom in theological teaching are examined in the section on Preaching and Teaching. In chapter 12, Paul Barker offers suggestions on preaching consecutive proverbs that appear to have no common theme. Barker proposes preaching like a sage, the use of humor and lively language, and preaching in the context of the book of Proverbs and the whole of life. In chapter 13, Tamie Davis explores the teaching of Tanzanian Bible teacher Ufoo Kassa George in her *Biblia Na Utajiri* (The Bible and Wealth). *Biblia Na Utajiri* was written in a context of poverty to combat myths around wealth creation in Tanzania, arguing that the world is orderly, and that Yahweh is in control. Davis seeks to hear this message in its own context and examines its connections to the teachings of the book of Proverbs. In chapter 14, Robin Payne argues that the Chinese proverb, "I hear and forget, I see and remember, I do and understand" is key to helping adults in Central Asia understand, teach, and preach from the Old Testament. Payne outlines strategies for teaching in oral, rote learning cultures, giving examples of active learning from the Pentateuch, Prophets, and Writings. Brian Rosner considers non-godly wisdom in the Old Testament and in 1 Corinthians 1–3 in chapter 15. Rosner then applies his insights to the teaching and study of theology in contemporary theological education.

5. Wisdom in Life (Chapters 16–19)

The final section addresses finding God's wisdom in everyday life, learning from Scripture and personal example. In chapter 16, Peter Adam suggests three keys to finding the fullness of God's wisdom. First, he suggests wisdom as a theological entity, which can be found throughout Scripture. Second, Christ is the fulfillment of biblical wisdom, is himself God's wisdom, and teaches wisdom. Third, the wisdom of God is supremely expressed in Christ's atoning death, and in the gospel of Christ. In chapter 17, Andrew Malone argues that Old Testament commands, liturgies, and narratives emphasize thankfulness. Malone draws attention to this strong theme in Old Testament teaching which can be overlooked in our contemporary interpretation and teaching from the Old Testament. Michelle Brennan examines Old and New Testament texts on waiting in chapter 18, and then applies these insights for today through real-life examples of Amy Carmichael, who became bedridden and was in constant pain, Soviet believer Liuba Ganevskaya, who reached out to her jailer, and Elizabeth Atwater, who was martyred in the Boxer Rebellion of 1900. The book concludes with a chapter compiled by Ruth Weatherlake, comprising individual reflections from colleagues and students on Lindsay Wilson's contribution and influence over the past thirty years, and a bibliography of his major publications.

Part I

Wisdom in Narrative

I

The Theological Purpose of Wisdom Elements in Exodus 1–2

Katherine Davis

Exodus 1–2 functions as a bridge between the Joseph narrative in Genesis 37–50 and Moses's commissioning narrative in Exodus 3:1—4:17. In Genesis 37–50, God used Joseph to preserve life in the midst of returning evil and brokenness with good. In this context, God showed his active favor to Jacob's sons and their families through the hospitality and welcome expressed to them in Egypt. By Exodus 3:1—4:17, however, the situation has dramatically changed. Rather than enjoying a favored status of hospitality in Egypt, the Israelites are enslaved and are in need of rescue. Yhwh's promise to Abram in Genesis 15:13–16—that his descendants will be enslaved in a land not their own—resounds in Exodus 3:1—4:17 where he finally announces his intent to make good on his promise to rescue his people from slavery. Between Genesis 37–50 and Exodus 3:1—4:17, Exodus 1–2 introduces the narrative upset forewarned in Genesis 15:13–16 and where reversal is foreshadowed in Exodus 3:1—4:17.

In light of the function Exodus 1–2 plays in its literary context, it is unsurprising that literary features characteristic of Genesis 37–50 also begin to emerge in Exodus 1–2. An example is the use of wisdom elements.[1]

---

1. Few scholars have acknowledged wisdom elements in Exodus 1–2 and so there is little treatment of the theological and rhetorical function these wisdom elements play at the beginning of Exodus's narrative and in relation to the Joseph narratives in

The term "wisdom element" refers in this chapter to "aspects of a text (ideas, motifs, forms, vocabulary etc.) [that] appear to mirror or remind the reader of similar aspects found in wisdom books."[2] Lindsay Wilson highlights that one purpose of exploring wisdom elements in the text "is to discover the relationship between wisdom and the other strands or streams of Old Testament thought."[3] Aligned with this view, this chapter explores the intersection of wisdom elements with other theological themes in a reading of Exodus 1–2. The goal of this chapter is to identify the theological function of wisdom elements within these beginning chapters of Exodus.[4]

Wisdom Elements within a Literary Reading of Exodus 1:8–14

Wisdom elements begin to emerge in Exodus 1–2 as the Egyptian king speaks directly to his people about the perceived threat of the Israelites in 1:9–10. Just prior to this speech, the book's preface accentuates the flourishing of the Israelites beyond the death of the first generation who came to Egypt, namely Jacob, his sons, and Joseph (1:1–7). This optimistic beginning, however, is soon overshadowed in 1:8 with the narrator's ominous remark that the new Egyptian king did not know Joseph, which sets the context then for the Egyptian king's speech in 1:9–10.

The king's speech begins in v. 9 by focusing upon the burgeoning Israelite numbers, which were highlighted positively in the book's overture. The king calls his people to observe the great number of the Israelite people and how the Israelites are now more numerous than the Egyptians. From the outset, the Egyptian king distinguishes "his people" from the "Israelite people" and, in making this distinction, seeks to instill fear about the growing Israelite numbers through the use of the comparison "than us" (מִמֶּנּוּ).[5] The king uses this fear as currency as he commands his people "come!" in v. 10a. This command is expressed by the Hebrew imperative

---

Genesis 37–50. For the few studies that acknowledge wisdom elements in Exodus 1–2, see Alexander, *Exodus*, 44–45, and Firth, "Wisdom," 157.

2. Wilson, *Joseph, Wise and Otherwise*, 29. See also Murphy, *Tree of Life*, 98–102.

3. Wilson, *Joseph, Wise and Otherwise*, 36.

4. The English translation used in this chapter is my own translation of the Hebrew text.

5. See also Dozeman, *Exodus*, 71; Durham, *Exodus*, 7; Houtman, *Exodus Volume 1*, 236; Utzschneider and Oswald, *Exodus 1–15*, 7. Contrary to Davies, *Exodus 1–18*, 139. Most English translations, such as the ESV, HCSB, NIV, translate the comparative as "for us," which conveys the idea that the Israelite numbers will soon be overwhelming for the Egyptians.

הָבָה, which, in the context of the speech as a whole, forms an invitation for "his people" to join him in taking the desired action justified through the scenario posed in the remainder of v. 10.[6] This initial invitation is then followed by the *hithpael* cohortative נִתְחַכְּמָה where the verbal root חכם ("to be wise") is usually rendered "to deal shrewdly."[7] However, חכם ("to be wise") is also within the semantic domain of wisdom language and the *hithpael* can equally be translated, "let us deal wisely."[8] Irrespective of how the *hithpael* is translated into English, the assumed idea of the verbal idea חכם ("to be wise") is that the outworking wise action is able to differentiate between good and evil. While the Egyptian king's speech does not evince the nature of this "wise" action, the king has already depicted the Israelites as more numerous than the Egyptians in vv. 9–10 to spark fear, which suggests his motives are not seeking good.

Immediately after the *hithpael* cohortative נִתְחַכְּמָה in v. 10, the Egyptian king states a series of consequences for the Egyptian people if collectively they fail to deal wisely with the Israelites. This sequence starts with the Israelites becoming great in number (יִרְבֶּה), but the king has already drawn attention to this first consequence as part of their present predicament in v. 9b. The repetition of the verbal idea רב ("to become great") between v. 9b and v. 10b suggests that the Egyptians have already failed to deal wisely with the Israelites and so they are already facing this consequence. The implication is that the rest of the verbal sequence in v. 10 will then swiftly happen if they do not act expediently; the Israelites will join force with Egypt's enemies, make war, and escape from Egypt.[9]

---

6. Alternatively, Houtman views the imperative as being imperfect. Although not common, this use of the imperfect tends to be used before a cohortative or jussive as a way of gathering attention (e.g. Gen 11:3, 4, 7; 38:16) and so is often translated as the imperative "come!". See Houtman, *Exodus Volume 1*, 237.

7. See the ESV, HCSB, KJV, NASB, NIV, NRSV. Dozeman, *Exodus*, 71, explains, "In the process, 'wise' actions (*ḥākām*) become perverted into 'shrewd' ones (*nithakmâ*). Pharaoh states: 'Come, we must deal shrewdly with them.' The Hebrew *nithakmâ*, 'deal shrewdly,' is a *Hithpael* form of the verb *ḥākām*, 'to be wise,' but it carries negative connotations. The author of Ecclesiastes illustrates the negative meaning of the word, and, in the process, he provides commentary on Pharaoh. He warns: 'Neither be overwise [shrewd], why destroy yourself?' (Eccl 7:16)." See also Sarna, *Exodus*, 5; Utzschneider and Oswald, *Exodus 1–15*, 7.

8. See also Davies, *Exodus 1–18*, 151.

9. Scholars often observe a dissonance between the Egyptians' fear of the Israelites leaving Egypt and yet the perceived threat by the Egyptians of the growing Israelite people in their midst. For example, see Dozeman, *Exodus*, 71. Yet, the sequence is not merely the Israelites escaping, but of war that causes Egypt to be conquered by a neighboring nation. Furthermore, the appeal to the growing number of Israelites to act strategically to mitigate this threat is really a justification for the conscription of

By connecting the present reality of the Israelites' growing numbers to the threat of war, the Egyptian king engages in antics to cause alarm and to justify the "wise" actions that are then implemented in vv. 11–14. For the hearer, however, the king's strategy represents a dissonance between the motives the king attributed to the Israelites in vv. 9–10 and the knowledge gained by the hearer from the Pentateuchal narrative framework and Exodus's overture that explains why the Israelites are flourishing. As Yʜᴡʜ promised to Abram in Genesis 15:13–16, Abram's descendants will become numerous, yet will be resident foreigners in a land not their own for four hundred years. While there is no explicit reference to God within Exodus 1:1–7, the verbal ideas used to describe the Israelites' numerical growth— פרה ("to be fruitful"), שרץ ("to move about"), and רבה ("to be great")—are within the semantic domain of creation language and echo God's blessing of humanity in Genesis 1:28 and Genesis 9:1–7.[10] The use of these creation verbs in v. 7 specifically implies that he is bringing about the Abrahamic promise of nationhood as the Israelites grow great in number and spread about.[11] Thus, the king's characterization of the Israelites flourishing is discordant with the hearer's understanding, which casts further ambiguity upon the king's motivations before 1:11–14 reveals the true nature of the king's "wise" strategy to deal with the Israelites.

Following the king's speech, the narrator recounts in vv. 11–14 how the Egyptians acted "wisely" to curtail the growth of the Israelites.[12] The Egyptian response unfolds in two stages. First, in v. 11, the Egyptians place taskmasters over the Israelites as they work on Pharaoh's building projects. The narrator describes this strategy as afflicting (עַנֹּתוֹ) the people "with heavy burdens" (בְּסִבְלֹתָם), which suggests conscripted service designed to humiliate and shame.[13] Even at this beginning stage, the Israelites' service to Pharaoh is forced. This situation escalates to the second stage in vv. 13–14 where the narrator relates that the forced labor now becomes slavery with

---

service. In light of this, the Egyptians may wish for the Israelites to remain, but only in a condition of conscription.

10. See also Alexander, *Exodus*, 42; Alter, *Five Books of Moses*, 308; Davies, *Exodus 1–18*, 148–149; Stuart, *Exodus*, 61; Utzschneider and Oswald, *Exodus 1–15*, 6.

11. See also Alexander, *Exodus*, 42–43; Childs, *Exodus*, 2–3.

12. The use of the *wayyiqtol* verb וַיָּשִׂימוּ ("they set") beginning in 1:11 continues the sequence of verbal actions in the text's foreground and thus creates a relationship between the previous *wayyiqtol* verb, which is וַיֹּאמֶר ("he said") beginning v. 9a, and this particular *wayyiqtol* verb in v. 11a. This sequential relationship is one of consequence, that is, the act of the Egyptians setting slave masters over the Israelites in v. 11a is a sequential outcome of the king's speech introduced by the quotative frame, "And he said to his people," in v. 9a.

13. See Meyers, *Exodus*, 34.

increased cruelty and hardship. The narrator identifies the catalyst of this escalating measure against the Israelites in v. 12.

Verse 12 begins with the temporal construction וְכַאֲשֶׁר + finite verb (יְעַנּוּ; "they were afflicted") that can be translated, "As soon as they were afflicted."[14] This type of temporal construction is used to make a strong connection between the action within the temporal clause ("they were afflicted"), with a following main clause, which, in this instance, is a sequence of three clauses, "so they became great and so they burst open and they scattered" (כֵּן יִרְבֶּה וְכֵן יִפְרֹץ וַיָּקֻצוּ)[15]; once more the Israelites grew in number to the point that they burst out and spread over the land. Ironically, the very problem that the Egyptians were trying to control through their aggression is the very consequence of their actions. Clearly, from a human perspective, the Egyptian strategy should have been effective. However, the failure of the Egyptians' strategy to accomplish the king's goal accentuates that, rather than being "wise," the action taken against the Israelites is futile and folly.[16] While God may not be mentioned explicitly in the text, the repetition of the verb רבה ("to be great") in v. 12b to describe how they grew in strength after the Israelites were afflicted by the Egyptians implies that God is superintending events so as to accomplish his purposes as promised in the Abrahamic covenant. However, this implication emerges into the foreground in Exodus 1:15–22.

Wisdom Elements within a Literary Reading of Exodus 1:15–22

The failure of Egypt's strategies to control Israelite numbers in 1:11–14 led to a third strategy being implemented in 1:15–22, which was once again initiated by the Egyptian king, yet delegated to a new set of characters within the Exodus narrative—the two midwives, Shiphrah and Puah. Verses 15–22 stand in stark contrast to vv. 8–14 as the motivation and actions of these two sets of characters are juxtaposed; whereas the Egyptian king has a pretense of acting wisely in vv. 11–14, the two midwives embody wisdom in vv. 15–22.

---

14. See Van der Merwe et al., *Biblical Hebrew Reference Grammar*, 347. See also Alter, *Five Books of Moses*, 309.

15. The verbal root יִפְרֹץ means "breaking out" or "bursting forth." See Dozeman, *Exodus*, 72; Houtman, *Exodus Volume 1*, 247; Propp, *Exodus 1–18*, 124.

16. See also Meyers, *Exodus*, 36: "The pharaoh intended to act shrewdly, but the futility of his policy calls that into question."

The introduction of Shiphrah and Puah in v. 15 suggests an underhandedness not apparent in the king's first strategy. The focus in v. 15 is solely upon the king speaking to the two midwives; the absence of others in the narrative lends a secretive quality to the exchange.[17] This same underhandedness is also apparent in the king's command to the midwives in v. 16. His command begins with a temporal clause that draws attention to their privileged task, which is attending to the Hebrew women as they are birthing. The clause וּרְאִיתֶן עַל־הָאָבְנָיִם ("and you see them upon the birthing stool") is slightly ambiguous as the meaning of הָאָבְנָיִם is unclear.[18] It can refer either to a kind of seat that the laboring woman sits upon as she gives birth or it is a stone that the newborn was laid upon immediately after the birth while the midwives attend to the mother.[19] Either way, the following command asks the midwives to betray their vocation of caring for women and their newborn at their most vulnerable.

This command is in two parts and each is a conditional statement introduced by the particle אִם ("if"). Each protasis focuses upon the baby's familial identity as either a son or a daughter, after which the apodosis declares whether the baby is to die or live. In the case of the first condition where the baby is a son, the king commands the midwives to put the newborn to death, whereas in the second situation where the newborn is a daughter, the king declares that she can then live. The stark contrast between the pronouncement of the death penalty for the son and yet the declaration of the daughter being free to live accentuates the chilling nature of the command where the declaration of life for the daughter almost sounds magnanimous. Irrespective of some ambiguity in v. 16, what is clear is that the king is commanding the midwives to kill the newborn immediately after, or even during, birth and possibly without the knowledge of the mother.[20]

After the king's horrific command in v. 16, the narrator immediately focuses upon the midwives' response in v. 17. Their response, though, was not directly to the king's command *per se*, but to God. For the first time in the Exodus narrative, God (הָאֱלֹהִים) is referred to explicitly as the narrator relates in v. 17a that the midwives feared (וַתִּירֶאןָ) God and that this

---

17. See also Durham, *Exodus*, 11.

18. For discussion on the interpretive options, see Alexander, *Exodus*, 52–53; Davies, *Israel in Egypt*, 65–66; Durham, *Exodus*, 11–12; Houtman, *Exodus Volume 1*, 253–54.

19. See Alter, *Five Books of Moses*, 310; Cassuto, *Exodus*, 14; Hamilton, *Exodus*, 13; Kaiser, "Exodus," 353–55; Sarna, *Exodus*, 7; Siebert-Hommes, *Let the Daughters Live!*, 46–47. Contrary to Durham, *Exodus*, 12; Houtman, *Exodus Volume 1*, 253; Propp, *Exodus 1–18*, 139; Stuart, *Exodus*, 77.

20. See Alexander, *Exodus*, 55; Houtman, *Exodus Volume 1*, 254.

disposition determined their decision not to follow the Egyptian king's command (v. 17b). The verb used in v. 17a to describe the midwives' response to God is יָרֵא ("to fear"), which Sarna observes represents, "a conception of God as One who makes moral demands on humankind; it functions as the ultimate restraint on evil and the supreme stimulus for good."[21] Sarna's explanation also depicts the meaning of the similar phrase in the book of Proverbs that attributes the fear of Yhwh as the beginning of knowledge and wisdom (1:7; 9:10).[22] In light of this, it is appropriate to view the reference to the fear of God in 1:17 as a wisdom element. This wisdom element is once more repeated in v. 21 as the narrator explains for the hearer why God showed his active favor towards the midwives by gifting them with their own families—they feared God. Thus, the use of יָרֵא ("to fear") to describe the midwives' motivation for not adhering to the king's command and letting the sons live suggests that their noncompliance that preserved life is an embodiment of wisdom.[23] Once more, Pharaoh's attempts to thwart the flourishing of the Israelites is confounded by two midwives who revered God. Thus, the contrast is stark. The Egyptian king's so-called "wise" action, which by nature of being wise is to exemplify a knowledge of good and evil, is shown to be folly as he opposes God's sovereign purposes for the Israelites and evil in his cruel and lethal strategies against the Israelites. This false wisdom is juxtaposed with the example of the midwives who refuse to be complicit in Pharaoh's evil as they act out of reverence for God as they save many lives.

The Theological Function of Wisdom Elements in Exodus 1–2

While wisdom elements are present in Exodus 1:8–22, it is true to say that these elements are not prolific. However, the two instances where wisdom elements are explicit in 1:10 and 1:17–20 are critical for the narrative's

21. Sarna, *Exodus*, 7. See also Hamilton, *Exodus*, 14; Houtman, *Exodus Volume 1*, 254; Stuart, *Exodus*, 82–83. Contrary to Davies, *Exodus 1–18 Volume 1*, 162.

22. Please note, the pattern of Exodus 1–2 is a deliberate omission of God's personal name, Yhwh. Alexander, *Exodus*, 43, explains the rhetorical impact of this omission as a deliberate contrast to the kings of Egypt. Leaving the kings of Egypt unnamed is a pattern from the beginning of the scene and renders each king as of no account in comparison with the sovereign God who will later be named as Yhwh in Exodus 3 (see also Dozeman, *Exodus*, 73). Contrary to Utzschneider and Oswald, *Exodus 1–15*, 7. For an alternate point of view built on the Elohistic and Yahwistic division, see Brueggemann and Wolff, *Vitality of Old Testament Traditions*, 67–82.

23. See also Kürle, *Appeal of Exodus*, 61; Stuart, *Exodus*, 83.

progression in the book's first two scenes (1:8–14; 1:15–22) that depict the unravelling situation for the Israelites. Previous to Exodus 1:8, the Israelites were granted a favored status in Egypt where they enjoyed the nation's hospitality as resident foreigners (Gen 47:1—Exod 1:7). Within this context, Exodus 1:8–22 explains how the situation for Jacob's descendants was reversed so abruptly that as resident foreigners they were shamed and dishonored; the Egyptians were threatened by their increasing numbers as God brought about his promise of nationhood to the patriarchs (see Gen 12:1–3; 15:1–21; 46:1–4). The wisdom elements in 1:8–22 reveal the character of both the Egyptian king and the two Hebrew midwives. The Egyptian king has a pretense of wisdom but is shown to be evil and displaying folly, whereas the two midwives embody wisdom as they use their resources to preserve life because of their fear of God.

Within this brief analysis, a major theme begins to emerge, which is that God in his hidden and revealed activity preserves life, to accomplish his purposes, as he superintended events and through wise human activity. Curiously, this theme echoes Wilson's conclusions from his analysis of the theological purpose of wisdom elements in Genesis 37–50. He finds that through the different stages of the Joseph narrative that God does not emerge into the foreground of the narrative and is often hidden.[24] Yet, in these same narratives, human actions and plans often result in the preserving of order and life, in reconciliation, and good, in such a way that exemplifies wisdom, especially where power is used for the sake of others.[25] Wilson states that throughout each scene where the hiddenness of God is juxtaposed with wise human action, these two dimensions are not in opposition, but rather go hand in hand.[26] God in his superintending divine activity uses wise human activity to accomplish his covenant purposes. Wilson concludes,

> In many covenant texts, God's rule is achieved either by divine intervention ("the mighty acts of God") or by human beings obediently carrying out God's instructions (for example, Moses, Joshua). God's sovereign ruling over his people and his world, is often promoted by hidden divine activity and evident human responsibility in wisdom literature and in the Joseph narrative. In the Old Testament it appears that the broader, all-encompassing category of God's kingly rule can be accomplished either by

---

24. Wilson, *Joseph, Wise, and Otherwise*, 295–96.
25. Wilson, *Joseph, Wise, and Otherwise*, 301–2.
26. Wilson, *Joseph, Wise, and Otherwise*, 303.

humans taking wise initiatives, by human obedience to God's instruction, or by God's direct activity.²⁷

Wilson's argument articulates what has been observed in this chapter pertaining to Exodus 1:8–22 in particular. As the new Egyptian king ascends the throne and seeks to control the population growth of the Israelites through harsh and cruel measures in 1:8–14, God is not mentioned once within the narrative; he remains hidden. Yet, despite the strategies taken against the Israelites, they continue to grow and flourish. As noted in our reading of Exodus 1:8–14, the verbs used to describe this continued growth echo creation language and so imply that God is present in his superintending activity—hiddenness does not mean absence. It is through this creative activity that God ensures that his covenant purposes are being achieved against all odds, from a human perspective.

It is noteworthy that there is a purposeful absence of wise human activity in 1:8–14. God does not work in this situation through a human agent to accomplish his covenant purposes. This contrast is deliberately absent to evince the folly of the Egyptian king's "wise" strategies to hinder God's covenant purposes. This depiction of Pharaoh's character as embodying folly is heightened in 1:15–17 when the two midwives foil the king's plans because they refused to obey his command out of their fear of God. Initially, God's presence in this scene is through his hidden superintending activity as the narrator relates the Israelites' continued numerical growth. In this instance though, God's hidden superintending activity to accomplish his covenant purposes is through the wise actions of the two midwives who fear God. Thus, wisdom elements in Exodus 1:8–22 intersect with the theme of God's hidden superintending activity both without and with human wise action, just as Wilson has demonstrated from Genesis 37–50.

Critical to Wilson's argument, however, is that a wisdom influence is not just present by the use of explicit wisdom language in the narrative, but also through motifs that reflect wisdom priorities.²⁸ The theme highlighted above—God, in his hidden superintending activity, uses wise human plans to preserve life and to bring about his sovereign purposes—is an example of such a wisdom theme.²⁹ This theme is at the foreground of the midwives' narrative in 1:15–22 and also in a second narrative immediately afterwards in 2:1–10.

In this second narrative, however, there are no explicit wisdom elements, but the same ideas are present as three women act to preserve the

---

27. Wilson, *Joseph, Wise, and Otherwise*, 302.
28. Wilson, *Joseph, Wise, and Otherwise*, 29–30.
29. See Wilson, *Joseph, Wise, and Otherwise*, 296–97, 301–4.

life of one Hebrew boy. The first woman is the boy's mother who, having given birth after the Egyptians adopt the policy of killing every Hebrew son (see 1:22), protects her son by hiding him in a waterproof basket among the reeds of a protected riverbank (2:1–3). The second woman enters as a surprise into the narrative in 2:5—Pharaoh's daughter—as she represents a threat to the mother's plans and to the boy's survival. However, instead of using her status to be complicit in Pharaoh's evil, she responds with compassion, bringing the boy into Pharaoh's household and adopting him as her son. The third woman is the boy's sister, who kept watch over the boy (2:4), and then responded shrewdly as she intervened with Pharaoh's daughter, suggesting the boy's mother as the Hebrew nurse (2:7–8). The cumulative response of the three women saw the life of one son preserved. While God is not mentioned in 2:1–10, the wise human plans of these three women were the means by which God in his hiddenness superintended the situation to preserve the life of one who is central to his plans within the rest of the book. Thus, the wisdom theme emerging in 1:15–22 with the midwives continues into 2:1–10. In each instance, there is the decision to defy Pharaoh's command, which goes in hand with the decision to use power for good, that is, for the saving of life, rather than for evil.

Therefore, just as Genesis 37–50 uses wisdom elements to evince the broader theme of God's hidden sovereign activity through wise human actions to preserve life and accomplish his covenant purposes, so too does Exodus 1:1—2:10. Within the literary and theological contexts of the Pentateuchal narrative, this thematic continuity through the use of wisdom elements reinforces the strong continuity between Genesis 37–50 and Exodus 1–2. These wisdom elements also serve a similar theological purpose in Exodus 1–2, as Wilson has argued for Genesis 37–50. In his hiddenness, God is superintending adverse circumstances to preserve life both through his sovereign power and through wise human actions.[30] Through preserving and sustaining the life of the Israelites, he upholds his covenant promise to the Patriarchs to create a nation from Abram's descendants, while also saving the life of the one that God will one day use to bring about another dimension of his covenant promises; the rescuing of the Israelites from slavery and bringing his nation to the land of promise.

Conclusion

In summary, the strong narrative continuity between Genesis 37–50 and Exodus 1–2 is evinced further still by the sustained use of wisdom elements

---

30. See Wilson, *Joseph, Wise, and Otherwise*, 296–97, 303–4.

from Genesis 37–50 into Exodus 1–2. These wisdom elements within Exodus 1–2 accentuate the sharp contrast between folly and evil and wisdom and good. The first set of attributes are exemplified by the Egyptian king who depicted his own actions as being "wise," yet are revealed by the narrator to be folly in opposition to God's sovereign power and with evil intent rather than seeking the good of those who are vulnerable. In contrast, the second set of attributes is exemplified by five women—the two midwives, Moses's mother, sister, and Pharaoh's daughter—who use their power to preserve life and thus embody wisdom and good. Thus, the wisdom elements function to set up this contrast within Exodus's narrative, which in turn evinces a key theological theme, that God in his hidden superintending activity preserves life through wise human actions and so brings about his covenant purposes in adverse circumstances. Wilson has also demonstrated that Genesis 37–50 uses wisdom elements to support this same theological theme in the Joseph narratives. Thus, the presence of this major theme in Genesis 37–50 and Exodus 1–2 is not a coincidence. This theological continuity functions to demonstrate the faithfulness of God to his word as he brings about the Abrahamic promise of nationhood. In the context of the book of Exodus as a whole, this emphasis at the book's beginning builds confidence that just as God is bringing about this promise of nationhood, so too he will make good on his word to Abram that he will rescue the Israelites and bring them to the land of their inheritance (Gen 15:12–21; Exod 3:1—4:17).

Bibliography

Alexander, T. Desmond. *Exodus*. ApOTC 2. London: Apollos: 2017.
Alter, Robert. *Five Books of Moses: A Translation with Commentary*. New York: W. W. Norton, 2004.
Brueggemann, Walter, and Hans Walter Wolff. *The Vitality of Old Testament Traditions*. Atlanta: John Knox, 1982.
Cassuto, Umberto. *A Commentary on the Book of Exodus*. Jerusalem: Magnes, 1967.
Childs, Brevard S. *Exodus: A Commentary*. OTL. London: SCM, 1974.
Davies, Gordon. *Israel in Egypt: Reading Exodus 1–2*. JSOTSup 135. Sheffield: JSOT, 1992. https://ereader.perlego.com/1/book/804040.
Davies, Graham. *Exodus 1–18 Volume 1: Chapters 1–10*. ICC. London: T. & T. Clark, 2020. https://ereader.perlego.com/1/book/1357000/184.
Dozeman, Thomas B. *Exodus*. EEC. Grand Rapids: Eerdmans, 2009.
Durham, John I. *Exodus*. WBC. Grand Rapids: Zondervan Academic, 1987.
Firth, David G. "Wisdom in Old Testament Narrative." In *Exploring Old Testament Wisdom*, edited by David G. Firth and Lindsay Wilson, 155–73. London: Apollos, 2016.
Hamilton, Victor. *Exodus*. Grand Rapids: Baker Academic, 2011.

Houtman, Cornelius. *Exodus Volume 1*. HCOT. Leuven: Peeters, 1993.
Kaiser Jr., Walter C. "Exodus." *Expositor's Bible Commentary*. Grand Rapids: Zondervan, 2008.
Kürle, Stefan. *The Appeal of Exodus: The Characters God, Moses and Israel in the Rhetoric of the Book of Exodus*. PBM. Milton Keynes: Paternoster, 2013.
Meyers, Carol. *Exodus*. NCBC. New York: CUP, 2005.
Murphy, Roland E. *The Tree of Life: An Exploration of Biblical Wisdom*. Grand Rapids: Eerdmans, 1990.
Propp, William C. *Exodus 1–18*. AB 2a. New Haven: Yale, 1999.
Sarna, Nahum M. *Exodus*. JPS Torah. New York: JPS, 1991.
Siebert-Hommes, Jopie. *Let the Daughters Live! The Literary Architecture of Exodus 1–2 as a Key for Interpretation*. Leiden: Brill, 1998.
Stuart, Douglas K. *Exodus*. NAC 2. Nashville: B&H, 2006.
Utzschneider, Helmut, and Wolfgang Oswald. *Exodus 1–15*. IECOT. Stuttgart: Kohlhammer, 2015. https://ereader.perlego.com/1/book/1074049/6.
Van der Merwe, C. H. J., et al. *A Biblical Hebrew Reference Grammar*. London: T. & T. Clark, 2018.
Wilson, Lindsay. *Joseph, Wise and Otherwise: The Intersection of Wisdom and Covenant in Genesis 37–50*. Carlisle, UK: Paternoster, 2004.

2

Judges 19 as Wisdom

Sitting with the Wise in Ambivalence and Discontinuity

Andrew Judd

Of all the horrors told in Judges, it is chapter 19 and the rape and murder of an innocent woman while her husband sleeps soundly inside that raises perhaps the most unsettling questions for interpreters. It marks the beginning of the end of a process we have been watching with increasing discomfort since the opening of Judges; the threat of the Canaanite "other" has gradually been displaced by an even more terrifying darkness *within*. That the Levite and his wife meet such a fate in Benjamin—having chosen, in a terrible moment of irony, not to lodge in a Canaanite town—shows that the "Canaanization"[1] of Israel is complete.

Genre-wise, there are many ways that we could take this story: as straight historical narration of an unhappy period; as prophetic commentary on pre-monarchical Israel; or perhaps even as a kind of ancient horror film, designed to shock the audience with the monsters within. The theme of this Festschrift, however, suggests a different—and, I think, productive—lens. In his provocative 2019 *Obituary for Wisdom Literature*, Will Kynes dares us to abandon the hard-edged nineteenth-century critical category of wisdom text, freeing us to see wisdom's intertextual connections with

---

1. Block, *Judges*, 58.

the entire canon.² Lindsay Wilson, never one to put dead Germans above Scripture, needed no such encouragement. His 2004 book *Joseph, Wise and Otherwise*, based on his doctoral thesis, brings out elements in Genesis 37–50 that suggest a "wisdom 'family resemblance.'"³ My reading, while slightly different in method, is inspired by Wilson's approach.⁴

My point of departure is modern genre theory's observation that texts do not "belong" to a single genre but have relationships with many genres.⁵ Readers use genres heuristically, forming a genre hypothesis and testing "alternative readings of the text *as* different genres."⁶ In part one, I test a reading of Judges 19 as if it were a wisdom text. What features stand out when we understand the chapter as something akin to Proverbs, Job, or Ecclesiastes? In part two, I explore how the wisdom genre helps us reconceive the discontinuities of the story—particularly in the disturbing bargain with the sons of Belial—as features, not flaws. Every genre requires something different from us as readers, and reading Judges 19 as a wisdom text demands that we sit with its discontinuities for longer than we might otherwise be comfortable. By refusing flat characterisation and trite moralizing, the text forces us to live with ambivalence—which is where wisdom is often to be found.

Reading Judges 19 as Wisdom

"His *pilegesh* was unfaithful to him."⁷ It is often noted that the woman at the center of this story is unnamed, the inference being that this enacts her erasure.⁸ Yet none of the characters in this story has a name. Verse 1 introduces the woman's husband simply: "There was a man, a Levite, a migrant (גר) in the far-off parts of the hill country of Ephraim." Tribe and spatial (dis)location alone identify the primary characters: the man from nowhere, and of a tribe distributed everywhere (Deut 14:27), who currently lives in Ephraim; the woman from Bethlehem in Judah (19:2); the old man in Gibeah, previously from the remote hill country of Ephraim.

2. Kynes, *Obituary*, 254.
3. Wilson, *Joseph, Wise and Otherwise*, 5.
4. In his engagement with the ethical questions raised by feminist hermeneutics about Judges 19, Nicholas Ansell also rereads the narrative in light of wisdom themes in the text, recovering the text as an ethical call for discernment. While my reading will arrive at a similar place, our paths will diverge at important points. Ansell, "Body."
5. Fowler, *Kinds*, 22; Frow, *Genre*, 2; Ricoeur, "Hermeneutical Function," 135.
6. Gerhart, "Generic Competence," 36; see also "Generic Studies," 316.
7. All translations mine unless otherwise noted.
8. So, e.g., Trible, *Texts*, 65, 80.

Introducing the characters with broad spatial references rather than names does not confine them to two-dimensional typecasts (they turn out, as we will see, to be very complex characters). Their anonymity may, however, position us to look for the broad principles at play in their lives. If so, this lends itself to wisdom's search for what is generally true.

Before we meet any of these characters, however, there is one figure—the king—who is significant because absent. The narrative opens: "In those days Israel had no king." This significant phrase from Judges 17:6 and 18:1 will return again in 21:25, bookending the story and hinting at the text's rhetorical goals. There is no further mention of kingship in this family tragedy, so why intrude by mentioning the king's absence? Because the absence of wise statecraft is one central wisdom theme of this episode. The narrator is inviting us to observe the spiritual and political state of pre-monarchical Israel and draw our own conclusions based on what we see. We are about to be taken into an ethical world which is slightly different—the narrator seems to assume, or why else tell us?—to the one we are familiar with. This field trip is designed to be instructive; we are meant to be asking, right from the beginning, "What can this story teach us about a nation's health?"

The first and last time the king's absence is noted in Judges the implications are spelled out for us: "In those days Israel had no king; a man [איש] would do what was right in his own eyes." The man who acts according to his own eyes is a regular feature of wisdom literature (Prov 12:15; 16:2; 21:2; 26:5, 12, 16; 28:11). Here in Judges 19:1 the following clause begins very similarly: "In those days Israel had no king; there was a man [איש] . . ." But at this point in the sentence the pattern is broken, and the man who does what is right in his own eyes becomes incarnate and enters the story as "a certain Levite" (NRSV). The role of the proverbial איש (*ish*) who does whatever seems right to himself will, in this episode, be played by this Levite in Ephraim.[9] A narrative or saga cycle centered upon an emblematic figure is a fitting vehicle for a wisdom text—we might think of Job, "a man in the land of Uz" (Job 1:1)—although it remains to be seen how righteous a sufferer this Levite is.

The first thing this man does is take an אשה (*ishah*) for himself, which would normally mean that he has married a "wife" (even in King Rehoboam's dark days: 2 Chr 11:18). Yet here the normal marriage customs are modified by a second description: the woman is a פילגש (*pilegesh*). This tricky word indicates some kind of wife of lower standing; back in Judges 8 we were told that apart from Gideon's many wives he also had

---

9. Later, by the mob: verse 24.

a "concubine" (NRSV) who bore him Abimelech, but here in Judges 19 no primary wife is mentioned.

This ambivalence is carefully and subtly drawn, and right from the start contributes to an air of unease about their relationship. We do well in English to avoid collapsing such studied ambivalence too quickly. The standard term "concubine," for instance, imports inaccurate connotations of a palatial sex worker, and has not done much to mitigate the history of interpretation's unfortunate bias against her. Instead, I will call her simply "the young woman" (נערה, na'arah). This is what she is called six times in verses 3–9, that short period in the story when she has taken refuge in her father's house, and the last time that she is safe and living out her own agency. It is only outside this temporary refuge, in verses 1–2 and 9–29, that she is referred to as the man's פילגש (pilegesh). The word נערה (na'arah) I think comes closest to how the narrator wants us to remember her: as a vulnerable young woman in the liminal space between the safety of her childhood and all the risks and opportunities of adult life.

Whatever her marital status, her new life with the Levite is clearly not straightforward or happy; we are perhaps not meant to be surprised when it breaks down. The MT tells us in verse 2 that the young woman then does something: ותזנה (vatizneh). Precisely what this means is also notoriously difficult. The root זנה (znh) normally means to "fornicate" or perhaps "act as a prostitute" (see Lev 21:9). If this is what the word means, then the young woman is unfaithful עליו ('alayv, "against him"). Yet we would usually expect the injured husband to be introduced by the preposition מן (min, see Ps 73:28); the preposition על ('al) would more naturally introduce the *cause* of the fornication (see Ezek 16:15).[10] No mention is made of whom she committed adultery with, so some take it that her unfaithfulness consisted merely in deserting her husband and returning to the family home. Others suggest an otherwise unattested alternative meaning for the root זנה (znh) might be "to feel repugnance,"[11] which would make more sense of the prepositional phrase "against him." This is partly by analogy with the Akkadian *zenû* and partly because the ancient versions more clearly take her side: in the Greek the young woman either ὠργίσθη ("became angry") or ἐπορεύθη ("departed") the Levite, and in Targum Jonathan she ובסרת (*uvasarat*, "despised") him.

This detail has become an unhealthy obsession for later commentators, who seek either to show that what happens to her is a kind of poetic justice for her adultery, or to form her into the perfect victim by expunging any

---

10. GCK, §249.

11. "זנה," *HALOT; DCH*. Alternatively, the verb can be amended to זנח ("to reject").

hint of wrongdoing from her backstory.[12] Neither project is well advised; the most we can say is that there was some fault on someone's side. Yet Ansell's sapiential reading of Judges 19 needs the young woman to be exonerated here so she can be fully disassociated from unwise Israel—otherwise his sapiential gender symbolism does not work.[13] In contrast, on my reading this finely balanced ambivalence actually serves the wisdom genre: presenting her, as Hamley describes it, as a complex character rather than a type character.[14] Much as wisdom literature requires us to give up trite ethical answers and walk through ambivalence and contradiction on the path to wisdom, the narrator here is inviting us to withhold judgment and sit with the complexity of her situation for a while.

The young woman returns to her father and spends four months there in Bethlehem in Judah (19:2) before her husband gets up and goes after her to speak "to her heart" (19:3), trying to convince her to return. This love poetry language (see Song 5:4) raises hope for a happy ending. Indeed, when the Levite arrives we are told that his "father-in-law, the young woman's father, rejoiced to see him" (19:3) and insists that he stay.

However, from this point on the young woman herself disappears from view; we have no idea how she feels about her husband's arrival and her father's lavish five-day hospitality. Four times the Levite tries to leave with her, but three times the father is successful in delaying him. This does several things at different levels of the story.

At the level of characterisation, this gives us pause to reflect on the character of the father.[15] Is he desperately trying to buy time for his daughter while he works out whether it is good for her to return? On the one hand, he seems pleased to see the Levite at first (19:3). Yet he must have sympathy for his daughter's cause in leaving the Levite, or else he presumably would not have provided her refuge in the first place. Then again, perhaps this is the kind of aggressively generous hospitality that an ageing father in that culture might be expected to lavish upon a man who is giving his daughter a second chance at economic security.

Whatever we make of the father's character and motivations, the delay underlines the theme of hospitality—a sharp contrast to the trio's treatment in Gibeah. His delaying tactics also serve the narrative arc by escalating the tension. The reader, like the Levite, is delayed here in Bethlehem, with repetition and reported speech slowing down the narrative time. The first

12. See Thompson, *Writing*, 179–221.
13. Ansell, "Body," 78.
14. Hamley, *Unspeakable*, 88 n. 251.
15. See Lapsley, *Whispering*, 41.

three days pass quickly, but on the fourth day comes the first of four direct speeches from the young woman's father to his son-in-law (verses 5, 6, 8, and 9). Each time the man urges him to "strengthen" (5, 8) or "gladden" (6, 9) his heart, just as he originally arrived with the intention of speaking to his wife's heart (19:3). While we never hear the Levite's reply, the first and third times the persuasion seems to work and the two men (the woman is never included) eat and drink (19:6), then eat (19:8) some more. The second time the Levite gets up to leave, but his father-in-law pressures him to stay the night. The final time, the speech from the father-in-law is much longer, yet is met with a wordless refusal as the man declines to stay the night and gets up one last time to leave (19:10).

Symbolically, an ill-advised journey is a fitting plot device for exploring wisdom's concern with choosing the right track—avoid the darkness of the wicked path (Prov 4:19) and the way of the fool (Prov 12:15) which "seems right to a man but its end is the way to death" (Prov 14:12; 16:25); choose the "way of the LORD" (Prov 10:29); trust him and he will "make your paths straight" (Prov 3:6). But it is not just symbolic journeys that require wisdom. If wisdom is the ability to form a successful plan,[16] then the Levite's departure serves the wisdom theme as a study in tragically poor logistics. He accepts the father's offer to stay as he is about to leave early on the morning of the fifth day, but then later that day rejects the father's observation that "night is coming" and leaves anyway—only now it is far too late to be setting off on a forty kilometer journey. Wisdom is partly "the ability to anticipate consequences."[17] His equivocation means they have not left nearly enough time to get home, and he sends them into the single most predictable danger of any journey: night. Mere hours into their daylong journey home, with darkness approaching, the servant suggests that they stop at Jebus, then a non-Israelite town. The Levite would prefer to stay with his fellow Israelites, and so he insists that they push on two hours further north to Gibeah. Here the street-smart servant's intuitions provide a tragic foil for the Levite's folly. In contrast to the journey in 1 Samuel 9 where, as Wilson observes, God's background activity is actuated through the wisdom of Saul's servant, here the wisdom of the servant is ignored.[18]

They must have been relieved to make it before sunset in the town square of Gibeah. Yet, in a breach of the obligations to any traveller—much more a Levite!—nobody offers them lodging for the night. There is here an unsettling reversal of expectations—the hostility of Canaanite Jebus and the hospitality

16. Wilson, *Joseph, Wise and Otherwise*, 240.
17. Davis, *Opening Israel's Scriptures*, 451.
18. Wilson, *Joseph, Wise and Otherwise*, 267.

of the Israelite Gibeah are reversed, as the narrator silently plays with expectations and stereotypes. Eventually an old man, himself a migrant from the Levite's home in Ephraim, comes back from working late in the fields. He asks them where they are coming from and going to, and the Levite explains, adding that nobody has offered them a place to stay, despite them having more than enough provisions for the party to ensure they do not impose. The old man greets them with peace and assures them he will indeed meet their needs and that they should not pass the night in the square (19:20).

Perhaps this, at last, is the wise man who can say with Job: "the stranger has not lodged in the street; I have opened my doors to the traveller" (Job 31:32 NRSV)? Yet the wisdom theme of hospitality is invoked only to be dramatically subverted. While they are enjoying his hospitality, the house is suddenly surrounded by townsmen who are described as בני־בליעל, "sons of worthlessness." They are an incarnation of the proverbial sons who have not listened to wisdom's advice but have thrown in their lot with the "worthless" man (Prov 6:12; 16:27; 19:28). They demand that the old man bring out the Levite so that they may ידע ("know") him. The intertextual connections with Genesis 19 have been building—the night scene, the visitors in the town square, the resident alien's hospitality—but the demand to "know" the strangers makes the echo into a shout (Gen 19:5). Yet "neither story is a blind reflection of the other" but rather each "is an independent and purposeful composition."[19] It is possible to focus too much on the linguistic similarities between the passages and ignore that with this repetition there is a more fundamental reversal. The dark melody of the Sodomite town has been transposed into a new, Israelite, key—and the effect is even more dissonant.

Any doubts commentators might have about the sexual connotations of the request to "know" the men in Genesis 19 are settled here in Judges 19 by what happens to the young woman when they "know her" in verse 25. Certainly, the old man understands their intention straight away, and he desperately tries to talk them out of it. Though he addresses them as "my brothers," the old man's speech to his neighbours begins with the tone of the father figure in Proverbs reasoning with his son: "do not be wicked; since this man has come into my house, do not do this stupid thing" (19:23). The two phrases אל־תרעו (*al-tareʿu*) and אל־תעשו את־הנבלה הזאת (*al-taʿasu et-hanvalah hazot*) offer an improvised bi-colon reminiscent of a sentence proverb's typical parallelism, and feature two words straight out of Proverbs: the root רעע (*rʿ*) echoes the admonishment of proverbial evildoers (Prov 4:16; 17:4; 24:8; 24:19) and the root נבל (*nbl*) reminds us of

---

19. Edenburg, *Dismembering*, 175.

the proverbial fool (Prov 17:7, 21; 30:32). We might expect God, as in the parallel story in Genesis 19, to intervene at this point: if not blinding them (Gen 19:11) then at least handing them over to someone like Jael, who has her own way of dealing with rapists (Judg 4:21; 5:30). But, as in the Joseph narrative, these chapters of Judges sit apart from the rest: in typical wisdom fashion God's agency is backgrounded.[20]

For the time being, at least, the moral order seems clear: the band of evildoers outside, threatening the old man and the Levite inside. It is an awful situation, but the line between good and evil is, up to this point, preserved. The horrifying twist in this story, however, is that in the end it is not the ravenous sons of Benjamin outside who are responsible for the greatest horror—it is the old man and the Levite inside. Without waiting for the men's response to his appeal to wisdom, the old man enters into exactly the kind of compromise and complicity with wickedness that wisdom figures like Joseph, Job, and Daniel would never have entertained:

> Look—my virgin daughter and his *pilegesh*, how about I bring them out to you; you rape them, do to them whatever is good in your eyes—but to this man do not do this disgraceful thing. (19:24)

The repetition of "in your eyes" reminds us of the wisdom theme invoked in verse 1. No longer shrouded in the crowd's euphemistic word "knowledge," the old man names exactly what they are here for: the word ענה (*'nh*) in the *piel binyan* implies affliction or, as here, the humiliation of forced sexual intercourse (see 2 Sam 13:12). Two women to save one man—it is an obscene offer, made all the more unthinkable by the fact that it is the father of one of the women making it. We are perhaps relieved to hear that the men are not willing to listen to it. But our horror at a father's words is quickly eclipsed by a husband's actions. Without another word, "the man seizes his *pilegesh*" and throws her outside to them (19:25).[21]

The family, like the royal court, is a classic "wisdom setting."[22] Yet within the supposed safety of the household we are confronted by two wicked men: the father who offers his own daughter, and the husband who casts out, abandons, perhaps murders (the Hebrew is ambiguous), and then mutilates his own wife. That the iniquity of the Canaanites materialises so dramatically in the domestic sphere reflects in a perverse way wisdom literature's interest in the family as a context for instruction: "Listen my

---

20. Wilson, *Joseph, Wise and Otherwise*, 259.
21. Though grammatically the subject could be the old man.
22. Wilson, *Joseph, Wise and Otherwise*, 28.

son to the discipline of your father, and do not abandon the *torah* of your mother" (Prov 1:8). Only here, the discipline on offer is a crash course in the deep depravity of the nation.

Betrayed by her husband, and abused all night, we are left with a haunting final image of the woman lying in the street with her hands towards the threshold of the door (19:26–27).[23] Here Ansell's identification of the young woman with Lady Wisdom herself is most persuasive:[24]

> Wisdom in the street cries out
>
> in the town squares (רחבות) she puts out her voice
>
> over the top of the bustle she calls out
>
> at the city gates, her words. (Prov 1:20–21, see also 8:3)

Yet nobody in this city's רחב (*rkhov*, 19:17) is listening to her. Not until the man (now "her master," 19:27) emerges in the morning and callously tells her to "get up" does anyone pay her even passing attention, and by then her voice is extinguished, and he receives no response. Lady Wisdom is abused and discarded—a martyr for the iniquities of her nation.

Is she alive or dead when he puts her on his donkey? Or when he takes her on the daylong journey home? Or when he takes the knife and divides her limb-by-limb into twelve pieces (19:29)? Unlike the LXX, which reassures us by commuting his crime to mutilation of his wife's corpse, the Hebrew does not tell us either way. The ambivalence is excruciating.

The story ends with outrage, and from here events escalate into the political arena, as the wisdom setting transitions from family to the realm of onlooking sages, or perhaps a (in those days, vacant) royal court. All who see her mutilated body say:

> It hasn't happened . . . such a thing hasn't been seen . . . not from the day the sons of Israel came up from the land of Egypt until this day. Get on top of it! Take counsel! And speak out! (19:30)

This rare moment of explicit commentary, placed in the mouths of an invisible chorus of onlookers, carries significant wisdom freight. "All who see it" is כל־הראה, "every seer"; the word elsewhere is used for those with prophetic insight, such as Samuel in 1 Samuel 9:11, and indeed keeping on the path of wisdom requires the skill of observing reality rightly. The mute, and now mutilated, body challenges the twelve tribes to respond wisely, in a process of judgment: get on top of it (שימו־לכם עליה), take counsel (עצו), and finally speak out about it (ודברו). This is the same challenge, in three

---

23. Lapsley, *Whispering*, 48.
24. Ansell, "Body," 81.

slightly different imperatives, as Proverbs 31:9: "Open your mouth! Judge righteously! Defend the rights of the poor and needy!"

We can read this as a strong invitation, like that of Proverbs 1:5–6, to seek wisdom in our public response to private evil, exercising judgment based on godly observation and reflection. Yet that is not what happens next in the story. The poor young woman's death will provoke, not wise and measured "speaking out," but even more horrific and ill-advised acts of violence in the following chapters. Lady Wisdom's warning from beside the road that "all who hate me love death" (Prov 8:34) comes true: her death leads to ever-escalating cycles of violence, genocide, and mass rape. Wilson observes that the goal of wisdom is to find life.[25] Joseph's wisdom is shown in his work saving life from famine, and his refusal to retaliate against his brothers by killing them when he has the perfect opportunity, instead bringing reconciliation and ensuring the continuation of the covenant family—especially Benjamin, whose fate is at one point in his hands (Gen 44). Here is the Joseph story almost in reverse: life is cheapened, retaliation is disproportionate, violence escalates into mass death—and as a result of this rejection of wisdom the covenant is imperilled, and Benjamin very nearly destroyed.

Ambivalence and Discontinuity

Throughout this reading I have noted some of the resonances that emerge in Judges 19 when read alongside the traditional wisdom texts. Yet there is more to genre than mere intertextuality.[26] One crucial dimension of genre is that it specifies strategies for readers—not just writers—for engaging with a text. It is here that the payoff of the wisdom lens becomes clear.

Commentators are routinely troubled by the gaps and inconsistencies in Judges 19—it seems almost riddled with them! I have noted some of these already. The starkest example of this is the negotiation at the center of the story's dark plotline. Faced with the threat of male-male anal rape of the Levite on his doorstep, the host desperately offers the men of the city two women who they can abuse as much as they like, so long as they do not commit this "outrageous thing" against the one man.

The terms of the bargain have rightly scandalized the history of reception—on what sick calculus is the abuse of two women less "outrageous" than that of a single man, especially when one of them is the man's own daughter![27] Besides, if these men are "sodomites" then why do they accept

---

25. Wilson, *Joseph, Wise and Otherwise*, 241.
26. Contra Kynes, *Obituary*, 110.
27. We might wonder if the old man even *has* a virgin daughter, or if this is a

a woman in place of the man if that is their true nature and desire? Leaving aside the ethical issues of the exchange, the sequence of the negotiations is simply odd—two women are refused, but one woman then accepted. Accordingly, commentators must either explain a complex motivation,[28] or see the discontinuity in the men's response as a defect owing to its dependence on Genesis 19.[29]

In contrast, the wisdom genre lens helps us see this discontinuity as a feature, not a flaw. The unexplained discontinuity between their refusal and their actions gives the reader pause—the detail is perhaps not important in the broader narrative, but nevertheless the discontinuity makes it hard not to get the scene stuck in our mind at this point. The men become a riddle, of sorts—but one that will never fall out in a simple "aha!" moment. What it does instead is force us to think about them over and over. Given the proverbial anthropology of the wicked, perhaps we are ultimately not meant to see these men as reasonable agents calmly negotiating to achieve their considered goals. This is a mob, after all, not a delegation. The nature of their sin is that it is opportunistic and irrational: that their stated intentions in verbal negotiations might be incoherent or might break down in their actions when suddenly given power over an actual woman's body, is entirely in keeping with the proverbial worldview. The nature of the path that they have chosen—the path of the violent and the wicked—is that it is impulsive, undisciplined, incoherent, and ultimately self-destructive. We should not be surprised by our own capacity for wickedness—that is why it is wise to keep far away from even the opportunity to do evil, particularly when it comes to the powerful forces of lust (Prov 5:8). The narrator could, of course, just have told us all this, but the ambivalence and discontinuity forces us to sit, and think it over for ourselves.

Conclusion

Ambivalence is a favourite tool of the wisdom texts. Proverbs 26:4–5 for example: should you rebuke a fool according to his folly, or not? Ellen Davis captures the rhetorical strategy of Proverbs as forcing us to "ruminate slowly on one saying and then another," which helps us to acquire the "habit of slowly reconsidering what once seemed clear."[30] Likewise, part of the genius of Job is the way each speaker leads us further down the garden path as

---

desperate ruse?

28. See Bal, *Dissymmetry*, 120; Hamley, *Unspeakable*, loc. 5342.

29. Edenburg, *Dismembering*, 179.

30. Davis, *Opening Israel's Scriptures*, 451.

the apparent coherence of each speech is met by discontinuity—one thing seems right, until another speaks (Prov 18:17).

This wisdom lens brings out what the ambivalence and discontinuity of Judges 19 invite the reader to do. The narrator constantly complicates things for us: the honorable Levite seeking his wife's heart becomes a callous monster, the hostile Canaanite and hospitable Israelite towns swap places, and the righteous outrage at Gibeah leads to a far greater outrage against Benjamin in the following chapters. In the broader context of the Former Prophets, we are required to sit with the ambivalence of political solutions: the monarchy is one answer to the escalating chaos of tribal retribution we see in Judges 19–21. But monarchy is a solution with its own discontinuities, and the wise do well to see those clearly as well. After all, knowing which of two contradictory statements applies to which situation is what Proverbs trains us in.

For my generation, raised on fairy tales and Facebook, it is impossible to understate how vital this is. Fairy tales present the world in black and white, with characters whose names reduce them to a single moral axis: the wicked stepmother, the beautiful princess, the wise king. Social media trains us through its relentless rituals to form judgments quickly—like, dislike, outrage, block. The wisdom genre requires something very different of us. At every turn it frustrates our attempts to make quick judgments about the characters, or jump to tidy ethical conclusions. We are invited to sit with the wise and observe the messiness of reality, with all its ambivalence and discontinuity; to get on top of it, take counsel, and then, only then, to speak out.

Bibliography

Ansell, Nicholas. "This Is Her Body: Judges 19 as Call to Discernment." In *Tamar's Tears: Evangelical Engagements with Feminist Old Testament Hermeneutics*, edited by Andrew Sloane, 65–103. Eugene, OR: Wipf and Stock, 2012.

Bal, Mieke. *Death and Dissymmetry: The Politics of Coherence in the Book of Judges*. Chicago: University of Chicago Press, 1988.

Block, Daniel I. *Judges, Ruth*. New American Commentary. Vol. 6. Nashville: Broadman & Holman, 1999.

Davis, Ellen F. *Opening Israel's Scriptures*. New York: Oxford, 2019.

Edenburg, Cynthia. *Dismembering the Whole: Composition and Purpose of Judges 19–21*. Atlanta: SBL, 2016.

Fowler, Alastair. *Kinds of Literature: An Introduction to the Theory of Genres and Modes*. Oxford: Clarendon, 1982.

Frow, John. *Genre*. The New Critical Idiom. 2nd ed. New York: Routledge, 2015.

Gerhart, Mary. "Generic Competence in Biblical Hermeneutics." *Semeia* 43 (1988) 29–44.

———. "Generic Studies: Their Renewed Importance in Religious and Literary Interpretation." *JAAR* XLV, no. 3 (1977) 309–25.

Hamley, Isabelle M. *Unspeakable Things Unspoken: An Irigarayan Reading of Otherness and Victimization in Judges 19–21*. Eugene, OR: Pickwick, 2019.

Kautzsch, Emil, ed. *Gesenius' Hebrew Grammar*. Translated by Arthur. E. Cowley. 2nd ed. London: Oxford, 1910.

Kynes, Will. *An Obituary for "Wisdom Literature": The Birth, Death, and Intertextual Reintegration of a Biblical Corpus*. Oxford: Oxford University Press, 2019.

Lapsley, Jacqueline E. *Whispering the Word: Hearing Women's Stories in the Old Testament*. Louisville: Westminster John Knox, 2005.

Ricoeur, Paul. "The Hermeneutical Function of Distanciation." *Philosophy Today* 17, no. 2 (1973) 129–41.

Thompson, John L. *Writing the Wrongs: Women of the Old Testament among Biblical Commentators from Philo through the Reformation*. Oxford: Oxford University Press, 2001.

Trible, Phyllis. *Texts of Terror: Literary-Feminist Readings of Biblical Narratives*. Philadelphia: Fortress, 1984.

Wilson, Lindsay. *Joseph, Wise and Otherwise: The Intersection of Wisdom and Covenant in Genesis 37–50*. Milton Keynes: Paternoster, 2004.

3

Critical Views of Wisdom in Samuel's Revolt Narratives

David G. Firth

Introduction

ALTHOUGH WE HAVE LEFT the time when Whybray could suggest that the Succession Narrative[1] could be considered as a work of wisdom literature[2] (not least because the question of whether or not there is a Succession Narrative is now a live question[3]), the value of his observation on the importance for wisdom as a motif in these chapters should still be acknowledged.[4] The presence of numerous references to wisdom cannot really establish a genre, but it is a significant factor which should be considered when noting the theology of the narrative. For the purposes of this chapter, a slightly narrower focus will be applied, considering only 2 Samuel 9–20 as a court narrative and thus setting aside the issue of succession. When this approach is followed, it becomes clear that these chapters offer a highly critical reading of David and his court. In part, this is because much of the text is given over

---

1. Understood broadly as 2 Samuel 9–20 and 1 Kings 1–2.
2. Whybray, *Succession Narrative*, 56–95.
3. See Firth, *Kingdom Comes*, 41–49. For a contemporary reading that presumes this model, see Miller, *King and a Fool*.
4. Auld, *I & II Samuel*, 478, points out that the words for "wisdom" and "wise" occur only in 2 Samuel 13–20, and not elsewhere in Samuel.

to working out the details of David's punishment for his murder of Uriah the Hittite following his adulterous relationship with Bathsheba. However, a consistent feature of this narrative is its use of what Yairah Amit has called "dual causality."[5] In this, human characters make free choices while at the same time they are fulfilling Yahweh's purposes. Through this technique, the narrative shows both that David's sin is reaping its inevitable outcome and that the sin of others continues to impact others negatively.

The court narrative can be divided into four principal sections. Two Samuel 9–10 provides the background to David's sin, with the sin itself and the content of the resultant punishment recounted in 2 Samuel 11–12. Following this, 2 Samuel 13–20 covers two revolt narratives, the long revolt narrative (2 Sam 13–19) which is concerned with Absalom's revolt, while the short revolt narrative (2 Sam 20) focuses on the revolt of Sheba ben Bichri.[6] Broken down this way, it quickly becomes evident that wisdom is not a significant feature in either the background (2 Sam 9–10) or the sin narrative (2 Sam 11–12). Wisdom is not prominent in the first two sections but then becomes a significant feature of the revolt narratives. Wisdom is highlighted through the role played in the revolt narratives by several characters who are, in various ways, said to be wise. Wisdom is a significant element in their characterization since in each case the narrator either describes them as being wise or places them in a role where giving advice is central.[7] On this basis, we will consider Jonadab and Ahithophel before briefly contrasting them with the wise woman from Tekoa, Hushai the Archite, and the wise woman from Abel. On the basis of dual causality, it will become apparent that much of this wisdom is applied to acts which are assessed negatively. This is because many of these characters contribute further to David's punishment, though more positive assessments of wisdom are also possible. But one particularly disturbing feature of the negative examples of wisdom is that they are associated with sexual violence against women. It soon becomes evident that the revolt narratives are showing the effects of David's sin,[8] and in particular how they are worked out in his own family.

---

5. Amit, *Art of Editing*, 105–21, and, applied to this narrative, Amit, "Absalom," 266.

6. Firth, *Samuel*, 37–39. Note that this means Samuel includes a long rivalry narrative (David and Saul, 1 Sam 16—2 Sam 1), and a short rivalry narrative (David and Ish-bosheth, 2 Sam 2:1—5:5), all of which pivot around the reflection on the whole of David's reign in 2 Samuel 5:17—8:14. For analogies from Mari for this model of reading Samuel, see Bodi, "David as an 'Apiru," 26–31.

7. On the crucial role played by characterization in the interpretation of Samuel, see Johnson, "Character."

8. Here, following, Keys, *Wages of Sin*, 127–41.

Within these more negative portrayals, wisdom is shown to be something which works with those in power, enabling the powerful to abuse the weak, especially women. That is, there are species of wisdom which collaborate with the powerful to act in ways which are destructive, though this is not the only form of wisdom. However, there is also a striking contrast in that those who demonstrate a more positive wisdom are themselves either women or foreign. Wisdom can resist sin, but wisdom that is too closely associated with power replicates the abuse of the weak that David had shown in his sin, and this is particularly damaging for women.

Jonadab and the Rape of Tamar

The events of 2 Samuel 13 are a low point in David's story. At the outset, we are introduced to Absalom and his beautiful sister Tamar, but then discover that Tamar was the object of the love of her half brother Amnon (2 Sam 13:1). Tamar's beauty is immediately noted, a factor which in Samuel is always important. David himself has been described as beautiful (1 Sam 16:12; 17:42), as also is Absalom, though in his case his beauty is only noted later (2 Sam 14:25, 27). Otherwise, only Abigail was said to be beautiful (1 Sam 25:3). Nevertheless, Kim is right to point to a connection to Bathsheba's good looks (2 Sam 11:2) since, although the wording is different, there is a conceptual link.[9] Just as Bathsheba's beauty attracted David, so also Tamar's attracts Amnon, though in both cases this was a forbidden union. But where David apparently had a compliant group of attendants who arranged for Bathsheba to be brought to him (2 Sam 11:2–5), and he apparently had no compunction in committing adultery, Amnon was clearly well aware that he could not have a sexual relationship with his sister, even to the point of becoming ill as a result (2 Sam 13:2). But just when it seems as if nothing inappropriate will happen, Amnon's friend Jonadab[10] is introduced. As will become clear in the case of Hushai the Archite, a "friend" was a counsellor. In Jonadab's case, this point is made immediately clear in the note that he was "very wise" (איש חכם מאד).[11] But what is the nature of his wisdom? As will become clear, it is wisdom that is prepared to work with Amnon to act with his sister in a way which could never be appropriate. Instead, Jonadab's wisdom will focus

---

9. Kim, *Identity*, 118–19.

10. LXX calls him "Jonathan," but the MT form of his name is used in this chapter.

11. Several versions (e.g., ESV) render this as "very crafty" in order to highlight the negative portrayal of his character. However, this reveals in advance something that the narrator will only disclose as the narrative proceeds, so the more neutral translation should be followed.

on giving Amnon access to his sister in a clearly inappropriate way, offering wisdom which supports the powerful abusing the weak.

Jonadab's astuteness is both flagged directly by the narrator and made evident when, immediately after his introduction, he engaged Amnon in conversation about his apparent ill health. He is a member of David's wider family, so we should assume that he has some access to Amnon in general, and not only as a member of the court. His question to Amnon, asking about his health, is apparently quite straightforward, and yet it elicits an excess of information about Amnon's problem, not only that he is in love with Tamar but that she is also Absalom's sister—indeed, as Amnon's response is phrased, it is Tamar's relationship to Absalom that is stated before his own desire for her (2 Sam 13:4).[12] In this way, the barrier to any relationship between Amnon and Tamar is stressed, as well as laying a foundation which will expose a stress point within the royal family since the conflict between Amnon and Absalom will also become more evident as the chapter proceeds, most notably when Absalom's response to Tamar's condition after being expelled from Amnon's room is simply to ask if Amnon has been with her (2 Sam 13:20). Amnon's response seems initially to show both his problem and that it was not capable of resolution.[13]

Despite this, Jonadab's wisdom is quickly employed, directing Amnon to lie on his bed and act ill. His language here is freighted with suggestion, the opening imperative שכב serving both as a perfectly regular word for lying down, and also one which can serve as a euphemism for sexual intercourse.[14] Suggesting that Amnon lie on the bed could be an entirely innocent statement, though it could also prepare for the sexual activity that will follow. This highlights a consistent feature of Jonadab's language, which is carefully ambiguous throughout, speaking in terms that could have an innocent meaning, but which within the larger context clearly prepare for sexual abuse. Although most versions suggest that Amnon is to "feign illness"[15] this would perhaps go beyond the intent of the verb here since it repeats the verb חלה from verse 2. Since in both cases the hithpa'el is used, the sense would rather be that Amnon was making himself ill because of his repressed desire, though perhaps in this case there is an emphasis on him making his illness more evident.[16] That is, Amnon was already making

---

12. This is a consistent feature of the opening of this chapter—note that 13:1 also introduces Absalom before Tamar and Amnon.

13. See also Long, *1 and 2 Samuel*, 378.

14. This interplay runs through four occurrences of this verb in 2 Samuel 11.

15. Here, using the hithpa'el of חלה, as also in 2 Sam 13:2.

16. Taking the verb in both cases as a reflective-factitive (Williams, *Syntax*, §154) provides a more coherent approach than is represented in most translations.

himself ill, and simply making it known that he was ill would apparently lead to a visit from David. David's visit would then enable Amnon to request a visit from Tamar so that she might bake some bread before him. Once again, his language is fraught with possible ambiguity since the verb "to come" (בוא) is a perfectly routine word for entering a place, but it is also a frequent euphemism for sexual intercourse. Nothing Jonadab says necessarily has any sexual overtones but given that Amnon has already admitted to a strong sexual desire for his half sister there are good reasons for thinking that Jonadab's language is open to the possibility that a sexual relationship between Amnon and Tamar is being set up. Indeed, his wisdom is perhaps shown in that although there might be plausible deniability for all he says, his words are still capable of a sexual interpretation.

This latent possibility in Jonadab's words may well be picked up by Amnon when he makes his request to David. Jonadab's plan has worked to this point so that immediately after directing Amnon to follow the plan, the narrative immediately moves to David's visit. David is not reported as speaking to Amnon, but we do have David's request that Tamar make some cakes in his sight so he can eat from her hand. A common feature of Hebrew narrative is that it uses repetition, so we might expect Amnon to use the actual words Jonadab had suggested. But although he clearly follows the contours of the plan, there are subtle changes. Jonadab had suggested simply that Tamar give him bread, preparing the food in his sight so he could eat from her hand. But rather than bread, he uses the word לבבות, usually understood as some sort of cake, and given the association of the word with the Hebrew for "heart" perhaps some sort of food for the ill. Yet along with this, he also uses the pi'el of the verb לבב to describe the preparation. The only other place we find this verb is in Song 4:9 where it speaks of a captivated heart in a clearly erotic context.[17] Amnon's words, like those of Jonadab, can be understood as an innocent request, but given the other connotations of the language used it is also possible that he speaks in a way that follows the lead established for him by Jonadab, a subtle acknowledgement of sexual intent that cannot be expressed directly because it is obviously unacceptable.

The subtle use of language in Jonadab's proposal and the way it is then developed by Amnon suggests that the narrator is carefully preparing readers for an illicit sexual encounter. Although Fokkelman thinks that Jonadab has only created a context in which Amnon and Tamar can be together,[18] it is more likely that he is shown as preparing for Tamar's rape.

---

17. Long, *1 and 2 Samuel*, 378, tentatively suggests that "enflame" could be an appropriate rendering for both settings.

18. Fokkelman, *King David*, 109.

This is clear from the fact that an assumed starting point is that a sexual relationship between Amnon and Tamar is regarded as impossible by Amnon from the outset. Irrespective therefore of whether the law in Leviticus 18:9 was in force, such a sexual relationship was clearly regarded as forbidden, otherwise the subterfuge proposed by Jonadab would have been unnecessary. If it is correct to read his speech as containing various *double entendre* (and Amnon's development of it would suggest he understood it in those terms), then this both demonstrates the nature of his wisdom and the ways in which it was applied to the goal of Amnon engaging in illicit sexual intercourse with Tamar. Admittedly, Jonadab could still claim that he had prepared for a sexual relationship, not rape—and we should of course acknowledge that rape as a specific category of illicit sex probably did not exist in Israel. But to prepare for something acknowledged by all as wrong means that would be only a very limited defence. In any case, Jonadab's wisdom is applied to the task of knowingly subverting established sexual relationships, and Tamar's rape is the outcome.

For the purposes of this chapter we do not need to consider the rape itself since Jonadab is not present for that. He only reappears at the end of 2 Samuel 13, after Amnon has been killed by Absalom. At this point, David has heard that Absalom had killed all David's sons, but Jonadab spoke up to tell him that this was incorrect (2 Sam 13:30–33). Rather, Absalom had only killed Amnon. His reasoning here is notable for the way it acknowledges the nature of Amnon's actions, noting that he had violated his sister Tamar. His use of the pi'el of ענה at this point indicates that he knows that Amnon had forced himself on his sister. The intriguing thing to note is that although he is not shown as having any particular information that would explain Absalom's actions, he was astute enough to work out that Amnon alone was the object of Absalom's anger because of the sexual abuse of Tamar. That is, he is shown as being aware of what had happened, but the only point at which he speaks of it is to calm David when David thinks his other sons have all been killed. His advice is soon shown to be correct as the other royal sons return (2 Sam 13:35). Jonadab seeks to ingratiate himself with the royal family, and Tamar's suffering can pass without comment. We do not hear of Jonadab again, but the effects of his wisdom are clear.

Ahithophel and the Concubines from Jerusalem

After Jonadab, the next major wise man is Ahithophel, a counsellor who was especially known for the quality of his wisdom and who aligned himself with Absalom in his rebellion against David. Indeed, we are first introduced to Ahithophel at the point where Absalom is launching his revolt with the note that Absalom sent for him while he was offering sacrifices in Hebron, his notional reason for going to the city (2 Sam 15:11–12). At this point, Ahithophel is introduced as David's counsellor, though given that this point is immediately followed by a note that Absalom's conspiracy continued to grow there may be an implication that Ahithophel was part of that. Ahithophel's significance is then gradually developed by the narrator. As David was making his ascent of the Mount of Olives in his flight from Jerusalem,[19] having left ten concubines behind (2 Sam 15:16), one of the key pieces of information he received is that Ahithophel has aligned himself with Absalom. This leads to one of the few prayers in 2 Samuel, this time a very brief one, as David prays that Yahweh would turn Ahithophel's counsel to foolishness (2 Sam 15:31). Although Ahithophel has only recently been brought into the story, his importance is emphasized by this note. David here clearly assumes that the advice that Ahithophel will give is good and that therefore the only way for it to be overcome is through Yahweh's intervention.[20] Narratively, this represents a decisive turning point for it is here that David begins to reconnect with Yahweh, though readers do not know this yet. But it also serves to characterize Ahithophel's wisdom as being of a high standard.

That David's prayer is being answered is hinted at by his next encounter, this time with Hushai the Archite. Hushai will later be described as David's "friend" (2 Sam 16:16), a title that links him to Jonadab and marks him as a close confidant of David's. But here, he is simply "the Archite." This gentilic identifies him as a descendant of one of the surviving Canaanite groups (Josh 16:2).[21] Although this might seem an unpromising designation, it is notable that in David's flight it is actually foreigners who mark the decisive points of change for him.[22] But at this stage, we are not told what Hushai's skill set might be. There may be a hint of his work as a counsellor in David's suggestion that he return to Jerusalem in order to defeat Ahithophel's counsel (2 Sam 15:34), but details of his characterization are withheld at this point to leave such matters open while again showing the strength of Ahithophel's counsel.

The importance of Ahithophel's counsel has thus been progressively developed through the narrative, and this is again stressed as the narrative

---

19. It should be stressed that although there will ultimately be battle between David and Absalom's forces, his flight is not presented as a military action, but rather as an expression of mourning. See Keys, *Wages of Sin*, 153, and Seiler, *Geschichte*, 145.

20. Cf. Mann, *Run, David, Run!*, 97.

21. Firth, *Including the Stranger*, 125.

22. Firth, "Foreigners," 248–53.

turns instead to Absalom's arrival in Jerusalem as it is immediately noted that Ahithophel was with him (2 Sam 16:15). David has not spoken against Absalom, but he has instead focused on Ahithophel, so his mention here reinforces the threat he posed and which Hushai had to address. Only at this point is Hushai's status as David's friend noted (2 Sam 16:16), showing that he too is a counsellor. Once Hushai has integrated himself into Absalom's household, the scene is set for the conflict between the counsellors. Nevertheless, it is immediately clear that Hushai is working from a disadvantage relative to Ahithophel. This is apparent as Absalom turns to Ahithophel for advice about how he should act now he has control of Jerusalem. His advice is direct—Absalom should make himself offensive to his father, and the way to do this is to have sex with the concubines David had left behind to keep his house (2 Sam 16:21). According to Ahithophel, this act would strengthen the hand of all that were with Absalom. Unlike Jonadab in his preparations for Amnon's rape of Tamar, for whom there might have been a degree of plausible deniability built into his speech, there is nothing like that here. Rather, this fits with what is an emerging pattern in 2 Samuel, where a perceived way of attacking another man is through sexual intercourse with a wife or concubine of his. This was the basis of Ish-bosheth's accusation of disloyalty against Abner, claiming that he had a sexual relationship with Saul's concubine Rizpah (2 Sam 3:7). The narrative never makes clear whether there was any truth in this claim, but it does form part of a picture that develops in Samuel of attacking another man who was a (perceived) rival through a sexual relationship. Ahithophel's advice, which amounts to a plan to rape ten women simply because of their association with David, is notable for its callous indifference to the women.[23] Like Jonadab, Ahithophel treats these women as a means to an end. As for these women, their mention in the short revolt narrative (2 Sam 20:3) shows that their suffering did not come to an end just because David was restored.

It is possible that the larger narrative hints at why Ahithophel makes this suggestion, though it is not one that readers can resolve at this point. According to 2 Samuel 11:3, Bathsheba's father's name was Eliam (2 Sam 11:3), while Ahithophel had a son with the same name (2 Sam 23:34). If the same Eliam is meant, then Ahithophel would have been Bathsheba's grandfather. This cannot be proved, but the connection is an intriguing one and at least shows that the revolt is still tied to David's sin in his sexual relationship

---

23. Quite how the rape of these women fits into the timeline of the larger narrative is uncertain, leading to suggestions of different redactional layers (nicely summarised by Seiler, *Geschichte*, 150–63). But once we recognize that Samuel often recounts matters in a dischronologized form, plausible solutions which work with the narrative integrity here emerge (see Firth, *1 & 2 Samuel*, 467–68).

with Bathsheba and murder of Uriah.[24] Nevertheless, we must still respect the text's silence as to Ahithophel's motivation, and in any case David's concubines are innocent of any involvement in his relationship with Bathsheba and Uriah. Instead, with a tent pitched on the roof so all in Jerusalem would know what was happening, Absalom raped each of these women.

Interpreters have understood the value of Ahithophel's advice differently,[25] but the one that matters here is surely the observation provided by the narrator in the observation that Ahithophel's advice was as if one had received a divine oracle (2 Sam 16:23). That is, Absalom would almost certainly have made himself odious to his father by such an action, and in so doing his supporters would know there was no going back. Only after this event has passed will there be an opportunity to challenge Ahithophel's advice in the contest of the advisors reported in 2 Samuel 17:1–14, though it should be noted that although Hushai offers advice contrary to that of Ahithophel, the narrator makes clear that it was not his advice that actually defeated that of Ahithophel. Rather, it was Yahweh who answered David's prayer, and that so that Absalom would be defeated. The failure of Ahithophel's advice to carry the day finally led to his suicide (2 Sam 17:23).

Conclusion

Ahithophel has clearly been presented as the wisest man of his generation, but his wisdom was too closely associated with the powerful, something that is also true of Jonadab. Both were undoubtedly wise, counsellors astute enough to ensure that the outcomes desired by the powerful people to whom they attached themselves were achieved. But such wisdom is hardly presented as something positive. That an alternative approach to wisdom is possible is something modelled in the narrative through other wise people who are mentioned. What is striking is that none of them represent the sources of wisdom to which the powerful might ordinarily be drawn. We have already noted Hushai, a descendant of the Canaanites who offers a more positive portrayal of what wisdom can achieve, but we should also note the role played by the wise woman from Tekoa (2 Sam 14:1–20) and the wise woman from Abel (2 Sam 20:16–22), one from each revolt narrative. Space precludes a detailed treatment of either, but their place within the revolt narratives and their general interest in wisdom should be noted. In both cases, these women come from relatively remote towns, yet both are shown seeking to minimize harm (even if neither can prevent it absolutely),

---

24. See Bodner, *David Observed*, 138.
25. See the summary in Mann, *Run, David, Run!*, 127–28.

and both are particularly noted for their wisdom. Together, Hushai and these two anonymous wise women demonstrate an approach to wisdom that is not so embedded with the desires of the powerful that they simply provide them with what they want. Rather, the species of wisdom which is encouraged is one that sees that the desires of the powerful must be challenged. But this is true of neither Jonadab nor Ahithophel. Instead, they are presented as men who made their own choices, even if those choices were part of Yahweh's punishment of David. In doing so, they were willing to work with those in power to abuse women sexually to achieve their own goals. But Samuel will not support such actions. Instead, these two are presented as a warning of wisdom gone wrong. It is not monarchy itself that is the problem, even if Samuel is aware that monarchy can be deeply problematic.[26] Rather, when wisdom is simply supporting the wishes of the powerful then it has subverted its own purpose, and it is women whose suffering is particularly noted when this happens.

Bibliography

Amit, Yairah. "Absalom: A Warrior for Justice—A Life Story in Seven Stages." In *Characters and Characterization in the Book of Samuel*, edited by K. Bodner and B. J. M. Johnson, 255–70. LHBOTS 669. London: T. & T. Clark, 2020.

———. *The Book of Judges: The Art of Editing*. Leiden: Brill, 1999.

Auld, A. Graeme. *I & II Samuel: A Commentary*. Louisville: Westminster John Knox, 2011.

Bodi, Daniel. "David as an 'Apiru in 1 Samuel 25 and the Pattern of Seizing Power in the Ancient Near East." In *Abigail, Wife of David and Other Ancient Oriental Women*, edited by Daniel Bodi, 24–59. HBM 60. Sheffield: Sheffield Phoenix, 2013.

Bodner, Keith. *David Observed: A King in the Eyes of His Court*. HBM 5. Sheffield: Sheffield Phoenix, 2005.

Firth, David G. *1 & 2 Samuel*. Nottingham: Apollos, 2009.

———. *1 and 2 Samuel: A Kingdom Comes*. London: T. & T. Clark, 2017.

———. "Foreigners in David's Court." In *Characters and Characterization in the Book of Samuel*, edited by Keith Bodner and Benjamin J. M. Johnson, 239–54. LHBOTS 669. London: T. & T. Clark, 2020.

———. *Including the Stranger: Foreigners in the Former Prophets*. NSBT. London: Apollos, 2019.

Fokkelman, Jan P. *Narrative Art and Poetry in the Books of Samuel: A Full Interpretation Based on Stylistic and Structural Analyses. Vol I: King David (II Sam. 9–20 & I Kings 1–2)*. Assen: Van Gorcum, 1981.

Johnson, Benjamin J. M. "Character as Interpretive Crux in the Book of Samuel." In *Characters and Characterization in the Book of Samuel*, edited by Keith Bodner and Benjamin J. M. Johnson, 1–13. LHBOTS 669. London: T. & T. Clark, 2020.

---

26. Against Westbrook, "*And He Will Take*," 206–7.

Keys, Gillian. *The Wages of Sin: A Reappraisal of the "Succession Narrative."* LHBOTS 221. Sheffield: Sheffield Academic, 1996.

Kim, U. Y. *Identity and Loyalty in the David Story.* HBM 22. Sheffield: Sheffield Phoenix, 2008.

Long, V. Philips. *1 and 2 Samuel: An Introduction and Commentary.* London: IVP, 2020.

Mann, Steven T. *Run, David, Run! An Investigation of the Theological Speech Acts of David's Departure and Return (2 Samuel 14–20).* Siphrut 10. Winona Lake: Eisenbrauns, 2013.

Miller, Virginia. *A King and a Fool? The Succession Narrative as a Satire.* Biblical Interpretation 179. Leiden: Brill, 2019.

Seiler, Stefan. *Die Geschichte von der Thronfolge Davids (2 Sam 9–20; 1 Kön 1–2): Untersuchungen zur Literarkritik und Tendenz.* Berlin: Walter de Gruyter, 1998.

Westbrook, April D. *"And He Will Take Your Daughters . . .": Woman Story and the Ethical Evaluation of Monarchy in the David Narrative.* LHBOTS 610. London: Bloomsbury, 2015.

Whybray, Roger Norman. The *Succession Narrative.* London: SCM, 1968.

Williams, Ronald J. *Williams' Hebrew Syntax.* 3rd ed. Revised and expanded by J. C. Beckman. Toronto: University of Toronto Press, 2007.

4

Honoring the Wise King

*The Solomonic Ideal in
1–2 Kings and Beyond*

ANDREW T. ABERNETHY

UPON JOINING RIDLEY'S FACULTY, I read Lindsay Wilson's *Joseph, Wise and Otherwise*.[1] He took a character who is rarely associated with wisdom, Joseph, and helped us see how wisdom is integral to Genesis 37–50. In this chapter, I consider a figure renowned for wisdom, Solomon. Although known for wisdom, Solomon is a mixed bag in 1 Kings 1–11. On the one hand, Solomon's wisdom is incomparable, he builds God a temple, and Israel expands its borders and experiences prosperity as never before under his leadership. On the other hand, Solomon acts with cruelty, is self-centered, has one thousand wives, and ends up worshipping foreign gods. So, is Solomon really wise or is he otherwise? How can someone who possesses such wisdom fail so miserably? Although valid questions, I would like to shift the direction of focus beyond merely evaluating the *person* of Solomon: "Is Solomon wise, foolish, or a hybrid?" We must also ask about

---

1. This chapter is dedicated to Lindsay Wilson, mentor, colleague, and friend. I had the privilege of being on faculty with him for three and a half years, my first stretch of full-time teaching. I am forever grateful for his encouragement and partnership in training students at Ridley. Although far more experienced than me, Lindsay made me feel like I belonged, which is no small thing in light of the imposter syndrome all new faculty experience.

the *purpose* of Solomon's wisdom as part of the book of 1–2 Kings: "What role does the account of Solomon's wisdom play in the purposes of 1–2 Kings?" I will argue that Solomon's wisdom contributes to the portrait of the ideal king in 1–2 Kings, one that looks beyond Solomon and subsequent kings to a greater (perhaps messianic) king.

A Negative View of Solomon?

A prominent strand within biblical scholarship is to see Solomon in an entirely negative light within 1–2 Kings. Two scholarly arguments will illustrate this negative view.[2]

J. Daniel Hays argues that subtle, ironic critiques of Solomon in the first ten chapters culminate in a burst of condemnation at the end in 1 Kings 10:26—11:13.[3] Hays amasses many convincing examples of subtle critique across the opening ten chapters. Solomon is harsh and vindictive in chapters 1–2.[4] He marries Pharaoh's daughter and sacrifices at high places at the start of chapter 3.[5] When it comes to God granting wisdom to Solomon, Hays interprets it negatively as well:

> I would suggest that the main purpose within the broad story of Solomon for including the narrative of Yahweh's appearance and his gift of wisdom to Solomon in 3.4–15 is to underscore Solomon's great culpability for his later apostasy. This text is not ultimately praising Solomon; it is underscoring the absurdity of his turning away from Yahweh.[6]

The critique continues in the second half of chapter 3 where Solomon associates with those engaged in the forbidden act of prostitution.[7] The idyllic depictions of life under Solomon (ch. 4) and preparations for temple building (ch. 5) stem from Solomon's oppressive ways, as Samuel had warned about in 1 Samuel 8. Amidst the building of the temple (chs. 6–8), the narrator tells us (6:38—7:1) that Solomon devoted nearly twice

---

2. Another negative example is Clements, "Solomon," 25–26. He argues that 1 Kings 3 was created and added later to justify the monarchy and how it took over the task of administering justice.

3. Hays, "Has the Narrator," 149–74.

4. Hays, "Has the Narrator," 158–60. For a more positive assessment of Solomon's succession in light of ANE succession narratives and Solomon's second name ("Beloved of Yhwh"), see Kalimi, "Love."

5. Hays, "Has the Narrator," 161.

6. Hays, "Has the Narrator," 164.

7. Hays, "Has the Narrator," 164–65.

as much time to building his own house (13 years) than to building God's house (7 years). Chapter 9 echoes the critique of 1 Kings 5. In chapter 10, a subtle critique by the Queen of Sheba gives way to presenting Solomon's failures (10:26—11:13) in light of the expectations of the king from Deuteronomy 17—he must not accumulate many horses, many wives, and great wealth. Solomon fails on all accounts. Thus, for Hays, the entire account is a criticism of Solomon: "The subtle narrator of 1-2 Kings has not come to praise Solomon but to bury him."[8]

While Hays makes his case by combing through the eleven chapters in search of subtle critiques,[9] Alison L. Joseph views Solomon negatively in view of how these chapters function within the overall purposes of 1-2 Kings.[10] Why are some kings said to be "upright" and others "evil" in 1-2 Kings? Why are some kings said to be like or unlike David throughout the book? Joseph argues that a Davidic prototype, fashioned in the image of Josiah, resides in the background throughout the entire work. The Solomon narrative contributes to this in two major ways. First, the Solomon narrative establishes a Josaianic-Davidic prototype via reference to David. David commands Solomon to keep the commands of Moses (1 Kgs 2:3-4), as does God (3:14; 6:12; 9:4-5), making success for a king contingent upon obedience to Torah. What is more, David is referred to on several occasions as a model for Torah observance in this part of the book (3:6; 3:14; 6:12; 9:4-5). The prototype, then, against which Solomon will be measured is a David who was faithful to God's Torah, like Josiah in 2 Kings 22-23. Second, Solomon's failures in chapter 11 make it clear that he does not meet these expectations, resulting in an assessment of him that will linger throughout the book: "Solomon did what was evil in the eyes of the LORD and he was not fully behind the LORD like David his father" (11:6).[11] Subsequent kings will be assessed in light of whether or not they were disobedient like Solomon, as the first king who did evil in the eyes of the Lord. Thus, the Solomon narrative introduces the prototype of the ideal king via recourse to David's

---

8. Hays, "Has the Narrator," 174. Conway, "Wisest Might Err," 43, draws a similar conclusion: "The enduring message of the Solomon narrative may not be to hold him up as an exemplar of wisdom and of piety, but it may be to warn subsequent generations of the dangers of misusing God's gifting and of failing to appropriate God's enabling."

9. See also Sweeney, "Critique," 613-17.

10. Joseph, *Portrait*, 58-76, 98-105. Sweeney, "Critique," argues that Josiah, not David, was the ideal king of the Deuteronomistic History and that Solomon's failure prepares for the remedy that comes in Josiah. Joseph's work extends the argument of Marvin Sweeney—her doctoral supervisor—by clarifying how the Davidic ideal of 1-2 Kings is modeled after Josiah. Neither Sweeney nor Joseph clarify how 1 Kings 3 fits into the picture, as they presumably interpret it as a later level of redaction.

11. All translations are my own unless otherwise noted.

obedience (fashioned in light of Josiah, not 1–2 Samuel) and presents Solomon as a failure in this regard, "initiating the model for how to evaluate bad kings—those who are not like David."[12]

By way of assessment, there is much to be said for these two studies. Hays, in my opinion, has dismantled a common notion that Solomon is presented in an entirely positive light in 1 Kings 3–8.[13] Similarly, Joseph's study is generally compelling, as Solomon does indeed provide the book's first window into what kingship is meant to entail and how Solomon fails with regards to Torah obedience. There are limitations, however, to both Hays's and Joseph's arguments. They both fall prey to an *all or nothing* sort of argumentation. To Hays, one must ask if the so-called Deuteronomist *only* wants to "bury" Solomon in condemnation. Could some of the positives in Solomon's reign endure beyond his failure? To Joseph, one must ask whether her myopic focus on the *Davidic ideal* causes her to overlook other aspects of the royal ideal that emerge from the positive parts of the Solomon narrative. Again, we can ask: Might the positives in Solomon's reign endure beyond his failure so as to infuse the ideal king of 1–2 Kings with a Solomonesque flavor? I will pursue this line of thought below.

Solomon's Wisdom

When read on its own, 1 Kings 3:4–15 can only be interpreted positively. Sure, this event occurs at the high place of Gibeon (3:4–5), but this does not prevent God from appearing to Solomon and inviting Solomon to make a request. The omniscient narrator tells us that Solomon's request for wisdom was "pleasing in the eyes of the Lord" (3:10). In the divine response, God specifies why he is favorable towards this request: ". . . you did not request for yourself length of days and did not request for yourself riches and did not request the life of your enemies, but you requested for yourself discernment to hear justice" (3:11). The author of Kings is unmistakably presenting Solomon's request for wisdom favorably. This becomes abundantly clear in the following verse: "Behold, I [God] have done according to your words, behold I have given to you a wise and understanding heart with the result that there was no one like you before you and after you no one will arise like you" (3:12). Gary Knoppers sets this statement of Solomon's extraordinary wisdom in its larger context of 1–2 Kings, where

---

12. Joseph, *Portrait*, 114.

13. See for instance, Parker, *Wisdom and Law*, who argues that chapters 3–8 assess Solomon positively and 9–11 assess Solomon negatively. Williams, "Once Again," attempts to ground Parker's schema in linguistic data.

there are only two other statements of incomparability after this in the entire book, applying to Hezekiah's trust (2 Kgs 18:5) and Josiah's religious reforms (23:25).[14] The narrator aims to present Solomon as exemplary in wisdom, and the divine speech confirms the positive vantage point a reader is invited to adopt when reading this account.

The Solomon narrative goes on to display this wisdom, thereby depicting how God's promise of wisdom is fulfilled (1 Kgs 3:16–28).[15] The emphasis on judicial wisdom is apparent in chapter 3. Solomon requests: "Give to your servant a listening heart to judge your people to understand between right and wrong, for who is able to judge this great people of yours!" (3:9). God has a similar judicial wisdom focus, as he affirms Solomon for requesting "discernment to hear justice (*mišpāṭ*)" (3:11). This judicial wisdom is illustrated in the case when Solomon wisely enables justice to prevail in a scenario involving two prostitutes (3:16–27). Hays claims that there is an implicit critique towards Solomon in that he entertains the case of prostitutes whose jobs put them at odds with Torah, but this could also show how Solomon's judicial wisdom is available to the most vulnerable in society, even those who are so desperate that they live in a house of prostitution. The narrator certainly interprets this account positively by offering a summative statement after the account: "All of Israel heard the judgment (*mišpāṭ*) which the king judged and they revered the king for they saw that the wisdom of God was in him to do (*laʿăśôt*) justice (*mišpāṭ*)" (3:28). Judicial wisdom is also in view in 1 Kings 10 when the Queen of Sheba comes to witness Solomon's wisdom. She declares: "May the LORD your God be blessed, who delighted in you to set you upon the throne of Israel, due to the love of the LORD for Israel forever, and he made you king to do (*laʿăśôt*) justice (*mišpāṭ*) and righteousness" (10:9). By concluding chapter 3 and the speech of the Queen of Sheba with awe over Solomon's God-given wisdom *laʿăśôt mišpāṭ* ("to do justice"), these two accounts link the local with the international. In Israel and abroad, Solomon is known for having been granted wisdom from God to ensure justice.

Although judicial wisdom is primary in the Solomon narrative, 1 Kings 4:29–34 [HB 5:9–14] describes other aspects of wisdom. Solomon was a sage, such that he spoke three thousand proverbs. Solomon's wisdom also included insight into nature, trees, hyssop, and all sorts of

---

14. Knoppers, "None Like Him," 411–31. In his estimation, it is an exilic redactor who incorporated this formula.

15. Our focus is upon God granting Solomon wisdom, but God also promises wealth and honor too. Porten, "Structure and Theme," and Knoppers, "None Like Him," both interpret chapters 3–10 through the lens of the fulfillment of God's promises of wisdom, honor, and wealth promised in the dream.

animals. The narrator again highlights the incomparability of Solomon's wisdom: "the wisdom of Solomon was greater than the wisdom of all the sons of the east and greater than the wisdom of Egypt" (4:30 [HB 5:10]). Such wisdom makes Solomon an international attraction (4:34 [HB 5:14]; cf. 10:1–2). It is difficult to interpret 4:29–34 [HB 5:9–14] other than in a positive vein. Indeed, the pericope opens with the narrator presenting God as the source of Solomon's wisdom: "God gave wisdom to Solomon, a very great understanding and a breadth of mind like the sand which is upon the shore of the sea" (4:29 [HB 5:9]). Thus, 1 Kings 3:4–28, 4:29–34, and 10:1–9 seem to be positive accounts of Solomon's divinely endowed judicial, sagacious, and "scientific" wisdom.[16]

Assessing Solomon's Wisdom in Kings

Although one can read the wisdom pericopes positively as individual texts (3:4–28; 4:29–34; cf. 10:1–9), the role of these texts within 1–2 Kings as a literary whole requires consideration. How are we to assess these accounts of Solomon's wisdom within the aims of 1–2 Kings?

Wisdom Not Grounds for Condemnation

There are several reasons to dismiss Hays's contention that the accounts of Solomon's wisdom establish grounds for indictment in view of his failures (see his argument above). First, we should not impose into 1 Kings 1–11 the act-consequence nexus of wisdom from Proverbs, whereby the righteous are the wise that deserve blessing and the wicked are fools that deserve judgment. In 1 Kings 3, 4, and 10, as argued above, the sort of wisdom in view is primarily judicial. Sure, one might argue that the ability to discern right from wrong in judicial cases and insights into the world should lead Solomon to obey Torah, but the accounts themselves do not connect these dots. When God grants Solomon's request for wisdom, there is no impression that the wisdom allotted to Solomon will give him any advantage in Torah obedience. After God declares his intention to grant Solomon judicial wisdom, God still exhorts him to obey Torah if he expects to live a long life (3:11–14). It seems possible that Solomon might possess great wisdom in the judicial realm yet struggle in the realm of Torah obedience. Throughout 1 Kings 1–11, the grounds for indictment against Solomon

---

16. Särkiö, "Struktur," interprets these wisdom passages positively and argues that they are later insertions aimed at legitimizing Solomon's rule.

are not in his betrayal of wisdom, but instead in his failure to heed David's (2:3–4) and God's (3:14; 6:12–13; 8:9; 9:4–5) admonitions to obey the commands of Moses. Both God (11:10, 11) and the prophet Ahijah (11:33) base Solomon's judgment in his disobedience to God's commandments. Thus, wisdom in 1 Kings 1–11 seems limited to judicial and creational wisdom, so it is not the basis for Solomon's indictment—instead, disobedience to the law of Moses is the basis.

Second, wisdom is not a basis for divine judgment toward any other king in 1–2 Kings. As one moves beyond 1 Kings 1–11, key terms for wisdom and justice do not occur in the rest of 1–2 Kings. Wisdom terms, such as "wisdom" (*ḥokmâ*; 3:28; 4:29, 30, 34; 5:12; 10:4, 6–8, 23–24; 11:41), "wise" (*ḥākām*; 2:9; 3:12; 5:7), "to be wise" (*ḥākam*; 4:31), and "to understand" (*bîn*; 3:9, 11, 12, 21), do not occur in association with any other king in 1–2 Kings. The basis for their judgment seems to be whether or not they have obeyed Torah. Thus, the narrative of 1 Kings 1–11 and the rest of 1–2 Kings does not utilize wisdom as a basis for condemning Solomon or any other king for disobedience.

Wisdom as Part of the Royal Ideal

If Solomon's wisdom is not meant to condemn him for his apostasy, it makes it more likely that the final form of 1 Kings 1–11 expects us to interpret Solomon's wisdom positively. What, then, is its purpose within the Solomon narrative (1 Kgs 1–11) and 1–2 Kings as a whole?[17]

Within 1 Kings 1–11, the wisdom of Solomon contributes to the construction of the book's royal ideal.[18] This ideal has at least four components within these chapters: (1) Torah obedience; (2) peace and prosperity; (3) temple centricity; and (4) wisdom. As Alison Joseph has demonstrated,[19] *obedience* to Torah surfaces as a significant component of the royal ideal in 1 Kings 1–11 in view of its portrayal of David and the failure of Solomon to heed the admonitions of David and God in this respect. This component becomes the key in the rest of 1–2 Kings for evaluating kings from the vantage point of obedience to Torah. Yet, there are other aspects of the royal ideal in 1 Kings 1–11, particularly when read in light of David in 2 Samuel. Solomon is portrayed as a greater David. Whereas David brings Israel rest

---

17. See Provan, "Messiah," who focuses on the contributions of Hezekiah and Josiah to the royal ideal, with only minor attention given to Solomon.

18. For a more developed account of the royal ideal in the Solomon narrative and the rest of Kings, see Abernethy and Goswell, *God's Messiah*, 67–84.

19. Joseph, *Portrait*, 58–76, 98–105.

from their enemies (2 Sam 7:1), the Deuteronomist presents Solomon as ushering in an idyllic age of *peace and prosperity* where Israel's boundaries reach from the Euphrates to Egypt and where there is peace throughout the land (1 Kgs 4:20–21, 25).[20] Whereas David brings the ark to Jerusalem and desires to build God a temple (2 Sam 6:12–19; 7:2), Solomon builds God's *temple* and the glory cloud of divine presence resides in the temple (1 Kgs 8:1–11). Whereas David "ruled over all Israel and was doing justice and righteousness for all his people" (2 Sam 8:15), Solomon receives an extraordinary endowment of divine *wisdom*, resulting in judicial, proverbial, and scientific wisdom that solicits awe from Israel and abroad (1 Kgs 3:28; 4:29–34 [5:9–14]; 10:1–9). These idyllic components in the Solomon narrative coordinate to offer an impression from 1 Kings 1–11 that life can be great for Israel in the land when a Davidic king governs with God's wisdom and centralizes the community around God's presence in the temple. The piece missing, however, from Solomon's example is obedience to Torah. As a foil in this respect, Torah obedience becomes the central concern throughout the rest of 1–2 Kings.

In 1 Kings 12—2 Kings 25, wisdom and justice are not part of the criteria for assessing whether kings after Solomon are "upright" or "evil." With Solomon's abysmal failure with regards to Torah obedience and its disastrous consequences, the rest of 1–2 Kings focuses primarily upon the ideal of obedience to Torah, particularly as it relates to the non-idolatrous worship of Yhwh in the temple. Josiah exemplifies this ideal of Torah obedience and temple reform. The Josianic ideal from 1 Kings 12—2 Kings 25 does not exhaust the royal ideal of 1–2 Kings; instead, the opening eleven chapters invite us to incorporate the Solomonic ideal into our understanding.

What would the purpose of a royal ideal be for the preexilic and exilic composition of 1–2 Kings? The main reason, in my opinion, why scholars focus on the Josianic ideal is because it more easily fits into an explanation of why Israel and Judah went into exile. In other words, a *Torah obedience* ideal exposes how the kings failed in this respect, resulting in divine judgment that culminates in the destruction of the temple, the absence of a ruler from David's line, and exile. There is, however, more to 1–2 Kings than explaining the *why* of judgment. Statements about God's unconditional commitment to David's lamp and the cryptic account of Jehoiachin receiving favor while in exile at the close of the book give rise to a hope that God's involvement with David might not be over.[21] The portrait of the ideal king lives on beyond the flesh and bones of Judah and Israel's kings soliciting hopes of a

---

20. Knoppers, "None Like Him," 416–17.
21. See Lovell, "Shape of Hope."

King with Solomonic wisdom and Josianic obedience that will lead to a new era of peace and blessing for God's people around God's temple.[22]

The Solomonic Royal Ideal Beyond 1–2 Kings

When one looks beyond 1–2 Kings, the ideal of a king receiving a divine allotment of wisdom for judicial purposes surfaces in the Latter Prophets.[23] In Isaiah, a sprig will spring forth from Jesse's stump,

> 2 And the spirit of the LORD will rest upon him,
>
> A spirit of wisdom and understanding,
>
> A spirit of counsel and might,
>
> a spirit of knowledge and the fear of the LORD.
>
> 3 His delight will be in the fear of the LORD,
>
> and not according to the appearance of things will he judge,
>
> and not according to whatever his ears hear will he reprove.
>
> 4 He will judge the poor with righteousness,
>
> and he will reprove the afflicted of the earth with uprightness.
>
> (Isa 11:2–4)

Isaiah's depiction of the future king is Solomonesque, as the new king from Jesse's stump will have a divine allotment of wisdom (11:2–3a) to bring about justice (11:3b–4).

Jeremiah also draws upon the Solomonic ideal. In Jeremiah 23:5, we read: "Behold, days are coming, declares the LORD, when I will establish for David a Righteous Sprout,[24] and he will reign as king and will deal wisely (*haśkîl*) and will do justice and righteousness in the land." Again, there is the intersection between wisdom and justice in this portrait of the ideal king in Jeremiah (cf. Jer 3:15; 9:23). Thus, Isaiah 11 and Jeremiah 23, like 1 Kings 3 and 10, draw upon judicial wisdom as a key component in their presentation of the ideal king, strengthening the likelihood that wisdom is understood positively in 1 Kings 1–11 and as contributing to its royal ideal.[25]

---

22. One might inquire further into how Hezekiah may contribute to the royal ideal in the area of trust. See Knoppers, "None Like Him"; Provan, "Messiah."

23. Parker, *Wisdom and Law*, 58–65, traces the place of justice in the Old Testament's depiction of the ideal king.

24. For an overview of scholarly debate on the phrase translated as "Righteous Shoot," see Abernethy and Goswell, *God's Messiah*, 107–10.

25. Of course, one might extend this to the association between Solomon and wisdom literature and the retention of Solomon's judicial wisdom, but not his scientific or sagacious wisdom, in Chronicles. Mitchell, "Ideal Ruler," 225–26, argues that

If one approaches the First Testament as a discrete witness to Christ, as I do, the Solomonic wisdom ideal bears witness to Jesus Christ, the greater wise king. Yes, the Queen of Sheba came to hear Solomon's wisdom, but Jesus is even greater (Matt 12:42). He is said to have been wise at an early age (Luke 2:40, 52). The people of Nazareth were astounded by Jesus, wondering where Jesus's wisdom came from (13:42; Mark 6:2). As fully God and fully man, Jesus's teaching and life would exude wisdom that inspires awe. He is the one in whom are hidden all of the treasures of wisdom and knowledge (Col 2:3). Yet, unlike Solomon, Jesus fulfills the other part of the 1–2 Kings royal ideal—Torah obedience. Unlike Solomon, Jesus did not depend upon horses, wealth, and one thousand wives. He did not go astray after foreign gods. Instead, as is revealed in the temptation narrative, he depended upon God alone and worshipped only God even when all the kingdoms of the world were offered to him (Matt 4:1–11). The ideal of a wise and obedient king centered around the temple from 1–2 Kings finds its fulfillment in Jesus Christ, and Christ's body today—the church—should draw upon the judicial wisdom of the Head to bring blessing to the vulnerable.

Conclusion

Although it has become increasingly common within scholarship to focus on the negative role wisdom plays as an indictment in the Solomon narrative in 1 Kings 1–11, Solomon's wisdom can only be interpreted positively. It contributes to part of an ideal emerging from 1–2 Kings where there is hope for a Solomonic and Josianic king, an expectation that God's people will find blessing as they center around God's presence in the temple under a king with astounding judicial wisdom who is also exemplary in Torah obedience.

Bibliography

Abernethy, Andrew T., and Gregory Goswell. *God's Messiah in the Old Testament: Expectations of a Coming King*. Grand Rapids: Baker Academic, 2020.

Clements, Ronald E. "Solomon and the Origins of Wisdom in Israel." *Perspectives in Religious Studies* 15 (1988) 23–35.

Solomon's wisdom in Chronicles is more mantic, styled after Daniel. Although she is correct that the terms for wisdom differ between 1 Kings 3 and 2 Chronicles 1:10–12, with the latter aligning more with Daniel, she overlooks the judicial element in both Solomon's request ("grant me wisdom and knowledge . . . to judge . . ." [1:10]) and God's response ("you have requested wisdom and knowledge for yourself that you may judge my people" [1:11]).

Conway, Mary. "'The Wisest Might Err': A Re-evaluation of Solomon's Character as Revealed by His Prayer for Wisdom in 1 Kings 3:1–15." *Canadian Theological Review* 1 (2012) 29–45.

Hays, J. Daniel. "Has the Narrator Come to Praise Solomon or to Bury Him?: Narrative Subtlety in 1 Kings 1–11." *JSOT* 28 (2003) 149–74.

Joseph, Alison L. *Portrait of the Kings: The Davidic Prototype in Deuteronomistic Poetics.* Minneapolis, MN: Fortress, 2015.

Kalimi, Isaac. "Love of God and *Apologia* for a King: Solomon as the Lord's Beloved King in Biblical and Ancient Near Eastern Contexts." *JANER* 17 (2017) 28–63.

Knoppers, Gary N. "'There Was None Like Him': Incomparability in the Books of Kings." *CBQ* 54 (1992) 411–31.

Lovell, Nathan. "The Shape of Hope in the Book of Kings: The Resolution of Davidic Blessing and Mosaic Curse." *JESOT* 3 (2014) 3–27.

Mitchell, Christine Karen. "The Ideal Ruler as Intertext in 1–2 Chronicles and 'Cyropaedia.'" PhD diss., Carleton University, 2001.

Parker, Kim Ian. *Wisdom and Law in the Reign of Solomon.* Lewiston, NY: Edwin Mellen, 1992.

Porten, Bezalel. "The Structure and Theme of the Solomon Narrative (1 Kings 3–11)." *Hebrew Union College Annual* 38 (1967) 93–128.

Provan, Iain W. "The Messiah in the Books of Kings." In *The Lord's Anointed: Interpretation of Old Testament Messianic Texts*, edited by Philip E. Satterthwaite, Richard S. Hess, and Gordon J. Wenham, 67–85. Carlisle: Paternoster, 1995.

Särkiö, Pekka. "Die Struktur der Salomogeschichte (1 Kön 1–11) und die Stellung der Weisheit in ihr." *BN* 83 (1996) 83–106.

Sweeney, Marvin A. "The Critique of Solomon in the Josianic Edition of the Deuteronomistic History." *JBL* 114 (1995) 607–22.

Williams, David S. "Once Again: The Structure of the Narrative of Solomon's Reign." *JSOT* 86 (1999) 49–66.

Wilson, Lindsay. *Joseph, Wise and Otherwise: The Intersection of Wisdom and Covenant in Genesis 37–50.* Carlisle: Paternoster, 2004.

Part II

Wisdom in Prophecy

5

Finding Relational Wisdom

*Terror, Shame, and Retribution
in the Book of Jeremiah*

JILL FIRTH

OUR WORLD IS NO stranger to terror, shame, and retribution. James Cone in *The Cross and the Lynching Tree* speaks of the pervasive terror of lynching in America in the nineteenth and twentieth centuries, where "blacks were too scared even to talk publicly about it."[1] National terror in Rwanda was tragically captured in a letter of Tutsi pastors who wrote to their church's president, "We wish to inform you that tomorrow we will be killed with our families."[2] A literature teacher in the former Yugoslavia was humiliated by her student who urinated into her mouth while a former colleague, a physics teacher, was shouting and hitting her, surrounded by a group of laughing men. She made a commitment to vengeance, "'To my second son who was just born, I gave the name "Jihad." So he would not forget the testament of his mother—revenge.'"[3]

In Australia's history, terror was experienced in 1916 by soldiers in France: "the anxiety and horror of it I cannot tell you. I had to drive men

---

1. Cone, *Cross and the Lynching Tree*, 15.
2. Gourevitch, *We Wish to Inform You*, 42.
3. Volf, *Exclusion and Embrace*, 111, quoting Serbian journalist Željko Vuković, *Killing of Sarajevo*.

who were in one trench ahead of us at one time, blocking the way, with my revolver," wrote Lieutenant J. A. Raws.[4] There was personal terror for Aboriginal girls of twelve and thirteen years of age who were sent out as "domestic servants," to work on cattle stations up till the 1960s, despite the acknowledgment of the Chief Protector in 1916 that "unscrupulous men" might take advantage of these girls. Girls who fell pregnant were returned to their settlement to have the baby, then contracted out again.[5] Hundreds of Aboriginal people were killed in retribution for offences against property: "no wild beast of the forest was ever hunted down with such perseverance," as one Victorian pastoralist wrote in 1856.[6]

Terror and shame are seen in current-day Australia in an abuser's tactics to shame his wife: "I raped her daughters—my stepdaughters—right in front of her. I made her watch . . . I had my .38 loaded and in my hand . . . I wanted her miserable. I wanted her to doubt herself as a mother, to think she was a bad mother. So I gave her the biggest failure a mother could have."[7] Behrouz Boochani wrote of shame in "Daddy's moustache," a moustache which was formerly a symbol of a father's strength, until he became a refugee on Manus Island, unable to protect his daughters from harm, and fearful that his choice to flee had harmed his family.[8] Terror and shame may be complex, and may lead to long-term moral injury, as one war veteran commented: "I have experienced a wide range of feelings including guilt, anger, shame and helplessness . . . Years later I am still processing the evil that I observed and, in a curious way, the evil to which I have been a party."[9]

Conventional wisdom about flourishing and the good life can be inadequate in extreme circumstances of trauma and chaos. We need a book like Job, which, as Lindsay Wilson writes, "does not simply arrive at propositional answers, but explores the process of loss and grief, the reworking of faith, and the transformation of Job."[10] Like Job, Jeremiah is a long book, a journey, not a postcard,[11] and it deals with "wheelchair" not "armchair" questions.[12] Jeremiah's world was torn by violence and warfare, and he and

4. Quoted in Tyquin, "Unseen Wound," 27.

5. Kidd, *Black Lives*, 20–21.

6. Broome, *Aboriginal Victorians*, 82, and see Atkinson, *Trauma Trails*, 23–92.

7. Hill, *Made Me Do*, 41.

8. Boochani, *No Friend but the Mountains*, 114–15. See also, Dale, "Shame and Honour," 5–18.

9. An Officer, "Combatant's View," 64. See also Firth, "Spirituality from the Depths," 122–23.

10. Wilson, *Job*, 27.

11. See Wilson, *Job*, 27, who cites Christopher Ash, *Out of the Storm*, 14.

12. See Wilson, *Job*, 216, who cites Christopher Ash, *Out of the Storm*, 12.

the people of Judah suffered terror and shame as they experienced forced migration, and the direct rule of foreign powers (21:2; 39:3; 40:1). Jeremiah endured death threats from family and political enemies (11:19; 18:20; 26:8; 38:25), public ridicule (20:7), assault, unjust arrest, imprisonment (20:2; 37:15, 21), and kidnap (43:4–7). Jeremiah desired vengeance on his enemies, and the people faced retribution for their sins. The book of Jeremiah proposes strategies for understanding and trusting God in circumstances of terror and shame, which can be described as relational wisdom: "the proper relationship between God and humanity or, to put it another way, the nature of true faith or righteousness."[13]

This chapter considers God's invitation to relational wisdom, Jeremiah's process of finding relational wisdom through apprenticeship, questioning, dialogue, and lament (1:1—20:18), and God's unexpected initiatives to Judah in her final days (21:1—52:34), where he continues to display his love, righteousness, and justice despite the people's persistent rejection of his offers of rescue.

1. Invitation to Relational Wisdom

The book of Jeremiah addresses Judah's lack of relational wisdom. God sums it up: "my people" (עמי) were wise (חכמים) in doing evil (4:22), but "they did not know" me (לא ידעו, 9:3).[14] The people were confident of God's steadfast love, relying on the temple (7:4), but did not see how God's love could be compatible with retribution on themselves (26:11; 36:29). God invites Judah into relationship, to trust in him, the fountain of living waters (מקור מים חיים) rather than other sources of apparent security, "cracked cisterns . . . that can hold no water" (2:13). He invites them to know him: to understand (השׂכל) and to know me (וידע אותי), "that I am the Lord; I act with steadfast love (חסד), justice (משׁפט), and righteousness (צדקה) in the earth, for in these things I delight (חפצתי, 9:23–24)."

The book of Jeremiah demonstrates the inseparability of God's steadfast love, justice, and righteousness, showing whom to trust, whom to fear, whose shame to accept, and how retribution is to be carried out. If Judah did not learn to fear God (ירא, 5:22, 24), they would experience terror all around (מגור מסביב, 6:25). God's people had chosen shameful behavior (3:3; 3:24–25; 6:15; 8:12), and if they persisted, this would result in further shame, for they would be dishonored by their conquerors (8:9; 9:19), go into

---

13. Wilson, *Job*, 10.

14. The NRSV is used for some Bible references. Versification follows English text. I also include my own translations in the chapter.

exile (2:36), and fail to receive proper burial (8:2). God calls the people to turn back (3:12, 14, 22; 4:1–4), and offers pardon (5:1), alongside warnings of retribution if they do not return to him (2:19, 35; 4:4, 27–28; 5:9, 29; 9:9). Promises of return begin in chapter 3 and continue through the book (3:18; 12:15; 16:15), and a new covenant is foretold to replace the one they have broken (31:31–34). Grace is even offered to Judah's "evil neighbors" after retribution (12:14–17; 46:26; 48:47; 49:6, 11, 39).

2. Relational Wisdom for Jeremiah (1:1—20:18)

Jeremiah also needed a personal relationship with Yhwh to fully grasp the connection between steadfast love, justice, and righteousness, even though, unlike Job, Jeremiah stands in the divine council (23:22), and knows the reason for his suffering and public shame from the outset. In his prophecy and confessions, Jeremiah comes to know God through apprenticeship, questioning, dialogue, and lament.

a. Apprenticeship

Jeremiah receives an apprenticeship in knowing God through prophecy. In the early chapters of Jeremiah, God is not "fluid, unstable, changing,"[15] but he demonstrates through warnings and tears that his steadfast love, justice, and righteousness are inseparable as he acts in the earth. Jeremiah declares God's anguish about the terrors of war (4:19), the devastation of the land (4:23–6; 12:4), the hurt of people (8:21), and the slain (9:1).[16] God weeps, and Jeremiah's tears mingle over the people's coming shame (2:37), and their shameless refusal to accept God's help (8:12). "My joy is gone, grief is upon me, my heart is sick" (8:18). "O that my head were a spring of water, and my eyes a fountain of tears" (9:1; see also 13:17; 14:17).[17] God calls for the mourning women to bring a dirge for the devastation of the earth and for the many deaths (9:10, 17–22). Yet God also calls for the covenant curses to be enacted (11:2–5), and Jeremiah signifies his assent, "So be it, Lord" (אמן יהוה, 11:5).

---

15. Contra O'Connor, "Tears of God," 184.
16. O'Connor, *Jeremiah*, 59–68.
17. Rowold, "Theology," 19.

b. Questioning and Dialogue

Jeremiah's confessions (11:18—20:18) focus on the prophet's own terror and shame, and his desire for retribution on his enemies.[18] In Jeremiah's call, God had encouraged Jeremiah, "do not be afraid" (אל־תירא, 1:8), and warned that Jeremiah would have to choose whether he acted on his fear of God or of his enemies, "do not be terrified before them (אל־תחת מפניהם), lest I terrify you before them" (פן־אחתך לפניהם, 1:17).[19] In the first two confessions, Jeremiah struggles to trust God's steadfast love for himself, and God enters into dialogue with Jeremiah.

In his first confession (11:18—12:13), Jeremiah expresses fears for his life when God reveals the plots of the men of Anathoth, his hometown (11:21). Public shame is implied in the threat to "cut him off from the land of the living," so that Jeremiah's name "will no longer be remembered" (לא־יזכר עוד, 11:19). Jeremiah calls for retribution on his enemies, "let me see your retribution upon them (נקמתך), for to you I have committed my cause (ריבי, 11:20)." Jeremiah affirms that Yhwh is righteous (צדקה) and yet he brings his charge against him (אריב, 12:1–4), raising questions of divine justice (משפטים), including the flourishing of the treacherous (בגדי בגד, 12:1). The prophet calls for a day of slaughter (יום הרגה, 12:3), conscious of the devastation and mourning of the land (תאבל, 12:4).

God replies to Jeremiah (11:21-23; 12:5–13), promising again to protect Jeremiah, and declares disaster (רעה) and punishment on the men of Anathoth (11:22-23). God likens the treachery (בגדו בך) of Jeremiah's brothers and father's house (בית־אביך, 12:6) to his own pain and the affront to his honor of seeing "my house" (ביתי, 12:7), "my heritage" (נחלתי, 12:7, 8, 9), "the beloved of my heart" (ידדות נפשי, 12:7) turning against him. God also grieves at the desolation of the land and its mourning (אבלה, 12:11), and he threatens destruction and shame (בש) for the wicked (12:13).

Jeremiah's second confession (15:10–18) focuses on public shame, beginning with the lament, "Woe is me" (אוי־לי), since everyone curses him (קלל, 15:10).[20] He calls for retribution (הנקם לי) on his persecutors (רדפי, 15:15), reaffirming that he has committed himself to Yhwh, suffering

---

18. The five texts used here are 11:18—12:13; 15:10-21; 17:14-18; 18:19-23; 20:7-18. For debate on the scope of the confessions, see O'Connor, *Jeremiah*, 81; Lundbom, *Jeremiah*, 634; Dell, "Cursed," 106. As we do not know the historical circumstances of the confessions, I discuss them in the order presented in the text.

19. I have chosen to translate חתת as terrify/be terrified, also see חתת in 8:9; 10:2; 17:17-18; 30:10; 46:27; 48:1; 49:37; 50:36. NRSV translates חתת as "*break down ... break you*" in 1:17, but often chooses "*dismay*" elsewhere.

20. I omit discussion of 15:11–14, see also Wright, *Jeremiah*, 106 n. 2.

disgrace (חרפה, 15:15), though he has delighted in being called by Yhwh's name (נקרא שמך עלי, 15:16), and he now sits alone (15:17).

In the Old Testament, questioning is an accepted aspect of relating to God (e.g., Psalm 88, and God applauding Job as speaking "what is right," נכונה, Job 42:8).[21] Jeremiah laments, "Why is my pain unceasing, my wound incurable?" (15:18). Jeremiah fears that Yhwh will turn out to be like a seasonal brook (כמו אכזב), waters that are not reliable over the longer term (לא נאמנו, 15:18).[22] This comparison of Yhwh with an unreliable stream has been interpreted as a complaint or accusation about God's past or present behavior.[23] But perhaps Jeremiah is expressing a fear about the future, that God may not always be reliable. I propose that היו תהיה לי is better translated, "will you be to me?" (ESV, see KJV),[24] with a modal imperfect plus the infinitive absolute (היו) conveying doubt, rather than certainty.[25]

God's response, "if you keep turning (אם־תשוב) to me" (15:19), can be read as a promise and encouragement to keep on trusting in him, understanding the imperfect verb "turn" in a repeated or durative sense,[26] rather than as a call to Jeremiah to "turn back" (to God) as in NRSV and other translations.[27] God's offer is rather, "then I will keep helping you to turn (ואשיבך) and you shall stand before me (לפני לעמד, 15:19)." This is not a rebuke, but a promise of faithful help in Jeremiah's prophetic office.[28] It reaffirms Jeremiah's role as a prophet who stands before him (see אם־עמדו, 23:22; יעמד, 15:1), and recalls God's call to Jeremiah to stand up and speak, and not be terrified (אל־תחת, 1:17).[29]

God's next words, to bring "what is precious (יקר) and not what is worthless (זולל, 15:19)," challenge Jeremiah to speak only God's precious word to the people, since God has put his words in Jeremiah's mouth (1:9).

---

21. Fretheim, *Jeremiah*, 241; Wilson, *Job*, 207.

22. God's trustworthiness is also questioned in 4:10 (השא השאת).

23. Translating the phrase היו תהיה לי (15:18) as "*you have been to me*" (see JPS, CSB) or "*you are to me*" (see NRSV, NIV). See Holladay, *Jeremiah*, 461; Wright, *Jeremiah*, 177; Lalleman, *Jeremiah*, 156; Fretheim, *Jeremiah*, 239–41.

24. See Lundbom, *Jeremiah*, 740. For modal imperfect, see Joüon and Muraoka, *Grammar*, §113.l.

25. Contra Holladay, *Jeremiah*, 231. For this use of infinitive absolute, see Joüon and Muraoka, *Grammar*, §123.f-h.

26. See Joüon and Muraoka, *Grammar*, §113.b.

27. Often translated as "*if you turn back*" (NRSV), or even, "*if you repent*" (NIV). See Thompson, *Jeremiah*, 397; Craigie et al., *Jeremiah*, 210–11; Lundbom, *Jeremiah*, 749; Wright, *Jeremiah*, 177; Lalleman, *Jeremiah*, 156.

28. Contra NRSV, "*I will take you back.*"

29. Similar also to the invitation to the people to "*not waver*" (ולא תנוד, 4.1).

Jeremiah is to continue to avoid the temptation to seek personal safety or social acceptance by bringing worthless words, unlike the false prophets who continually brought lies (שֶׁקֶר, 5:31; 7:4; 13:23). It is unnecessary to assume that Jeremiah's previous words were worthless.[30]

In the next verse, God's words can be translated in a past tense, "and I have made you" (15:20), confirming Jeremiah's call, and encouraging Jeremiah to persevere, as the verb form (וּנְתַתִּיךָ, 15:20, qal perfect) is the same as in God's original affirmation to Jeremiah that he has made him as a fortified city (נְתַתִּיךָ, 1:18).[31] God then repeats his earlier promises to be with Jeremiah, and to save and deliver him (לְהוֹשִׁיעֲךָ וּלְהַצִּילֶךָ, 15:20–21, see 1:19).

In these first two confessions, Jeremiah receives God's words of comfort and assurance as he pours out his terror, shame, and desire for retribution to God, then he continues to process his concerns before God in three further monologues.

c. Continued Lament

In the next three confessions, Jeremiah again expresses terror and fear of shame, showing that his anxious feelings are not resolved despite the direct assurances he has received in his call (1:1–19) and in the first two confessions (11:18—12:13; 15:10–21). It is possible that God gave further personal assurances, but none are recorded after chapter 15.

In his third confession (17:14–18), Jeremiah responds to God's earlier warning not to be terrified (אַל־תֵּחַת) of his opponents, lest God terrify him (פֶּן־אֲחִתְּךָ, 1:17). He requests that God not be a terror to him (מְחִתָּה), as he has made God his refuge (17:17). He prays against shame (אַל־אֵבֹשָׁה) and terror (אַל־אֵחַתָּה) for himself but continues to pray that his persecutors (רֹדְפַי) are shamed (יֵבֹשׁוּ) and terrified (יֵחַתּוּ), and will receive a day of disaster (יוֹם רָעָה) and double destruction (מִשְׁנֶה שִׁבָּרוֹן, 17:18), though he does not desire to hasten the fateful day (17:16).

---

30. Contra Wright, *Jeremiah*, 178; Holladay, *Jeremiah*, 462. Earlier preaching is suggested by Lundbom, *Jeremiah*, 750. Fretheim, *Jeremiah*, 241, comments on 15:19, "Jeremiah has not sinned."

31. Whether the *vav* has a connective (past) or converting function (future) is dependent on interpretation, not morphology, as in both 1:18 and 15:20, the stress on the verb נְתַתִּיךָ has moved to the third syllable with the addition of the pronominal suffix (see Joüon and Muraoka, *Grammar*, §62.e). וּנְתַתִּיךָ is often translated as a future promise, "*and I will make you*" (see JPS, NRSV, NIV, ESV, KJV), interpreted as conditional on Jeremiah's turning back to him, see explicit conditional in CSB, "*then I will make you*." Holladay, *Jeremiah*, 465, contrasts what he sees as the "conditional" promise (15:18–19) with an "unconditional" promise (15:20–21).

Jeremiah's fourth confession (18:19–23) abandons his former prayers for mercy for his enemies (18:20), and this has been interpreted as "a violent swing from love to hate."³² However, Jeremiah may simply be obeying God's command, "do not pray on behalf of (בעד) these people" (7:16; 11:14; 14:11).³³ Many scholars argue that God now prohibits intercession because repentance has become impossible,³⁴ or because judgment is now inevitable.³⁵ An alternative explanation is that Jeremiah is now forbidden to intercede, because God will no longer accept prophetic intercession in place of repentance. The time for intercession alone is now past (15:1), though, formerly, God had chosen to be swayed by the prayers of prophets such as Moses (Exod 32:11–14; Num 11:2; 21:7; Deut 9:15, 29) and Samuel (1 Sam 7:8–9; 12:23), and perhaps by Jeremiah's first twenty-three years of ministry (25:3–7; see 26:1).³⁶ Now, when there still is no true repentance, God is weary of relenting (נלאיתי, 15:6), and Jeremiah aligns himself with God's command to cease this type of prophetic intercession (18:20).³⁷ Jeremiah's prayer that the children be given to famine and the sword, and that their wives become childless and widowed (18:21–23), echoes God's own declaration that "the young men shall die by the sword, their sons and their daughters shall die by famine, and not even a remnant shall be left of them" (11:21–22), and may reflect Jeremiah's obedient acquiescence to God's judgment. Jeremiah does not plan to take vengeance on his own enemies but continues to surrender retribution to God (11:23).³⁸

In the final confession (20:1–18), terror, shame and retribution continue as key themes. In the first two confessions, God revealed his own heart, and gave patient assurances, even when Jeremiah expressed his fear that God would fail him like a deceitful brook (15:18), and in the third and fourth confessions, Jeremiah spoke with greater assurance of God's trustworthiness. The opening words of the final confession (פתיתני, 20:7) can be translated as God having "enticed" (NRSV),³⁹ "deceived,"⁴⁰ or even

32. Kidner, *Jeremiah*, 78.
33. "*Do not pray for these people*" (NRSV).
34. Holladay, *Jeremiah*, 253, 354.
35. McConville, *Judgment and Promise*, 51; Lalleman, *Jeremiah*, 109; Fretheim, *Jeremiah*, 137, 183.
36. This fourth confession follows the determination of the people to reject God's plans (18:12), and their plot against Jeremiah's life (18:18). It might relate to the fourth year of Jehoiakim (25:3–7).
37. Jeremiah continues to pray for the people, e.g., 42:4.
38. McCaulley, *Reading While Black*, 21–23.
39. Lundbom, *Jeremiah*, 855.
40. Wright, *Jeremiah*, 226; Holladay, *Jeremiah*, 552.

"seduced"[41] Jeremiah, but I suggest that the translation "persuaded"[42] (as in Prov 25:15), or "allured" (as in Hos 2:14) is more consistent with the dynamics of the previous confessions, which expressed his growing trust. Similarly, the next phrase may perhaps be translated "you have strengthened me" (חזקתני, 20:7),[43] rather than the common translation, "you have overpowered me" (NRSV),[44] since Jeremiah has not mentioned any fear of God's power in the earlier confessions. Jeremiah then affirms that "you have prevailed" (ותוכל, 20:7, NRSV), as Yhwh's persuasion has prevailed over the prophet's fears, or perhaps the translation nuance "you are able" contains a play on words, in contrast to Jeremiah's inability to hold in the words of God (ולא אוכל, 20:9), and the inability of his persecutors to persuade him (לא יכלו, 20:11).[45]

Jeremiah continues to speak of terror and shame. Terror is all around (מגור מסביב), with danger from Judah's leaders (20:3), the enemy (6:25), and his friends (20:10). Jeremiah grieves that he is a laughingstock (שחוק, 20:7), mocked (לעג, 20:7), and receiving constant reproach and derision (חרפה, קלס, 20:8), though he affirms that his persecutors will be shamed (בשו) and permanently dishonoured (כלמת עולם, 20:11). He laments that the continuing price of his obedience will be toil (עמל), sorrow (יגון), and shame (בשת, 20:18), though he has been faithful to Yhwh (20:11–13). Jeremiah's final confession ends with cursing the day he was born (20:14–18). Such a return to lament is also found in some lament psalms, illustrating the range and movement of emotions in a faithful relationship.[46] Jeremiah holds his loyalty together with a realistic awareness of the cost.[47] This "ending in a minor key" fits the trajectory of Jeremiah's life,[48] and fits his awareness that there will be no resolution to his suffering.[49]

---

41. Heschel, *Prophets*, 113–14; see also, discussion in Firth, "Desert Spring."

42. Craigie et al., *Jeremiah*, 273; Lalleman, *Jeremiah*, 177.

43. For similar though rare uses of חזק in *qal*, see Jer 10:4; 2 Chr 28:20. This translation of the *qal* of חזק with object suffix is rare in the OT, but the translation "overpowered" (NRSV) of חזק in *qal* usually requires a preposition, such as מן or על (see Wakely, "חזק," 65).

44. See Fretheim, *Jeremiah*, 298; Wright, *Jeremiah*, 226; Craigie, *Jeremiah*, 273; Holladay, *Jeremiah*, 553.

45. All three of these verbs are from the same Hebrew root, *ykl*. In 20:7, יוכל lacks a suffixed preposition (as in Gen 32:28), unlike 20:10, ונוכלה לו.

46. For example, Psalms 31 and 35, see Villanueva, *Uncertainty*, 202–4.

47. Luke 14:28.

48. Rah, *Prophetic Lament*, 190.

49. Villanueva, *Uncertainty*, 210.

As in the earlier confessions, Jeremiah calls for retribution on his enemies. In fact, he uses the exact wording in the first and final confessions, "Let me see your retribution upon them (אראה נקמתך מהם), for to you I have committed my cause (ריבי, 11:20; 20:12)," and he repeats that God tests "the heart and the mind" (בחן כליות ולב, 11:20; 20:12).[50] However, he has deepened his trust in YHWH, who is with him "like a dread warrior" (אותי כגבור עריץ, 20:11) who delivers (הציל) "from the hands of evildoers" (מיד מרעים, 20:13), echoing God's earlier promises to be "with you to deliver you" (1:8, 19; 15:20) "from the hand of the wicked" (מיד רעים, 15:21) and "the ruthless" (ערצים, 15:21).[51]

The confessions reveal Jeremiah's personal development in relational wisdom. Far from finding God "hard-nosed and unyielding,"[52] Jeremiah has found God is steadfast, showing his heart, and reminding Jeremiah of the promises in his call. Jeremiah is not "scarred" by God in the confessions, nor is he "compelled to offer" his prophecies "against his own will."[53] Rather, he has gained confidence in YHWH through apprenticeship, questioning, dialogue, and the freedom to lament. Jeremiah will gain even more relational wisdom in seeing how God's retribution in Judah is inseparably linked to his steadfast love.

3. Relational Wisdom for Judah (21:1—52:34)

Judah continued to reject God's invitation to know and trust him, even after the exile of Jehoiachin in 597 BC. In chapters 21–52, alongside his justice and righteousness, God demonstrates his steadfast love in surprising ways to those who are still rebelling against him. He offers unexpected safety to anyone who surrenders to the Babylonians (21:9), and reconfigures Babylon (24:4-7; 29:4-7) and Judah (42:10-12) as sites of blessing during the exile, as well as continuing to offer an end to terror, shame, and retribution in the future return from exile (30:10; 32:37-41; 33:9).[54]

---

50. NRSV translates בחן כליות ולב as "*you see the heart and the mind*" in 20:12, but the same words are translated as "*who try the heart and the mind*" in 11:20.

51. These connections are less easy to see in NRSV which translates עריץ as "*dread*" in 20:11, and ערצים in 15:21 as "*ruthless*." NRSV translates מרעים as "*evildoers*" in 20:13, but רעים as "*wicked*" in 15:21.

52. Brueggemann, *Theology*, 33.

53. Brueggemann, *Theology*, 34.

54. See Firth, "Shaping and Smashing."

a. Receiving Life as a Prize of War

During the rebellions described in chapters 21–45, unexpected safe passes are offered to Baruch and Ebed-melech, and to anyone who surrenders to the Babylonians. In the fourth year of King Jehoiakim, the very year that retribution was announced to Judah (25:1–7), Jeremiah conveyed to Baruch a personal promise of receiving his life "as a prize of war" (45:5). In the midst of retribution in the reign of Zedekiah, God extends a promise to anyone who would surrender to Nebuchadnezzar to receive their life as a prize of war (את־נפשך לשלל, 21:9), and this promise is repeated to all (21:8–10; 38:2), to Zedekiah himself, if he would surrender (38:17, 20), and to Ebed-melech (39:18), and some did surrender during the final siege (38:19). This gracious offer of life as a prize of war bookends the narrative in chapters 21–45 (21:8–10; 45:5).[55]

Another sign of the inseparability of God's steadfast love from his just retribution is the honor shown to Jehoiachin in Babylon (52:31–34).[56] Perhaps the book of Jeremiah subtly signals that Jehoiachin's surrender allowed the king to receive his life as a gift. Jehoiachin had surrendered to Nebuchadnezzar during the first siege (2 Kgs 24:12), and though we have no evidence that Jeremiah counselled Jehoiachin to surrender, Jehoiachin's surrender may possibly be interpreted as obedience to God.[57]

b. Revealing Babylon as a Temporary Site of Blessing

In another surprising twist, Babylon is revealed as a temporary site of blessing for the exiles (24:1–10; 29:4–32). In earlier chapters (1–23), the message about the exile was uniformly negative, such as where God says, "I will show you no favor" (לא אתן לכם חנינה, 16:13) and the exile was configured in terms of shame, punishment, and bereavement (2:37; 5:29; 10:20; 12:14; 13:17, 19, 24; 15:2; 16:13; 20:4; 22:26, 28). Hope in these chapters was reserved for a future return to the land (3:14–18; 12:15; 16:15; 23:3, 8).

However, after the exile of King Jeconiah in 597 BC, God gives a vision of good and bad figs at the temple, revealing that he now regards the exiles in Babylon as "good figs" (24:4), while the rotten figs are identified with Zedekiah, his officials, those who remain in the land, and those who live in

---

55. In MT, also see LXX (21:9; 51:35).
56. Kidner, *Jeremiah*, 162.
57. The wording in Jeremiah 29:2 that Jehoiachin "*went out*" (צאת) echoes the wording in the invitations to "*go out*" in Jer 21:9 (והיוצא), 38:2 (והיצא), 38:17 (יצא תצא), and 38:21 (לצאת), and uses the same verb.

the land of Egypt (24:8). God now says of the exiles in Babylon, "I will build them up and not tear them down; I will plant them and not pluck them up" (24:6). The letter to the exiles commands them to "build houses ... plant gardens ... take wives" (29:4–7). This language is like the future return when Jerusalem will be rebuilt (30:18; 31:4, 38), vineyards and grain planted (31:5, 12, 24; 33:12) and marriages celebrated (33:11). Jeremiah's letter reconfigures the Babylonian exile as a "heterotopia," an alternate real location where the blessings of the return are temporarily experienced in advance.[58]

c. Remaining in the Land after the Fall of Jerusalem

Another unexpected move extends the offer of blessing to those who remain in the land after the fall of Jerusalem. These were formerly designated as "bad figs" (24:8) destined to be a horror (לזועה) and disgrace (לחרפה, 24:9), but God once again shows how his steadfast love is inseparable from his justice and righteousness: "I will build you up and not pull you down; I will plant you and not pluck you up; for I am sorry for the disaster that I have brought upon you" (42:10). God's punishment is neither disproportionate nor interminable, but "in just measure" (למשפט, 30:11).[59]

Jeremiah shares God's commitment to those who are still in need of grace by electing to remain in the land (40:1–6),[60] but he is unable to receive the blessings promised to those who remain in the land (42:9), because he is kidnapped to Egypt by the rebels (43:1–7). Tragically, the rebels continue to refuse to trust in Yhwh, and only a small remnant survive (44:14, 28). Hope remains primarily with the Babylonian exiles who are promised a future return to the land (30:10; 32:37–41; 33:9). The book of Jeremiah shows how God's just retribution is drenched in his tears and framed by offers of mercy to his people.

Conclusion

God invites Judah to relational wisdom in the midst of terror and shame, as he offers them a choice of whom to fear, whose shame to accept, and how retribution is to be executed. Jeremiah accepts an apprenticeship in God's steadfast love, justice, and righteousness, but he still struggles to trust God in his own life. In his confessions, Jeremiah voices his terror of his own

---

58. For "heterotopia," see Foucault, "Of Other Spaces," 4.
59. See also 2 Sam 24:16; Ps 103:9–10; Isa 40:2.
60. See Luke 15:3.

enemies and fear of public shame, but through questioning, dialogue, and lament, he deepens his trust in God. In the midst of retribution to Judah, God shows his surprising mercy, offering safety and flourishing to anyone who surrenders to Nebuchadnezzar, to the exiles in Babylon, and even to those who remain in the land, and promising the end of shame, terror, and retribution in the return from exile.

We too are invited to find relational wisdom by getting to know God, and by trusting him in our own terror, shame, and desire for retribution. Many have identified with Jeremiah's story of loss of what usually makes up the "good life," such as family, popularity, and wealth.[61] Jeremiah's confessions show that we are permitted to "remember and feel,"[62] and to speak out our terror and shame in lament.[63] We can take time to tell our story to God or a sympathetic listener, just as Jeremiah tells his long and complex story. Externalizing shame can be helpful, as with the innovative "shame mat" used in Aboriginal narrative practice.[64] We can reconfigure the impact of social shame, as Martin Luther King Jr. said about those who wished to make him ashamed, "I am ashamed of the people who were so sinful to make me a slave."[65] Like Jeremiah, we may protest against injustice, but like him, we are also to surrender retribution to God and to legal authorities.[66] We learn from the book of Jeremiah that God's steadfast love, justice, and righteousness are inseparable, so there can be no reconciliation without truth telling,[67] but there also can be "just mercy."[68]

Bibliography

Atkinson, Judy. *Trauma Trails, Recreating Song Lines: The Transgenerational Effects of Trauma in Indigenous Australia*. North Geelong: Spinifex, 2002.

Boochani, Behrouz. *No Friend but the Mountains: The True Story of an Illegally Imprisoned Refugee*. Translated by Omid Tofighian. Sydney: Picador, 2018.

Broome, Richard. *Aboriginal Victorians: A History Since 1800*. Crows Nest: Allen and Unwin, 2005.

---

61. See Wilson, *Proverbs*, 30–43.
62. McCaulley, *Reading While Black*, 126.
63. Katongole, *Born from Lament*, 63.
64. Wingard et al., *Aboriginal Narrative Practice*, 10.
65. Quoted in McCaulley, *Reading While Black*, 113.
66. Wilson, *Job*, 10.
Edwards, *Might from the Margins*, 165; see Jeremiah 21:11—23:4.
67. Volf, *Exclusion and Embrace*, 252, 259–62, 304.
68. Stevenson, *Just Mercy*, 314.

Brueggemann, Walter. *The Theology of the Book of Jeremiah*. Cambridge: Cambridge University Press, 2017.
Cone, James H. *The Cross and the Lynching Tree*. Maryknoll: Orbis, 2013.
Craigie, et al., *Jeremiah 1–25*. WBC 26. Grand Rapids: Thomas Nelson Inc., 1991.
Dale, Moyra. "Shame and Honour: Blunt Instrument or Useful Lens?" *When Women Speak* . . . 6, no. 1 (2020) 5–18.
Dell, Katherine. "'Cursed Be the Day I Was Born': Job and Jeremiah Revisited." In *Reading Job Intertextually*, edited by Katharine Dell and Will Kynes, 106–17. LHBOTS 574. London: Bloomsbury, 2012.
Edwards, Dennis R. *Might from the Margins: The Gospel's Power to Turn the Tables on Injustice*. Harrisonburg: Herald, 2020.
Firth, Jill. "Desert Spring, Dead Dog Waterhole, Disappointment Creek: Is the God of the Book of Jeremiah Bad for Women?" In *Grounded in the Body, in Time and Place, in Scripture: Papers by Australian Women Scholars in the Evangelical Tradition*, edited by Jill Firth and Denise Cooper-Clarke, 121–136. ACT Monograph Series. Eugene: Wipf and Stock, 2021.
―――. "Of the Shaping and Smashing of Pottery: Grace and Judgment in the Book of Jeremiah." Unpublished paper from Tyndale Fellowship Old Testament Study Group, Wolfson College, Cambridge, June 26, 2019.
―――. "Spirituality from the Depths: Responding to Crushing Circumstances and Psychological and Spiritual Distress in Jeremiah." In *The Bible and Mental Health: Towards a Biblical Theology of Mental Health*, edited by Christopher C. H. Cook and Isabelle Hamley, 115–27. London: SCM, 2020.
Foucault, Michel. "Of Other Spaces: Utopias and Heterotopias." ("Des Espaces Autres," March 1967). Translated from the French by Jay Miskowiec. *Architecture/Mouvement/Continuité* (1984). http://web.mit.edu/allanmc/www/foucault1.pdf.
Fretheim, Terence E. *Jeremiah*. SHBC 15. Macon: Smyth & Helwys, 2002.
Gourevitch, Philip. *We Wish to Inform You That Tomorrow We Will Be Killed With Our Families: Stories from Rwanda*. London: Picador Classic, 1999.
Heschel, Abraham J. *The Prophets: An Introduction*. New York: Harper Torchbooks, 1962.
Hill, Jess. *See What You Made Me Do: Power, Control and Domestic Abuse*. Carlton: Black Inc., 2019.
Holladay, William L. *Jeremiah 1 (1–25)*. Hermeneia. Philadelphia: Fortress, 1986.
Joüon, P., and T. Muraoka. *A Grammar of Biblical Hebrew: Second Reprint of the Second Edition, with Corrections*. Roma: Gregorian Biblical, 2009.
Katongole, Emmanuel. *Born from Lament: The Theology and Politics of Hope in Africa*. Grand Rapids: Eerdmans, 2017.
Kidd, Rosalind. *Black Lives, Government Lies*. Sydney: University of NSW Press, 2000.
Kidner, Derek. *The Message of Jeremiah: Against Wind and Tide*. BST. Downers Grove, IVP, 1987.
Lalleman, Hetty. *Jeremiah and Lamentations: An Introduction and Commentary*. TOTC 21. Nottingham: IVP, 2013.
Lundbom, Jack R. *Jeremiah 1–20*. AYB 21. New Haven: Yale University Press, 1999.
McCaulley, Esau. *Reading While Black: African American Interpretation as an Exercise in Hope*. Downers Grove: IVP Academic, 2020.
McConville, J. G. *Judgment and Promise: An Interpretation of the Book of Jeremiah*. Leicester: Apollos, 1993.

O'Connor, Kathleen M. *Jeremiah: Pain and Promise*. Minneapolis: Fortress, 2002.

———. "The Tears of God and Divine Character in Jeremiah 2–9." In *God in the Fray: A Tribute to Walter Brueggemann*, edited by Tod Linafelt and Timothy K. Beal, 172–85. Minneapolis: Fortress Press, 1998.

An Officer. "A Combatant's View." In *Moral Injury: Unseen Wounds in an Age of Barbarism*, edited by Tom Frame, 63–78. Sydney: UNSW Press, 2015.

Rah, Soong-Chan. *Prophetic Lament: A Call for Justice in Troubled Times*. Downers Grove: IVP, 2015.

Rowold, Henry. "Theology of the Pain of God: Reflections from Scripture." *Missio Apostolica* 12 (2004) 17–23.

Stevenson, Bryan, *Just Mercy: A Story of Justice and Redemption*. New York: One World, 2014.

Thompson, J. A. *The Book of Jeremiah*. NICOT. Grand Rapids: Eerdmans, 1980.

Tyquin, Michael. "In Search of the Unseen Wound." In *Moral Injury: Unseen Wounds in an Age of Barbarism*, edited by Tom Frame, 18–34. Sydney: UNSW Press, 2015.

Villanueva, Federico G. *The Uncertainty of a Hearing: A Study of the Sudden Change of Mood in the Psalms of Lament*. Leiden, Brill, 2008.

Volf, Miroslav. *Exclusion and Embrace: A Theological Exploration of Identity, Otherness, and Reconciliation*. Nashville: Abingdon Press, 1996.

Wakely, Robin. "חזק." In *NIDOTTE* 2:65.

Wilson, Lindsay. *Job*. THOTC. Grand Rapids: Eerdmans, 2015.

———. *Proverbs: An Introduction and Commentary*. TOTC 17. Downers Grove: IVP Academic, 2017.

Wingard, Barbara, et al. *Aboriginal Narrative Practice: Honouring Storylines of Pride, Strength and Creativity*. Dulwich Centre, 2015.

Wright, Christopher J. H. *The Message of Jeremiah: Grace in the End*. BST. Nottingham: IVP, 2014.

6

The Gracious Absence of the Love of God in the Book of Ezekiel

A Missional Reading

Andrew Sloane

"For God So Loved . . ." Except in Ezekiel

God's love is central to most evangelicals' understanding of the gospel—the *evangel*—that stands at the heart of our name and our self-understanding. God's love and mercy are equally central to the message of the Old Testament. It is at the heart of God's identity, as evident in the "character creed" of Exodus 34:6–7. Trust in that love is at the heart of the theology and spirituality of the Psalter, as evident in Psalm 107. Despite what some cultured despisers of Christianity (or at least the OT) might say, "God is love" is a whole-Bible affirmation, not an invention of New Testament faith; it is witnessed throughout the canon of Scripture. Except in the book of Ezekiel. There, God's love is puzzling in its absence.[1]

---

1. This chapter arises out of classroom discussions of this phenomenon over a number of years teaching the exegesis and theology of Ezekiel at Morling College. I am grateful to the persistent questioning of many students for prompting the questions that generated this piece. I am equally grateful for Dr. Jill Firth's invitation to contribute to this volume, and for the stimulating discussion of the Morling College research seminar at which it was first presented.

Of course, that is not the only puzzle in this book. We are puzzled by the strange and intricate vision-reports, the powerful and often bizarre metaphor and imagery, and the prevalence of (at times quite peculiar) symbolic actions. And we can now add this to them: while there is a clear message of hope in the book, it is neither grounded in nor motivated by God's love or compassion for Israel. This is particularly perplexing given the prominence of divine love elsewhere in the OT, especially in its message of hope as seen, for instance, in the book of Isaiah's message to exiled Israel (e.g., Isa 40:1–2, 11; 49:15–16; 54:4–8). How do we as believers in the *evangel* make sense of that? That's the question I want to come to grips with here. So, having first demonstrated the absence of love in Ezekiel's message of hope, I will outline typical responses to it, and their inadequacy. I will seek to show that the absence of God's love for Israel in Ezekiel's message of hope plays an important role in the book's persuasive strategies. It aims to reorient sinful exiles to God's larger purposes and their role in them, ultimately serving to restore the focus of God's people to God's mission of restoring a broken world. This is, I will suggest, a *missionally loving* absence, a puzzle that (perhaps paradoxically) opens up for us, as for Israel, a bigger vision of the love of God.

Where Is the Love? The Absence of God's Love in Ezekiel's Message of Hope

Let me begin by showing the ways in which God's love is absent from Ezekiel's message of hope to exiled Israel. The positive use of love language is rare in Ezekiel.[2] "Covenant love/mercy" (חֶסֶד) is entirely absent from the book, as is the cognate verb, in stark contrast to Jeremiah and Isaiah 40–55. "Love" (אהב) is both rare, and never used positively in the book.[3] In 16:33–37 it is used of Jerusalem's bribing of her adulterous lovers and their

---

2. I leave aside the two occasions where עגב (*'agab*, to lust) is used in the book, as it is negative in both its denotation and its rhetorical force. The verb עגב in Qal (and one fem noun form) is found in 23:5, 7, 9, 11, 12, 16, 20 in the extended metaphor of the adulterous sisters. The noun עֲגָבִים (*ʿagabim*, "love" [NIV], "lustful talk" [ESV]) is found in 33:31, 32, to speak (most likely, as in the ESV) of lustful speech and song. This lexeme, only otherwise found in Jer 4:30 with similar force, is never used positively of human or divine love, and so can be discounted from this analysis—except inasmuch as it casts a negative light on the capacity for "love" of Jerusalem and the exiles, and the way that even Ezekiel's powerful words of judgment (and eventual hope) can be perverted to their sinful interests.

3. As my colleague Anthony Petterson helpfully pointed out, this is particularly striking given the prominence of אהב ("love") in Hosea, the book that immediately follows Ezekiel in the Hebrew Bible, and one with which, along with Jeremiah, it has many theological affinities.

turning on her in violence. In 23:5, 9, and 22, it similarly speaks of her lust for foreign powers and their violent rejection of her. "Comfort, console" (נחם) is only ever used ironically in a "positive" sense. In 14:22–23, the (very) few survivors of Jerusalem will come to the elders of Israel in exile and "comfort" them about the disaster that befalls the city, inasmuch as their shameful ways will demonstrate the justice of Yhwh's action. In 31:16 the descent of Pharaoh and his hordes into the pit brings (ironic) consolation to the trees of Eden, while a bevy of fallen kingdoms that join Egypt in the pit in 32:29–30 will bring corresponding consolation to Pharaoh and his army in 32:31. Similarly, in 16:54, נחם (*naḥam*, "comfort") speaks of the shameful comfort Jerusalem gave to Sodom in view of the fact that Sodom's sins paled into insignificance in comparison with Jerusalem's. The verb only otherwise appears with the meaning of "comfort" (as opposed to "relent/repent") in 24:14 where it is used with "pity" (חוס) in the characteristic *negation* of compassion by Yhwh.

This brings us to the two most common words for love or compassion used in the book: pity (חוס) and spare (חמל). They are introduced to us in 5:11 in the oracle that explains the strange sequence of symbolic actions that opens Ezekiel's public ministry. And they horrify and terrify us with their remorseless force: "I, myself, will cut off/shave; my eye will not spare (וְלֹא־תָחוֹס עֵינִי), and also I myself will not have pity (וְגַם־אֲנִי לֹא אֶחְמוֹל)." This particular locution (or close variants of it) appears in the announcements of impending judgment in 7:4, 7:9, 8:18, 9:10, and in corresponding commands to the executioners in 9:5 that *their* eyes should not spare, *they* should have no pity.[4] There is no pity, no sparing of Jerusalem in the future. True, there are moments in the *past* where the language is used with positive force. Yhwh states in 20:17, "But my eye did spare them (וַתָּחָס עֵינִי עֲלֵיהֶם)" and so Yhwh did not destroy them for their sins in the wilderness. That, of course, is all in the past, as the chapter now declares both the impending judgment on Israel, and Yhwh's future rescue of them for the sake of Yhwh's own name (20:44).

This locution has a similar (preliminary) positive force in relation to Jerusalem's past in 16:5, even if it is couched negatively. There we hear, "no eye spared you (לֹא־חָסָה עָלַיִךְ עַיִן) . . . no one had pity for you (לְחֶמְלָה עָלָיִךְ)" when Jerusalem was a despised, abandoned baby, in contrast to Yhwh's action in adopting and then wedding her, thus bringing her into Yhwh's own kinship network so as to be the recipient of Yhwh's care.[5]

---

4. And note the way it echoes the command to execute idolaters in Deut 13:9 (v. 8 in Eng.).

5. I am aware of the debate that surrounds the depiction of Yhwh in Ezekiel 16 and 23, and have discussed it extensively elsewhere, for which see Sloane, "Aberrant

That care was spurned (and worse), which precipitates the judgment. And so we have an interesting instance of this language. Couched negatively, used positively to highlight Yʜᴡʜ's own action, but in the context of a (brutally) negative metaphor-driven oracle of inevitable disaster. Any pity is all in the past. The future is one of unsparing judgment. Almost. On the other side of the horrors of judgment, exile, and the destruction of city and temple, there is a word of hope.

And it is there, where we would most expect to hear words of love, compassion, of *ḥesed* (חֶסֶד) and mercy, that we hear none. In 11:16–21, the first clear message of hope-after-judgment, we hear of God's unilateral action for Israel in restoration and transformation. But no words of love or of comfort. In 16:59–63, there is again a message of hope-after-judgment. Yʜᴡʜ will (re)establish covenant with them; but Jerusalem will know, not the love of God, but shame at their past actions in light of the terms and means of the everlasting covenant into which they will be brought. Almost identical ideas are found in 20:42–44 (where "feel disgust," קוט is used of their response to the knowledge of their past failures), with the addition now that Yʜᴡʜ will act "for the sake of my name (לְמַעַן שְׁמִי)" and not on account of their past deeds. That, of course, makes sense, for their past ways were evil (רע), their past deeds were corrupt (שחת), and so judgment is the only kind of action that Yʜᴡʜ could undertake in response to them. In Ezekiel there is restoration, covenant renewal, acceptance, and a new exodus; but no love.

Now, in one sense that is to be expected, for in each of those instances, the word of hope is a coda to a word of judgment. Important, and I would argue integral to Ezekiel's message from the start,[6] but given in a context of indictment and a warning of judgment. So, there might be contextual reasons for muting, or even silencing, God's love in those passages. But no such explanation can account for the absence of love in chapter 36. For there, not only is the context (of both book and oracle) the turn to hope after judgment has come upon the nation, but the motivation for God's future action for Israel is explicitly tied to a concern for Yʜᴡʜ's own name

---

Textuality?"

6. This stands in contrast to those who see it as a late (redactional) addition to his original message of doom. On chs. 8–11 and the role of 11:14–21 see, for instance, Wevers, *Ezekiel*, 78; Eichrodt, *Ezekiel*, 112–19, 142–43; Zimmerli, *Ezekiel 1*, 230–37; Allen, *Ezekiel 1–19*, 129–37; Jenson, *Ezekiel*, 78. Joyce, *Ezekiel*, 109–11, 154–55, sees passages such as this as possibly written prior to the fall of Jerusalem, but still secondary additions to the text. For arguments supporting the integrity of chs. 8–11 and its theology (albeit involving the possible combination of originally separate elements into an edited whole), see Greenberg, *Ezekiel 1–20*, 192–205; Block, *Ezekiel 1–24*, 272–76, 342–46; Tuell, *Ezekiel*, 65; Kelle, *Ezekiel*, 115.

and not for Israel's sake, and in the most striking possible manner. Ezekiel 36:16–38 is the longest, and one of the more complex of Ezekiel's salvation oracles.[7] There is a sustained concern for the name of Yhwh, which was profaned both in Israel's past (sinful) life in the land, and in Israel's present (shameful) dispersion amongst the nations (36:16–20). And in that context the word "pity" (חמל) returns. That which was explicitly repudiated in Yhwh's prior act of judgment is now explicitly tied to Yhwh's future act of restoration. But it is directed not at suffering exiles, but towards Yhwh's own long-suffering name. Having seen how Yhwh's name has been dishonored amongst the nations, Yhwh now says: "And I had pity on my holy name (וָאֶחְמֹל עַל־שֵׁם קָדְשִׁי) which the house of Israel profaned in the nations where they went. Therefore say to the house of Israel, 'This is what the Lord Yhwh says, "Not because of you am I acting O house of Israel, but for my holy name that you profaned in the nations where you went" (36:21–22, my translation). Not only is the language of pity reserved for Yhwh's own name and not for Yhwh's people, but Yhwh explicitly excludes concern for them from Yhwh's motivations. And Yhwh does so in order that now, and in the future, Israel will be shamed and disgraced for both their past actions, and also recognize that Yhwh's concern for Yhwh's name is the basis on which a future of hope is held out to them (36:32). And so even here, in the turn to hope in the book of Ezekiel, there are no words of love, compassion, pity, or mercy.

Well, almost none. There is one, single, perplexing and passing exception: the positive use of "compassion" (רחם) in 39:25. At the end of the puzzling—and puzzlingly located—oracle concerning Gog of Magog, when security seemingly established in the return from exile (38:8) is disrupted by an ancient axis of evil (38:10–16), Yhwh will destroy this great military coalition (38:17—39:24). The resultant knowledge of Yhwh and Yhwh's purposes will encompass both the recognition of Israel's past sin and the justice of their judgment-in-exile, and of Yhwh's power in restoring them and their covenant relationship, and the holiness of Yhwh's name in both sets of action. But now, and uniquely in Ezekiel, this is connected with the language of love.[8] For in 39:25, Yhwh will bring Israel back from captivity (again?), and "I will have compassion on the house of Israel (וְרִחַמְתִּי כָּל־בֵּית

---

7. For the rhetorical complexity of the unit, and a variety of redactional explanations, see Zimmerli, *Ezekiel 2*, 244–46; Allen, *Ezekiel 20–48*, 176–78; Greenberg, *Ezekiel 21–37*, 733–35; Block, *Ezekiel 25–48*, 337–43; Tuell, *Ezekiel*, 245, 259–61; Bowen, *Ezekiel*, 221.

8. So, also, Wright, *Message of Ezekiel*, 322–23; Bowen, *Ezekiel*, 237. For the notion that this singular usage is not original to Ezekiel, but is the work of a later redactor, see (characteristically), Zimmerli, *Ezekiel 2*, 320.

יִשְׂרָאֵל) and I will be zealous for my holy name (וְקִנֵּאתִי לְשֵׁם קָדְשִׁי)."⁹ So, there is *some* language of love in the message of hope in Ezekiel. But only here. And still, it's connected with shamed remembering of the past of sin that necessitated their judgment, and a future salvation such as this. As an aside (well, almost an aside), I think it important to note that the NIV, NRSV, and even ESV all err in their translation of 39:26 ("they shall *forget* their shame"), on the basis of a dubious textual emendation. In line with the NET Bible, ASV, and a few others, I would suggest that the MT is to be preferred ("they shall *bear* their shame").¹⁰ Even in the future state of restoration, the house of Israel will bear their shame (וְנָשׂוּ אֶת־כְּלִמָּתָם), they will not forget it. And that, as we will see, is in line with the rhetoric of Ezekiel, and the role of future hope in it.

Why Don't You Love Me? Explaining a Deafening Silence

Now, I am not the first to notice the absence of love in Ezekiel, nor that future salvation is grounded in God's own character, in a concern for God's holy name. Zimmerli, for instance, notes the absence of the normal love-language of the OT in Ezekiel. He states regarding chapter 36: "Here too Ezekiel is devoid of all soft-hearted features and warmer tones. There is no mention of mercy, love, covenant faithfulness, the justice that brings salvation. This whole vocabulary is missing . . . In place of these in Ezekiel the dominant concept is that of the majesty of Yahweh and the revelation of his honor and glory. To a period and a nation who believed that they can willfully manipulate Yahweh, he is presented in all his majesty."¹¹ Similarly, Block states: "The modern reader may find Yahweh's apparent heartlessness at this point disturbing, if not offensive . . . Absent is any compassion towards a bleeding nation, any mercy, or any hint of forgiveness. Absent also is any reference to the covenant promises . . . When Yahweh begins to work, his concern will be the vindication of his own name, not theirs, among the nations."¹² The phenomenon is well recognized.¹³ Less clear is the reason for it.

---

9. Zeal/jealousy (קנא) is only found here in Ezekiel and in 8:3 (in relation to an idolatrous practice in the temple precincts) and 31:9 in relation to the jealousy of the trees of Eden towards Assyria, the once-lofty cedar of Lebanon.

10. For this, see Block, *Ezekiel 25–48*, 478; Zimmerli, *Ezekiel 2*, 295, 320.

11. Zimmerli, *Ezekiel 2*, 247–48.

12. Block, *Ezekiel 25–48*, 352.

13. Similar comments can be found in Joyce, *Divine Initiative*, 89–107; Kelle, *Ezekiel*,

There have been a number of approaches that have typified attempts to explain this absence. Probably the most common amongst evangelical interpreters is to read it into the text. It is such a deeply engrained expectation that God's saving work is motivated by God's loving that it is illegitimately imported into Ezekiel. For instance, Mackay states: "It is often argued that the conception of God in Ezekiel is deficient in that nothing is said of God acting in love, or even mercy towards his people . . . [But] Recognition that salvation comes despite human rebellion and incapacity is the greatest tribute which can be paid to the love and grace of God, and provides a sure ground for pleading with him."[14]

Others, in stark contrast, recognize this absence but see it as (further) evidence of the dangerously distorted theology of the book. Schwartz argues that Yhwh, having been humiliated by Israel's sinful rejection in the past and in the exposure of their sin to the watching nations in the exile, imposes Yhwh's will on Israel and forces their obedience.[15] This is an egocentric, loveless act of spite, a forced restoration against Israel's will, purely for Yhwh's own ends.[16] Tiemeyer echoes this view and, while not simply rejecting the "troubling" sections of Ezekiel, calls on us to resist this portrayal of God.[17] A somewhat different strategy is adopted by Mein, who claims that

---

294; Eichrodt, *Ezekiel*, 496; Darr, "Book of Ezekiel," 1492; Mein, "Ezekiel," 201–2. Tuell, *Ezekiel*, 248, speaks of Ezekiel's "bleak, cold, loveless view"; Greenberg, *Ezekiel 21–37*, 737–38, speaks of the restoration as "not a gracious response to human yearning for reconciliation . . . [but] an imposition on wayward Israel of a constraint necessary for saving God's reputation . . . Ezekiel remains true to his ruthless focus on the majesty of God, the safe-guarding of which is, in his view, the prime motive of Israel's history."

14. Mackay, *Ezekiel 25–48*, 252–53. Similar sentiments can be found in Eichrodt, *Ezekiel*, 496. Similar, if somewhat muted, statements are found in Duguid, *Ezekiel*, 414–15. Block speaks of God's grace for Israel in past, and present, and future. While recognizing the absence of the vocabulary of mercy, he argues that it is evident, both in the shepherd oracle of ch. 34, and in the logic of unmerited divine favor directed towards Israel in the future, for which see Block, "God Ezekiel Wants," esp. 188–92.

15. Schwartz, "Ezekiel's Dim View." It is important to note at this point that his notion that Yhwh has been (or could be) humiliated is deeply flawed. In Ezekiel true honor or shame relate to one's standing not in the public court of reputation (as in classical honor-shame theory), but the divine court of reputation, and so Yhwh cannot actually be shamed. See Wu, *Honor, Shame, and Guilt*, esp. 130–31, 69–73.

16. Schwartz, "Ezekiel's Dim View," 49, 59, 66, 67. Koller endorses Schwartz's "loveless" view of the relationship between Yhwh and Israel, but argues that, in fact, this frees up the possibility of grace in the present (see Koller, "Ezekiel 16," esp. 420–21). I'm not persuaded that Ezekiel 16 works quite the way he suggests, nor that "grace" is the best term to use of the possibility of restoration in Ezekiel (drawing, as it does, on affectional language foreign to the book). Nonetheless, it is an interesting observation that rhetorical force and apparent emotional loading may differ.

17. Tiemeyer, "To Read," see esp. 484, 486. She argues that we should adopt a

Ezekiel's repugnant presentation of God should prompt us to a *via negativa*, seeing Ezekiel's—and all other portrayals of God in language—as idolatrous, justifying a multiplicity of images in order to demonstrate the inadequacy of our theological constructions.[18] Bowen goes further, sharply criticizing the picture of God that emerges from this passage.

> The strategy employed in this unit is an extreme application of social control. Unilaterally forcing a new heart and new spirit on the people, God exerts total control over them. In the human realm those who use extreme social control to coerce people's obedience are called "tyrants," and their acts of control are viewed as "coercive" and "evil." That God is the one controlling only makes it more problematic and often provides legitimacy for humans to engage in similar behavior.[19]

For them, Ezekiel's is a poisonous, dangerous, misogynistic and abusive picture of God. We must expose, unmask and resist it, for our own sake and that of others.[20]

In their own, very different way, each of these approaches is deeply problematic for evangelical hermeneutics and theology. The first, because it reshapes Scripture into our own image, according to our likes. It fails to look carefully at what Ezekiel, and so God, might be saying through this book. The second, because it refuses to sit under the authority of Scripture. It believes we are in a position to discern on our own authority what is good and life-giving, and how God must go about God's purposes. Neither allows for the *evangel* to be good news about who God really is and how God actually works. They are also unnecessary, for I believe we can see how this sharp, abrasive presentation of God's promise of restoration presents not only a true picture of God, but serves to further God's loving, missional purposes in and for the world, for and through Israel.

---

strategy of lament, and resist the portrayal of God (and Israel) entailed in Ezekiel. Kelle is somewhat more nuanced, suggesting that we hold these depictions in tension with other, more love-oriented portrayals of God's character, and that they operate out of an ANE metaphorical world, and as ways in which the trauma of exile was integrated into Israel's (and Ezekiel's) understanding of God and themselves (see Kelle, *Ezekiel*, 105–9, 147–48, 201–4, 241–43).

18. Mein, "Ezekiel's Awkward God," esp. 271–77. His view is echoed and endorsed in O'Brien, "Metaphorization," 254–55.

19. Bowen, *Ezekiel*, 226.

20. I have discussed this perspective and the literature associated with it in some detail elsewhere. See Sloane, "Aberrant Textuality?"

An Immodest Proposal: Missional Grace and the Absence of God's Love in Ezekiel

I propose that the absence of God's love in Ezekiel's message of hope is neither an oversight nor a problem to be solved but is fundamental to the rhetorical function of the book. This is hinted at in the commentaries.[21] For instance, Block states: "God's actions in human history are driven by revelatory aims: that his people and the world may know that he is Yahweh. The recipients of divine grace are easily deluded into thinking that they are the center of the universe, that their desires determine God's agenda . . . But the universal Lord is concerned that all may see his glory and his grace. He acts to preserve the sanctity of his reputation."[22] Christopher Wright (characteristically) connects this to God's mission. "There is also a strong missiological current flowing in these lines, as they touch on the ultimate and universal mission of the God of the Bible to be known to his whole creation." He notes that God's reputation was impugned both by Israel's sin (Ezek 5) but also by their judgment, requiring a solution that dealt with both their character and Yahweh's public reputation.[23] But these occasional comments are not tied to the larger persuasive purposes of the book.

This brings me to the work of Thomas Renz on the rhetoric of the book of Ezekiel. His fundamental thesis is clear and, in the main, compelling.[24] Renz argues that the book of Ezekiel has been purposefully shaped to persuade its exilic readers to turn from their past affiliations (to sin, idolatry, defiled Jerusalem, foreign allegiances, and the like) to a new commitment to Yhwh. The book addresses an audience in exile in Babylon who know the fall of Jerusalem as a past reality, calling them to dissociate from the original (resisting) audience.[25] They are called to acknowledge that the past judgment of Yhwh on Jerusalem is just, which functions as an implicit call to repentance to the exilic community.[26] He states: "The argument of the book of Ezekiel is that the exilic community is to define itself not by the

---

21. See Zimmerli, *Ezekiel 2*, 247–48; Block, *Ezekiel 25–48*, 352.

22. Block, *Ezekiel 25–48*, 366. See also Glatt-Gilad, "Yahweh's Honor at Stake"; Wong, "Profanation/Sanctification," 217–18, 22, 29–30, and the connection with holy war traditions and Yhwh's character and power.

23. Wright, *Message of Ezekiel*, 292. See also his insightful (but passing) comments on Ezekiel in *Mission of God*, 88, 472.

24. I think further work could be done on the various illocutionary levels present in the book, and I have questions about some points of detail, but his fundamental thesis stands.

25. Renz, *Rhetorical Function of Ezekiel*, 41, 55.

26. Renz, *Rhetorical Function of Ezekiel*, 57, 59.

past but by the future promised by Yahweh. The author dissociates the exiles from their past by motivating them to regard the fall of Jerusalem as the just punishment for Israel's former disloyalty to Yahweh."[27] The new orientation called for requires a radical "acknowledgement of Yahweh's kingship as the beginning and end of Israel's future" which entails "a transformation from a rebellious people to a people that is loyal to Yahweh is like a heap of dry bones being transformed to a living assembly," through the dual agency of the Spirit and the prophetic word.[28]

Ezekiel's rhetoric, then, is a rhetoric of *displacement*. Israel has, most obviously, been displaced from both city and land, and this because of their (past) wrongly disposed hearts and allegiances. This community displaced from the center of their affection (Ezek 24:21) needs to see that they have exhausted God's patience, and are now also displaced from the center of God's affection. Moreover, they need to understand both those displacements in order to function again as the people of God. The word of judgment explains their geographical displacement as the work of a sovereign God who, in response to sin and disloyalty, enacts God's purposes in the world in and against and through Israel, amongst and through and against the nations. The pattern of the word of hope enacts another displacement, even as it speaks of the return of the exiled community to the space from which they were displaced. It requires that they see that they are not at the center of God's affections, nor are they the ones for whom God acts: the center of God's affections, the one for whom God acts, is God's own holy name.[29]

The language of Yhwh's compassion, pity, concern (חמל) for Yhwh's holy name makes that clear. To understand this, we need to go back to Ezekiel's first public words and actions, which serve to show the inextricable connection between Jerusalem and God's name—God's identity as demonstrated in God's actions in the world. At the center of the argument of the complex sequence of sign-acts is Jerusalem—and in a number of ways. In sign-acts Jerusalem is besieged, enfamined (so to speak), burned and beaten and scattered (4:3, 16; 5:2). In the prophecy Jerusalem is indicted in the third person (5:6), and indicted, condemned, and judged in second-person divine speech (5:6, 7, 8–12, 14–17). Jerusalem is the focus of the rhetoric of both sign-acts and prophecy. And it is so because it is the focus of God's actions in the world. "This is Jerusalem. In the midst of the nations I set her, and [set] around her lands" (5:5, my translation).

27. Renz, *Rhetorical Function of Ezekiel*, 249.
28. Renz, *Rhetorical Function of Ezekiel*, 249–50.

29. This is particularly important given that, as 33:30–32 shows, they are able to turn even Ezekiel's message into self-serving lust-filled entertainment (see the brief discussion in n. 2 above).

This is a statement not of simple geography (which would, in any case, be something of a stretch) but of divine intention—a *missional* intention. Jerusalem was intended to be a "model city," an expression in God's world of God's intentions for all humanity and every human community. It was intended to be a place where the watching nations would be drawn to say: "Oh! So *this* is what human flourishing looks like!" And, given Israel's call to reflect the very character of God, to then say: "Oh! So this is what *God* looks like!" As Dumbrell, and Goheen, and Wright (amongst others) have shown, Israel was intended to be a *missional* nation (Exod 19:5–6); called to experience relationship with God and its benefits, to be sure, but for the sake of the world.[30]

And Jerusalem, the locus of the rule of the Davidic king as agent and exemplar of God's reign (Ps 72), the locus of the presence of God and the place from which God chose to reign over God's whole-earth domain (Ps 24), was intended to be a *missional* city. It was meant to embody what a properly governed human community would look like—a missional politics through the *mashiach* (מָשִׁיחַ, "messiah")—and what a properly formed human community would look like, so drawing the nations into the ambit of God's saving, sovereign rule (Isa 1:21; 2:1–4). Jerusalem's special position, Israel's elected love, was always for others, not (just) for themselves. They were chosen, *for* the nations, that God's redeeming love might transform a broken world and bring healing and wholeness to broken communities. They were chosen for God's purpose; indeed, to *enact* God's purposes in the world. God's love for Israel was always tied to God's name and God's glory. It was always connected to who God is and how that is manifested in the world.

Thus, the absence of God's love in Ezekiel's message of hope helps us see that this story is not about Jerusalem. It is not about Israel. It is not about us. It is about God. God's name, God's reputation, God's purposes, God's glory, all of which are in question, even under threat, by the besmirching sinfulness of God's people—exemplified in that city that was meant to exemplify God's character and purposes. God is not glorified, God's name is not sanctified by Jerusalem, but dishonored and profaned. And so God's *name* is in need of being pitied. God's *name* is in need of rescue. God's *name* needs to be restored, even as God's purposes are reaffirmed.[31] Displacing Jerusalem from the heart of God's affection and replacing it with God's name serves to

---

30. Dumbrell, *Faith of Israel*, 34–35; Wright, *Mission of God*, 57, 254–57. They read the כִּי of v. 5 as explanation, not concession—"*for/because* all the nations are mine . . ." See also Goheen and Wright, "Theological Interpretation" (esp. 181 on Ezek 5:5); Bauckham, *Bible and Mission*.

31. Goheen and Wright, "Mission and Theological Interpretation," 180, 182–83.

reorient Jerusalem and the exiled Jewish community away from themselves and back to God and to God's call for them to demonstrate who God really is, and what human flourishing really looks like. It reorients them so that they can see that God's name and reputation are at stake in this Jerusalem project, that God's love for the world is at the center of God's purposes, and that, important as they are, theirs is a being-for-others, not for themselves. It is a call to forsake a small, self-centered, selfish love, in favor of a big love. Perhaps there are other ways of achieving this purpose (indeed, Isaiah 40–55 suggests there are); but this is how *Ezekiel* achieves it.

"For God So Loved *the World*"—The *Big* Love of the Book of Ezekiel

Ezekiel is an uncomfortable book. We struggle to make sense of it and, when we do, we often don't like what we see. We certainly don't like seeing the striking absence of God's love in this book, and we struggle to make sense of it. This is my suggestion: that this is a deliberate theological strategy aimed at fostering the central rhetorical function of the book. To call the exiled Israel community to renounce those past practices, vices, and affections that led rightly to them being judged, and to embrace God's transforming work to enable them to function once again as God's own people. Exemplars of God's character and purposes, agents of God's missional love in a needy and broken world.

In the end, we come to see that God's love and God's glory are inextricably connected, and that they need to be coordinated in both our picture of God and our understanding of our task as God's people (as Jesus so memorably taught, exemplified, and enabled in John's Gospel). Evangelical Christians, so often cultural captives to moralistic therapeutic deism, need to hear and heed this message just as much as did captive Israel. Ezekiel's focus on God's holiness and name, rather than God's love for Israel, is a reflection of God's love for a broken world. For Yhwh's name relates to Yhwh's reputation and Yhwh's plan. That plan is the choice of Israel and Jerusalem for the nations, and for restoration of corrupted human agency for the benefit of the world God called humans to rule-in-service. A focus on God's love for Israel at this point could easily return them to their sinful self-orientation. Ezekiel's bracing message of hope says: "this story is not about us; it's about God's plan for the world—and we are caught up in that, and only for that grander purpose."

Bibliography

Allen, Leslie C. *Ezekiel 1–19*. WBC. Dallas: Word, 1994.

———. *Ezekiel 20–48*. WBC. Waco: Word, 1990.

Bauckham, Richard. *Bible and Mission: Christian Witness in a Postmodern World*. Grand Rapids: Baker, 2003.

Block, Daniel I. *The Book of Ezekiel: Chapters 1–24*. Grand Rapids: Eerdmans, 1997.

———. "The God Ezekiel Wants Us to Meet: Theological Perspectives on the Book of Ezekiel." In *The God Ezekiel Creates*, edited by Paul M. Joyce and Dalit Rom-Shiloni, 162–92. London: T. & T. Clark, 2016.

Block, Daniel Isaac. *The Book of Ezekiel: Chapters 25–48*. New International Commentary on the Old Testament. Grand Rapids: Eerdmans, 1998.

Bowen, Nancy R. *Ezekiel*. Nashville: Abingdon, 2010.

Darr, Katheryn Pfisterer. "The Book of Ezekiel." In *The New Interpreter's Bible, vol. 6*, edited by Leander E. Keck, 1073–607. Nashville: Abingdon, 2002.

Duguid, Iain M. *Ezekiel*. NIV Application Commentary. Grand Rapids: Zondervan, 1999.

Dumbrell, William J. *The Faith of Israel: Its Expression in the Books of the Old Testament*. Leicester: Apollos, 1989.

Eichrodt, Walther. *Ezekiel: A Commentary*. Old Testament Library. London: SCM, 1970.

Glatt-Gilad, David A. "Yahweh's Honor at Stake: A Divine Conundrum." *Journal for the Study of the Old Testament* 26, no. 4 (2002) 63–74.

Goheen, Michael W., and Christopher J. H. Wright. "Theological Interpretation and a Missional Hermeneutic." In *A Manifesto for Theological Interpretation*, edited by Craig G. Bartholomew and Matthew Y. Emerson, 171–96. Grand Rapids: Baker, 2016.

Greenberg, Moshe. *Ezekiel 1–20*. AB. New York: Doubleday, 1983.

———. *Ezekiel 21–37*. AB. New York: Doubleday, 1997.

Jenson, Robert W. *Ezekiel*. Brazos Theological Commentary on the Bible. Grand Rapids: Brazos, 2009.

Joyce, Paul. *Divine Initiative and Human Response in Ezekiel*. Sheffield: JSOT, 1989.

———. *Ezekiel: A Commentary*. Library of Hebrew Bible/Old Testament Studies. New York: T. & T. Clark, 2007.

Kelle, Brad E. *Ezekiel: A Commentary in the Wesleyan Tradition*. New Beacon Bible Commentary. Kansas City: Beacon Hill, 2013.

Koller, Aaron. "Pornography or Theology?: The Legal Background, Psychological Realism, and Theological Import of Ezekiel 16." *Catholic Biblical Quarterly* 79, no. 3 (2017) 402–21.

Mackay, John L. *Ezekiel, vol. 2: Chapters 25–48*. Mentor Commentary. Fearn, UK: Christian Focus, 2018.

Mein, Andrew. "Ezekiel: Structure, Themes, Contested Issues." In *The Oxford Handbook of the Prophets*, edited by Carolyn J. Sharp, 190–206. New York: Oxford University Press, 2016.

———. "Ezekiel's Awkward God: Atheism, Idolatry and the Via Negativa." *Scottish Journal of Theology* 66, no. 3 (2013) 261–77.

O'Brien, Julia M. "Metaphorization and Other Tropes in the Prophets." In *The Oxford Handbook of the Prophets*, edited by Carolyn J. Sharp, 241–57. New York: Oxford University Press, 2016.

Renz, Thomas. *The Rhetorical Function of the Book of Ezekiel*. Boston: Brill, 2002.
Schwartz, Baruch J. "Ezekiel's Dim View of Israel's Restoration." In *The Book of Ezekiel: Theological and Anthropological Perspectives*, edited by Margaret S. Odell and John T. Strong, 43–67. Atlanta: Society of Biblical Literature, 2000.
Sloane, Andrew. "Aberrant Textuality? The Case of Ezekiel the (Porno) Prophet." *TynBul* 59, no. 1 (2008) 53–76.
Tiemeyer, Lena-Sofia. "To Read—Or Not to Read—Ezekiel as Christian Scripture." *Expository Times* 121 (2010) 481–88.
Tuell, Steven Shawn. *Ezekiel*. New International Biblical Commentary. Peabody: Hendrickson, 2009.
Wevers, John W. *Ezekiel*. Century Bible—New Series [RSV]. London: Nelson, 1969.
Wong, Ka Leung. "Profanation/Sanctification and the Past, Present and Future of Israel in the Book of Ezekiel." *Journal for the Study of the Old Testament* 28, no. 2 (2003) 210–39.
Wright, Christopher J. H. *The Message of Ezekiel: A New Heart and a New Spirit*. Leicester: IVP, 2001.
———. *The Mission of God: Unlocking the Bible's Grand Narrative*. Nottingham: IVP, 2006.
Wu, Daniel Y. *Honor, Shame, and Guilt: Social-Scientific Approaches to the Book of Ezekiel*. Bulletin for Biblical Research Supplements. Winona Lake: Eisenbrauns, 2016.
Zimmerli, Walther. *Ezekiel 1*. Translated by R. E Clements. Philadelphia: Fortress, 1979.
———. *Ezekiel 2*. Translated by J. D. Martin. Philadelphia: Fortress, 1983.

7

Knowledge and Rebellion, Judgment and Grace

An Examination of the Impact of the Portrayal of Yhwh in the Golden Calf Narrative on Joel and Jonah

Heather Reid

It is difficult to overestimate the importance of Yhwh's words in Exodus 34:6–7, given that they are "the longest and most complete description of the Lord's character to be found in Scripture, and canonically later Scriptures often return to them."[1] However, the surrounding narrative in Exodus 32–34 is also a profound theological exploration that shaped the thought-world of much of the Hebrew canon. Any attempt to explore this influence must include the unique hypertexts which occur in Joel and Jonah since these not only cite Yhwh's self-declaration from Exodus 34:6 but also highlight the importance of the golden calf narrative itself in understanding the self-declaration. In the following chapter, after examining the role of the Exodus 34:6–7 self-declaration within the narrative of Exodus 32–34, we will then track its impact on the Old Testament writers, with a specific focus on its use in Jonah and Joel.

---

1. Blackburn, *Makes Himself Known*, 15.

Exodus 34:6–7 Within the Narrative of Exodus 32–34

The context of Exodus 32–34 is set by the events of the Exodus from Egypt, that is, the rescue (1:1—5:21); journey to Sinai (15:22—19:2); and Yhwh's initiation of the covenant (19:3—23:33). Following unequivocal acceptance by the people (24:1–23), plans are put into place to establish the tabernacle as a permanent symbol of Yhwh's presence amongst them (24:12—31:17). The golden calf narrative then intrudes, raising questions about sin, forgiveness, and the viability of Israel's relationship with their holy God (31:1—34:35). Covenant renewal is made possible by Yhwh's revelation of himself as not only holy and just, but also "merciful and gracious, slow to anger, and abounding in spontaneous, unobligated love (חסד) and faithfulness" (34:6), allowing the tabernacle to be constructed (35–40) so that Yhwh can dwell amongst his people.

The calf narrative lies at the center of a chiasm within Exodus 24:12—40:38:[2]

    A Cloud/Glory (Offering)

        B Ark/Furnishings

            C Tabernacle

                D Bezalel

                    E Sabbath

                        F Golden Calf (31:18—34:35)

                    E^1 Sabbath (Offering)

                D^1 Bezalel

            C^1 Tabernacle

        B^1 Ark/Furnishings/Miscellaneous

    A^1 Cloud/Glory

The key to understanding the theological significance of the chiasm is the Sabbath pericopes, which bracket the calf narrative. Since Sabbath observance points both back to God's initial creative work and forward toward the new creation which God is bringing into being in and through Israel, the golden calf apostasy represents a threat to the shape of God's creative work.[3]

When 32:1 is read with this context in mind, the request for Aaron to "make us gods who shall go before us" is a covenantal calamity! The parallels

---

2. Waring, *Nature of Yahweh*, 45.
3. Fretheim, *Exodus*, 277–78.

between Yhwh's words in 32:31, "they have made for themselves gods of gold" (ויעשו להם אלהי זהב), and the prohibition in 20:23, "gods of gold, you shall not make for yourselves" (ואלהי זהב לא תעשו לכם), adds emphasis to this.[4] For, as the people sought to make for themselves what Yhwh had already provided, they forfeited "the very divine presence they had hoped to bind more closely to themselves" (25:8; 29:45–46).[5]

Exodus 32–34, therefore, presents a theological framework of sin and forgiveness.[6] While the breaking of the tablets (32:19) demonstrates Israel's breaking of covenant, the rewriting of the tablets indicates covenant restoration by Yhwh (34:1, 4, 28). Similarly, the intercession of Moses that begins in 32 and climaxes in 34 highlights the ongoing presence of Yhwh.[7] His presence bridges the gulf between Israel's disobedience and punishment in 32 and their forgiveness and restitution in 34.

The fundamental question underlying 32:7–14 is: "In light of their sin (32:1–6), can Israel continue to be the people of Yhwh?" The resolution of this question is critical for both the narrative as a whole and the declaration of 34:6–7.[8]

Yhwh's description of the people's actions (32:7–8) stresses the seriousness of their sin.[9] He begins by subtly disowning them—they are Moses's people! They have acted corruptly (שחת).[10] Not only have they turned aside from the way he commanded them but have done so quickly.[11] The seriousness of this is accentuated by Moses's threefold use of the phrase "great sin" (חטאה גדלה) to describe Israel's actions (32:21, 30–31).[12]

Thus it is remarkable that as Yhwh speaks in judgment, he makes such dependent on the agreement of Moses—"now, therefore, let me alone, that ... I may consume them" (32:10), paradoxically leaving a possible escape.[13] This "invitation" to Moses does not diminish the reality of Yhwh's wrath and judgment. Instead, it introduces the paradox at the heart of the character of Yhwh, which is to be revealed in 34:6–7.[14] The notion that Yhwh

---

4. Josipovici, *Book of God*, 93–107.
5. Fretheim, *Exodus*, 280–81.
6. Childs, *Exodus*, 557–58.
7. Stuart, *Exodus*, 40–42.
8. Moberly, *Mountain of God*, 49.
9. Caudill, *Presence of God*, 161.
10. Cf. Genesis 6:11–12.
11. Moberly, *Mountain of God*, 49.
12. For example, Genesis 20:9. Caudill, *Presence of God*, 163.
13. Moberly, *Mountain of God*, 50.
14. Sarna, *Exodus*, 205.

is both a jealous judge (34:7, 14; 20:5) and "gracious and compassionate, slow to anger, and abounding in spontaneous, unobligated love and faithfulness" (34:6) receives further emphasis when Moses's appeal to Yhwh's faithfulness to the Abrahamic covenant—an idea Yhwh first introduced in 32:10—becomes the reason the people are spared (32:13–14).[15] Just as 32:1–6 presents a paradigm of sin and apostasy, so 32:7–14 presents a paradigm of judgment, intercession, and forgiveness.

The paradoxical nature of Yhwh's character in Exodus 32 is also apparent in the descriptions of Yhwh's relationship with Israel. In 32:7, the people are no longer "*my* people (עַמִּי)" (3:7; 5:1; 7:4; 8:16–19; 9:1; 20:14; 22:24), but rather "*your* people (עַמְּךָ), whom *you* brought up out of the land of Egypt," and "*this* people (אֶת־הָעָם) . . . a *stiff-necked* people (עַם־קְשֵׁה־עֹרֶף)" (32:9).[16] Hence the statement that "Yhwh relented from the disaster that he had spoken of bringing on *his* people (לְעַמּוֹ)" (32:14), powerfully demonstrates the complete reversal Yhwh's forgiveness entails.[17] Instead of walking away from his covenant with Israel, as they have done to him, Yhwh turns "from his fierce anger" and acts in חסד—unexpected, surprising, unobligated mercy and love.[18] Despite their "great sin" against Yhwh, the narrator acknowledges what Moses has argued: that *this* people are still *his* people. Such confidence is subsequently affirmed in Leviticus 26:12, although the term "*my* people" is not used again in Exodus. Thus, 32:14 provides both a context in which to read the judgments in 32:15—33:11, and a promise that "God will be merciful and restore his people."[19]

In Exodus 32:30, Moses again approaches Yhwh on behalf of the people hoping to make atonement. However, the relationship between Yhwh and the Israelites has changed. Although Yhwh's acceptance of a future with Israel is implied at the beginning of 32:34, the end of Yhwh's statement indicates that Israel must still suffer for their sin. Such is achieved by a wordplay on פקד: "when I *visit*, I will *visit their sin* upon them." In 3:16; 4:31 and 13:19, פקד is used when Yhwh's visitation is favorable. Now, because of Israel's sin, Yhwh's visitation has turned from blessing to curse.[20] The plague Yhwh sends (32:35) links the plight of the Israelites with that of the Egyptians. Now he is their judge (7:4–5) rather than their redeemer (6:6–7).

---

15. Moberly, *Mountain of God*, 50. Cf. Genesis 12:3; Sarna, *Exodus*, 205.
16. Reid, *Exodus*, 313; Sarna, *Exodus*, 205.
17. Moberly, *Mountain of God*, 52.
18. Andersen, "Yahweh, the Kind," 81–82.
19. Moberly, *Mountain of God*, 53.
20. Moberly, *Mountain of God*, 58.

Although Israel mourns (33:4), Yhwh's distancing is a protective measure.[21] He will not go with them because his presence is dangerous to the sinful (33:3; cf. 12:33 and 20:5).[22]

Moses's intercession in 33:12–16 displays that more is needed for Israel: a fuller revelation of Yhwh's nature as a gracious and merciful God (cf. 33:18–19; 34:6–7). Only because of Yhwh's abundant "spontaneous, unobligated love" (חסד) can he deal mercifully with Israel's sin, renew covenant, and not destroy them. Hence the theophany in which God reveals his grace, mercy, and חסד.[23]

Since "*who* God is, determines *how* he will act," the request by Moses to know Yhwh's ways (33:13) is a request to understand the personal attributes and norms that guide Yhwh's actions in the world.[24] He wants to see Yhwh's glory—to see a visible demonstration of who Yhwh is and what makes him this.[25] However, appropriately for Yhwh, who is revealed in his word, this will come in words.[26] Instead of Moses *seeing* what Yhwh *looks like*, Yhwh *proclaims* who he *is*.[27] Yhwh's words show Moses the truth about what makes him glorious (33:19). Unlike the time Yhwh passed through (עבר) Egypt in judgment (12:12), here (33:22) he passes (עבר) in benevolence, showing that his glory lies primarily in his benevolent goodness.[28]

The natural division of Yhwh's self-declaration in 34:6–7 is into two opposing theological declarations split at 34:7b by the adversative *vav*. This split emphasizes the rhetorical weight falling on Yhwh's merciful attributes and also highlights the reversal of the judgment and mercy sequence in 20:6. Such is picked up by Lane's structure below.[29]

A   Yhwh, Yhwh,

B   God, merciful and gracious,

      slow to anger,

      and abounding in spontaneous, unobligated love and faithfulness.

---

21. Gowan, *Theology in Exodus*, 229.
22. Lin, *Golden Calf*, 187.
23. Moberly, *Mountain of God*, 68.
24. Moberly, *Mountain of God*, 73, emphasis his.
25. Sarna, *Exodus*, 214.
26. Reid, *Exodus*, 319.
27. Durham, *Exodus*, 452.
28. Hamilton, *Exodus*, 570.
29. Lane, *Compassionate but Punishing*, 26.

C	a	Keeping spontaneous, unobligated love for thousands (of generations),[30]
	b	forgiving iniquity, transgression, and sin,
	b₁	but who will by no means clear the guilty,
	a₁	visiting the iniquity of the fathers on the children and the children's children, to the third and fourth generation.

The double reference to Yhwh at "A" followed by a series of appositions is unique in the Hebrew canon. Elsewhere, when repetition occurs with Yhwh as the subject, it is followed by a descriptive string of predicates.[31]

"B" then contains a threefold affirmation of Yhwh's merciful attributes. The three words, "merciful and gracious God" (אל רחום וחנון) only occur together in Nehemiahi 9:31, Psalm 86:15, and Jonah 4:2, and appear to be an aspect of Yhwh's sovereignty (see Exod 33:19).[32] ארך אפים is an idiom meaning "slow to anger," indicating that Yhwh's mercy is not easily taken back from the people. The key to ורב־חסד ואמת (abounding in spontaneous, unobligated love and faithfulness) is the word חסד. In this context of broken covenant, חסד carries the sense of "unexpected, surprising, unobligated mercy and love."[33] It provides reassurance that Yhwh will uphold his relationship with his people *despite* their sin.

The chiasm in "C" highlights the vertical nature of Yhwh's judgment. It emphasizes his חסד, noting that it is "the foundation of Yhwh's dealings with humans, 'to the thousandth generation,' whereas his wrath is transitory by contrast, lasting only for four generations."[34] Significantly, the second participial phrase includes "iniquity, transgression, and sin" (עון ופשע וחטאה); encompassing all kinds of sin and thereby indicating the scope of Yhwh's forgiveness.[35] The clause and the following participial phrase, then articulate Yhwh's judgment on the unrighteous. Again Yhwh uses the term "visit" (פקד) to reference judgment. Here also, the relationship change triggered by the people's sin is highlighted, as a phrase generally

---

30. See Deuteronomy 5:9–10.
31. Andersen, "Yahweh, the Kind," 47.
32. Lane, *Compassionate but Punishing*, 28.
33. Snaith, *Distinctive Ideas*, 102; Reid, *Exodus*, 328. See also Dentan, "Literary Affinities," 43.
34. Andersen, "Yahweh, the Kind," 49.
35. Lane, *Compassionate but Punishing*, 29; Cassuto, *Exodus*, 440.

used to describe reward for righteousness—"to the third and fourth," is applied to Yhwh's wrath.³⁶

However, while this section of Yhwh's self-declaration begins by elucidating Yhwh's mercy, forgiveness, and "spontaneous, unobligated love" (חסד), it concludes with a warning that this should not be exploited lest Yhwh extend his wrath on the culprits for three or four generations.

This revelation of Yhwh's character summarizes the previous narrative. But it also prefaces the continuation of Israel's story after the golden calf incident, thus demonstrating Israel's deserved wrath and judgment being overwhelmed by Yhwh's mercy (34:10–28). Only on this basis can Yhwh dwell among his people.³⁷

Joel, Jonah, and Exodus 32–34

Gérard Genette uses the analogy of the *palimpsest* to describe the relationship between the texts: "on the same parchment, one text can become superimposed upon another, which it does not quite conceal but allows to show through."³⁸ Thus, Genette proposes that every text is a hypertext, for all texts evoke some other text: imitating or transforming it.³⁹ Moreover, although it is possible to understand a hypertext without reference to its hypotext, a richer reading is possible if the hypertext is read *palimpsestuously* with an awareness of the hypotext that sits behind it.⁴⁰

Other than the parallel passages in the Torah, there are eight instances listed in the table below, where *hypertextual* use of Exodus 34:6–7 presents as *intertextuality*, or a citation.⁴¹ Each of these reconceptualizes the message with an emphasis on either divine justice or divine mercy.⁴²

---

36. Sarna, *Exodus*, 111. See Genesis 50:23; 2 Kings 10:30; Job 42:16.
37. Dozeman, "Inner-Biblical Interpretation," 218.
38. Genette, *Palimpsests*, 398–99.
39. Genette, *Palimpsests*, 9.
40. Genette, *Palimpsests*, 399. The adverb, *palimpsestuously*, has been derived from an adjective coined by Philippe Lejeune—*palimpsestuous*. Lejeune used the term "a *palimpsestuous* reading" to describe a reading which engages with both the text and its hypotexts.
41. Genette, *Palimpsests*, 1–2 defines intertextuality as "the actual presence of one text in another."
42. Kim, "Jonah Read Intertextually," 513.

Transtextual Use of Exodus 34:6–7 in the Hebrew Canon

	Compassionate (רחום)	Gracious (חנון)	Slow to anger (ארך אפים)	Abundant in loving-kindness (חסד)	Faithfulness (אמת)	Steadfast love (חסד) to thousands	Forgiving (נשא עון ופשע וחטאה)	Not clearing the guilty (לא ינקה)	Visiting iniquity (פקד עון) to third and fourth
Exodus 34:6–7	•	•	•	•	•	•	•	•	•
Parallel Intertextual use of Exodus 34:6–7 spoken by Y<small>HWH</small> in the Torah									
Exodus 20:5–7						•			•
Exodus 33:19	•	•							
Deuteronomy 5:9–11						•			•
Obvious *hypertextual* citations of Exodus 34:6–7 in the Hebrew canon									
Numbers 14:16–19			•	•			•	•	•
Joel 2:13	•	•	•	•					
Jonah 4:2	•	•	•	•					
Nahum 1:3			•					•	
Psalm 86:5, 15	•	•	•	•	•	•			
Psalm 103:8–13	•	•	•	•					
Psalm 145:8	•	•	•	•					
Nehemiah 9:16–19, 30–32	•	•	•	•					

Significantly, of Y<small>HWH</small>'s attributes listed in 34:6–7, those most frequently cited outside of Torah are the positive attributes in 34:6.

Unique amongst these citations are Joel 2:13 and Jonah 4:2. Both have nearly identical wording, recording the first two attributes of Y<small>HWH</small>

in reverse—"gracious and compassionate" (חנון ורחום), followed by "slow to anger" (ארך אפים) "and abounding in spontaneous, unobligated love" (רב חסד) as in 34:6. However, both then omit "faithfulness" (אמת) and finish instead with the statement "and relents concerning disaster" (ונחם על־הרעה). Since the phrase "Who knows—he may turn and relent" (מי־יודע ישוב ונחם) also occurs in both Joel 2:14 and Jonah 3:9, the presence of hypertextual links between Exodus 32:12, 14 and Exodus 34:6 is apparent, indicating that the authors are referencing the golden calf narrative as a whole.

Joel 2:13–14 in Context

Joel's prophecy begins with an encouragement to look back to "the days of your fathers" (1:2) and "tell your children" (1:3) of a judgment taking the form of a locust plague, pointing to the hypotexts Exodus 10:2–6 and the generational language of Exodus 34:7. The rhetoric describing the coming plague highlights the nature and intensity of the catastrophe (1:4), as does the call for the people to lament and grieve.[43] The judgment day of Yhwh is near (1:15). Food has been cut off, and therefore the presentation of offerings is no longer possible (1:16). Their joy is shamed (בוש) in the eyes of the nations (1:12, 15).[44] Such language reflects Exodus 32–34, particularly Moses's plea in Exodus 32:12, leaving the only solution: to "cry out to Yhwh" (1:14).

The urgency increases in 2:1b, with the words, "the day of the Lord comes; it is near!"[45] This new warning focuses on invading destroyers, describing them as an army, the like of which "has never been before, nor will be again . . . through the years of all generations" (2:2b). These words both parallel and answer the question of 1:2–3, while the Exodus 10:6, 14 hypotext highlights the irony.[46] What Yhwh had once done to Egypt in order to save Israel, he now prepares to do to Israel.[47] Israel is under Yhwh's judgment: "who can endure it?" (2:11; Exod 15:6–7).

In 2:12, Yhwh speaks, providing hope and calling his people to repentance and worship—*with* all your heart, *with* fasting, *with* weeping, and

---

43. Allen, *Joel, Obadiah, Jonah*, 49, notes that the intensity of the catastrophe is achieved by "piling up four different terms for locusts" (1:4). Cf. Achtemeier, "Book of Joel," who suggests that these "may refer to the four stages in the locust life cycle." This may support the previous generational allusion (1:2–3). See also Prior, *Joel, Micah and Habakkuk*, 22.

44. Simkin, "Return to Yahweh," 46–47.

45. Prinsloo, *Book of Joel*, 41. See also Dillard, "Joel," 1:1271.

46. Fleer, "Exegesis of Joel 2:1–11," 155.

47. Dillard, "Joel," 1:271; Fleer, "Exegesis of Joel 2:1–11," 160.

with mourning (2:12b).⁴⁸ This call is about inward change rather than a superficial show (2:13a). Subsequently, there is a reminder of the paradox revealed in Yhwh's self-declaration (2:13b): if they are to flee from Yhwh's judgment, it must be toward Yhwh. Return is only possible because Yhwh is as he is revealed in Exodus 34:6.⁴⁹

Joel's use of the words "Yhwh your God" (2:13a) points to whom they must return: "Yhwh *your* God." This term complements "*his* people" in Exodus 32:14, a link which is then emphasized by the final clause following the Exodus 34:6 intertext: "he relents over disaster" (ונחם על־הרעה). Substituting this phrase for "faithfulness" (אמת) provides another link to Exodus 32:14, where Yhwh "relented from the disaster that he had spoken of bringing on his people."⁵⁰

Thus, as occurred in Exodus 32–34, recognition of Yhwh's propensity to mercy in Joel 2:13 shifts the focus of the book from the judgment of 1:1—2:11, to a future hope (2:18—4:21).⁵¹ Such hope is emphasized by Joel's poignant question: "Who knows whether he will not turn to relent and leave a blessing behind him?" (2:14a).

The phrase, "Who knows?" (מי יודע), occurs within the Book of the Twelve only here and in Jonah 3:9. It undermines arrogance and presumption. Yhwh has already pronounced judgment against Israel, so one cannot assume that an act of repentance can force him to change. It is a reminder that Yhwh "acts in sovereign freedom"—he will be gracious to whom he will be gracious and will show mercy on whom he will show mercy (Exod 33:19).⁵²

Similarly, the occurrence of the words "return and relent" (ישוב ונחם), referencing Yhwh (2:14), are "an extremely infrequent combination."⁵³ When spoken into this context of judgment and mercy, they function as a hypertext to Exodus 32:12 and Moses's plea to Yhwh, "turn from your burning anger and relent" (שוב מחרון אפך והנחם). As Yhwh's willingness to relent at Moses's behest (Exod 32:12–14) allowed the golden calf narrative to reach its culmination in Exodus 34, so here Yhwh's willingness to relent and provide food for an offering can remove the cause of Israel's shame amongst the nations (1:11–16; 2:17; cf. Exod 32:11–13). This idea is subsequently

---

48. Prinsloo, *Book of Joel*, 50.
49. Wolff, *Joel and Amos*, 41.
50. Andersen, "Yahweh, the Kind," 48–52, 76, 81.
51. Lane, *Compassionate but Punishing*, 81.
52. Crenshaw, *Joel*, 138. See also Crenshaw, "Expression Mi Yôdēaʿ," 274–88.
53. Dozeman, "Inner-Biblical Interpretation," 221. The only other place "return and relent" referencing Yhwh occurs in Jonah 3:9.

developed in Joel's prayer for mercy (Joel 2:15–17), where it is "couched in an argument about the effects that Yahweh's withholding of compassion would have on the other nations" (cf. Exod 32:11–13).[54]

It therefore appears that Joel's citation of Exodus 34:6 in 2:13, and other Exodus 32–34 hypotexts, amounts to an exploration of the theology underpinning the golden calf narrative as a whole.

Jonah 4:2

The scope of the narrative in Jonah is comprehensive, exploring Yhwh's relationship to Jonah, gentile sailors, Israel's enemy (Nineveh), and creation (wind, storm, sea, dry land, fish, vine, worm, sun, and cattle). Hence, although the message of Jonah might be reduced to "Don't be like Jonah," its broad scope suggests that the book is "in many ways, a microcosm of God's relationship to his whole creation in history."[55]

The narrative is set in two locations: the western sea (chs. 1 and 2) and Nineveh to the east (chs. 3 and 4).[56] These locations are then further divided into two scenes. The first describes Jonah's adventures amongst "nameless foreigners" who come to call upon Yhwh (1:16; 3:7–9), while the second shows Jonah alone with Yhwh.[57] Within each of the four chapters of Jonah, there is also a general repeating structure.[58]

> A crisis presents itself (1—Sailor/2—Jonah/3—Ninevites/4—Jonah)
>   Those affected cry to Yhwh (1,2,3,4)
>   Yhwh is merciful and saves them (1,2,3,4)
>   They offer praise and thanksgiving (1,2)

This structure demonstrates that although the narrative deals with Jonah, the main message is about Yhwh and his character as a sovereign God who acts to show that he is still the God of Exodus 32–34—a God who will have mercy on whom he will have mercy (Exod 33:19), despite Jonah's disobedience.

---

54. Dozeman, "Inner-Biblical Interpretation," 212.

55. Stuart, *Hosea-Jonah*, 434; Bruckner, *Jonah*, 17.

56. Trible, *Rhetorical Criticism*, 109–11 notes that this is emphasized by the parallel between 1:1–3 and 3:1–3a.

57. Sasson, *Jonah*, 16–17. However, within this structure there is variation in narrative styles, Kidner, "Divine Names," 126–28.

58. Reid, *Postcard from Palestine*, 85.

The repetition of two verbs highlights the connections between the book of Jonah and the critical themes of YHWH's mercy and grace in the golden calf narrative (Exod 32–34). The first of these is נחם (*relent*).[59] It occurs twice in 3:9–10, where the king of Nineveh expresses a hope that "God may turn and relent . . . and we will not perish," followed by the statement that "God relented of the disaster that he had said he would do to them." Such language is almost identical to that used in Exodus 32:12, 14.[60] Hence, when נחם occurs in 4:2, it points back to 3:9–10 and beyond that to its hypotext in Exodus 32:14.[61]

Second, שוב (*turn*) occurs five times. Two of these speak of YHWH's *turning* to relent and *turning* from his burning anger (3:9). Exodus 32:12 and Joel 2:14 are the only other places to combine these elements when speaking about YHWH. However, this occurrence "is startling since this . . . idea that was formerly restricted to the relationship between God and Israel is (now) expanded to embrace the 'pagan' world."[62]

Jonah's anger at YHWH's compassion toward the gentile Ninevites leads to his prayer involving the retrospective revelation that he had fled because he knew of YHWH's propensity to mercy (4:2–3). Landes notes various parallels between this prayer and that in 2:2–10 despite their different form, type, and content:[63]

Each one:

- is introduced with the words, "he prayed to YHWH . . . and said"

- refers back to earlier distress (2:3–7a: "in the deep"; 4:2a: "in my country")

- reflects on YHWH's חסד (spontaneous, unobligated love). In 2:7b–8, idolaters forsake their hope of חסד, while in 4:2, YHWH's abundant חסד (spontaneous, unobligated love) is the reason Jonah gives for fleeing

- concludes with Jonah's response to YHWH's action. In 2:10 thanksgiving, sacrifices, and vows, because "Salvation belongs to YHWH," and in 4:3; "it is better for me to die than live"

---

59. Sasson, *Jonah*, 262.

60. Magonet, *Form and Meaning*, 71. The extension of this idea of YHWH relenting towards another nation outside of Israel also occurs in Jeremiah 18:8, but in the context of Jonah "it is still the shock of the similarity of the 'Jonah' verse to Exodus which predominates, and the contrast that it emplies (sic)."

61. Cf. Joel 2:13–14.

62. Magonet, *Form and Meaning*, 71; Dozeman, "Inner-Biblical Interpretation," 222–23.

63. Landes, "Kerygma of Jonah," 16–17.

- concludes with a response from Yhwh, who acts so that Jonah may respond favorably to the divine mission.

Such parallels highlight Exodus 32–34 as a hypotext. First, in 2:9, the idea of idolatry is linked to forsaking Yhwh's loving-kindness (חסד). Second, in Jonah 4:2–3, Jonah is identified with the disobedient Israelites through a hypertextual reference to Exodus 14:12 (see below). Where the Israelites preferred slavery to death, Jonah prefers death to life.[64]

Exodus 14:2	Jonah 4:2a, 3
"*Is this not the word* which we spoke to you in Egypt?" saying:	"*Is this not my word* while I was in my land? . . .
"Let us alone that we may serve Egypt! *For it is better for us to serve Egypt than to die in the wilderness.*"	So now Yhwh, please take my life from me. *For better is my death than my life.*"

Andersen maintains that Jonah's use of Exodus 34:6 in 4:2 is "the powerful climax to the book of Jonah," since it makes the point, "somewhat disapprovingly, that repentance and forgiveness are more central to God's desires than justice and retribution"—an idea supported by the Jonah narrative as a whole.[65]

Conclusion

Yhwh's self-declaration in Exodus 34:6–7 is not only a theological reflection on the golden calf narrative of 32–34 but also a high point upon which the narrative is dependent and up to which it leads.[66] It reveals that it is *who God is* that determines *how he will act*, a concept displayed in all Exodus 34:6–7 hypertexts. It is in Joel 2:13 and Jonah 4:2 that this synthesis of word and action in the character of Yhwh shows itself most clearly. By substituting the words "relents from disaster" (נחם על־הרעה) for "faithfulness" (אמת), these texts share a unique relationship with both Exodus 34:6 and with the divine mercy shown in Exodus 32:12–14.

Joel's and Jonah's re-presentations of the theological truths of the golden calf narrative provide a glimpse of the importance of Exodus

---

64. Magonet, *Form and Meaning*, 75 notes that this also echoes Elijah in 1 Kings 19:4.

65. Andersen, "Yahweh, the Kind," 76.

66. Moberly, *Mountain of God*, 130; Wright, *God Who Acts*, 86.

32–34 for biblical theology, in its promise that when called on, Yhwh will act with mercy and grace amid judgment. Such led Joel to call the people to "Return to the Lord your God" in the face of judgment (Joel 2:13) and also triggered Jonah's flight from Joppa to Tarshish to block Yhwh's mercy from the enemies of Israel.

Joel and Jonah's use of the theologically rich conflation of the golden calf narrative and Yhwh's self-declaration (Exod 34:6) lays the groundwork for central theological themes that find their expression in the New Testament in the overwhelming display of God's חסד—his "spontaneous, unobligated love" in the cross and the inclusion of gentiles into the kingdom (Acts 10).[67] It exposes Yhwh as a God of abundant "spontaneous, unobligated love" whose "mercy triumphs over judgment" (James 2:13). He may be a jealous God (20:5; 34:14) who "punishes the children and their children for the sin of the parents to the third and fourth generation" (34:7b), but he is also the God who will show "spontaneous, unobligated love" to thousands; the God who forgives "wickedness, rebellion, and sin" (34:7a).

Bibliography

Achtemeier, Elizabeth. "The Book of Joel." In *The New Interpreter's Bible: A Commentary in Twelve Volumes*, 7:299–336. Nashville: Abingdon, 1996.
Allen, Leslie C. *The Books of Joel, Obadiah, Jonah, and Micah*. NICOT. Grand Rapids: Eerdmans, 1976.
Andersen, Francis I. "Yahweh, the Kind and Sensitive God." In *God Who Is Rich in Mercy: Essays Presented to Dr. D. B. Knox*, edited by Peter T. O'Brien, and David G. Petersen, 41–88. Homebush West: Lancer, 1986.
Blackburn, W. R. *The God Who Makes Himself Known: The Missionary Heart of the Book of Exodus*. Nottingham: Apollos, 2012.
Bruckner, James K. *Jonah, Nahum, Habakkuk, Zephaniah*. Grand Rapids: Zondervan, 2004.
Cassuto, Umberto. *A Commentary on the Book of Exodus*. Jerusalem: Magnes, 1967.
Caudill, Norma W. *The Presence of God in the Exodus Narrative: Purposes, Means and Implications*. Ann Arbor: ProQuest, 2006.
Childs, Brevard S. *Exodus: A Commentary*. OTL. London: SCM, 1974.
Crenshaw, James L. "The Expression Mî Yôdēaʿ in the Hebrew Bible." *VT* 36 (1986) 274–88.
———. *Joel: A New Translation with Introduction and Commentary*. AB 24C. New Haven: Yale University Press, 2008.
Dentan, Robert C. "Literary Affinities of Exodus XXXIV 6f." *VT* 13 (1963) 34–51.
Dillard, Raymond B. "Joel." In *The Minor Prophets: An Exegetical and Expository Commentary*, edited by Thomas E. McComiskey, 1:239–313. Grand Rapids: Baker, 1992.

---

67. Acts 10 presents Peter as an "anti-Jonah" who receives a call in Joppa to go to the gentiles, but unlike Jonah, he obeys.

Dozeman, Thomas B. "Inner-Biblical Interpretation of Yahweh's Gracious and Compassionate Character." *JBL* 108 (1989) 207–23.
Durham, John I. *Exodus*. WBC. Waco: Word, 1987.
Fleer, David. "Exegesis of Joel 2:1–11." *ResQ* 26, no. 3 (1983) 149–60.
Fretheim, Terence E. *Exodus*. Interpretation. Louisville: John Knox, 1991.
Genette, Gérard. *Palimpsests: Literature in the Second Degree*. Lincoln: University of Nebraska Press, 1997.
Gowan, Donald E. *Theology in Exodus: Biblical Theology in the Form of a Commentary*. Louisville: Westminster John Knox, 1994.
Hamilton, Victor P. *Exodus: An Exegetical Commentary*. Grand Rapids: Baker Academic, 2011.
Josipovici, Gabriel. *The Book of God: A Response to the Bible*. New Haven: Yale University Press, 1988.
Kidner, Derek. "The Distribution of Divine Names in Jonah." *TynBul* 21 (1970) 126–28.
Kim, Hyun C. P. "Jonah Read Intertextually." *JBL* 126, no. 3 (2007) 479–528.
Landes, George M. "Kerygma of the Book of Jonah: The Contextual Interpretation of the Jonah Psalm." *Interpretation* 21, no. 1 (1967) 3–31.
Lane, Nathan C. *The Compassionate but Punishing God: A Canonical Analysis of Exodus 34:6–7*. Eugene: Pickwick, 2010.
Lin, Tsai-Yun. *The Golden Calf, God's Nature, and True Worship in Exodus 32–34*. Deerfield: ProQuest, 2010.
Magonet, Jonathan. *Form and Meaning: Studies in Literary Techniques in the Book of Jonah*. Sheffield: Almond, 1983.
Moberly, R. W. L. *At the Mountain of God: Story and Theology in Exodus 32–34*. JSOTSup 22. Sheffield: JSOT, 1983.
Prinsloo, Willem S. *The Theology of the Book of Joel*. BZAW 163. Berlin: De Gruyter, 1985.
Prior, David. *The Message of Joel, Micah and Habakkuk*. Leicester: Inter-Varsity, 1998.
Reid, Andrew. *Exodus: Saved for Service*. RBTS. Sydney: Aquila, 2013.
———. *Postcard from Palestine*. 2nd ed. Kingsford: Matthias Media, 1989.
Sarna, Nahum M. *Exodus*. Philadelphia: Jewish Publication Society, 1991.
Sasson, Jack M. *Jonah: A New Translation with Introduction, Commentary, and Interpretations*. New Haven: Yale University Press, 1990.
Simkin, Ronald A. "'Return to Yahweh': Honor and Shame in Joel." *Semeia* 68 (1994) 41–54.
Snaith, Norman H. *The Distinctive Ideas of the Old Testament*. London: Epworth, 1944.
Stuart, Douglas K. *Exodus*. 2 vols. Nashville: Broadman & Holman, 2006.
———. *Hosea-Jonah*. Dallas: Word, 1989.
Trible, Phyllis. *Rhetorical Criticism: Context, Method, and the Book of Jonah*. Minneapolis: Fortress, 1994.
Waring, Dawn E. "The Nature of Yahweh's Relationship with His People: A Literary Analysis of Exodus 32–34." PhD, Fuller Theological Seminary, 1985.
Wolff, Hans W. *Joel and Amos*. Hermeneia. Philadelphia: Fortress, 1977.
Wright, G. E. *God Who Acts: Biblical Theology as Recital*. London: SCM, 1952.

8

Habakkuk's Calling for a Faithful Response to a Faithful God

Lwin Thida

There are elements of theodicy in the book of Habakkuk, but theodicy does not explain the theology of the book as a whole. Patterson rightly observes that the theological context of Habakkuk is God's person and work, the nature of human relationship with God, and the possibility of an intimate relationship between the believer and God.[1] The book is very relevant to the world in times of trouble. Specifically, Habakkuk focuses on God's relationship with the righteous and with the world rather than God's relationship to evil, although it does also describe the end of the wicked. It has a broad concern with how to live and respond to God in the reality of this broken world. The teaching of the book emphasizes God's faithful character rather than justifying God's ways. It is painting a bigger picture of God's character: the character of God embodies its theology as a whole, emphasizing the faithfulness *of* God and faithfulness *to* God in crisis. This contribution will explore a bigger understanding of God's faithful character and human response.

---

1. Patterson, *Habakkuk*, 134.

1. The Portrayal of the Faithfulness of God

Since there is a dialogue between two speakers in the book—the prophet Habakkuk and God himself—the character of God is presented from both the human view and through God's self-revelation. The faithful character of God is revealed as God responds faithfully by showing that he is at work and in control as the giver of life and salvation.

a. The Faithful Responsive Character of God Who Keeps Relationship With Humankind

The book presents the enduring faithful character of God as the one who keeps relationship with humankind, especially with the righteous by responding to their prayers even though they are irritated complaints. Habakkuk seeks a response from God who appears unresponsive and inactive in relation to his people (1:2–4). Habakkuk pleads with God to pay attention, and to act when he pays no attention to his prayer. Baker puts it this way, that Habakkuk complains that his understanding of God as just and righteous is not matched by his experience of God.[2] Cathcart summarizes the issue as "the apparent absence of God is the cause of the lament."[3] Sweeney insists that 1:2–4 is concerned with the breakdown of justice and the Torah in Judean society as the wicked oppress the righteous.[4] Of course, these three expressions are not mutually exclusive.

I argue that Habakkuk's anxiety in his first complaint focuses on God's behavior as irresponsible because it contains an implication of blame and rebuke.[5] Habakkuk accuses God of betraying his own character, and Habakkuk's encounter with God has put him in distress. The prophet's first prayer shows that he is already in a state beyond intercession, for he has tried that without result. His prayer starts with "How long" (עד־אנה) and lists the complaints of a very desperate person who can tolerate no more. Also verse 3a states, "Why do you make me look at injustice? Why do you tolerate wrong?" Barr observes that in biblical Hebrew, the Israelites asked "Why?" (למה) when they saw that something was deeply wrong and were characteristically

---

2. Baker, *Nahum, Habakkuk and Zephaniah*, 51.
3. Cathcart, "Law is Paralysed," 345.
4. Sweeney, *Twelve Prophets*, 453–67.
5. According to Broyles, a complaint means it addresses the one who is responsible, it focuses on the one responsible, and contains a note of blame and rebuke. See Broyles, *Conflict of Faith*, 38.

complaining to God about his neglect.⁶ According to Haak, in 1:13 Habakkuk's rhetorical question to Yahweh is accusing God of "betraying his own nature by allowing [various] evils to remain."⁷ Andersen also states that Habakkuk's accusation and complaint to God (1:2–4) are made because Yahweh has failed to live up to his covenant commitment.

In the OT, Israel used the term "Rock" (1:12) to refer to the faithfulness of God and to celebrate the delivering, protecting power of Yahweh that points out that ultimate security belongs to God (cf. Deut 32:4, 30–31).⁸ The book simply shows how Habakkuk deals with God's silence at a time when God is seemingly inactive in response to Habakkuk's prayer and his people's current issues. It depicts God as above human control and human manipulation. Andersen states that Yahweh is the living God, not to be controlled by humans. Yahweh is always free and interacts freely with human freedom.⁹

Therefore, Yahweh in Habakkuk reveals that he has his own divine timing and can respond as he wishes. It shows the divine freedom to choose whether to talk or to be silent, even though God is capable of conversation because he breaks his silence in 1:5–11.¹⁰ Therefore the crisis that Habakkuk undergoes is not doubt in the saving power of God. What troubles him is God's silence and that he "was not on prayer-answering ground."¹¹ What concerns him even more than his people's sin is God's silence (1:2).¹² Szeles rightly observes the question of Habakkuk here is why God has taken so long to respond to his cry.¹³

However, the book presents God's two responses to Habakkuk (1:5–11 and 2:2–20). Both of God's responses express some characteristics of himself as faithful and affirm that Habakkuk's accusation of God ("you do not listen") in 1:2 is not true. Even though the book does not reveal how long God takes to respond, he really does answer the one who confronts him and pleads for a just outcome (cf. 1:5–11 and 2:2–20). It affirms that God values his relationship with the righteous. The unanswered prayer cannot be interpreted to mean that God is unaware of what is happening,

---

6. Barr, "Why? In Biblical Hebrew," 8, 33.

7. Haak, *Habakkuk*, 32.

8. Johnson, "Paralysis of Torah." See also Wright, *Knowing God the Father*, 198–211.

9. Andersen, *Habakkuk*, 131.

10. Other scholars including Renz, *Habakkuk*, 230–52, do not believe that 1:5–11 is to be read as a divine response but as a citation of an earlier divine oracle within Habakkuk's prayer.

11. Patterson, *Habakkuk*, 141.

12. Blanchard, *Major Points*, 177.

13. Szeles, *Wrath and Mercy*, 11.

that he does not care about the oppressed, or that he is betraying the covenant with his people. God's two responses (1:5–11 and 2:2–20) show his faithful character and that he is listening and knows what is happening in this world, but that he responds and says what he is doing in his own time. God in Habakkuk clearly proclaims that he never changes. He has a plan. He remains enthroned in his holy temple. And the whole earth is called to remain silent before him (2:20). When God calls the whole earth to be silent before him, it is a call to worship and respect the Almighty God. It underlines the fact that God in Habakkuk is a faithful God who values relationship with humankind (all the earth).

b. The Faithful Character of God Who Is at Work and in Control

The faithful character of God is also revealed in his responses to Habakkuk declaring that he is at work and in control. When Yahweh makes himself known to be at work and in control, the reader perceives his faithful character that does not change. He is still the sovereign God, the just God, the Creator, the God of all nations, and the holy God because he is at work and in control.

The book proclaims that God is intimately involved in everything that happens in history and that he is in control. Sweeney, Smith, and many other scholars emphasize the righteousness of God as the ground for God's ultimate punishment of the wicked Babylonians[14] and the ultimate vindication of the righteous.[15] However, they cannot deny that the book reveals more than that about God. Sweeney notes that "the book upholds that God controls world events and employs nations for divine purpose."[16] House claims that three prophetic books (Nahum, Habakkuk, and Zephaniah) move beyond the account of sin and proclaim the judgment day of the Lord.[17] Patterson observes that the book testifies to God's continuous concern for his people and his dealing in the affairs of all humanity.[18]

Habakkuk shows that the holy and sovereign character of God goes beyond sin and punishment. Boadt rightly holds that "the Lord is always faithful to the just and acts on their behalf"[19] is one of the messages of Habakkuk.

---

14. Sweeney, *Twelve Prophets*, 453–67.
15. Smith, "Habakkuk," 96–97.
16. Sweeney, *Twelve Prophets*, 453.
17. House, *Old Testament Theology*, 346. See also House, "Character of God," 129.
18. Patterson, *Habakkuk*, 129–30.
19. Boadt, "Jeremiah and Habakkuk," 168.

I agree with Boadt that the character of God in Habakkuk is unchanging, faithful, and just. Habakkuk has no doubts about the justice of God or the presence and power of God even from the beginning of his first complaint. According to Andersen, there is no expression of "disbelief about the justice of God."[20] Yahweh shows that he is a living God and his behavior is "a consistent inconsistency."[21] He is not under the control of humankind. Habakkuk wants consistency in God's behavior to match his reputed character as just in dealing with injustice in the world, but Yahweh makes himself known as in control—humankind, even the righteous, cannot put him in a box. He knows what he is doing, "For I am going to do something in your days that you would not believe, even if you were told" (1:5b).

Moreover, the book delineates the faithful character of God in his deeds. In Habakkuk Yahweh makes himself known, not only in his caring and listening to individuals who cry out to him, but also as the sovereign God of all the nations of the earth. Yahweh is the one who lifts his prophet's sights from a local to a world view, and from a national to an international perspective (1:5; 2:6–20), and then to a cosmic scale (1:12–17; 2:14; 3:3–15). In addition, Yahweh's act of "raising up" the other nation, Babylon (1:6a), and the aggressive nature of the Babylonians (1:6–11), also point to God's sovereignty over all people and all nations of the earth. It is clear that Yahweh is a just God who does not tolerate misconduct between human beings, and his vindication of the righteous is regardless of their nationality (2:4–19). Notably, Habakkuk's usage of the word "humankind" (אדם) in the second prayer (1:14) refers to the creation of the human race and so God lifts the prophet's eyes to the universal stage.[22]

More importantly, 2:14 depicts Yahweh as the one who is working out his purpose to fill the earth with the knowledge of his glory even though this world has turned away from his ways and purpose. He calls all the earth to be silent before him and worship him (2:20). It also highlights the sovereignty of God over all peoples, all nations, and all the earth. According to Wright, the glory of Yahweh will be completely public and not confined to private devotion or individual spiritual aspirations because he will be exalted among the nations and the whole earth (2:14). Wright believes that what Habakkuk says about the fullness of the glory of the Lord on the whole earth does not refer to a time in the future. Rather, all the people on the earth will see and know this glory every day by living in the creation of God. "The God who will be universally exalted will be the God who

---

20. Andersen, *Habakkuk*, 109.
21. Andersen, *Habakkuk*, 131.
22. Andersen, *Habakkuk*, 184.

will be universally known."[23] Gowan insists that Habakkuk mainly deals with the suffering of the righteous and the justice of God.[24] However, the book presents not merely the traditional dogma of the justice of God by which righteousness is rewarded and wickedness is punished. It teaches, and gives a bigger picture of, the sovereignty of God who is at work and in control, not only in Israel's affairs but also in world history. God brings all nations and peoples into his plan and is faithful to the world that he, the holy and sovereign God of all, created.

c. The Faithful Character of God as Giver of Life and Savior of the Righteous

In Habakkuk, Yahweh makes himself known as the faithful and trustworthy God who has authority to give life to the righteous. Although the book includes the faith of the righteous (2:2–4), it stresses more the faithfulness of God to the righteous and his deliverance of his people (2:2–4; 3:2–19). House discusses 1:12—2:11 under the heading "the God who Inspires Faith in Crises."[25] Faith is not self-generated by the righteous individual but comes ultimately from God himself. According to Andersen, "each event in which God is involved has lasting value as a revelation of God's true being and as an expression of his holiness and righteousness that people can trust (2:4)."[26] I believe that God's unfailing promise in 2:3–4 highlights the divine faithful character. In verse 4 the statement, "Behold, swollen, his soul is not straight in him, but the righteous in his (its) faithfulness will live" (הנה עפלה לא־ישרה נפשו בו וצדיק באמונתו יחיה) expresses the contrast between the arrogant and the righteous person in their respective attitudes and ways of living.[27] There are different translations and interpretations of the Hebrew באמונתו ("his/its faithfulness") in verse 4b and it is necessary to clarify whose faithfulness it refers to.

A number of scholars think that the suffix of "its/his faithfulness" (באמונתו) addresses the trustworthiness of the vision (Haak, Robertson, and Andersen).[28] They claim that the reliability of the vision refers to God's

---

23. Wright, *Knowing God*, 211.
24. See Gowan, *Prophetic Books*, 91 and Gowan, *Triumph of Faith*, 16.
25. House, *Old Testament Theology*, 377.
26. Andersen, *Habakkuk*, 131.
27. The Hebrew word אמונה can be translated as faithfulness, trustworthiness, firmness, steadfastness, fidelity, and truth. See *HALOT, I*, 62–63 and *BDB*, 595.
28. See Haak, *Habakkuk*, 55; Robertson, *Nahum, Habakkuk, and Zephaniah*, 111; and Andersen, *Habakkuk*, 213. Also note that the first part of this verse first talks about

reliability, not the fidelity of human righteousness. Haak explains that "the antecedent is understood as the vision, since it is the reliability of the vision which is in question (cf. 2:3a)."[29] Andersen argues simply but rightly that God tells Habakkuk all he needs as a righteous man is to know that "the righteous will live because the vision is certain, God is reliable." This statement expresses that "the dependability of God is inseparable from the certainty of his word."[30] Verse 2:4b centrally affirms that there is an assurance of life and salvation for the righteous as a result of the faithfulness of God. Hutton rightly states that God's answer (2:4b) has a promise of life which reveals the salvation of God according to his faithful character and is simultaneously a challenge to be righteous by being called "to live a life of trust."[31] The righteous will live because there is the reliability or trustworthiness of the vision which points to the faithfulness of God. Therefore, the faithfulness of 2:4b belongs to God. This verse is concerned mainly with the faithfulness of God and his promise of life to the righteous person. The one who has faith in God and is faithful to God, the righteous person, will survive because of the trustworthiness of God.

In contrast, the proud who rely on their own strength will perish and have no life. Habakkuk has been shown the truth that God is the giver of life. This leads him to remember Yahweh in his prayer (3:3–15) as the deliverer who saved his people's lives, and to recall God's faithfulness and salvation to the oppressed in the past. The prophet highlights the exalted savior God (3:17–19), rather than divine judgment or divine justice. This makes clear Habakkuk's realization that God's trustworthy faithfulness leads the righteous to life and salvation (2:4b; 3:17–19).

2. Human Responsibility as Faithful Response to God

The book presents not only the faithful character of God but also the righteous person's reactions on receiving God's promise and the challenge to play a role in God's mission (2:2–4; 3:1–19). In Habakkuk there are various human responses to God (1:2–4, 12–17; 2:2; 3:2–19). Habakkuk's last prayer

---

the inconsistent and violent desire of the wicked. It echoes 1:11 which is about the arrogant Babylonians who rely on themselves and whose god is their own strength.

29. Haak, *Habakkuk*, 59.

30. Andersen, *Habakkuk*, 215.

31. Hutton, *Introduction to the Prophets*, 60. Hutton points out that there is a misunderstanding of the text and Hab 2:4b has been taken "to mean that eternal life comes to the one who is made righteous by faith." Taylor also sees it as a challenge to the righteous person to live in the light of the faithfulness of God. Taylor, "Faith, Faithfulness," 478–93.

(3:2–19) expresses his faithful response to the faithfulness of God with perseverance and the confidence of faith.

It is important to note that the book does not end with God's solution to Habakkuk's dilemma. The book clearly teaches the responsibility of human beings. This can be seen in God's challenge (2:2–20) to live as one who knows the faithfulness of God (cf. 2:4b). Some scholars, such as Hiebert, maintain that chapter 3 is not an integral part of the book but was added after the exile.[32] In Floyd's form criticism, chapter 3 may simply be read as a vision or a liturgical psalm to use in temple worship. However, this chapter is Habakkuk's personal response to God with words of trust in the form of a prayer psalm, as well as a call to worship. Here I follow scholars like Baker and Pakula, who state that chapter 3 is Habakkuk's response to what he has experienced of the presence of the Lord as he placed himself to wait and respond to what Yahweh would answer (2:1).[33] He has no more questions regarding God's identity, for his focus is more on the saving character of God (3:2, 16–19) than on his problems and circumstances (1:2–4, 12–17; 3:16–19). Habakkuk plays his role as a paradigm of the suffering righteous who, in times of crisis, act responsibly in faithfulness to God. His response to God has developed because his later emphasis and attitude are completely different from his responses to God in the first chapter. He has engaged with the community's concerns on ethical social issues (Hab 1). He has raised his questions directly with God, rather than with human beings (1:2–4, 11–17), and he has waited in God's presence seeking understanding (2:2).

In the final chapter Habakkuk is silenced in his complaint but responds in prayer and praise to the word of the Lord that he has received. This is because he had received "comfort, consolation, and reassurance" from God (2:3–4), "instead of stern rebuke for his personal audacity in complaint."[34] His response in chapter 3 begins with a petition (3:2) to God to renew his work ("give it life," בקרב שנים חייהו) and compassion ("in the time of turmoil declare yourself compassionate," תודיע ברגז רחם תזכור). It expresses his comprehension of the unchanging faithful character of God which relates to his ironic questions about God's character in 1:12–17, i.e., is God the everlasting one, the holy one, the giver of life, and the compassionate one in the time of turmoil? It also expresses his acceptance of God's promise in 2:4b, i.e., "the righteous will live because the vision is certain, God is reliable."[35] Broyles states that 3:2 is by implication a call for new intervention in the

---

32. Hiebert, *God of My Victory*, 136–43.

33. Baker, *Nahum, Habakkuk and Zephaniah*, 68. See also Pakula, *Nahum, Habakkuk and Zephaniah*, 117.

34. Robertson, *Nahum, Habakkuk, and Zephaniah*, 212.

35. Andersen, *Habakkuk*, 215.

near future.³⁶ In his prayer response describing the theophany (3:3–15), Habakkuk expresses his knowledge of the glory of God as he remembers the faithfulness of God and past salvation.³⁷ In this he responds to the glory of God as almighty; the God of history; the deliverer; the God of nature; divine warrior; and the God who is with his people (cf. 2:14). Chisholm claims that, for Habakkuk, God's devastation of the oppressors is nothing less than salvation history repeated. His portrayal of the Lord's deliverance (3:2–15) recalls Israel's early experiences that affirm Habakkuk's trust in God as an everlasting God who is ever working in history (3:6) and always capable of intervening for his people.³⁸ His prayer and response in chapter 3 focus on the character of God as faithful savior. He exalts and addresses God as savior no matter what transpires in this world (3:16–18). Moreover, Habakkuk recognizes his own role as a messenger of Yahweh (3:19b).

Habakkuk learned that faithfulness meant more than defeat over foreign invaders (Babylon). He realizes the sovereignty of God as preserver in times of crisis when God's protection and blessings appear to be absent (3:16–18). Watts rightly sees that the joy Habakkuk expresses is the fruit of faith and hope rooted in God himself rather than in what God has given. As a prophet, Habakkuk speaks and prays in confident trust on behalf of the faith community. In addition, he has confidence and stresses that God's victory also brought about his personal salvation.³⁹ The book concludes (3:16–19) by using the first-person perspective, for example: "I will wait patiently" (אנוח); "I will rejoice" (אעלוזה); and "I will be joyful" (אגילה).

The book highlights the development of human response which is presented in how Habakkuk encountered God. From his first complaint, his prayer and questions are a prayer of faith because he trusts that God is good and expects that God will save his people. However, his prayers in 1:2–4 and 1:12–17 reveal his desperation and audacity in complaining to Yahweh. Andersen states that Habakkuk's distress is rooted in "his theological convictions" because he has no doubt about the justice of God but raises his right to know why God has delayed helping and delivering the victims who are in need.⁴⁰ According to Childs, Habakkuk's faith is a faith seeking understanding when life is under threat.⁴¹ But it is also a faith seeking

---

36. Broyles, *Conflict of Faith*, 43.

37. ". . . if the prayer is now integral to the prophecy . . . it is entirely possible that Habakkuk himself found this ancient composition appropriate for personal use and as a vehicle for his timely message." Andersen, *Habakkuk*, 268.

38. Chisholm, "Minor Prophets," 415.

39. Watts, *Books*, 151–52.

40. Andersen, *Habakkuk*, 130.

41. Childs expresses the meaning of the threat from the biblical perspective, that "it was not a momentary phase or an introductory stage, but a recurring danger of catastrophic proportions, always present and continuously to be faced." See Childs, *Old*

understanding when life is under promise. Habakkuk received a response from a faithful God about his purpose and his timing in this world. The book does not end with the final judgment of the wicked and the righteous, but with the prophet's response to Yahweh (chapter 3). In his final response Habakkuk does not mention anything about whether the ways of God are right or wrong; instead, his response is a prayer of exaltation which attributes righteous responsibility to God. This is the proper thing to do: it is one of the teachings of the book. The faithful response to God rejoices in hope and perseveres in affliction. It is not easy, but Habakkuk can do it because he lives in God's promise and challenge (2:2–4, 20). His hope is founded in the Lord's assurance of ultimate victory and deliverance no matter what his current situation is. Even though Gowan argues that theodicy (God's justice and the suffering of the righteous) is a dominant subject of the book and believes that Habakkuk does not get an answer from God,[42] he cannot deny that it presents Habakkuk's commitment to God who gives him strength to remain faithful no matter what happens.[43]

Boadt rightly states that the book teaches how to live with uncertainty and its message is that "the Lord is *always faithful* to the just and acts on their behalf; they in response must be *patient and trust* entirely and solely in him."[44] I also argue that Habakkuk's faithful response to God is a commitment to be God's messenger (2:2–3; see also 3:19 above) even at a time of darkness (3:16, 19). Habakkuk is aware of God's historical presence and action in the affairs of Israel, in those of other nations and of all creation.[45] He remains personally convinced of the eventual victory of God over all forces of violence and chaos (3:17–19).

Therefore, it is right to affirm that the book presents God's relationship with human beings through the experience of Habakkuk. The communication is presented in a dialogue, not in a monologue. Habakkuk's responses in the book highlight human freedom and the right to make a response to God. However, the book discloses that God's promise comes with challenges (2:2–20) to action, and so people should be aware that they have a role to play in God's mission (2:2–4; 3:2–19). Habakkuk plays his role as a righteous person, a messenger and a prophet. He knows himself and his right to call upon God. He is aware of current affairs including the social,

---

Testament Theology, 232–34.

42. See Gowan, *Triumph of Faith*, 10, 16.

43. Gowan, *Triumph of Faith*, 83.

44. Boadt, "Jeremiah and Habakkuk," 168.

45. Even though it is true that the word "faithfulness" refers to reliable, honest conduct that conforms to Yahweh's moral and ethical standards, the verb "live" in 2:4b refers to the physical preservation of the righteous through the coming invasion (cf. 1:12; 3:17–19) rather than eternal life in an eschatological concept. See Chisholm, *Minor Prophets*, 414.

political, and spiritual situation of his community. He continues to communicate with God even though he received an unexpected answer. After he gets his answer, he does not demand a reward, but praises and worships God with a joyful heart and trusts in the salvation of God. This is the right response of faithfulness to God.

As mentioned, the book includes human responsibility as a faithful response to God. The focus on human response highlights that the book is more than a theodicy. If the book is only a theodicy it ought to be entirely focused on how God's ways can be justified. But the fact that the book itself urges people to respond to this understanding of God in certain ways, makes it more than theodicy.

Conclusion

In the book of Habakkuk, the prophet is asking the theocentric question of when God will respond and act. God's answer focuses not on justice, but on revealing what he is doing in this world (1:5–11) and on resolving Habakkuk's theological tension between his preconceptions and present reality (2:2–20; cf. 1:12–17). Although the idea and elements of theodicy are present in the questions of the prophet, it is not the principal theme of the book but is part of the outworking of God's purposes. God's answers are an explanation neither of the existence of evil nor of the suffering of the righteous in order to justify himself. If Habakkuk is only about the intellectual questions of evil and the suffering of righteous people, there is no room for God to expect a response in action and worship from all the earth (2:20; cf. 3:1). The book presents Habakkuk's experience in understanding God's ways and character not only intellectually, but also experientially and responsively. The principal theme of the book is God's faithful involvement in human history especially in relation to the faithful righteous. The book also highlights the responsibility of humanity and the proper response of the faithful righteous to God. These all point to the broader theology and purpose of the book—the faithfulness of God and faithfulness to God in times of crisis.

Bibliography

"אמונה." In *HALOT, I*, 62–63.
"אמונה." In BDB, 595.
Andersen, Francis I. *Habakkuk: A Translation with Introduction and Commentary*. AB 25. York: Doubleday, 2001.
Baker, David W. *Nahum, Habakkuk and Zephaniah*. TOTC. Leicester: Inter-Varsity, 1988.

Barr, James. "Why? In Biblical Hebrew." *JTS* 36 (1985) 1–33.

Blanchard, John. *Major Points from the Minor Prophets*. Darlington: EP, 2012.

Boadt, Lawrence. "Jeremiah 26–52, Habakkuk, Zephaniah, Nahum." In *Old Testament Message: A Biblical Theological Commentary*, edited by Carroll Stuhlmueller and Martin McNamara, 157–98. Wilmington: Michael Glazier, 1982.

Broyles, Craig C. *The Conflict of Faith and Experience in the Psalms*. JSOTSup 52. Sheffield: Sheffield Academic Press, 1989.

Cathcart, Kevin J. "'Law is Paralysed' (Habakkuk 1.4): Habakkuk's Dialogue with God and the Language of Legal Disputation." In *Prophecy and the Prophets in Ancient Israel: Proceeding of the Oxford Old Testament Seminar*, 339–53. New York: T. & T. Clark, 2010.

Childs, Brevard S. *Old Testament Theology in a Canonical Context*. Philadelphia: Fortress, 1989.

Chisholm, Robert B., Jr. "A Theology of the Minor Prophets." In *A Biblical Theology of the Old Testament*, edited by Roy B. Zuck, 397–433. Chicago: Moody, 1991.

Gowan, Donald E. *Theology of the Prophetic Books: The Death and Resurrection of Israel*. Louisville: Westminster John Knox, 1998.

———. *The Triumph of Faith in Habakkuk*. Atlanta: John Knox, 1976.

Haak, Robert D. *Habakkuk*. VTSup. Leiden: E. J. Brill, 1992.

Hiebert, Theodore. *God of My Victory: The Ancient Hymn in Habakkuk 3*. Atlanta: Scholars, 1986.

House, Paul R. "The Character of God in the Book of the Twelve." In *Reading and Hearing the Book of the Twelve*, edited by James D. Nogalski and Marvin A. Sweeney, 125–45. SBL Symposium Series 15. Atlanta: SBL, 2000.

———. *Old Testament Theology*. Downers Grove: Inter-Varsity, 1998.

Hutton, Rodney R. *Introduction to the Prophets*. Minneapolis: Fortress, 2004.

Johnson, Marshall D. "The Paralysis of Torah in Habakkuk 1.4." *VT* 35, no. 3 (1985) 257–66.

Pakula, Martin. *Nahum, Habakkuk and Zephaniah: The End of Evil*. Edited by Paul Barnett. Sydney: Aquila, 2014.

Patterson, Richard D. *Nahum, Habakkuk, Zephaniah*. WEC. Chicago: Moody, 1991.

Renz, Thomas. *The Books of Nahum, Habakkuk, and Zephaniah*. NICOT. Grand Rapids: Eerdmans, 2021.

Robertson, O. Palmer. *The Books of Nahum, Habakkuk, and Zephaniah*. NICOT. Grand Rapids: Eerdmans, 1990.

Smith, Ralph L. "Habakkuk." In *Micah–Malachi*, 92–119. WBC 32. Waco: Word, 1984.

Sweeney, Marvin A. *The Twelve Prophets*. Vol. 2. Minnesota: Liturgical, 2000.

Szeles, Maria E. *Wrath and Mercy: Habakkuk and Zephaniah*. ITC. Grand Rapids, MI: Eerdmans, 1987.

Taylor, Stephen S. "Faith, Faithfulness." In *NDBT*, 478–93.

Watts, John D. W. *The Books of Joel, Obadiah, Jonah, Nahum, Habakkuk and Zephaniah*. CBC. London: Cambridge University Press, 1975.

Wright, Christopher J. H. *Knowing God the Father through the Old Testament*. Oxford: Monarch, 2007.

Part III

Wisdom in the Writings

9

Dusted Off and Polished to Fresh Luster
David's Crown in Psalm 132

CHARLIE FLETCHER

IN A COURSE ON the Psalms at Ridley College in 1998, Lindsay Wilson introduced me to the emerging scholarly interest in a canonical approach to reading the Psalter, and it fired my imagination. I had never heard anyone ask the kinds of questions in relation to the Psalms that seemed so obvious when reading other books. How is it structured? How does it begin? How does it end? How does it progress from start to finish?

The seminal work of Gerald H. Wilson (no relation) on the shape and shaping of the Hebrew Psalter provided a methodological foundation and a hermeneutical sparring partner,[1] leading me to postgraduate research, supervised by Lindsay, on the Davidic motif in Book V of the Psalms and its interpretive significance. In response to Gerald Wilson's contention that the kingly figure of David is displaced by a model of dependence on Yahweh or a suffering, dependent messiah in Book V,[2] I argued for the presence and positive reappropriation of the kingly Davidic motif at the Psalter's end.

Drawing on that work, my contribution to *Honoring the Wise* is a reflection on neither wisdom literature nor wisdom as a biblical theme,

---

1. See Wilson, *Editing*, and subsequent works in the bibliography.

2. Wilson, *Editing*, 215, and Wilson, "King," 400 respectively present the two distinct views.

but rather on an aspect of Old Testament scholarship opened up for me by a wise teacher.

Part of Lindsay's wisdom as a supervisor was to gently guide my unbridled enthusiasm for the subject towards a modest and achievable project. Now with more restrained ambitions, employing a canonical approach and focusing on the Masoretic Text, I offer some thoughts about Psalm 132 and its portrayal of Davidic kingship.

Introductory Comments on Psalm 132

Form, Setting, and Date

Psalm 132's rich Davidic content justifies its common classification as a royal psalm, while the Zion theme is also prominent in this climactic song of ascents. The psalm's structure highlights the Davidic motif, supporting this designation.[3]

Psalm 132 presupposes the existence of the Davidic monarchy and the temple, suggesting an original setting during the period of the monarchy at some point between David and the exile. Cross claims that archaic language indicates an early date,[4] but the psalm apparently incorporates earlier material, which could account for archaisms in a later text. Various cultic settings are possible, in connection with the ark, the temple, or the monarchy, but the text specifies none. The placement of Psalm 132 in Book V, its petition to remember David, and the promise that God will cause a horn to sprout for David are consistent with a postexilic editing or even composition of the psalm in its final form. In any case, the setting of primary concern for the present chapter is the Psalter's canonical form.

Structure

Some details in Psalm 132 are notoriously difficult to interpret, and the psalm's structure is also a point of contention, with scholars divided over

---

3. *Pace* Tucker and Grant, *Psalms*, 839, who regard the Zion theme as definitive in categorizing the psalm and see the Davidic motif as playing a supporting role. Certainly, the two themes are mutually reinforcing in Psalm 132. DeClaissé-Walford et al., *Psalms*, 936 note the importance of God's presence and Davidic kingship, temple, and court for ancient Israelite identity. Hossfeld and Zenger, *Psalms 3*, 457 state that Psalm 132 is both a royal psalm and a Zion psalm, although they emphasize the Zion motif and take the view that "the election of Zion precedes the election of David and in a sense implies it" (465).

4. Cross, *Canaanite Myth*, 97.

whether the main sections are vv. 1–9 and 10–18 or 1–10 and 11–18.⁵ Broyles suggests a structure organized around the petitions of vv. 1 and 10, "each followed by two quotations, all of which have a narrative introduction."⁶ Distinguishing narrative from citation in vv. 6–9 is difficult, however, and a break between vv. 10 and 11 is more likely, marking a shift from petition to promissory response and from second person to third. Also, on this division, each half begins with a verb followed by לדוד יהוה (Yahweh to/for David).⁷ I suggest the following structure:

Superscription

vv. 1–10		A prayer to Yahweh concerning David
	v. 1	A prayer for Yahweh to remember David's hardships favorably
	vv. 2–5	David's oath to find a dwelling place for Yahweh
	vv. 6–9	The entry of the ark into Jerusalem recalled
	v. 10	A prayer for Yahweh to answer his anointed one on account of David
vv. 11–18		A promise from Yahweh concerning David
	vv. 11–12	Yahweh's oath to David to establish David's dynasty
	vv. 13–16	Yahweh's choice and promise regarding Zion
	vv. 17–18	Yahweh's promise to make a horn sprout for David in Zion⁸

The parallels between the halves are striking. The first contains a prayer to Yahweh relating to David, the second a promise from Yahweh relating to David. The first contains David's oath concerning a place that belongs to Yahweh, the second Yahweh's oath concerning a throne that belongs to David. Both halves begin and end with references to David. The Davidic motif is highlighted emphatically by this structure. It is significant that both the prayer and the promise of Psalm 132 are ultimately concerned with David's dynasty rather than with David himself.⁹ Each half of the psalm is also

---

5. Indeed, somewhat amusingly, in Hossfeld and Zenger, *Psalms 3*, 457–58, Zenger cites Hossfeld as the most recent defender of breaking the psalm into vv. 1–9 and 10–18, and then argues for the alternative view!

6. Broyles, *Psalms*, 471.

7. Mitchell, *Message*, 123.

8. The divisions follow Allen, *Psalms 101–150*, 270.

9. The anointed one of v. 10 is distinguished from David and is apparently a Davidic

concerned with Yahweh's settlement in Jerusalem and mentions the priests being clothed with righteousness or salvation and the saints singing for joy with regard to Yahweh's dwelling in Zion.[10]

If the psalm contains fragmented citations of earlier texts, as often suggested, they have been integrated into a carefully crafted composition.[11]

Exegetical Observations on Psalm 132

Superscription

Given Psalm 132's Davidic content, the absence of לדוד in the superscription is surprising, and may suggest a postexilic date for the composition.

Verses 1–10

The psalm opens with a prayer (spoken by king, priest or people) for Yahweh to remember David's hardships favorably. The hardships are probably to be understood as self-imposed.[12] The noun עני (hardships) with this sense is applied to David in 1 Chronicles 22:14, where he describes the great pains he has taken to provide materials for the house of the Lord.[13]

Verses 2–9 undergird the plea of v. 1, which is reformulated in v. 10's prayer for Yahweh to remember David's successor on David's account.

What is the subject of David's oath? Allen suggests that the dwelling place (משכן) of v. 5b, in parallel with David's "house" in v. 3 (note the use of אהל, "tent" in the expression) refers to the tent (אהל) David set up for the ark in Jerusalem (2 Sam 6:17). The term "place" (מקום) in v. 5a also occurs in 2 Samuel 6:17, strengthening the connection with David's placement of the ark in a tent in Jerusalem.

This association fits with vv. 6–9, which apparently describe the ark's collection from Kiriath-Jearim and its triumphant entry into Jerusalem, whether in historical action or liturgical recollection. On this reading, vv. 6–9 describe the fulfillment of David's pledge.[14]

---

successor, like the sons of vv. 11–12.

10. Goldingay, *Psalms 90–150*, 542 highlights these parallels.

11. Crow, *Songs of Ascents*, 105.

12. Compare the *pual* of ענה (to oppress, humiliate, be afflicted) in Leviticus 23:29, where it clearly has this sense.

13. Tucker and Grant, *Psalms*, 840.

14. Allen, *Psalms 101–150*, 271. The feminine singular pronouns of v. 6 have no antecedent, suggesting that this passage may be an extract from an earlier text. They

There are also various allusions to the temple in connection with David's oath. The two-part structure of Psalm 132, shaped around David's concern to establish a place for Yahweh and Yahweh's promise to establish a dynasty for David, alludes unmistakably to 2 Samuel 7, where David's concern is that the ark remains in a mere tent while he lives in a house. As noted, the use of ענה ("to be afflicted") here in v. 1 and the related noun in 1 Chronicles 22:14 encourages us to understand David's hardships in terms of the effort he expended in preparation for the temple's construction. Similarly, the appearance of מנוחה ("resting place") here in vv. 8 and 14 and in 1 Chronicles 28:2 connects David's oath with his desire to build a house as a permanent place of rest for the ark. Furthermore, 2 Chronicles 6:41–42 quotes vv. 8–10 in connection with Solomon's dedication of the temple.

The first half of Psalm 132 thus draws on two elements in the narrative of 2 Samuel 6–7, the entry of the ark into Jerusalem at David's initiative, and David's concern to see a house built as a permanent resting place for it, and thereby presents David as the temple's founder (not builder).[15]

Verses 11–18

The psalm's halves contain responsive parallels. The promise of vv. 17–18 answers the prayer of vv. 1 and 10. Yahweh's oath in vv. 11–12 requites David's oath in vv. 2–5. Yahweh's choice of Zion in vv. 13–16 confirms the ark's entry into Jerusalem in vv. 6–9.[16]

Yahweh's sure oath to David offers a strong hope for the Davidic kingship's future. It is reinforced by the concluding promise of vv. 17–18 to make a horn sprout or flourish for David and the assurance that Yahweh has prepared a lamp for the anointed Davidic successor.[17] Yahweh's commitment not to turn back from his oath in v. 11 echoes and answers the petition not to turn away the face of his anointed one in v. 10.[18]

Set against the ebulliently positive outlook of vv. 11–18 regarding Yahweh's promises and the Davidic dynasty's future, the condition in v. 12, of

---

should be understood as referring to the ark, not explicitly mentioned until v. 8. Hossfeld and Zenger, *Psalms 3*, 456 note that the term ארון, "ark," while usually masculine, is feminine in 1 Samuel 4:17 and 2 Chronicles 8:11.

15. Hossfeld and Zenger, *Psalms 3*, 457.

16. Allen, *Psalms*, 265–66.

17. David and the anointed one are presumably to be distinguished in v. 17 as they are in v. 10.

18. Mays, *Psalms*, 410 notes that the verb "turn" (שוב) in vv. 10–11 binds the two halves of the psalm.

which only the positive outcome is expressed,[19] sets Yahweh's oath alongside the requirement of covenant keeping by David's successors without making explicit the relationship between them.[20] The resultant tension looks forward implicitly to a Davidic king who will fulfill the condition, whether one understands the covenant in question to be Davidic or Mosaic, as the language of עדתי, "my testimonies," may imply.[21] This is one way in which the Psalter connects torah piety and Davidic kingship.[22]

Yahweh's choice of Zion as his resting place (vv. 13–16) confirms David's initiative in moving the ark as Yahweh's desire.[23] Thus Yahweh's enthronement serves not to undermine but to affirm David and the Davidic monarchy.[24]

The Davidic and Zion motifs are bound by several cords in the second half of Psalm 132. Yahweh's oath concerning the Davidic dynasty responds to David's oath concerning the place of Yahweh's dwelling. The use of ישׁב ("sit" in v. 12, "dwell" in v. 14; note also the derivation מושׁב—"dwelling"—in v. 13) in vv. 12–14 pictures both Yahweh and the Davidic king as sitting enthroned in Zion.[25] Moreover, v. 17 brings the Davidic and Zion themes together explicitly as Yahweh specifies, "There I will make a horn to sprout for David."

Grogan asserts that the promise of a horn and a lamp in v. 17 "strongly implies the postexilic break in the succession of actually reigning Davidic kings, so that it seems to be messianic."[26] Alternatively, Goldingay argues that "the full growth of David's horn is not something that will have to wait until the end; it will be a continuing reality in Israel's experience."[27] The latter interpretation fits awkwardly with the lack of Davidic kingship in the postexilic context of the Psalter. Whether or not one accepts Grogan's assertion of postexilic composition, the exalted language of Psalm 132 and its location in the canonical shape of the Psalter indicate that the final editors viewed the psalm as an expression of messianic hope for the future fulfillment of Yahweh's promises to David.

---

19. Tucker and Grant, *Psalms*, 844, write, "The statement assumes, conversely, that disobedience will result in the end of the monarchy in Jerusalem." The silence regarding the negative consequence in the case of the condition's being unfulfilled, however, may be another literary clue to the rehabilitation of Davidic kingship in this psalm.

20. Goldingay, *Psalms 90–150*, 560.

21. See discussion of the covenant in Allen, *Psalms 101–150*, 268.

22. I am grateful to my former colleague Andrew Abernethy for this suggestion.

23. Mays, *Psalms*, 411.

24. *Contra* Wilson, "King," 397.

25. Huwiler, "Patterns and Problems," 209.

26. Grogan, *Psalms*, 210.

27. Goldingay, *Psalms 90–150*, 557; see also Hossfeld and Zenger, *Psalms 3*, 466.

Nowhere is that hope clearer than in the final verse, with its promise that, whereas God will clothe the king's enemies with shame, the king will wear a shining crown. The final clause, ועליו יציץ נזרו, might be woodenly translated, "but on him will shine his crown."

The Hebrew noun for crown here (נזר) is, perhaps surprisingly, a rare word, occurring only twenty-five times in the Old Testament, and only eight times outside the Pentateuch.[28] Most significantly for present purposes, it occurs only twice in the Psalter, the other instance being in Psalm 89:39, which declares, at the beginning of a bitter lament on the apparent failure of the Davidic covenant, that God has defiled the crown of his anointed one in the dust (חללת לארץ נזרו, "you have defiled in the dust his crown"). The allusion is unmistakable. After the bitter despair of Psalm 89, here in Psalm 132 David's crown has been dusted off and polished to fresh luster. No longer defiled in the dust, it will again sit radiantly on the king's head.

Canonical Reflections on Psalm 132

In Relation to Adjacent Psalms

The לדוד ("by/to/for David") superscriptions of Psalms 131 and 133 tie Psalms 131–133 together as a triad of Davidic psalms at the conclusion of the Songs of Ascents. Two short psalms with Davidic titles flank a long psalm with distinctive Davidic content. Thus, the literary focus falls on Psalm 132. At the center of the hope of Psalm 131 and the blessed gathering of Psalm 133 stands the future Davidic rule promised in Psalm 132.

Following Psalm 132, references in Psalm 133 to Hermon and Zion, combined with a focus on Zion as the place where Yahweh commands blessing, may allude to a reunification of the northern and southern kingdoms under a future Davidide. The blessing of Psalm 133 is bound up with the future of David's dynasty, for Zion is where Yahweh promises both.[29]

---

28. Thirteen instances in Numbers 6 deal with Nazirite vows and two occurrences each in Exodus and Leviticus refer to the consecration of priests. Outside the Pentateuch, seven of the eight occurrences refer to a royal diadem, all but Jeremiah 7:29, where the word refers to the prophet's hair.

29. Psalms 132:17; 133:3. Note the adverb שם ("there") in both verses.

Within the Songs of Ascents

Psalm 132 is "the longest and most theologically considered"[30] of the otherwise brief Songs of Ascents, and its royal theme is distinctive among them. Placed towards the end of the collection, it occupies a very prominent place among the Songs of Ascents. Its inclusion in the collection "may well indicate that pilgrims marching to Jerusalem were eager to connect the two themes: Zion and David's dynasty."[31] Indeed, the presentation of Zion as the seat of both divine presence and Davidic rule offers a twin theological rationale for pilgrimage to Jerusalem.[32]

Zenger observes a division of the Songs of Ascents into three groups of five, and at the center of each group "a psalm that has been influenced by royal theology and the theology of Zion: 122, 127, and 132."[33] Describing the theme of these psalms as Jerusalem, the temple, and David respectively, he states that "these three psalms produce a coherent theological view which acclaims Zion as the place of blessing and salvation to which Israel should go in 'ascents.'"[34] While Zenger makes nothing of the Davidic motif in the Songs of Ascents, his structural observation is suggestive of a wider alignment of the Davidic and Zion motifs in the collection as a whole, an alignment that climaxes in Psalm 132.[35]

Within Book V

To consider the place of Psalm 132 within Book V more broadly, some reflection on the book's structure is useful. While the structure of Book V is still debated,[36] for present purposes, I offer some brief remarks based on the following structural analysis:

30. Hossfeld and Zenger, *Psalms 3*, 457.
31. Terrien, *Psalms*, 847.
32. McCann, "Psalms," 1211.
33. Zenger, "Composition," 92.
34. Zenger, "Composition," 92.
35. The alignment suggested by Zenger's observation becomes more striking when one notes that Psalm 122 bears a Davidic superscription and speaks about Jerusalem as the place where the thrones of the house of David were set (v. 5).
36. See Fletcher, "Return" for a range of structural approaches to Book V; also, Zenger, "Composition," and Snearly, *Return of the King*, 57–78. Snearly surveys a range of proposals, opting for a "variegated approach" on the basis that "it can accommodate the evidence of Book V better than the הודו/הללויה taxonomy" (78). Whether one sees in a variegated approach the virtue of methodological sensitivity or a lack of methodological control will depend in large part on how persuaded one is that the הודו/הללויה ("Give thanks"/"Praise the LORD") taxonomy adequately delineates the

Section I Psalms 107–117	A	Psalm 107	"Give thanks to the LORD, for he is good; for his love endures forever"
	B	Psalms 108–110	Davidic, including the royal Psalm 110
	C	Psalms 111–117	"Praise the LORD"
Section II Psalms 118–135	A	Psalm 118	"Give thanks to the LORD, for he is good; for his love endures forever"
	B	Psalm 119	Torah
		Psalms 120–134	Songs of Ascents, including Davidic Psalms 122, 124, 131–133, among them the royal Psalm 132
	C	Psalm 135	"Praise the LORD"
Section III Psalms 136–150	A	Psalm 136	"Give thanks to the LORD, for he is good; for his love endures forever"
		Psalm 137	Further introduction to Psalms 138–145, establishing the exile and its aftermath as the interpretive backdrop for the final Davidic group
	B	Psalms 138–145	Davidic, including the royal Psalm 144
	C	Psalms 146–150	"Praise the LORD"

This proposal provides a literary approach to the structure of Book V which has a clear, objective, and tightly-defined basis in the lexical data of the text itself (especially the distinctive distribution of the plural imperatives הודו ליהוה, "Give thanks to the LORD," and הללו־יה, "Praise the LORD," and identical first verse of Psalms 107, 118, 136), accounts for all the psalms in the book's final form, and does not depend upon hypothetical reconstruction of the origins and use of Book V.

The caesurae introduced between Psalms 117 and 118, dividing the traditional Egyptian Hallel (Psalms 113–118), and between Psalms 135 and 136, separating two clearly related historical psalms, represent a possible

structure of Book V.

objection to this structure.³⁷ In response to the former, the lack of the praise formula that binds Psalms 111–117 together begs the question of whether the Egyptian Hallel reflects the intentions of the Psalter's final editor(s). Regarding the latter, Psalm 136 is more universal in flavor than Psalm 135 and the Songs of Ascents, and the prominent word חסד, "steadfast love," in Psalm 136 occurs only once in the Songs of Ascents, but eight times in Psalms 138–145. If the grouping of Psalms 113–118 and 135–136 precedes the final form of the Psalter, it would seem that these two psalms have been editorially loosened from their moorings in prior collections to serve a new function as structural hinges in the final collection.

This proposal offers a suggestive solution to the cartographic challenge of mapping the towering peak of Psalm 119 within the wider terrain.³⁸ Following our observations regarding Psalm 132 and the Davidic motif in the Songs of Ascents, the pairing of Psalm 119 and the Songs of Ascents, bracketed by Psalms 118 and 135, might be a deliberate parallel to the pairing of Psalms 1–2 in the introduction to the Psalter, a torah psalm followed by a focus on the reign of God through his appointed king in Jerusalem.³⁹

A further consequence of this structural proposal is the highlighting of a prominent royal psalm in each of the three major sections, and of parallel Davidic clusters in the first and third sections, each framed between calls to thanksgiving and choruses of praise.

Within this structure, the number, placement, and content of Davidic psalms indicate a strong editorial rehabilitation of Davidic kingship in the final book of the Psalter's final form.⁴⁰

---

37. Zenger, "Composition," 87.

38. The other psalm that poses a particular conundrum for structural explanations of Book V is Psalm 137.

39. In contrast to the view of Wilson, *Editing*, 143, 204–7 that Psalm 1 alone constitutes the introduction to the final form of the Psalter, I regard Psalms 1 and 2 together as the introduction to the Psalms. There are several reasons for this conclusion. First, Psalms 1 and 2 are both untitled (a rarity in Books I–II of the MT, and unique in the LXX Psalter). Second, אשרי ("blessed") in Psalm 1:1 and 2:12 creates an inclusio. Third, הגה ("meditate," "plot") occurs in 1:2 and 2:1. Fourth, the psalms present two ways for individuals and nations respectively. Fifth, Yahweh's anointed king in Psalm 2 exemplifies the righteous one of Psalm 1 (compare Deuteronomy 17:14–20, where devotion to the law of the Lord is the charter for kingship). Sixth, wisdom and kingship motifs occur throughout the Psalter. See Howard, *Psalms 93–100*, 202–3, and for supplementary arguments, Taylor, "Psalms 1 and 2," 48–50.

40. For some examples of other scholars who reach similar conclusions, see Allen, *Psalms*; Grogan, *Psalms*; Howard, *Structure*; Mays, *Psalms*; Mitchell, *Message*; and Snearly, *Return*.

Within the Psalter

Psalm 132 contains many echoes of Psalm 89.[41] Yahweh's oath and promises in vv. 11–12, 17–18 recall Psalm 89's positive opening, but the two psalms end in stunningly different ways. Whereas Psalm 89:38–46 describes God as having rejected his anointed, renounced the covenant, defiled his crown in the dust, turned back the edge of his sword, made his splendor cease, cast his throne to the ground, and covered him with shame, Psalm 132 ends with the bright confidence that Yahweh will keep his sure oath to David, that David's offspring will sit on his throne forever, that the anointed one's enemies will be clothed with shame and that his crown will shine. Grogan observes: "Although it has points of similarity with Psalm 89, it ends not in perplexed distress but in triumphant expectation. Nothing could more clearly show the difference between the overall tone of books 3 and 5."[42]

Psalm 2 introduces the theme of kingship in terms of God who reigns from heaven and his appointed king who reigns from Zion. Snearly comments from the vantage point of Book V:

> [T]he content and subject matter at the end of the Psalter is integrally related to the content and subject matter at the beginning. The trajectory of the storyline is consistent throughout: Yahweh is king; he has appointed an earthly vice-regent who represents his heavenly rule on earth; the earthly vice-regent and his people travail against the rebellious of the earth.[43]

He further specifies in regard to Psalm 132:

> By linking Zion with the king, Psalm 132 demonstrates that the program outlined in Psalm 2 still stands: Yahweh's reign will be represented by an earthly king whose throne is on Zion.[44]

I would add that, in response to the crisis of the exile and the seeming failure of the Davidic covenant and kingship, Books IV and V function as a twin theological response in line with Psalm 2, with the reassertion of Yahweh's reign in Book IV and, after the glaring absence of David in Books III and IV, the prominent reaffirmation of Davidic kingship in Book V.[45]

---

41. Tournay, *Seeing and Hearing*, 206, identifies sixteen identical words or phrases.
42. Grogan, *Psalms*, 208–9.
43. Snearly, *Return*, 1.
44. Snearly, *Return*, 153–54.
45. David's name is ubiquitous throughout Books I–II, occurs in only five psalms in Books III–IV, then returns in sixteen psalms in Book V: Psalms 108–10, 122, 124, 131–33, 138–45.

In Book V, while David is presented as a model of torah piety, the Davidic motif moves beyond this exemplary function to messianic hope for the future of the Davidic monarchy.[46] This hope finds its strongest expression in the royal Psalms 110, 132, and 144. The structure of Book V gives shape and direction to this eschatological hope as the Davidic king returns from exile, welcomed home to a victory march and the resounding trumpet blast of Yahweh's praise. To interpret David in Book V as a model of torah piety or a suffering servant only, without seeing the rehabilitated king, is to hear the music and miss the parade.

Looking at David in Book V through a different lens, the doctoral research of Jill Firth on Psalms 140–143 elegantly and persuasively demonstrates that the suffering servant of Book V, the David beset by enemies and dependent on God, rather than being an innovation or a dramatic shift of perspective in the Psalter's presentation of the Davidic motif, is consistent with the portrait of David earlier in the Psalms.[47] Firth observes that, lodged between triumphant images of future royal victory in Psalms 110 and 132 on the one hand, and a crescendo of final praise in Psalms 146–150 on the other hand, the final cluster of Davidic psalms in the Psalter (Psalms 138–145) foregrounds the suffering, dependent David.[48] These psalms provide a haunting anticipation, even after the glittering promise in Psalm 132:18, of the king who would wear a crown of thorns.

Psalm 144, the last royal psalm, entwines the two Davidic threads. There we see David, acutely aware of human frailty and pleading once more for divine rescue from enemies, placing his trust in the LORD who trains his hands for war, who rescues his servant David, and who gives victory to kings and blessings to God's people.

The Davidic motif in Book V does not reflect a shift from conquering king to suffering, faithful servant. Rather, it marks the reappearance and rehabilitation of the conquering, suffering, faithful king who dominates the opening books, then disappears amid the ruined hopes of exile, before returning to be crowned anew in the final act. In both his exaltation and his humiliation, what we witness in Book V is the return of the king.

---

46. *Contra* Goswell, "Non-Messianic," who supports Gerald Wilson's view of David in Book V as a model of loyal devotion to God's kingship.

47. Firth, "Re-Presentation."

48. Firth, "Re-Presentation," 151–52.

In Relationship to 2 Samuel 7

As previously observed, Psalm 132's two-part structure, set around David's concern to establish a place for Yahweh and Yahweh's commitment to establish a dynasty for David, alludes unequivocally to 2 Samuel 7, and the relationship between the two passages throws more light on the radiant crown of Psalm 132. As with our reflections on Psalm 89, so also with 2 Samuel 7, the points of difference are more noteworthy than the connections. As already discussed, the conditional covenant-keeping language of Psalm 132:12 contrasts with the language of discipline in the context of unconditional promises in 2 Samuel 7:14–16. Two other differences are important.

First, Psalm 132 omits the pun on the word "house" (בית) that is so prominent in 2 Samuel 7, where David is told that he will not build a house (temple) for Yahweh, but Yahweh will build a house (dynasty) for him, and David's son will eventually build a house (temple) for Yahweh.[49] By way of this pun, David does not fulfill his intention to build a temple, and Yahweh reorients him, but that play on words is absent from Psalm 132.

Second, the language of oaths present in Psalm 132 is absent from 2 Samuel 7. In Psalm 132, Yahweh's oath appears to mirror and requite David's oath. As noted in the exegetical comments, David's oath alludes to both the temple and the ark's entry into Jerusalem. The allusion to the ark allows David's oath to be represented as fulfilled in vv. 6–9, which contrasts with his unfulfilled intention to build a temple in 2 Samuel 7, and adds to the expectation that Yahweh's corresponding oath will also be fulfilled.

In 2 Samuel 7 David is confronted by Yahweh; in Psalm 132 he is confirmed.[50] Yahweh's actions and promises are here presented as responsive to David's, not corrective. Given the postexilic canonical placement of Psalm 132, and the exilic anguish of Psalm 89, it is extraordinary to find David presented more brightly here than in the Davidic covenant's foundational passage! Truly David's crown shines with fresh luster at the end of Psalm 132.

Conclusion

Psalm 132 links the Davidic and Zion motifs. On the one hand, it pairs David's oath to establish a permanent place for Yahweh with Yahweh's oath to establish a permanent dynasty for David. On the other hand, it connects Yahweh's choice of Zion with Yahweh's choice of David. It thus provides the

---

49. Huwiler, "Patterns and Problems," 209.
50. Goldingay, *Psalms 90–150*, 561.

Songs of Ascents with a twin theological rationale for pilgrimage to Jerusalem, the seat of divine presence and Davidic rule. In the Psalter's postexilic final form, Psalm 132 rehabilitates the Davidic kingship with bright hope and confidence, forming part of a wider reappearance and restoration of the Davidic motif in Book V of the Psalms, a return of the king so resplendent that David's crown shines more brightly at the end than the beginning.

Bibliography

Allen, Leslie C. *Psalms*. WBT. Waco, TX: Word, 1987.

———. *Psalms 101–150*. 2nd ed. WBC 21. Waco, TX: Word, 2002.

Broyles, Craig C. *Psalms*. NIBC. Old Testament Series 11. Peabody, MA: Hendrickson, 1999.

Cross, Frank Moore. *Canaanite Myth and Hebrew Epic: Essays in the History of the Religion of Israel*. Cambridge, MA: Harvard University Press, 1973.

Crow, Loren D. *The Songs of Ascents (Psalms 120–134): Their Place in Israelite History and Religion*. Atlanta, GA: Scholars, 1996.

DeClaissé-Walford, Nancy L. et al. *The Book of Psalms*. NICOT. Grand Rapids, MI: Eerdmans, 2014.

Firth, Jill. "The Re-Presentation of David in Psalms 140–143." *TynBul* 70, no. 1 (2019) 149–52.

Fletcher, C. J. "The Return of the King: The Davidic Motif in Book V of the Psalter." Unpublished MTh Dissertation, Australian College of Theology, 2012.

Goldingay, John. *Psalms, Volume 3: Psalms 90–150*. BCOTWP. Grand Rapids, MI: Baker Academic, 2008.

Goswell, Gregory. "The Non-Messianic Psalter of Gerald H. Wilson." *VT* 66, no. 4 (2016) 524–41.

Grogan, Geoffrey. *Psalms*. THOTC. Grand Rapids, MI: Eerdmans, 2008.

Hossfeld, Frank-Lothar, and Erich Zenger. *Psalms 3: A Commentary on Psalms 101–150*. Translated by Linda M. Maloney. Hermeneia: A Critical and Historical Commentary on the Bible. Minneapolis, MN: Fortress, 2011.

Howard, David M., Jr. *The Structure of Psalms 93–100*. Biblical and Judaic Studies 5. Winona Lake, IN: Eisenbrauns, 1997.

Huwiler, Elizabeth F. "Patterns and Problems in Psalm 132." In *The Listening Heart: Essays in Wisdom and the Psalms in Honor of Roland E. Murphy*, edited by Kenneth G. Hoglund, Elizabeth F. Huwiler, Jonathan T. Glass, and Roger W. Lee, 199–215. JSOTSup 58. Sheffield: JSOT, 1987.

Mays, James L. *Psalms*. Interpretation. Louisville, KY: Westminster John Knox, 1994.

McCann, J. Clinton. "Psalms." In *NIB* 4:641–1280. Nashville, TN: Abingdon, 1996.

Mitchell, David C. "Lord, Remember David: G. H. Wilson and the Message of the Psalter." *VT* 56 (2006) 526–48.

———. *The Message of the Psalter: An Eschatological Programme in the Book of Psalms*. JSOTSup 252. Sheffield: Sheffield Academic, 1997.

Snearly, Michael K. *The Return of the King: Messianic Expectation in Book V of the Psalter*. Library of Hebrew Bible/Old Testament Series. London: T. & T. Clark, 2016.

Taylor, J. Glen. "Psalms 1 and 2: A Gateway into the Psalter and Messianic Images of Restoration for David's Dynasty." In *Interpreting the Psalms for Teaching and Preaching*, edited by H. W. Bateman and D. B Sandy, 47–62. St Louis, MO: Chalice, 2010.

Terrien, Samuel L. *The Psalms: Strophic Structure and Theological Commentary*. ECC. Grand Rapids, MI: Eerdmans, 2003.

Tournay, Raymond Jacques. *Seeing and Hearing God with the Psalms: The Prophetic Liturgy of the Second Temple in Jerusalem*. JSOTSup 118. Sheffield: JSOT, 1991.

Tucker, W. Dennis Jr., and Jamie A. Grant. *Psalms, Volume 2*. NIVAC. Grand Rapids, MI: Zondervan, 2018.

Wilson, Gerald H. *The Editing of the Hebrew Psalter*. Chico, CA: Scholars, 1985.

———. "Evidence of Editorial Divisions in the Hebrew Psalter." *VT* 34 (1984) 337–52.

———. "A First Century C. E. Date for the Closing of the Hebrew Psalter?" *Jewish Biblical Quarterly* 28 (2000) 102–10.

———. "King, Messiah, and the Reign of God: Revisiting the Royal Psalms and the Shape of the Psalter." In *The Book of Psalms: Composition and Reception*, edited by Peter W. Flint and Patrick D. Miller, 391–405. Leiden: Brill, 2005.

———. *Psalms*. Vol. 1. NIVAC. Grand Rapids, MI: Zondervan, 2002.

———. "The Qumran Psalms Manuscripts and the Consecutive Arrangement of Psalms in the Masoretic Psalter." *CBQ* 45 (1983) 377–88.

———. "The Qumran Psalms Scroll Reconsidered: Analysis of the Debate." *CBQ* 47 (1985) 624–42.

———. "The Shape of the Book of Psalms." *Interpretation* 46 (1992) 129–42.

———. "Shaping the Psalter: A Consideration of Editorial Linkage in the Book of Psalms." In *The Shape and Shaping of the Psalter*, edited by J. Clinton McCann, 72–82. JSOTSup 159. Sheffield: JSOT, 1993.

———. "The Structure of the Psalter." In *Interpreting the Psalms: Issues and Approaches*, edited by Philip S. Johnston and David G. Firth, 229–46. Leicester: Apollos, 2005.

———. "Understanding the Purposeful Arrangement of Psalms in the Psalter: Pitfalls and Promise." In *The Shape and Shaping of the Psalter*, edited by J. Clinton McCann, 42–51. JSOTSup 159. Sheffield: JSOT, 1993.

———. "The Use of Royal Psalms at the 'Seams' of the Hebrew Psalter." *JSOT* 35 (1986) 85–94.

Zenger, Erich. "The Composition and Theology of the Fifth Book of Psalms, Psalms 107–145." *JSOT* 80 (1998) 77–102.

10

Jesus, Job, and the Suffering Image of God
An Exploration in Biblical Anthropology

Andrew R. Prideaux

Peter Singer and the Bible's Dangerous Idea

In his book *Rethinking Life and Death*,[1] the secular ethicist Peter Singer outlines his shockingly consistent ethical vision. Not only late-stage abortion and euthanasia, but the infanticide of unwanted infants, who no longer qualify as "persons"—are all permissible. As he sees it, his is a moral vision not hampered by the "speciesism"[2] of the traditional Western worldview, which would privilege human life above other sentient life-forms.

---

1. Singer, *Rethinking Life and Death*. Lindsay Wilson together with a number of former lecturers at Ridley, contributed to a very helpful volume edited by Gordon Preece, *Rethinking Peter Singer*.

2. Wilson, "Human Beings," 107. For Singer, "speciesism" (a term coined by Richard Ryder and popularized by Singer) is as indefensible a moral act as racism. Singer follows Jeremy Bentham (1748–1832) in his "preference utilitarianism," and ethical distinction between sentient and non-sentient beings (a "sentient being" demonstrates the ability to experience suffering and happiness; and to have a sense of its own existence over time). Trueman, *Rise and Triumph*, 320: "Human beings are, according to Singer, generally in thrall to speciesism, which, like racism, posits an innate superiority of one group over others on an ultimately unjustifiable foundation." That is, human exceptionalism.

> Science has helped us to understand our evolutionary history, as well as our nature and the nature of other animals. Freed from the constraints of religious conformity, we now have a vision for who we are, to whom we are related, the limited nature of the differences between us and other species, and the more or less accidental manner in which the boundary between "us" and "them" has been formed.[3]

Singer traces the direct source of this outmoded worldview regarding human exceptionalism, to the Judeo-Christian teaching of human beings as created *imago Dei*.

> There have been cultures, especially in the east, that have held that all life is sacred, including the lives of nonhuman animals . . . The western tradition is unusual in its emphasis on the sanctity of every human life, but only of human life. The origins of this distinctive western view are not difficult to trace. The starting point is the Hebrew view of creation, as put forward in Genesis . . . Human beings are here seen as special because they alone of all living things were made in the image of God. In addition God gave them power over all the other living things.[4]

Singer pulls no punches as he maps out the implications of his anthropology to his utilitarian ethics, surrounding the beginning and ending of human life: "Once we remove the assumption that an animal must be human in order to have some kind of right to life, then we will have to start looking at the characteristics and capacities that an animal must possess in order to have that right . . . if we set the standard anywhere above the bare possession of life itself, some human beings will fail to meet it."[5]

For Singer, the idea that human beings are made in the image of God is the most pernicious lie ever to deceive the human race. The environmental disasters that the world now faces as a result of the destruction of biodiversity, which has led to the loss of species through extinction, are the direct result of the god-like elevation of human beings over other lifeforms. The traditional Western ethic, which privileges human life above all other life, has been exposed by the undeniable ecological devastation which it has largely caused. For Singer, it is time to recognize the obvious: we must finally surrender the irresponsible and morally reprehensible commitment to our god-like status in the world.

---

3. Singer, *Rethinking Life and Death*, 182–83.
4. Singer, *Rethinking Life and Death*, 165–66.
5. Singer, *Rethinking Life and Death*, 183.

An Inescapable Worldview

And yet getting past the *imago Dei* has proved extremely difficult—even for modernists. In an interview with Michael Parkinson, Stephen Fry, himself no friend of Christianity, spoke of the relationship between human beings and the (wider) animal kingdom in this way:

> There is an animal kingdom and a plant kingdom, and we belong to the animal kingdom. And yet we are so interested in them . . . but no animal—unless it's hungry—is interested in us! We are always trying to define the human difference to animals—be it consciousness, wit, self-awareness . . . *but this difference has to do precisely with our interest in other animals.* Kangaroos have no concern for cockroaches . . . and yet we care about them all. *In a sense Genesis is right . . . we're so guilty . . .* Bears don't wake up feeling guilty; a bear spends all its time being a bear. We spend all our time trying to be someone else . . . whereas animals are supremely themselves.[6]

There are a number of implications that could be drawn from this quote. What is fascinating for our purposes is Fry's concession that the Genesis account says *true things* about the reality of being human:

- We are interested in and take responsibility for other species; and the web of life in the world that surrounds us
- We experience strong feelings of guilt
- We are restless and don't know how to be ourselves.

This relational and therefore moral sense of responsibility is a universally persistent feature of human experience. Behind scientific questions concerning an ages-long *process* in the development of human life lies the foundational and fundamental theological question concerning the *purpose*, and *telos* of human being.[7] The great turn of the century philosopher and theologian P. T. Forsyth observed:

> Our footing . . . is not in the process, which is too changing, and even fleeting, but in the latent purpose, the goal, the destiny prescribed by the interests of the one good thing, great end, and

---

6. Author's transcript of Stephen Fry interviewed by Michael Parkinson, https://www.youtube.com/watch?v=39ya2Drpj3s&t=1226s, emphasis added.

7. Cf. Forsyth, *Principle of Authority*, 198. Further to this he writes, "The method of science; and science cannot give us contact with super-empiric reality. Scientific history cannot give us the super-historic in history. No induction can prove a miracle. Evidence could prove the fact, but not that it was a miracle."

final cause in the world—a good will. Existence is a kingdom of ends—*i.e.*, of persons, of souls and not of mere movements. If we raise this to the Christian temperature we have the reality of things in a kingdom of moral relations infused with love . . . The kingdom of moral affection casts us upon the King of holy love.[8]

There is a reason for Singer's outrage at the state of the planet; and his just complaint against his own species.[9] There is a reason why the documentaries of another famous atheist, David Attenborough, are so widely enjoyed. We *are* like God. To again quote Forsyth, "In history, human beings are at once dependent on Nature and above it, a product of it and yet a personality who descends on it from their partnership in the personality of God."[10] We enjoy the world God enjoys. We rejoice in the wonder of the myriad creatures that populate the earth, we enjoy their beauty, we are awed by their furies, and we recognize our responsibility to wisely care for and manage the world around us. When that responsibility is betrayed, we see it as a crime.

Thus, in responding to the goodness of creation, we also implicitly acknowledge human greatness. We reveal that we know that we are called to exercise a "responsible dominion" over the world—even though we are constantly frustrated by our failure to do so. Philosophical theorists might boldly assert that we are just a random collection of atoms assigning other random collections of atoms arbitrary values. Yet when we see, for example, the effects of human greed-fueled consumption leading to the loss of ecosystems; and the consequent animal and especially human suffering that results, we sense that things are "not the way they are supposed to be." We *know* that as human beings we cannot deny our own culpability in this.[11] We sense what Marilynne Robinson calls "the *givenness* of things": that there is a Creator, that we are his creatures, and that we have a unique responsibility in his world. We are answerable to him who made us together with the whole universe in line with his own *good* purpose.

> We are singular among creatures precisely in our capacity to refine and elaborate our understanding in the awareness of its

---

8. Forsyth, *Principle of Authority*, 180.

9. Wilson, "Human Beings," 108–9, 120. While acknowledging the contribution that Singer has made in raising awareness concerning the misuse of human dominion (e.g., animal cruelty, and environmental problems related to the widespread dietary dependence on meat), Wilson also points out some clear contradictions. E.g., "while the Bible shows a concern for species; animals created *according to their own kind* (Gen 1:24), Singer's view gives few grounds for preferring one species to another, or preserving endangered species or a diversity of species, provided that utility is maintained."

10. Forsyth, *Principle of Authority*, 199.

11. Plantinga, *Not the Way*, 26.

shortfall. It is this in us that has made tiny blue earth a singular, seraphic presence in the great cosmos, watching and pondering, rapt with wonder. We can feel deficiency in what we know or do, we can hear inadequacy in our most painfully considered phrases. And gracious and chimerical beauty will bless us with the certainty that there is more to be hoped for, more to be tried. The theologian can say all this implies divine intention and also continuous, loving engagement. Because God has created the universe, humankind is at the center of it all.[12]

This glorious position we occupy as God's vice-regents, also highlights the devastation we have caused now that we have both rejected our Maker and betrayed our high calling. Christ's apostle Paul wrote, "For although they knew God, they neither glorified Him as God nor gave thanks to Him, but their thinking became futile and their foolish hearts were darkened" (Rom 1:21, NIV). Andrew Moody, another former student of Lindsay Wilson writes: "When we understand the original significance and glory of human beings, it helps us to grasp both the magnitude of the disaster that we've brought on ourselves and the astonishing achievement of Jesus. We had everything and we threw it away. We converted ourselves from kings and queens into skulking hypocrites. We traded innocence for pride and self-deception. We lost God and threw away our lives."[13]

Whatever worth atheistic philosophers and ethicists may or may not ascribe to their fellow human creatures, none of us can avoid what we are. We cannot help but live out our high calling as men and women who are "fearfully and wonderfully made," *imago Dei*. For better, and certainly for worse, we inevitably exercise our God-like dominion over his world (Gen 1:27; Ps 8, cf. Job 31:13–15; Ps 139:13–14). As Calvin famously asserted, we have no true knowledge of ourselves apart from a true—that is, *a divinely revealed*—knowledge of God. "It is certain that man never achieves a clear knowledge of himself unless he has first looked upon God's face, and then descends from contemplating Him to scrutinize himself."[14]

We come now to God's revelation through the biblical description of human identity, vocation, and destiny.

---

12. Robinson, "Beautiful Changes," 33.

13. Moody, *In Light*, 97.

14. Calvin, *Institutes*, I.i.2. Christian apologetics appeals to the knowledge that every human being actually has, but willfully suppresses (Rom 1:18–20). Cf. VanTil, *Defense of the Faith*, 101. "At bottom man [sic.] knows that he is the creature of God. He knows that he is responsible to God. He knows that he should live to the glory of God. He knows that in all that he does he should stress that the field of reality which he investigates has the stamp of God's ownership upon it."

The Image of God in Human Beings—Psalm 8

The opening chapters of Genesis are not the only place in the Scriptures that such a high view of humanity is articulated. It is everywhere assumed, as human beings are the only creatures whom God speaks and relates to in the deeply personal and intimate way that he does. There are also a number of places where the dignity and purpose of human beings is explicitly celebrated. The most famous of these comes in Psalm 8.

> O Lord, our Lord, how majestic is your name in all the earth!
> You have set your glory above the heavens.
> Out of the mouth of babes and infants,
> You have established strength because of your foes,
> to still the enemy and the avenger.
> When I look at your heavens, the work of your fingers,
> the moon and the stars, which you have set in place,
> what is man that you are mindful of him, and the son of man that you care for him?
> Yet you have made him a little lower than heavenly beings
> and crowned him with glory and honor.
> You have given him dominion over the works of your hands;
> you have put all things under his feet,
> all sheep and oxen, and also the beasts of the field,
> the birds of the heavens, and the fish of the sea,
> whatever passes along the paths of the seas.
> O Lord, our Lord, how majestic is your name in all the earth!
> (Psalm 8, ESV).

The ideal human dominion described here is a delegated authority. The world and all its creatures are the work of *God's hands* (v. 6), made in accordance with God's purposes. This means that the way we "rule" the world was never intended to be a license to exploitation and destruction; whereby we are drunk on power and driven by greed. But rather, the kind of loving care and responsible dominion and development of creation that God in his mercy demonstrates hour by hour, day after day, and year after year.

Yet the Psalm is not a hymn of praise to *humanity*, but *a hymn of praise to God*, bookended with identical acknowledgements of God's glory and sovereignty: "O Lord, our Lord, how majestic is your name in all the earth!" (Ps 8:1, 9).

This perspective is fundamental to a right understanding of God, his image bearers and their role in the world. As Packer and Howard put it,

> We were made to worship God. Worshiping is our supreme achievement and privilege, and our dignity is fullest as we do the thing we were made for. We enter into our own glory when we glorify God . . . the truest dignity, nobility, and glory are seen, not in heroes, pioneers, great rulers, great artists, or any other of the world's celebrities as such, but rather in holy men and women of God who have learned the lesson of worship. Their powers and weaknesses, their successes and failures, their exultation and grief, all go up continually to the throne as an offering . . . In humbling themselves before God . . . and acknowledging their constant need of his grace, and in disclaiming any form of self-righteousness or self-sufficiency.[15]

When we reject God's kingship and his purposes for human life, we not only dishonor God, we also lose our crowns. We undermine the exalted role we have been given in the world. Like King Nebuchadnezzar—who, in his quest for greatness denied God and was reduced to a beast (cf. Dan 4:19-33)—we too dehumanize ourselves. "Humanity's lie . . . is that our dignity justifies our egoism. God's truth is that our dignity is only realized as we love and serve God for himself, and mankind for God's sake . . . The alternative is to demean and dehumanize ourselves by the sort of manipulative self-centeredness that rots the soul."[16]

The demolition of the divine image which Singer and others recommend is not a new project. It is just the old story of the human race estranging itself from its Maker and losing its way in the world. Without the elevating concept of the divine image, we drag the rest of creation down with us. It is the true story that Peter Singer along with every other human being is both frustrated by and implicated in.

The Suffering Image—The Story of Job

Many commentators see the great theophany and creation speeches of Job as a divine "slap-down." Job must shut up and mind his place; his questions and laments dismissed. The final word is simply, "you are not in charge, I am!"[17] As Virginia Woolf famously remarked, "I read the book of Job last night—I

---

15. Packer and Howard, *Christianity*, 152, 153.
16. Packer and Howard, *Christianity*, 154.
17. E.g., Crenshaw, "Form and Content," 78–85.

don't think God comes well out of it."[18] Penchansky makes this point even more strongly, "He blusters and bullies Job, never effectively answering his questions . . . Yahweh's speeches . . . represent not the answer but the final desolation of Job, the failure of his last hope of redress."[19]

Yet the LORD's speeches are better seen as an invitation to Job to wonder at his work in the world, so that his vision of God's works in creation is enlarged. More than anything else, Job yearned to hear the voice of his Maker, to be assured by him that God was for and not against his world, including his creature Job. God meets that longing, and at the same time deepens his faith—which, from the very beginning, the LORD had recognized as sincere (1:1, 8; 2:3). Lindsay Wilson writes, "The playful irony of the Yahweh speeches preserves a right balance. Job's longings are met, enabling him then to proceed in a new direction. God also broadens Job's understanding so that he will continue to persevere in faith."[20]

The Anthropology of the Yahweh Speeches

The LORD lifts Job's eyes both to his creation and kingly reign of the world. He highlights, in particular, those realities which appear to demonstrate no direct benefit to human beings, and those which make the world feel strange and inhospitable. Examples include, sending "rain on a land where no human lives" (38:25–26), the wild animal discourse (39:1–30), and the description of the mysterious, frightening, and untamable Behemoth and Leviathan (40:15–24; 41:1–34). In speaking of these things, the LORD reframes Job's questions of justice and retribution within a wider view of his governance of the created order. Wilson writes, "God's ordering of the world is more complex than Job had imagined, and is certainly more nuanced than simply rewarding human righteousness and punishing human wickedness."[21]

As a number of commentators have observed, with the exception of 40:15, the creation of human beings is not even mentioned in the four chapters which make up the Yahweh speeches. Kathryn Schifferdecker writes of their "radical non-anthropocentricity." "The world is not a safe place, but it is indeed an ordered one. Forces of chaos and wildness are given a place in the world, but they are also given boundaries so that they cannot overwhelm it . . . Job must acknowledge that God's sovereignty does not exclude forces indifferent towards, and even dangerous to, humanity

---

18. Quoted in Schifferdecker, *Out of the Whirlwind*, 1.
19. Penchansky, *Betrayal of God*, 48, 53.
20. Wilson, *Job*, 181.
21. Wilson, *Job*, 201. Cf. Scholnick, "Meaning of *Mishpat*," 521–29.

... Job must learn to live in the untamed, dangerous, but stunningly beautiful world that is God's creation."²²

A High Anthropology

While Job gets more than he bargained for in the theophany and the Lord's speeches, God's very act of appearing to, and speaking with him, uniquely honors Job within creation as the divine image bearer. The Lord's characteristic way of addressing Job in both the prologue and the epilogue is with the honorific title עֶבֶד/*ebed* (servant, 1:8; 2:3; 42:7, 8).²³ Indeed the book begins with an unusual word order for the beginning of a Hebrew clause, in that the noun comes before the verb. From the first, our attention is drawn to the key relationship that the book will focus upon: the Lord and his honored servant Job.²⁴

> A man there was in the land of Uz, Job was his name.
>
> That man was blameless and upright.
>
> He feared God, and turned from evil. (1:1, author's translation)

The theme of the book of Job is announced in the very first verse. Lindsay Wilson brings this into sharp focus, helpfully providing a topic sentence for our study: "At the outset, the writer hints at the issue of *what it means to be human before God*. In an atypical Hebrew word order (commonly used for emphasis), the word 'man' is at the beginning of the first

---

22. Schifferdecker, *Out of the Whirlwind*, 123, 125. Cf. Fretheim, *Creation Untamed*, 78–90. Although beyond the scope of our discussion, the divine and human relationship to the "wild world" described in the Yahweh speeches, speaks into key environmental questions that we currently face (e.g., McKibben, *Comforting Whirlwind*, 42–63). In his 2020 Netflix documentary, *A Life on Our Planet*, the 93-year-old David Attenborough shares his "witness statement" concerning the ecological devastation caused by humanity during his lifetime. The scientific findings are unanimous: biodiversity must be restored. In his words, human beings must "re-wild the world." In the debate, humanity vs. wild, Marilynne Robinson, "Wilderness," 253–54, offers this provocative nuance: "Wilderness has for a long time figured as an escape from civilization, and a judgment upon it. I think we must surrender the idea of wilderness, and accept the fact that the consequences of human presence in the world are universal and ineluctable, and invest our care and hope in civilization, since to do otherwise risks repeating the terrible pattern of enmity against ourselves, which is truly the epitome and paradigm of all the world's most grievous sorrows."

23. Carpenter, עבד (*ebed*, servant/slave), 306–7. An honorific title which describes persons "of a distinctive character or role . . . it did not mean degradation but exaltation in Yahweh's service." E.g., Abraham, Isaac, Jacob (Exod 32:13; Deut 9:27); Moses (Exod 14:3; Num 12:7; Deut 34:5; 1 Kgs 8:53; Mal 4:4); David (1 Sam 23:10; 25:39).

24. Keil and Delitzsch, *Job*, 45.

verse. This suggests that *the book will teach us not only about God but also about humanity.*"25

Almost the first words we hear from the LORD himself are his boasting of his *servant*, before angelic powers—and particularly before the accuser (השׂטן, *hasatan*, "the satan," 1:6)—"Have you seen my servant Job, that there is no one like him on the earth?" (1:7, cf. 2:3). It is this favorable verdict concerning his servant which leads God to invite the accuser to "consider Job" (1:8, cf. 2:3).26 And while the accuser responds to that invitation in a sinister way, it is the LORD's sovereign purpose for it which will prevail: God will be glorified, the faith of his servant vindicated, and the accuser's cynical accusation will be rejected27 (1:9–12; 2:4–8, cf. 42:7, 8). As the accuser acts with malice, "inciting the LORD to (lit.) swallow him up without cause" (2:3b), the LORD spares Job's life and sets limits on the harm he experiences. At the last God proves Job's faith, bringing him "glory and honor." In this the creator God is exalted (42:7–17, cf. 1 Peter 1:7; James 5:11). The LORD is committed to the increase of Job's faith, and final experience of superabundant blessing (1:8–12; 2:4–6, cf. 42:12–17).

Job's relationship with God is precious to his Maker. As Job continually turns to God in his physical and spiritual suffering, the LORD draws him into a deeper dependence upon him.28 Throughout the dialogues, in his prayers and laments, Job's genuine *fear of the LORD*—expressed in his deep desire for a greater assurance of God's love—vindicates God's assessment of him. With the divine verdict in 42:7, 8, Job himself is vindicated, implicitly before the accuser, and explicitly before the accuser's unwitting allies: Eliphaz, Bildad, and Zophar. These are key verses for understanding "God's" verdict on Job's

---

25. Wilson, *Job*, 28–29 (emphasis added). The construction also highlights Job's gentile origins. He is not linked verbally or narratively into Israel's salvation history. Keil and Delitzsch, *Job*, 45, "The writer does not begin with וַיְהִי (*wayhi*/"now it came to pass/now it happened that," *etc.*), as the writers of the historico-prophetical books, who are conscious that they are relating a portion of the connection of the collective Israelitish history." Cf. Seow, *Job 1–21*, 263, "Job 1:1 introduces an account, the context of which is not already familiar. Indeed, ancient Jewish interpreters placed Job in various historical contexts." Calvin, *Sermons on Job*, 2. Calvin's comments are pertinent. "We know not, neither can we guess in what time Job lived; saving that we perceive he was of great antiquity . . . and that the children of Abraham might know that God had showed favour to others who were not of the same line."

26. Brown, "Introducing Job," 237.

27. A similar picture of the limits of Satan's influence within the sphere of God's sovereign grace for his people is seen in Paul's experience described in 2 Corinthians 12:7–10; and that of Peter and the other disciples in Luke 22:31–32.

28. Thielicke, *Prayer*, 126: "What does the Devil accomplish except to drive Job straight into the arms of the very God from whom he was trying to separate him?"

life and faith: while the LORD condemns the speech of the friends throughout the dialogues, he upholds the words of Job.[29]

As the New Testament letter of James interprets it; Job's experience is an example for Christian believers of God using their suffering to grow faith that perseveres, and of God's mercy and compassion towards his people who "wait for the Lord." "As you know, we consider blessed those who have persevered. You have heard of Job's perseverance and have seen what the Lord finally brought about. The Lord is full of compassion and mercy" (Jas 5:11, NIV). In Ephesians, Paul shows that the pattern we see with Job—wherein God refutes his enemies, including all cosmic and angelic opposition, through faithful suffering—is also true for his new people redeemed through Christ, ". . . that through the church the manifold wisdom of God might now be made known to the rulers and authorities in the heavenly places . . . according to the eternal purpose that he has realized in Christ Jesus our Lord . . ." (Eph 3:10–11, ESV).

The Disproportionate Attention of God

In line with the majority report of human beings throughout history, Job is never given an explanation from God for exactly why it is that he must suffer in this way. He remains painfully unaware of the conversation between the LORD and the accuser in the prologue. Job experienced incredible pain in his lifetime. The tragic loss of his children, his physical anguish, and psychological torment frequently brought him to the brink of the abyss. But for this man of faith, the deepest source of his distress came in the form of the silence of God; his Maker whom he loved. The divine silence continues throughout the whole of the dialogues, by far the longest section of the book.

As the prologue comes to a close and the dialogues begin, Job finds himself estranged from all those who were close to him, and who once honored him (e.g., 30:1–15), including his wife and his extended family (e.g., 19:13–20). All that is left for him are long days and nights filled with suffering, and his very real but confusing relationship with God. Job's experience provides a test case in the most extreme circumstance, for whether it is possible for a human being to ". . . fear God for nothing" (1:9, cf. 2:4–5). From Job's opening soliloquy (3:1–10) and on through the dialogues, Job wonders whether the focused attention of the Maker upon his human creatures is really such a good thing after all. He questions the "disproportionate attention" God has paid to this one human being who, in the larger scheme

---

29. Cf. Prideaux, "Job 42:7–17," 174–76.

of things, is as transitory as a breath.³⁰ In verses which could almost be a parody of Psalm 8,³¹ he asks whether God is mistaking him for a great sea monster that needs to be tamed,³² rather than a feeble, fragile human being.

> Am I the sea, or a sea monster that you set a guard over me?
> I loathe my life; I would not live forever.
> Leave me alone, for my days are a breath.
> *What is man, that you make so much of him,*
> *and that you set your heart on him,*
> *visit him every morning and test him every moment?*
> (Job 7:12, 16–18, ESV, emphasis added)

But the LORD refuses to "leave Job alone." Moreover, through his complaints, Job persists in crying out for God; for assurance that (appearances not withstanding) God is for him and with him; that he is not alone in the vastness of creation (cf. Jesus's words in Luke 12:7/Matt 10:31—see also Luke 12:24; Matt 6:26; 12:12).

Gird Up Your Loins Like a Man!

When the LORD does finally break his silence in the great theophany, he treats Job like a new Adam. He takes him on a tour of creation, showing him his kingly rule through the many wonders and threatening realities of the world (38:1—41:34). That is, God addresses Job as a human being: "Gird up your loins like a man; I will question you, and you make it known to me" (38:3, ESV). While the LORD's speeches humble Job (40:3–5), it is also true that of all the creatures which he has made, it is this image-bearer alone whom God directly addresses. As another Job scholar and former vice-principal of Ridley wrote, "The mere fact that God converses with [Job] gives him a dignity above all the birds and beasts, assuring him that it is a splendid thing to be a man."³³

As the LORD speaks to Job of his loving care and concern for every part of creation and exposes the limits of human understanding as to the true

---

30. Clines, *Job 1–20*, 194.
31. The relevant issues are discussed in Van Leeuwen, "Psalm 8:5," 205–15.
32. Cf. Leviathan in 3:8–10, cf. [Eng.] 41:10–11.
33. Andersen, *Job*, 271. Cf. Janzen, "Creation and the Human," 52: "Job is given no human figure with which to identify in the cosmos because he is being summoned to relate himself vocationally to the cosmos."

"*way of things,*"[34] the Creator also reminds Job of his love and care for him, as well as of Job's exalted position as a human creature who is inside, but also stands apart from, the wider creation as God's vice-regent. Job is at one and the same time *humbled* and *exalted* by God. Professor Frank Andersen put this point in his characteristically eloquent way:

> Job is satisfied. His vision of God is expanded beyond all previous bounds. He has a new appreciation of the scope and harmony of God's world, of which he is but a small part. But this discovery *does not make him feel insignificant* . . . The world is beautiful and terrifying, and in it all God is everywhere, seen to be powerful and wise, and more mysterious when He is known than when He is but dimly discerned. The Lord has spoken to Job. That fact alone is marvellous beyond all wonder. Job has grown in wisdom. *He is at once delighted and ashamed.*[35]

The True Image, the Suffering Image, and the Image Restored—Psalm 8 in Hebrews 2

According to the New Testament gospel, the mystery of human existence—our dignity, purpose and destiny—finds its realization in the new Adam, Jesus Christ. He alone succeeds where we have failed (e.g., Luke 3:23—4:13, cf. Romans 5:12–21). God's purpose for human life in the world is finally accomplished through his Son. The writer to the Hebrews picks up Psalm 8 and applies it to Jesus's life, death, and resurrection, and then through this Christotelic lens, applies it to Christ's people. After the quotation from Psalm 8:4–6, which refers to God "putting everything in subjection under his feet" (Hebrews 2:6–8), we read,

> Now in putting everything in subjection to him, he left nothing outside his control. At present, we do not yet see everything in subjection to him. But we see him who for a little while was made lower than the angels, namely Jesus, crowned with glory and honor because of the suffering of death, so that by the grace of God he might taste death for everyone. For it was fitting that he, for whom and by whom all things exist, in bringing many

---

34. Habel, "Implications of God," 288, notes that the word דרך/*derek* "road/way" is used in wisdom writing to denote *the way* of things; "laws," "dimensions," "the interrelationships between different aspects of the cosmos" (e.g., Job 28:26). It is these interrelationships; these "ways" which the Lord describes in his speeches.

35. Andersen, *Job*, 291 (emphasis added).

sons to glory, should make the founder of their salvation perfect through suffering. (Heb 2:8–10, ESV)

Neither Job nor the Psalmist could know that the answer to all their prayers of lament would finally and fully come through Jesus. Jesus Christ is the true pattern of human life; he is *the* Suffering Servant of the Lord *par excellence*. He is the realization of all God's creative and redemptive purpose for human dominion; the one in whose image we were made, and into which his people will one day be perfectly restored (1 John 3:1–3).[36]

Robert Gordis wrote a study of the book of Job entitled, *The Book of God and Man*. The key which unlocks the mystery of human existence, achieving the perfection of relationship between God and those who bear his image, ultimately comes in *the Man who is God*. In this way the great theophany which crowns the book of Job, can be seen as an anticipation of God's final answer to the suffering and struggle of the human race; and the happy ending in the epilogue (42:7–17) as a "rehearsal" for the final accomplishment of God's purpose to "bless" creation, in the new heavens and the new earth (Rev 21–22).[37] In the person of the true image, the man Jesus Christ, God himself appears and enters the world which he made and which he maintains through him (e.g., Col 1:15–17; Heb 1:2–3). The final and full revelation of the word of God has been declared in the appearing of Jesus Christ, the eternal Son; the Lamb who was slain for the sins of the world, and who now reigns with God in glory (John 1:14; Heb 1:1–4, cf. Rev 4 and 5).

Glorious Scars

Peter Singer is scandalized by the suffering image of God. From his point of view, suffering removes our value from us, redefining us as "non-persons." In this worldview, very young and very sick humans have less of a claim on life than a healthy animal. "The old commandment: 'Treat all human life as always more precious than non-human life,' should be replaced with: 'Do not discriminate on the basis of species.'"[38] "The right to life is not a right of members of the species *Homo sapiens* . . . Not all members of the species *Homo sapiens* are persons, and not all persons are members of the species *Homo sapiens*."[39]

---

36. Hughes, *True Image*, 47, "Christoformity was the intention of God in the creation of man [sic]. As his origin is christomorphic, so also is his destiny. The end, however . . . will be more splendid than the beginning."

37. Cf. Prideaux, "Job 42:7–17," 183.

38. Singer, *Rethinking Life and Death*, 202–3.

39. Singer, *Rethinking Life and Death*, 206.

In his *Practical Ethics*, Singer allows for the possibility of experimentation upon severely disabled adults and very young children, placing them in the same category as non-sentient animals. The reason being, "that they would not know what was happening to them."[40] To most people who have enjoyed the privilege and protection of living in a culture shaped by the Judeo-Christian worldview, such an ethic cannot be viewed as progressive in any real sense of the word.[41] The historian Tom Holland, at the time of writing a professed atheist, contrasts the Roman Empire's regressive social hierarchy—particularly its dehumanizing treatment of the weak and vulnerable, with the revolution that Jesus and the Christian movement produced. "Roman culture was built on systematic exploitation. The entire economy was founded on slave labor; the sexual economy built on free Roman males having sex with anyone they wanted in any way they liked."[42] "It was not just the extremes of callousness [as seen in a] Caesar, who was reported to have killed a million Gauls and enslaved a million more, that I came to find shocking, but the lack of a sense that the poor or the weak might have any intrinsic value . . ."[43]

The Bible's vision of universal human dignity and worth has always been a radical one. Job himself, who was once a wealthy man and public figure, understood this well as is evidenced in his attitude towards those who had been servants in his household: "Did not he who made me in the womb make them? Did not the same one form us both within our mothers?" (Job 31:15, NIV).

In short, in cultures and societies where the biblical gospel took root, men, women, and children from every social stratum were effectively given back their humanity. The most recent findings of historians such as Tom Holland, O. M. Bakke, Rodney Stark, and John Dickson show that it was neither Greek philosophy nor Roman imperialism, but the person of Jesus Christ and the teaching of the New Testament, which account for values such as human rights that inform international law. Many historians would argue that the widely held virtues of humility and

---

40. Cited in Wilson, "Human Beings," 109.

41. Trueman, *Rise and Triumph*, 337. "Neither abortion nor infanticide are unprecedented in history, but they have not been widely sanctioned in the West since ancient times, and Singer's argument is predicated on two very modern notions; the rejection of human exceptionalism and the imperative of personal happiness."

42. https://www.youtube.com/watch?v=AIJ9gK47Ogw. Cf. Harrison, *Better Story*, 167, who describes the common Greco-Roman practice of *expositio*—the abandoning of unwanted infants to die or be "rescued" into slavery. Many of these children became sex slaves in brothels, "which were legal, thriving, public enterprises in Rome."

43. Holland, "Why I Was Wrong."

self-sacrifice, which are so fundamental to the assumed ethical framework of the modern world, find their origin in the person and the teaching of Jesus Christ.[44] It would seem that Singer and others like him are committed to a return to a former pagan state. These words from a sermon on Job by G. Campbell Morgan tell a better, a truer story:

> Jesus . . . confronted human beings as he found them, with degraded conceptions of themselves, and he demanded that they deny, not the essential fact of their personality, but the sum-total of their thinking about themselves, resulting from their sin and rebellion against God. He did this, moreover, in order that they might discover the true majesty of their life according to Divine purpose. The mastery of Jesus which first humbles a person to the dust in abnegation lifts them, when yielded to, into the realm of the glory and the majesty of their being.[45]

The only hope for the world now, as in the first century and as it has always been, is that found in the gospel of redemption through the atoning death of our Lord Jesus Christ. If we view ourselves and one another from the perspective of our Maker, Judge, and Savior, such wicked folly as Singer pronounces will be silenced as from "the mouth of babes and infants" (Ps 8:2, cf. Job 31:13–15).[46] For the true man, *the* image of God and final Adam, the person Jesus Christ, the one through whom our true destiny as God's image bearers is restored, was himself wounded and disfigured beyond recognition (cf. Isa 52:14; 53:2–3). The risen and glorified Son still bears the glorious scars of his death on the cross for our sin (John 20:24–27). The Father is not embarrassed or ashamed of the disabling and suffering of his Son, for these scars reveal his glory and "by his wounds we are healed" (Isa 53:5). P. T. Forsyth put it this way: "Our sin brought us into a collision course with a moral universe; and our salvation can therefore only be by communion with the absolutely holy . . . In a Christian faith we descend on creation from redemption, we do not descend on redemption from creation . . . There is no final footing for the soul in the universe [apart from] the holiness of God's love . . . the supreme revelation of the Crucified."[47]

---

44. E.g., Holland, *Dominion*; Bakke, *When Children Became People*; Stark, *Rise of Christianity*; Dickson, *Humilitas*.

45. Morgan, *Answers of Jesus*, 106–7. Emphasis added.

46. The Ur texts of the dangerous folly of twentieth-century thought, and its offspring in the twenty-first century, are found in the writings of Malthus (1798), Darwin (1838), Marx (1867), Nietzsche (1910), and Freud (1932). See Robinson, "Darwinism," 28–75.

47. Forsyth, *Principle of Authority*, 183, 184.

The suffering and struggle; the brokenness and disabling that every person experiences in different ways throughout the course of their lives, does not disqualify us from being the honored image bearers of God. And none of these things can separate us from the committed love of God for us in Christ Jesus our Lord (e.g., Rom 8:18–39; Heb 2:14–18). This is why God's children, ransomed from sin and judgment; who on the last day will be perfectly conformed into the image of his Son in a restored and transformed new creation (e.g., 2 Cor 4:16–18; Rev 21:1–5), will forever worship the Lamb who was slain and is now alive forevermore (Rev 5). And why in the meantime, the prayers of God's people echo Job's yearning prayers and faithful laments, by which he cried out to the Lord God his Maker:

> Come, Lord Jesus! (Rev 22:20, NIV)

Bibliography

Andersen, Francis I. *Job*. TOTC. Leicester: InterVarsity, 1976.
Attenborough, David. *A Life on Our Planet*. Netflix Original, 2020.
Bakke, O. M. *When Children Became People: The Birth of Childhood in Early Christianity*. Minneapolis: Fortress, 2005.
Brown, William P. "Introducing Job: A Journey of Transformation." *Interpretation* 53 (1999) 228–38.
Calvin, John. *Institutes of the Christian Religion*. Edited by John T. McNeill. Translated by Ford Lewis Battles. LCC. Philadelphia: Westminster, 1960.
———. *Sermons on Job*. Translated by Arthur Golding. Edinburgh: Banner of Truth Trust, 1993.
Carpenter, Eugene. "עבד." In *NIDOTTE* 3:304–9.
Clines, David J. A. *Job 1–20*. WBC 17. Waco: Word, 1989.
Crenshaw, James L. "When Form and Content Clash: The Theology of Job 38:1—40:5." In *Creation in the Biblical Traditions*, edited by R. J. Clifford and J. J. Collins, 70–84. CBQ Monograph Series 24. Washington DC: Catholic Biblical Association of America, 1992.
Dhorme, E. *A Commentary on the Book of Job*. London, UK: Nelson, 1967.
Dickson, John. *Humilitas: A Lost Key to Life, Love and Leadership*. Grand Rapids, MI: Zondervan, 2010.
Forsyth, P. T. *The Principle of Authority: In Relation to Certainty, Sanctity and Society*. Blackwood SA: New Creation, 2004.
Fretheim, Terence E. *Creation Untamed: The Bible, God, and Natural Disasters*. Grand Rapids, MI: Baker Academic, 2010.
Fry, Stephen. Interview with Michael Parkinson. Accessed August 5, 2020. https://www.youtube.com/watch?v=39ya2Drpj3s&t=1226s.
Gordis, R. *The Book of God and Man*. Chicago: University of Chicago Press, 1965.
Habel, Norman. "The Implications of God Discovering Wisdom in Earth." In *Job 28: Cognition in Context*, edited by Eugene van Wolde, 281–97. Leiden: Brill, 2003.

Harrison, G. *A Better Story: God, Sex and Human Flourishing*. London: InterVarsity, 2017.
Holland, Tom. Discussion with Tom Wright and Justin Brierly. Accessed August 17, 2020. https://www.youtube.com/watch?v=AIJ9gK47Ogw.
———. *Dominion: How the Christian Revolution Remade the World*. Boston: Little, Brown, 2019.
———. "Why I Was Wrong about Christianity." *New Statesman*, September 14, 2016. Accessed August 17, 2020. https://www.newstatesman.com/politics/religion/2016/09/tom-holland-why-i-was-wrong-about-christianity.
Hughes, Philip E. *The True Image: The Origin and Destiny of Man in Christ*. Leicester: InterVarsity, 1989.
Janzen, J. Gerald. "Creation and the Human Predicament in Job." *Ex Auditu* 3 (1987) 45–53.
Keil, Carl Friedrich, and Franz Delitzsch. *Commentary on the Book of Job*. Translated by Francis Bolton. Grand Rapids, MI: Eerdmans, 1949.
McKibben, Bill. *The Comforting Whirlwind: God, Job and the Scale of Creation*. Grand Rapids, MI: Eerdmans, 1994.
Moody, Andrew. *In Light of the Son: Seeing Everything Through the Father's Love for the Son*. Sydney: Matthias Media, 2015.
Morgan, G. Campbell. *The Answers of Jesus to Job*. London: Marshall, Morgan & Scott, 1934.
Packer, James I., and Thomas Howard. *Christianity: The True Humanism*. Berkhamsted, Herts: Word, 1985.
Penchansky, David. *The Betrayal of God: Ideological Conflict in Job*. Literary Currents in Biblical Interpretation 1. Louisville: Westminster John Knox, 1990.
Plantinga, Cornelius Jr. *Not the Way It's Supposed to Be: A Breviary of Sin*. Grand Rapids, MI: Eerdmans, 1995.
Preece, Gordon, ed. *Rethinking Peter Singer: A Christian Response*. Downers Grove, IL: InterVarsity, 2002.
Prideaux, Andrew. "Job 42:7–17 and the God of the Happy Ending." *RTR* 71, no. 3 (2012) 170–84.
———. "The Repentance of Job in 42:1–6: Another Look at a Perplexing Text." *RTR* 70, no. 1 (2011) 26–36.
———. "The Yahweh Speeches in the Book of Job: Sublime Irrelevance or Right to the Point?" *RTR* 69, no. 2 (2010) 75–87.
Prideaux, Andrew R. "The Relationship between the Creator and the Creature in the Book of Job: An Exploration of the Theme of the Book of Job." Unpublished MTh thesis, Australian College of Theology, 2006.
Robinson, Marilynne. "The Beautiful Changes." In *What Are We Doing Here? Essays*, 127–33. London: Virago, 2018.
———. "Darwinism." In *The Death of Adam: Essays on Modern Thought*, 28–75. New York: Mariner, 1998.
———. "Wilderness." In *The Death of Adam: Essays on Modern Thought*, 245–54. New York: Mariner, 1998.
Schifferdecker, Kathryn. *Out of the Whirlwind: Creation Theology in the Book of Job*. Cambridge, MA: Harvard University Press, 2008.
Scholnick, Sylvia Huberman. "The Meaning of *Mishpat* in the Book of Job. *Journal of Biblical Literature* 101 (1982) 521–29.

Seow, C. L. *Job 1–21: Interpretation and Commentary.* Grand Rapids, MI: Eerdmans, 2013.

Singer, Peter. *Practical Ethics.* Cambridge: Cambridge University Press, 1993.

———. *Rethinking Life and Death: The Collapse of Our Traditional Ethics.* Melbourne: Text, 1994.

Stark, Rodney. *The Rise of Christianity: How the Obscure, Marginal Jesus Movement Became the Dominant Religious Force in the Western World in a Few Centuries.* UK: Harper Collins, 1997.

Thielicke, Helmut. *The Prayer That Spans the World: Sermons on the Lord's Prayer.* London: James Clarke, 1965.

Trueman, Carl R. *The Rise and Triumph of the Modern Self: Cultural Amnesia, Expressive Individualism, and the Road to Sexual Revolution.* Wheaton, IL: Crossway, 2020.

Van Leeuwen, Raymond C. "Psalm 8:5 and Job 7:17–18: A Mistaken Scholarly Commonplace?" In *The World of the Arameans. I. Biblical Studies in Honor of Paul-Eugene Dion*, edited by P. M. Michele Daviau et al., 211–15. JSOT Sup 324. Sheffield: Sheffield Academic Press, 2001.

Van Til, Cornelius. *The Defense of the Faith.* Phillipsburg, NJ: Reformed and Presbyterian, 1967.

Wilson, Lindsay. "Human Beings—Species or Special? A Critique of Peter Singer on Animals." In *Rethinking Peter Singer: A Christian Response*, edited by Gordon Preece, 106–21. Downers Grove, IL: InterVarsity, 2002.

———. *Job.* THOTC. Grand Rapids, MI: Eerdmans, 2015.

———. "Job 38–39 and Biblical Theology." *RTR* 62 (2003) 121–38.

———. "Job, Book of." In *Dictionary for the Theological Interpretation of the Bible*, edited by K. J. Vanhoozer, 384–89. Grand Rapids: Baker Academic, 2005.

11

A Study of the Relational Construct Behind the Discipline of the Lord (Proverbs 3:11–12)

David C. Ray

As clear as day, I remember being caught red-handed by my Year 10 history teacher writing music to words penned by my dopey bandmates. The problem was the name of the said piece—unmentionable! I never saw the text again, but a few days later I was called before the vice-principal. He delivered his verdict: "Right, you can take four, sonny. And if you do it again, I'll tan your backside myself." I remember the school marshal walking me to his office to serve out the punishment. His words were few but most poignant, "You did the wrong thing, but I know you won't do it again." I remember showing my bandmates the welts—the sergeant stripes were a work of art!

Here is an example of two approaches to discipline in one event. An act of folly brought its own well-deserved natural consequence. The consequent act of punishment did nothing but reinforce the school's authority over me, which I already recognized yet could have come to resent. But as a naive youth trying to walk in Christ's ways, I recognized this incident as God's correction for me, in the setting of a denominational boys' school through the school marshal's act of fatherly care.

I think the author of Proverbs wanted to capture this idea succinctly in the plea:

> The discipline of the LORD—my child, may you not reject nor detest his rebuke; because whomever the LORD loves, he rebukes, just as a parent (does of) a child (in whom) they delight. (Prov 3:11–12)[1]

My main argument in this chapter is that "the discipline of the LORD" is an act of correction which presupposes a relational construct behind the receipt of divine instruction; that is, the naive *child* is an "active participant" in the process of being shaped by *God* as mediated by the *parent*-like sage.[2] On the one hand, the receipt of an act of discipline is inherently unpleasant because it involves personal and perhaps physical submission to an authority figure, whether willingly or forcibly. However, the way that one conceives of the circumstances that gave rise to the exercise of discipline can derive divinely appointed benefit. On the other hand, the manner in which divine wisdom is mediated by the authority figure ought to be directed as if to a learner. The key distinction as to whether an experience of discipline is constructive or destructive is correlated with one's capacity to submit to the teaching of another.[3]

The purpose of this brief study is to explore discipline (מוסר) in the Hebrew Bible (HB), which ultimately comes from the LORD, albeit most often indirectly. It evaluates how one's relationship with God and human authorities causes discipline to take the form of backward-looking punishment with destructive effect or forward-looking instruction with a constructive effect.[4] First, I intend to use Proverbs 3:11–12 as an example of the relational construct which underpins the concept of discipline (מוסר) in MT and how it relates to counterpart references to the wandering generations in Deuteronomy. Second, the uses of מוסר and its verbal form יסר in MT are examined with particular attention to texts which reveal the

---

1. My translation of MT. For the purpose of this study, I use "discipline" as the English derivate of מוסר and יסר as this translation can symbolize both its alternate core meanings of positive instruction or negative chastisement (Soanes and Stevenson, *Concise Oxford English Dictionary*, 318; cf. Brown et al., BDB, 415; Köhler and Baumgartner, *HALOT*, 418). For similar reasons, I use "rebuke" as a standard rendering of both יכח and תוכחת.

2. Cf. Cottingham, "Philosophy of Punishment," 774. Whilst the text is arguably set in a patriarchal world, the disciplining parental role is not limited to the father figure in Proverbs but is undertaken by both father and mother (Prov 1:8; 6:20; 10:1; 15:20; 23:22, 25). Accordingly, I take the gender-inclusive perspective that parenthood (cf. אב), as proxy for human authority, connotes God's wisdom and understanding and that childhood (cf. בן) reflects the learning conditions of the pupil.

3. Gilchrist, "Proverbs 1–9," 138–39.

4. Cottingham, "Philosophy of Punishment," 763–64.

distinction between constructive and destructive discipline in conjunction with key human relationships.

Relational Construct Underpinning Discipline in Proverbs 3:11–12

An analysis of the example in Proverbs 3:11–12 demonstrates that discipline is the theme of this proverb and reveals relational assumptions behind discipline as well as its closing effect on the wider discourse:

מוּסַר יְהוָה בְּנִי אַל־תִּמְאָס וְאַל־תָּקֹץ בְּתוֹכַחְתּוֹ׃

כִּי אֶת אֲשֶׁר יֶאֱהַב יְהוָה יוֹכִיחַ וּכְאָב אֶת־בֵּן יִרְצֶה׃

(Prov 3:11–12)

First of all, the theme of this proverb pertains to the relationship between God and the naive child.[5] It is noteworthy that מוסר יהוה ("the discipline of the Lord") appears in the emphatic opening position as the central theme of the dual-verse proverb.[6] This theme is paralleled to בתוכחתו prefixed with a *beit*-adversative connoting an action "against the rebuke" of either the theme or the genitival source of that discipline (Yhwh) in the emphatic closing position of verse 11. Either way, the theme of Proverbs 3:11–12 is the content and/or the process of the impartation of divine wisdom and understanding (cf. Prov 1:8; 15:33; 16:22).

Second, the relationship between God and the naive child is mediated by a parent-like sage, who in turn seeks to maintain relationship so as to impart wisdom. The proverb is directed to "my child" (בני, cf. Υἱέ μου, Heb 12:5, but Υἱέ, LXX) with a common syntactic pattern in Proverbs comprising the אל (ʾăl) volitive negation followed by a *yiqtol* verb.[7] Given the phrase is followed with explanatory information, I interpret this phrase with a modality such that the imperatival sense of the phrase is essentially one of a negative petition ("may you not . . .").[8] Accordingly, the parent figure expresses their desire that the child does not "reject" or "detest" that discipline and rebuke (תוכחת) respectively, but with some tact.

---

5. By "naive child," I mean the young person who has yet to be shaped by the impartation of God's wisdom, often referred to as נער (cf. Prov 1:4) and here as בני.

6. Cf. Longman, *Proverbs*, 41.

7. This syntactic form occurs 84 times in Proverbs compared with 668 instances across HB.

8. Cf. Joüon and Muraoka, *Grammar*, 568.

Importantly, nearly all instances מוסר and יסר are rendered παιδεια and παιδευω respectively in LXX as derived from παις ("child").[9] Etymologically, the concept of discipline then imports an inherent relational construct based on a prototypical dynamic between a child-like figure and their natural parents, in that the parents "rear" the child (cf. "*Zucht*" as the most common rendering of מוסר in LUT84). In the context of Proverbs 1–3, this speech is issued by the sages acting under the auspices of a parent of a child (Prov 1:8, 10, 15; 2:1; 3:1). Accordingly, the process of impartation of divine wisdom and understanding occurs by means of a human mediator issuing מוסר as tradition (cf. Prov 1:2–3; 4:1–4; 8:10)[10] as if it were directly from God (cf. Deut 4:36, cf. 5–6), the source of all wisdom and knowledge (Prov 1:7). This authorized wise sage of God's wisdom is a parent-like figure, who is able to nuance this teaching process with a more amenable tone of suggestion to a naive yet obedient child.

Third, the parent-like sage passes down their understanding about relating to God, possibly based on past experience. It is a common formal characteristic that "calls to remember and obey" in Proverbs 1–9 are ordered such that warnings as negations are followed with explanatory clauses marked with the causal *ki*-conjunction.[11] In verse 12a, the sage alters the typical biblical Hebrew word order to place the child as direct object in the emphatic first position. The "rebuke" (יכח, cf. ἐλεγχω, LXX, but Heb 12:6, παιδευω) of the child is then a manifestation of God's love for the child (cf. Prov 6:23; Job 5:17).

The nexus between God's love and rebuke is not obvious to the child, who has a natural inclination to avoid placing himself under the teaching of another and therefore requires discipline, even by means of a rod (Prov 22:15). Also, the parent does not explain here why God disciplines the beloved ones. Suffering comes with discipline regardless of one's approach to it. However, it is conceivable that this piece of wisdom was passed down in a similar fashion by earlier generations. For instance, the lexemes יסר/מוסר and discourse pattern of instruction and explanation in this proverb is "remarkably similar" to Deuteronomy 8:5.[12] In particular, the Moses figure calls Israel to recognize how God was מיסרך ("the one disciplining you," cf. מוסר יהוה, Deut 11:2), both the humility of hunger and divine provision of food and clothing in the desert (Deut 8:1–4), just as a man disciplines his child:

---

9. "παιδεια," in *LEH*, n.p.
10. Cf. Longman, *Proverbs*, 76.
11. Pemberton, "Rhetoric of the Father," 67, 69.
12. Spellman, "Drama of Discipline," 498.

וְיָדַעְתָּ עִם־לְבָבֶךָ

כִּי כַּאֲשֶׁר יְיַסֵּר אִישׁ אֶת־בְּנוֹ יְהוָה אֱלֹהֶיךָ מְיַסְּרֶךָּ׃

(Deut 8:5)

This probable intertextual reference functions rhetorically by likening the divine discipline of the wandering generation to that which the child shall encounter in pursuing torah-piety.[13] Accordingly, the sage highlights the parental nature of God in that the human familial relationship is synonymous for the relationship between God and his people as one body (i.e., by means of the second person singular pronoun).

Fourth, the pericope closes with a clause comparing God with the parent figure with the rhetorical purpose of managing the affections of the child. Whereas Deuteronomy 8:5 compares the respective acts of parental and divine discipline, the comparison in verse 12b is made between the love of God (אהב) and the delight (רצה) of a parent for their child, out of which correction is made (יכח, v. 12a). The powerful expression of affection for the child from God *and* the parent figure is aimed at assuring the child of the parent's affinity with the child as well as God's favour, subject to submission to acts of correction as fulfillment of covenant expectations (Deut 4:23; 5:2; 6:3).

Fifth, this proverb closes the lecture from Proverbs 3:1 about the fortuitous promises of obeying the parent's teaching with a *caveat*.[14] Not only divine favour (vv. 1–4) and well-being (vv. 8–10) are concomitant with following the parent's teaching to trust and fear God (vv. 5–7), but also suffering through the process of discipline. Verses 11–12 have the significant effect of placing a religious impetus behind the parent's teaching.[15] It is expected that the pursuit of torah piety results in the painful process of being *shaped*, which Lindsay Wilson succinctly summarizes:

> . . . the pupil may be undergoing hard times, which are described as times of discipline and rebuke . . . while they [discipline and rebuke] may both refer to setbacks and obstacles, the focus is on using these sufferings to redirect or shape a person's life.[16]

The notion that life's disappointments ought to be reoriented as divine instruction is consistent with the distinctive HB concept of the

---

13. Spellman, "Drama of Discipline," 499.
14. Pemberton, "Rhetoric of the Father," 79.
15. Fox, *Proverbs 1–9*, 152.
16. Wilson, *Proverbs*, 19.

Tun-Ergehen-Zusammenhang ("act-consequence relationship").[17] The core idea behind Koch's construct might be best defined as an ancient Hebraic understanding as to how justice is meted out in a manner similar to the natural law established by God. Here the parent is seeking to assure the child and leaves no room for doubt as to God's intention behind the problems faced by the naive but obedient child. Wrongdoing has its own consequences which bring into effect God's discipline. The choice remains as to whether the child accepts the consequences in deference to God's ultimate benevolence or rejects any nexus between act and consequence outright by seeking to be independent of God's will.

In addition, the negative petition in verse 1 not to *carelessly* "forget" (שכח) about the parent's instruction (תורתי) is juxtaposed to the warning not to *actively* "reject" and "detest" God's discipline, as if they were one in the same. The effect of the parent's teaching must become entrenched in the child's lifestyle so as to ensure that the discipline of the LORD is not rejected or resented. Discipline requires submission to God's and the wise parent's divinely appointed authority for one's ultimate benefit.[18]

In summary, Proverbs 3:11–12 comprises a parent's caveat to their child's expectations of well-being before God. The benefits of keeping God's commands and torah piety will involve the painful process of allowing oneself to be shaped by life's misfortunes, which ought to be accepted as God's own discipline. The use of negative petitions and explanations are rhetorical devices which aim at managing the child's openness to teaching through warnings and also to bind the teaching of the parent with that appointed by God himself. Accordingly, this proverb is a good example of how discipline is underpinned by a relational construct—one must make themselves vulnerable to the influence of another so as to gain the wisdom which comes with life's experiences *coram deo*. In this manner, "reproof becomes a constructive instrument."[19]

Constructive and Destructive Approaches to the Discipline of the LORD

In this section, the study is widened to survey uses of lexemes יסר/מוסר (i.e., nominal and verbal forms of "discipline") across HB. In particular,

---

17. Koch, "Vergeltungsdogma," 68–72. I would advance an amplified translation of *Tun-Ergehen-Zusammenhang* as "actions and what they yield from social and theological perspectives."

18. Brown, *Wisdom's Wonder*, 26.

19. Bland, *Proverbs*, 27.

I explore how the way one approaches the parental figure and God respectively affects the outcome of discipline, whether as instruction toward wisdom and/or punishment even toward death. In general, the Writings present discipline as having the potential to cause harm and/or help, contrasting the texts from Deuteronomy, Deuteronomistic history, and the Prophets which more often convey discipline as outright punishment for Israel's failure to comply with God's covenant expectations. Both forms of text are mediated by their respective writers to the current "child" generation by a parent/royal sage or prophetic figure.

Association Between Discipline, Rebuke, and Wisdom, and the Role of the Human Mediator

In the book of Proverbs, discipline and rebuke are invariably related to each other, in that a response to rebuke might result in either constructive or destructive forms of discipline. Either way, discipline arises by making mistakes and having them corrected.[20]

It is common for the sage to use antithetical parallelism to contrast the one who rejects or accepts discipline or rebuke. Most of the examples of antithetical parallelism between מוסר and תוכחת are found in the wise sayings ascribed to Solomon in Proverbs 10–15. Importantly, this section opens with a comparison of the wise child who gladdens and the foolish child who represents grief to their parents (Prov 10:1ab–b), which sets the relational dynamic across the entire section.

In this context of the child being a source of honor or shame for their parents, instances of antithetical parallelism compare wise and foolish approaches to encountering acts of discipline. In particular, the sage uses the image of paths leading to life or death (Prov 10:17) as well as abstractions of seeking or spurning knowledge (Prov 12:1), receiving honor and shame (Prov 13:18), and demonstrating prudence and recklessness (Prov 15:5).

In addition, a final example of the collocation of discipline with rebuke in Proverbs 15:32–33 is particularly poignant. It both closes this collection of sayings in Proverbs 10–15 and establishes a causal relationship between discipline and the reified objects of divine wisdom and understanding (cf. Prov 12:1; 16:22; 19:20, 27; 23:12, 23). Whereas the child who rejects discipline abandons their very own being, the child who listens to rebuke "gains a heart" (קונה לב); that is, "the thinking, feeling, believing center of the person who is coming into full being before God."[21] This rebuke is "discipline for

---

20. Longman, *Proverbs*, 77.
21. Davis, *Getting Involved with God*, 69.

wisdom" (מוסר חכמה with imputed genitive of purpose),²² which requires one to submit humbly in the fear of the Lord before attaining the status of a having a wise, godly, and shaped character:

פּוֹרֵעַ מוּסָר מוֹאֵס נַפְשׁוֹ
וְשׁוֹמֵעַ תּוֹכַחַת קוֹנֶה לֵּב׃
יִרְאַת יְהוָה מוּסַר חָכְמָה
וְלִפְנֵי כָבוֹד עֲנָוָה׃

(Prov 15:32–33)

Accordingly, the naive child is called by their parents to pursue God's own wisdom, such that the child becomes an "inquirer" of their parents' wise sayings and thus allows their own identity and character "to be transformed by the power of God."²³

In summary, it is ultimately up to the individual who encounters an act of discipline to recognize both the authority causing that act and that the authority can be trusted as "possessing" wisdom, understanding, and knowledge such that the parental figure has the individual's ultimate interests at heart. The role of the parental figure is then to present God's wisdom in a manner which the child will not automatically reject nor accept without consideration, evidenced by the regular use of negative petition, antithetical parallelism, and language conveying affective commitment to the child's cause.

Corporal Discipline

As a part of ANE social order, Proverbs 3:11–12 demonstrates that the hope of the parent figure is that the naive child will approach God's discipline. This hope is nested in a form of constructive criticism with the forward-looking aim of shaping the character of the child, equipping him for life's blessings and challenges. Defining discipline as having "dual modes of . . . content and process," Goldstone claims that מוסר in Proverbs "connotes a unified and wholly positive enterprise oriented toward the improvement of individuals . . . nearly conflated with Proverb's (sic) core theme of wisdom."²⁴ I would complement Goldstone's argument with the claim that the process of discipline is one which is inherently relational. However, I would note that discipline is not entirely positive in all circumstances in

22. Joüon and Muraoka, *Grammar*, 438.
23. Bland, *Proverbs*, 3–4.
24. Goldstone, "Dual Dimensions," 118.

Proverbs nor in the warnings of impending mutiny in the former prophets nor of exile in the latter prophets. In particular, physical punishments are conceivable as harsh discipline. Indeed, physical punishment is by no means normative for today's discipline.

An example from Deuteronomistic history demonstrates how discipline (יסר) is a means of exerting a form of human authority over the people. King Rehoboam seeks to exert his divinely appointed authority in the face of Jeroboam's treachery by comparing the impost of King Solomon (cf. 1 Sam 8:11–18; 1 Kgs 4:7) to his own:

וְעַתָּ֗ה אָבִי֙ הֶעְמִ֤יס עֲלֵיכֶם֙ עֹ֣ל כָּבֵ֔ד וַאֲנִ֖י אוֹסִ֣יף עַֽל־עֻלְּכֶ֑ם

אָבִ֗י יִסַּ֤ר אֶתְכֶם֙ בַּשּׁוֹטִ֔ים וַאֲנִ֕י אֲיַסֵּ֥ר אֶתְכֶ֖ם בָּעַקְרַבִּֽים׃

(1 Kgs 12:11, cf. 14; 2 Chr 10:11, 14)

It is noteworthy that the term "whips" (שׁוֹט, cf. μαστιξ, LXX) is associated with a better experience of authority than that of Rehoboam's "scorpions," the latter form being a curious reference to capricious discipline.[25] By contrast to Solomon's harsh but fair maintenance of monarchic order, Rehoboam's threat is clearly negative and designed only to oppress and drive fear into those plotting the division of the kingdom, perhaps as a projection of Rehoboam's own fear of the shame of losing his exclusive kingship. The relational construct behind negative discipline of God's supposed representative is one of brokenness between divine and human authorities and their subjects (cf. Prov 19:18).

Nonetheless, the use of corporal punishment is also associated with positive acts of discipline. The verbal form of μαστιξ ("he scourges") parallels παιδειας κυριου ("discipline of the LORD") in the LXX version of our key example (italicized), albeit as a textual addition to MT:

Υἱέ, μὴ ὀλιγώρει *παιδείας Κυρίου*,

μηδὲ ἐκλύου ὑπ' αὐτοῦ ἐλεγχόμενος·

ὃν γὰρ ἀγαπᾷ Κύριος ἐλέγχει,

μαστιγοῖ δὲ πάντα υἱὸν ὃν παραδέχεται.

(Prov 3:11–12, LXX)

In addition, the positive relationship between discipline and "scourging" (μαστιγοω) is demonstrated here as a sign of God's acceptance

---

25. It could be levelled that the author is transforming metaphorically the physical pain of corporal punishment into another domain (e.g., hard labour, taxation). Nevertheless, one must consider the domain of domination by means of physical pain before its cognitive transformation.

(παραδέχομαι). Further, uses of this same lexeme in Ben Sira (Sir 22:6; 23:2; cf. Pss. Sol. 7:8; 10:2) indicate that corporal disciplinary measures were used to correct pupils in at least Hellenized-Jewish circles.[26]

The issuing of corporal discipline by the parental figure is also found in Proverbs MT. The denominative verb נכה ("to strike") is used in conjunction with parent's discipline for the child's ultimate good in that the use of שבט ("rod") will not result in death (cf. Prov 13:24; 22:15):

אַל־תִּמְנַע מִנַּעַר מוּסָר כִּי־תַכֶּנּוּ בַשֵּׁבֶט לֹא יָמוּת

(Prov 23:13)

It is noteworthy that the same connection between discipline and striking is found in Jeremiah, particularly in the recounting of God striking Judah like an enemy as a disciplinary measure (Jer 30:14, cf. 11; 2:30; 5:3), which would result in both devastation of Jerusalem and its inhabitants through exile but also consolation upon its return (Jer 30:18–23, cf. Jeremiah's "Book of Consolation").[27] In a similar way, the child who is incapable of accepting the discipline of their parents (Deut 21:18) is ultimately served with capital punishment (Deut 21:19–21a), which in turn serves as an *example* to all of Israel to fear God and shun evil (Deut 21:21b, cf. Prov 3:7b). To discipline a mocker or a wicked person has no effect but to bring dishonor to the one who attempts to impart God's wisdom (Prov 9:7).

Physical pain appears to have been associated with a positive and building experience in ANE. This educative process is underpinned by a positive relational construct between the subject, God, and the divine mediator (whether parent figure, prophet or sage). However, the child who rejects the authority of parents and is not able to be disciplined represents "evil in the midst" of Israel and a tangible example of that which one should turn from (Deut 21:21b).

Benevolence and Malevolence of Discipline

An analysis of the instances of discipline also reveals a grading of different acts of discipline; that is, there are types of discipline which seem to be beneficial or detrimental to the experiencer. For example, grades of discipline are set out in Proverbs 15:10 which relate to the manner in which one approaches discipline and correction:

---

26. Goldstone, "Dual Dimensions," 119–20.
27. Feinberg, "Jeremiah," 558, 564.

מוּסָר רָע לְעֹזֵב אֹרַח שׂוֹנֵא תוֹכַחַת יָמוּת

(Prov 15:10)

The sage qualifies discipline which is literally "bad" or "evil" (רע), rendered as "grievous punishment" (NASB, 1995), "severe discipline" (NRSV), or perhaps "vicious chastisement" (cf. LUT84). This example demonstrates the tendency to distinguish the lexeme מוסר between "instruction" and "punishment."[28] Here מוסר is malevolent to the one who is lured by the way of the wicked (cf. Prov 15:9a) to the point of death, all because they hate correction (תוכחת). This passage then demonstrates that discipline is a wholly negative experience to the one who rejects the parent's discipline (מוסר אב, Prov 15:5a) and therefore submission to God's will for their life (cf. Prov 5:12; Ps 39:12; of Judah, Jer 2:19; Ezek 5:15).

Another example of the grading of discipline is found in the book of Jeremiah. In Jeremiah 10, the prophet juxtaposes of the nations' idolatry and Judah's waywardness (which most likely also included idolatry, cf. Jer 11:10) as sin of equal significance.[29] Jeremiah calls on the righteous God to "discipline with justice, not your anger" (interpreted as a jussive, cf. Pss 6:2; 38:2, יכה), lest Judah be brought to nought:

יַסְּרֵנִי יְהוָה אַךְ־בְּמִשְׁפָּט

אַל־בְּאַפְּךָ פֶּן־תַּמְעִטֵנִי׃

(Jer 10:24)

It is most noteworthy that God's discipline could be conceived as being *either* benevolent *or* malevolent in the eyes of Judah, albeit in the context of a strong prophetic critique. The intention of the prophet is to express a plea for divine mercy on behalf of Judah, rather than a treatise on divine discipline. Nevertheless, the notion that God could discipline with wrath also points to the centrality of the relational construct behind the issuance and receipt of discipline. Where the discipline of the LORD is perceived as being benevolent, even in the context of the exile, it ultimately serves as beneficence, albeit with the benefit of hindsight which might be visible only to future generations. However, if the broken relationship between God and humanity is not recognized by the recipient of divine discipline, that discipline might well be wrongly perceived as being capricious.

---

28. E. H. Merrill (#3579) in VanGemeren, *NIDOTTE*, 2:479.
29. Feinberg, "Jeremiah," 445.

Discipline as a Reflection of Certain Types of Relationship

It is from the vantage point of a broken relationship with God that the *nifal* imperative of יסר is used to exhort the hearer to accept divine discipline and, most importantly, to return to relationship with God. For instance, Jeremiah conveys a divine exhortation for Jerusalem to return to relationship with God, even at its impending fall so that God might not abhor it in perpetuity (Jer 6:8). Also, a most poignant example is found in royal Psalm 2:10, where the psalmist warns the kings and judges of the earth to have insight (שׂכל, cf. משׂכיל "proverb") and to "be disciplined" by serving the divinely appointed and empowered Davidic king:

וְעַתָּה מְלָכִים הַשְׂכִּילוּ הִוָּסְרוּ שֹׁפְטֵי אָרֶץ

(Ps 2:10)

A more universal perspective of God's discipline is found in Psalm 94:10–12, where the psalmist muses on God's discipline of the nations as being an example as to how God's people might receive divine instruction through correction as a blessing. By contrast, the sage distinguishes the idea of disciplining a slave from that of a free person (Prov 29:19), in that the slave is at all times subject to the master. The power imbalance inherent in this specific human-to-human relationship is normalized, leading to homogeneity in the issuing of instruction and punishment; that is, the master will always have the upper hand over the slave.[30]

There is also homogeneity in the relationship between God and Israel as well as the child and their parents in HB, given that the LORD has set his order over the cosmos as well as the divinely appointed social order (Deut 6:4–9). The verb לקח is associated with the human acceptance of divine discipline (Prov 8:10; 24:32), but more often in the prophetic texts in the context of Judah's refusal to accept God's discipline (Jer 2:30; 5:3; 7:28; 17:23; 32:33; 35:13; Zeph 3:2, 7). Part of the divine order is humanity's freedom to reject that order yet paradoxically remain within it. The corollary of this choice of acceptance or rejection of discipline is that it is not the human power that is the ultimate source of discipline but that of God alone, who is the only righteous one capable of consistent issuance of discipline to the one who submits to God's will.

---

30. Foucault, *Discipline and Punish*, 184.

Conclusion

This study has sought to demonstrate that the child figure of Proverbs is naive and requires discipline in order to follow the upright path set before them by God. The shaping of the character of an individual toward that which reflects God's own righteousness, justice, and equity requires a human mediator, who is in the most trusted human relationship to the individual. The key textual example in Proverbs 3:11–12 provided a foretaste of some of the more common attributes of calls to follow divine discipline in Proverbs generally. First, it presented the learning process as one which comes from the LORD, such that the ideal parent-child relationship then crystallizes the role of instruction in divine-human relations. Second, the parent-child relationship is a reflection of that between God and Israel of the wandering generations, wherein the parent has gained divine wisdom through their own process of discipline and rebuke, such that the child requires that same instruction. Third, the parent-sage presents divine discipline using negative petitions, antithetical parallelism, explanatory statements, and expressions of affinity such that the child is likely to seriously consider their exhortations and warnings and bring honor upon the family and God's people rather than shame. Fourth, the content and process of discipline is presented by the parent as a necessary process of learning from life's mistakes, which are akin to a natural consequence from human actions under God's divinely appointed order. Fifth, physical punishment as a part of the process of discipline was a part of ANE social order but by no means normative for today's discipline. Sixth, divine discipline is a necessary response to the broken relationship between humanity and God. Finally, the writings present the naive one with a choice to accept or reject discipline, whereas the prophetic texts present discipline as an unavoidable consequence of repeated and endemic failure of Israel to meet its covenant expectations. If wisdom, knowledge, and understanding are key *ends* which reflect the righteousness of God, discipline (and correction) are the key *means* by which they are brought about in the life of the child, who is brought into right relationship with the Father-in-heaven through the mediation of a loving earthly parental figure. No one need remain a fool forever so long as one remains teachable—I now remember my school marshal most fondly (Prov 9:8).

Bibliography

Bland, Dave. *Proverbs and the Formation of Character*. Eugene, Oregon: Cascade, 2015.
Brown, Francis, et al. *Enhanced Brown-Driver-Briggs Hebrew and English Lexicon*. Oxford: Clarendon, 1977.

Brown, William P. *Wisdom's Wonder: Character, Creation, and Crisis in the Bible's Wisdom Literature*. Grand Rapids, MI: Eerdmans, 2014.
Cottingham, John G. "The Philosophy of Punishment." In *An Encyclopaedia of Philosophy*, edited by G. H. R. Parkinson, 762–83. London: Routledge, 1988.
Davis, Ellen F. *Getting Involved with God: Rediscovering the Old Testament*. Cambridge, MA: Cowley, 2001.
Die Bibel Nach Der Übersetzung Martin Luthers. Stuttgart: Deutsche Bibelgesellschaft, 1984.
Feinberg, Charles L. "Jeremiah." In *The Expositor's Bible Commentary: Isaiah, Jeremiah, Lamentations, Ezekiel*, edited by Frank E. Gaebelein, 355–692. Grand Rapids: Zondervan, 1986.
Foucault, Michel. *Discipline and Punish: The Birth of the Prison*. Edited by Alan Sheridan. London: Allen Lane, 1977.
Fox, Michael V. *Proverbs 1–9: A New Translation with Introduction and Commentary*. New York: Doubleday, 2000.
Gilchrist, Margaret Odell. "Proverbs 1–9: Instruction or Riddle." *Proceedings* 4 (1984) 131–45.
Goldstone, Matthew. "Dual Dimensions of Discipline in Jewish Wisdom and Early Rabbinic Sources." *Shofar: An Interdisciplinary Journal of Jewish Studies* 35, no. 3 (2017) 115–33.
Joüon, Paul, and Takamitsu Muraoka. *A Grammar of Biblical Hebrew*. Subsidia Biblica 27. Rome: Pontifical Biblical Institute, 2006.
Koch, Klaus. "Gibt es ein Vergeltungsdogma im Alten Testament?" In *Spuren des hebräischen Denkens: Beiträge zur alttestamentlichen Theologie*, edited by Bernd Janowski and Martin Krause, 65–103. Neukirchen-Vluyn: Neukirchener Verlag, 1991.
Köhler, Ludwig, and Walter Baumgartner. *The Hebrew and Aramaic Lexicon of the Old Testament*. Leiden: Brill, 2001.
Longman, Tremper, III. *Proverbs*. Grand Rapids, MI: Baker Academic, 2006.
Lust, Johan, et al. "παιδεια." In *LEH*, n.p.
Pemberton, Glenn D. "The Rhetoric of the Father in Proverbs 1–9." *Journal for the Study of the Old Testament* 30, no. 1 (2005) 63–82.
Soanes, Catherine, and Angus Stevenson. *Concise Oxford English Dictionary*. 11th ed. Oxford: Oxford University Press, 2008.
Spellman, Ched. "The Drama of Discipline: Toward an Intertextual Profile of *Paideia* in Hebrews 12." *Journal of the Evangelical Theological Society* 59, no. 3 (2016) 487–506.
VanGemeren, Willem A. *New International Dictionary of Old Testament Theology and Exegesis*. 5 vols. Grand Rapids: Zondervan, 1997.
Wilson, Lindsay. *Proverbs: An Introduction and Commentary*. Downers Grove, IL: Inter-Varsity, 2017.

Part IV

Wisdom in Preaching and Teaching

12

Wise Preaching from Proverbs 10–29

Paul A. Barker

Approaches to Preaching Proverbs 10–29

While there is a coherent flow or narrative in each of the first nine chapters of Proverbs that makes preaching those chapters relatively straightforward, as well as in Proverbs 30–31, that is not the case in Proverbs 10–29. In these chapters, with some exceptions, there appears little connection between consecutive verses. As Garrett says, the preaching of Proverbs 10–29 is "notoriously difficult."[1]

When I first approached preaching from these chapters many years ago, I turned to the late Derek Kidner's Tyndale commentary to find that he largely grouped the proverbs within these chapters thematically.[2] This thematic approach is reflected in a look at any of the sermon archives of evangelical churches. Sermons on Proverbs 10–29 are few and far between anyway, and those that do exist are almost all thematic.

Several articles and chapters that discuss preaching Proverbs 10–29 take the same thematic approach. Bullock simply suggests focusing on the theme of righteousness in Proverbs and offers no other ideas or help for preaching from the book.[3] Longman thinks the most successful preaching

---

1. Garrett, "Preaching," 108.
2. Kidner, *Proverbs*, 31–56.
3. Bullock, "Preaching," 302–3.

on Proverbs 10–29 is topical and Achtemeier only seems to consider topical sermons.[4] Doriani's brief article mentions a few clusters of proverbs on a common theme, links several proverbs back to themes in Proverbs 1–9, but otherwise assumes preaching on Proverbs 10–29 will be topical.[5] Similarly Chris Wright, "I think that the best way to preach from the book of Proverbs is probably thematically . . . It's not easy to preach a coherent sermon with a single main point from a whole chapter, and it's probably too much to preach a whole sermon on one single verse."[6] He gives an example of a sermon from Proverbs 11 using righteousness as the key unifying theme.[7] Waltke alludes to rhetorical groupings of proverbs, but commends topical sermons and even suggests that preaching on consecutive but thematically disconnected proverbs would in fact be wrong.[8]

Rare among commentaries on Proverbs, Lindsay Wilson's Tyndale commentary has an introductory section on preaching from Proverbs. On Proverbs 10–29, he commends a topical approach, understood in the context of chapters 1–9, suggesting a "string of beads" approach, stringing together a number of proverbs on a particular theme.[9] But even with Wilson there is no discussion about preaching consecutive proverbs that have no apparent common theme.

Even as keen an expositor as Kaiser recommends preaching clusters of proverbs that focus on similar topics. However, he also acknowledges there are more connections between consecutive proverbs than is often acknowledged and preaching a textual cluster of proverbs is possible.[10] He gives examples of 11:1–21, which begin and end with the theme of an abomination or delight to the Lord, 6:20–35, a warning against adultery, 19:16–23, with the theme of a disciplined life.[11] However even Kaiser makes no comment on preaching what are disconnected proverbs in consecutive verses. He focuses on the exceptions rather than the norm, in my opinion.

While there is merit in a thematic approach, there remains for me a lingering dissatisfaction. There are many proverbs that do not fit simply or

---

4. Longman, "Preaching Wisdom," 106; Achtemeier, *Preaching*, 172–73.

5. Doriani, "How to Preach."

6. Wright, *Sweeter than Honey*, 251.

7. Wright, *Sweeter than Honey*, 256–58.

8. Waltke, "Fundamentals," 7. See 389–92 for his analysis of connecting theme in Proverbs 10:6–14.

9. Wilson, *Proverbs*, 49.

10. Kaiser, *Preaching and Teaching*, 89. Kaiser, *Towards an Exegetical Theology*, 19, wrote that "he has been advising his students for some years now to preach a topical sermon only once every five years—and then immediately repent!"

11. Kaiser, *Preaching and Teaching*, 89–92.

easily into a major theme and would be overlooked in a topical approach. A topical approach disregards the canonical order, even if we cannot detect a structure. Can we, indeed ought we, preach consecutive verses of Proverbs 10–29? Garrett suggests preaching on consecutive verses from these chapters would be "tedious" and "bewildering."[12] Gowan almost implies that we cannot preach on proverbs at all: "Their very nature suggests they ought not to be taken as texts to be expounded in a sermon."[13]

Another approach, of course, is what is sometimes called textual preaching, namely preaching just one verse. These days evangelicals tend to shy away from this style, though it was much more common in earlier times, on the grounds of context. In the vast majority of the Bible, it is evident that verses find meaning in the context of what precedes and succeeds. But in Proverbs 10–29, if the individual proverbs are independent of each other, then preaching one proverb, one verse, may be legitimate. Arthurs gives a few examples of preaching on a single proverb.[14] McKenzie suggests preaching on one proverb as a "roving spotlight" shedding light on a particular focus, rather than as a floodlight lighting up everything.[15]

Yet, this lingering dissatisfaction remains for me. Even if we do not see verbal, structural or thematic connections between consecutive proverbs, they are in our canon consecutively, so there seems to be a case for considering how to preach a section of these proverbs.

Are There Connections between Proverbs in Proverbs 10–29?

Recent scholarship has investigated links between proverbs in these chapters. "It is possible, however, that the proverbs of Proverbs 10–29 are not nearly as random as they appear to be."[16] Garrett goes on to summarize that some connections are structural, in a chiasm, for instance, or follow a theme or use repetition of a word of phrase. The key point he makes is that connections show that "the whole is greater than the sum of the parts."[17] He illustrates his point from 10:1–5 with a common theme of economic security. Similarly, Longman refers to the work of Heim who argues for

---

12. Garrett, "Preaching," 108.
13. Gowan, *Reclaiming the Old Testament*, 104. When he more generally addresses what to preach from wisdom literature, he answers with topics.
14. Arthurs, *Preaching with Variety*, 145.
15. McKenzie, *Preaching Proverbs*, 103.
16. Garrett, "Preaching," 109.
17. Garrett, "Preaching," 110.

connections on phonological, semantic, syntactic, and thematic grounds which form larger units.[18] Bland likewise argues that clusters based on macrostructure such as chiasm, macroparallelism, catchwords, and inclusio, are "frequently found."[19]

It remains unproven though that the vast bulk of Proverbs 10–29 has coherence and connections in consecutive proverbs. While Garrett suggests there are many coherent groups of proverbs, he makes no comment on preaching those where there is no connection. Arthurs urges the preacher to look, and look hard, using good commentaries, to find the connections which are often subtle. He gives no examples of this, and goes on also to commend topical preaching of proverbs.[20] On the other hand, some scholars, such as Ryken, remain unconvinced about the coherence of groups of proverbs.[21]

How, then, do we preach proverbs where there is no obvious connection between them? Before addressing that question directly, there are some other key issues to address concerning the nature of a proverb, whether proverbs are merely observations of what is the case, their limitations, and the context of Proverbs 10–29. These matters are critical to get the thrust and style of preaching a proverb right, before we offer suggestions for preaching a sequence of proverbs.

Preaching the Narratives behind a Proverb

Miguel de Cervantes described a proverb as "a short sentence founded upon long experience." Ricoeur put it, "Without being a narrative, the proverb implies a story."[22] Similarly, Walter Kaiser says, "Recurring patterns of stories gave rise to a short sentence that tended to wrap up the truth of the narrative in a memorable phrase or line."[23] As Thomas Long suggests, this opens the way to envisage the background narratives of proverbs, the past experiences, and then the wise person's gathering of narratives into a proverb.

---

18. Longman, "Preaching Wisdom," 106–7, referring to Heim, *Like Grapes of Gold*.

19. Bland, "New Proposal." Bland gives a few examples, though not enough to prove the point of frequency.

20. Arthurs, *Preaching with Variety*, 142.

21. Ryken, *How to Read*, 127.

22. Quoted in Long, *Preaching*, 57.

23. Kaiser, *Preaching and Teaching*, 84.

Long uses the example of 15:17, "Better is a dinner of herbs where love is than a fatted ox and hatred with it."[24] He then explores his memory for parallels to the two sides of the proverb in his own experience. He uses an example of a farmer's simple but generous hospitality. He recalls an episode from a book. He cites a conversation with a fellow minister's experience of communion. All simple but loving table fellowship. Then he recounts a few brief examples of strained, unloving meals, including Judas leaving the last supper early to betray Jesus. He concludes, "Narratives, vignettes, story-like threads that the proverb tugs from the fabric of everyday life would be told, each thread punctuated by the proverb itself, quoted as an interpretive refrain."[25]

Proverbs thus give creative licence to the preacher to recall past experiences or narratives that might give rise to the proverb.[26] What feasts lacking love has the preacher participated in? If there is "long experience" behind a proverb, then that experience will draw in numerous narratives, illustrations from all works of life. What an opportunity to tell stories!

But preaching proverbs is more than storytelling because proverbs are more than observations.

Preaching More than Observations

A proverb is neither a law nor a promise but states what is usually the case. So 9:11 is not a promise that if you fear the Lord, you will live longer.[27] Nor is 16:3 a promise that if you pray about your plans, they will always succeed. But are they mere observations?

This is a crucial question. A parishioner once came to me in distress over Proverbs 22:6. Their son was no longer a Christian and she felt that she and her husband had failed to train their son in the way he ought to go. So, I explained to her this was neither a promise with a guaranteed outcome, nor even a law, but a general observation.

However, as I have pondered over the years, the proverb is more than just an observation. Wisdom is not just hearing or understanding, but obeying, as Jesus said in a different context in Matthew 7:24. Embedded within the observation is at least an urging to recognize the wisdom in bringing up children in the right way, in fearing the Lord, in committing all plans to

---

24. Long, *Preaching*, 62–64.

25. Long, *Preaching*, 65.

26. See McKenzie, *Preaching Proverbs*, 105–12, for an example of this from Proverbs 13:2.

27. See Duguid, "Preaching Christ," 177–78, further on this point.

the sovereign Lord.[28] Unlike a command, this proverb is an invitation to observe, ponder, and then act wisely.

So proverbs do observe what is often the case, but more importantly they are empirically guiding people to live wisely. The wise person is not the person who knows the proverbs or even sees narratives behind them. Rather the wise person employs proverbs towards changed behavior. Longman defines biblical wisdom as "skill of living."[29] That is, wisdom is not academic knowledge but applied knowledge, in the relational context of the fear of the Lord. Indeed, a proverb in a fool's hands is dangerous (26:7b). The wise person will need to know when and how to apply proverbs. That skill for life is true wisdom.

Proverbs are making moral statements, often with implied application. Thus Long, "the rhetorical function of the proverb is to provide a general ethical guideline."[30] However Long sees this as a secondary role of the proverbs, their primary role being to describe succinctly the way things are. He concludes that the key question for the proverbs is not, "What should we do? But rather the question, What is really going on here?"[31]

This is where Long does not go far enough in my opinion. So, using the example above on 15:17, the sermon is not simply to describe what is the case, but to encourage a person to cultivate love above feasting and to value people more than food. So, what meals will we host? Will we be loving? Will we value loving relationships above glamorous hospitality? The moral pathway to walk in chapters 1–9 underscores that the individual proverbs do more than merely describe.

Kaiser, on the other hand, rightly sees the proverbs as espousing morality and ethics, representing in proverbial form what has been announced in the laws of the Torah.[32] So it is right and essential for the preacher to expose the moral guidance of the proverbs.

Many proverbs clearly urge moral application, encouraging the reader to be wise by not being lazy and being careful in speech, for example. Proverbs 10:4, "diligent hands bring wealth," is not merely an observation of what is often the case but is a commendation and encouragement to be diligent. "The Lord detests the sacrifice of the wicked . . ." (15:18) is not information about God's likes and dislikes but is prodding the hearer to act

---

28. Duguid, "Preaching Christ," 184, makes the same point for Proverbs 6:6–11; 26:13–16.
29. Longman, "Preaching Wisdom," 105.
30. Long, *Preaching*, 56.
31. Long, *Preaching*, 56.
32. Kaiser, *Preaching and Teaching*, 85.

wisely by not thinking that religious piety can cover wickedness. Proverbs 14:21, "happy are those who are kind to the poor," is clearly urging the reader to be kind to the poor.

The comparative proverbs, structured as "better than . . ." are also clear enough in urging wise character and behavior. So 28:6, "Better to be poor and walk in integrity than to be crooked in one's ways even though rich," is clearly enjoining integrity. Proverbs 30:33 compares churning milk and twisting the nose to stirring up anger. The first produces butter, the second blood, and anger produces strife. We can note the striking similes and the vivid pictures, but the point of the proverb is neither humor nor ordering things. It is not something to learn, but rather something to apply. We are being nudged not to stir up anger for anger once stirred leads to strife.

Some commentators suggest that certain proverbs are even immoral.[33] However such an assessment fails to grasp both the nature of observation about a fallen world (this is what the world is like) and the subtlety of the moral guidance in Proverbs. For example, Achtemeier suggests 14:20 is immoral, "the poor are disliked even by their neighbors, but the rich have many friends."[34] However she fails, firstly, to note the next verse, that those who despise their neighbors are sinners. Secondly, even by itself, 14:20 is not commending wealth or befriending the wealthy. In our society we can observe celebrity weddings with lengthy guest lists of friends. But the shallowness of befriending wealth and the wrongness of disliking the poor in light of the Mosaic law, for example Deuteronomy 15:1–11, shows the gentle way Proverbs probes and exposes what wise people need to do.

Similarly, 10:15, "A rich man's wealth is his strong city; the poverty of the poor is their ruin," is not immoral, commending wealth. While it is an observation of what is often the case, it is also subtly a rejection of this status quo. Far from being immoral, the proverb gently provokes moral guidance to love the poor and not be drawn to wealth.

For every proverb, the preacher needs to find what is being commended in the proverb, and not simply what is being observed.

Limitations of a Proverb

Most commentators note that proverbs are not always true.[35] They might be the norm, but there will always be exceptions. So, the wise person will

---

33. For example, 14:20; 17:8; 11:16, 22; 18:16; 25:20.

34. Achtemeier, *Preaching*, 171, though admittedly she later, 172, explores this proverb in a wider setting.

35. Hildebrandt, "Proverb," 246–48.

know that while the fear of the Lord adds years to life (9:11), many faithful people die young or are martyred.[36]

Long says, "A proverb is larger than one case, but not large enough to embrace all cases."[37] Similarly Stuart, "The briefer a statement is, the less likely it is to be totally precise and universally applicable."[38] Gowan says proverbs contain "fragments of truth."[39] Therefore, when preaching, we must guard against implying a universal truth. The preacher needs to be aware that though there are normal patterns, this world is full of exceptions, and so proverbs are not making iron-clad guarantees or promises.[40]

Wilson suggests a "sometimes but not always" approach to proverbs, exposing its limitations and balancing one proverb with others.[41] Proverbs 26:4–5 makes that clear in juxtaposing proverbs about answering a fool and not answering a fool. There is a time for one, and a time for the other, and the wise person knows the difference. McKenzie calls this approach "duelling proverbs," placing contrasting proverbs alongside each other.[42]

While diligent hands might often bring wealth (10:4), a sermon might tease out exceptions. The preacher can use narratives of long experience to explore the exceptions also, and thus how to apply the proverb. Give examples of a lazy wealthy person, for example, maybe one whose wealth was inherited or won in gambling. Give examples of a diligent poor person. Then play around with the value of diligence regardless of the outcome.

Scholars often speak of Proverbs as promoting order in the world, which Ecclesiastes and Job correct. That misunderstands proverbs and the limitation on any proverb. A wise person would not follow such scholars. Proverbs often need prodding, to expose the exceptions and thus to gather the kernel of moral guidance lying underneath.

The Context of Proverbs 1–9

Proverbs 19–29 needs to be read in the context of the themes and thrust of Proverbs 1–9, often called the gateway to the rest of the book. This point

---

36. Arthurs, *Preaching with Variety*, 136.
37. Long, *Preaching*, 55.
38. Fee and Stuart, *How to Read*, 196.
39. Gowan, *Reclaiming the Old Testament*, 103.
40. Arthurs, *Preaching with Variety*, 141.
41. Wilson, *Proverbs*, 50. See McKenzie, *Preaching Proverbs*, 113–19, for an example of this based on Proverbs 15:1.
42. McKenzie, *Preaching Proverbs*, 127, gives examples of verses in Proverbs in this category but her example sermon is from Matthew's Gospel.

is frequently made so we will be brief here.[43] Fear of the Lord is the theme that bookends chapters 1–9 (1:7; 9:10). Long says, "To listen to a proverb without at the same time hearing its covenantal background is to pry a gem from its setting."[44] The wisdom espoused in chapters 10–29 must be preached in the covenantal context of fearing the Lord and following the right moral pathway, and thus preachers must avoid preaching selfishness, humanism or materialism.[45]

One point worth noting for preachers is that a key aspect of the context of Proverbs 1–9 is that a father or mother or teacher is instructing their child (see 1:8; 2:1; 3:1; 4:1; 22:17; 31:1–3, etc). Even though a son is the focus in chapters 1–9, as Longman notes, Proverbs is for any young person (1:2–7), male or female, and indeed is also for the wise (1:5).[46] Indeed, Woman Wisdom shows that we ought not read Proverbs only through the lens of father/son or male teachers. The parents and teachers are teaching their children godly wisdom by learning from life. Hildebrandt says, key contexts for proverbs in the ANE included family and schools.[47] Both those settings can be very helpful in considering how to preach Proverbs. How can a preacher of proverbs reflect the style of a parent or teacher or sage?

Preaching Like a Sage

Given the reflective and observant nature of the proverbs, in contrast to the laws, how they are preached ought to reflect their style.

Proverbs admonishes and encourages through the back door, as Arthurs puts it, calling us to observe, think, and then act.[48] Eswine suggests the preacher invites the congregation to go outside, with Bible, notebook, and pen, and watch the ants, and discuss it the following Sunday.[49]

Arthurs uses the example of Proverbs 18:21, "The tongue has the power of life and death, and those who love it will eat its fruit." He comments that the sage has seen parents criticize children who are then alienated, has watched the coach belittle her team and seen the players give up in response, and has heard the boss yell at employees with a consequential

43. Wilson, *Proverbs*, 45.
44. Long, *Preaching*, 59.
45. Arthurs, *Preaching with Variety*, 141–42.
46. Longman, "Preaching Wisdom," 104.
47. Hildebrandt, "Proverb," 237–38.
48. Arthurs, *Preaching with Variety*, 135–36.
49. Eswine, *Preaching*, 144.

rise in sick days.[50] Such narratives in a sermon reflect a back door towards learning the lesson of the proverb.

Longman suggests that the preacher can take the role of the parent father to the congregation as the child, though he doesn't elaborate on this.[51] Or the sermon could take the voice of the parent/teacher and give a proverb to the child. Arthurs commends this approach, asking how a preacher can reproduce the pedagogical tone and attitude. The answer is not to be authoritarian but to encourage listeners to ponder and draw conclusions for themselves. In other words, to preach like a sage.[52] How can we do that?

Much ancient wisdom, and indeed in many communities today, wisdom is taught informally, by the watercooler, around a campfire, in casual conversations, amid everyday life. How can such informal settings and styles be embraced in a more formal sermon?

Let me suggest a couple of ways that this can be expanded, deductively or inductively. Deductively, beginning with the proverb, consider using an imaginary dialogue in a sermon along these lines. The preacher takes the stance of a parent addressing the child.

> Parent: My child, "the poor are disliked even by their neighbors but the rich have many friends" (14:20). At school today I want you to think about the wisdom of this proverb.
>
> Sermon cuts to the end of the day.
>
> Parent: So, my child, what do you see at school?
>
> Child: Mum, I realized that Sarah has lots of friends and she is rich but Freddy doesn't have much lunch. I think he is poor. That might be why he doesn't have lots of friends. He cannot invite them to his home perhaps because he is embarrassed.

Or this can be done inductively, making observations and leading to the proverb.

> Parent: Child, which people in class have the most friends?
>
> Child: Dad, Sarah has the most.
>
> Parent: Why do think that is?
>
> Child: She has the best clothes and toys so it feels good to be with her.

---

50. Arthurs, *Preaching with Variety*, 136.
51. Longman, "Preaching Wisdom," 105.
52. Arthurs, *Preaching with Variety*, 147.

> Parent: Who in your class does not have friends?
>
> Child: Freddy doesn't.
>
> Parent: Why is that? Is that a good thing? How do you think Freddy feels?
>
> Child: I think it is not nice for Freddy.
>
> Parent: What sort of person makes the best friend?

Probing and teasing at the proverbs in a sermon conveys the same style that the collection carries. Then read the proverb and explain its purpose.

Since proverbs do more than make observations, this is where the moral nudges need to be teased out.

> Parent: So, my child, what did you do when you thought about Freddy?
>
> Child: I shared my lunch with him. Mum, can Freddy come over after school to play?

Or, on 10:4:

> Parent: Son, who gets the best grades in your class?
>
> Child: Stephen does.
>
> Parent: Does he study hard?
>
> Child: Yes, he's always studying.
>
> Parent: So, son, this proverb encourages us to be diligent.

The imaginary dialogue should also consider the exceptions to the rule too.

> Child: But Mum, what about Julie? She's lazy but brilliant. She doesn't need to study.
>
> Parent: So, what about you, my daughter? Do you need to study hard?
>
> Child: Yes, Mum, I should do more.
>
> Parent: Julie might be an exception. But God sees us as wise when we are diligent.

Several proverbs are comparisons: better is this than that. The preacher could frame this as a question to the congregation, or to the hypothetical child in your sermon.

Parent: My child, what do you think is better, this or that? Why?

In order to avoid the application being limited to children, the so-called parent in the sermon could then add their own experiences. I suggest you can imagine your sermon as a family discussion over the dinner table one night, each person contributing with both examples, exceptions to the rule, and applying the lessons.

Parent 1: Have you seen how often the guests at a famous person's wedding or party are always rich?

Child: Why don't we invite Freddy's family for a meal?

Parent 2: I should work harder in my job.

Parent 1: At work I see everyone wants to get to know the boss.

Humor and Style

What is important in the examples above is that preaching proverbs ought to reflect the style and genre of proverbs. Such preaching will be observational, helping the congregation to observe, ponder, reflect, and think about the world around them. It will also be suggestive, nuanced, encouraging pondering and nudging thought, and not simply commanding obedience.[53]

Estes suggests proverbs guide by indirection rather than authoritative commands. Poetic language recreates experience, and that such compressed language invites pondering and meditation. Proverbs challenge the listener to infer the principle which they teach and thus the listener is drawn in to be an active listener, participating in the learning process.[54] How does a preacher convey and create that?

Proverbs uses humor to startle and make the hearer think. Expose the humor of proverbs when you preach for the same purposes. Whether it is a dog returning to its vomit (26:11), a lazy person afraid of lions (26:13), sluggards too lazy to withdraw their hands from the dish (26:14–15), or even a gentle tongue breaking a bone (25:15), let the humor cause people to think and ponder. A sermon could ask rhetorically, what is the laziest thing you can imagine? Offer some suggestions. Then come to 26:14–15 and allows its humor and absurdity to hit home.

---

53. For other suggestions for how a preacher might reflect wisdom in their sermon preparation and preaching style, see Eswine, *Preaching*, 154–62, which goes beyond preaching Proverbs itself.

54. Estes, *Hear, My Son*, 102–3.

Similarly, don't water down the strong and evocative language of some proverbs. The path of the lazy is not just thorny but "overgrown with thorns" (15:19). The Lord is not just opposed to the proud but "tears down the house of the proud" (15:25).

Several similes and comparisons in Proverbs make us sit up and take notice by their striking associations. "Like a gold ring in a pig's snout is a beautiful woman without good sense" (11:22) is hilarious and shocking. So too is the comparison of a lazy guy with "vinegar to the teeth" (10:26). A door turning on its hinges is a striking image of a lazy person turning on their bed (26:14). Is it really better to live in a desert land than with a contentious and fretful wife (21:19)? Imagine how heartbreaking it is to be the partner of a thief (29:24).[55] A sermon could encourage people to think of the most striking comparison to drive home the point.

Preaching Consecutive Proverbs

Having addressed key points in preaching proverbs in general, we return to our opening question about consecutive unrelated proverbs. Where there is no obvious connection between consecutive proverbs, how can they be preached together? What is the added benefit for preaching consecutive proverbs?

We can preach consecutive proverbs, even if they seem, and are, disconnected, because they add to a larger composite picture, not of a topic, but of a wise life with a godly worldview. Stuart says, "the more in isolation one reads a proverb, the less clear its interpretation may be."[56] Proverbs is not teaching wisdom in regard to a list of topics. It is teaching wisdom as a whole for a whole world.

As an example, Goldsworthy uses 10:1–32, using the theme of a contrast between wicked and righteous behavior and sees a "cumulative effect to this chapter." "(B)ecause wisdom involves perception in the whole order of creation, righteousness is seen to be far more than ethical conformity. It encompasses a person's relationship to God, to people, and to the world of nature."[57] He gives no practical guidance for preaching, but his point about the breadth of worldview of wisdom and the cumulative effect of dealing with several proverbs is important. Bartholomew suggests an overall progression in Proverbs, from moral guidance for the young with basic rules in chapters 10–15 progressing to more and more complex

55. The list goes on. See also, 19:24; 25:18–19; 26:13, 15; 27:14.
56. Fee and Stuart, *How to Read*, 200.
57. Goldsworthy, *Preaching the Whole Bible*, 189–90.

issues and exceptions to the basic rules in chapters 16–22. He calls this "developmental pedagogy."[58]

Hildebrandt comments that "if one is going to approximate the complexities of real life, all the proverbs must be taken together as a canonical whole. A single proverbial sentence is not meant to be taken as a comprehensive statement of life." This both limits the temptation to take an individual proverb as a universal truth but also points the preacher to preach on a range of proverbs.

A preacher could extend the suggested dialogue above of a parent and child by imagining a similar discussion for the hypothetical next day, a new proverb for the child to consider or new reflections leading to the next proverb. The sermon could be like a week in the life of a family, each day a different proverb and issue. Each imaginary day the parent invites the child, or even each family member, to a proverb a day.

Because each proverb takes some time to explore and probe, I suspect it would be hard to preach a full chapter. Five to seven verses might be sufficient, one for each hypothetical day of the working week or week, though see Bartholomew's sensible caution against a proverb a day.[59] Nonetheless, five to seven verses would then be sufficient to make the point that anything and everything needs to be considered and pondered in order to bring our worldview and all areas of our lives under the fear of the Lord.

Proverbs is encouraging the hearer to take every thought captive to the Lord in fearing him. It is encouraging the whole of life to be drawn into walking in wise ways. So-called disconnected proverbs help expand our perception to see God's wisdom everywhere. It doesn't matter that the proverbs address seemingly unrelated topics. We are training people to reflect on all of life. We ought not be afraid of preaching consecutive though disconnected proverbs.

The conclusion for such a sermon could be along these lines. The parent may invite the child to recap on the proverbs of each day of the week. The child could recite them with a concluding comment:

> Child: Mum and Dad, everything in my life is worth thinking about because God is over everything. I realize if I fear the Lord, it will affect my view on friends, hard work, and . . . the preacher can list the issues that the proverbs in the sermon have touched on. Mum and Dad, there is so much to think about if I am to be wise in God's eyes.

---

58. Bartholomew, *Reading Proverbs with Integrity*, 13.
59. Bartholomew, *Reading Proverbs with Integrity*, 5.

Bibliography

Achtemeier, Elizabeth. *Preaching from the Old Testament.* Louisville: Westminster John Knox, 1989.

Arthurs, Jeffrey D. *Preaching with Variety: How to Recreate the Dynamics of Biblical Genres.* Grand Rapids: Kregel, 2007.

Bartholomew, C. G. *Reading Proverbs with Integrity.* Grove Biblical 22. Cambridge UK: Grove, 2001.

Bland, Dave. "A New Proposal for Preaching from Proverbs." https://www.preaching.com/articles/a-new-proposal-for-preaching-from-proverbs/.

Bullock, C. Hassell. "Preaching in the Poetic Literature." In *Handbook of Contemporary Preaching*, edited by Michael Duduit, 293–305. Nashville: Broadman & Holman, 1992.

Doriani, Daniel. "How to Preach Proverbs." https://www.thegospelcoalition.org/article/how-do-i-preach-expository-sermons-from-proverbs/.

Duguid, Iain. "Preaching Christ from Proverbs." *Unio Cum Christo* 5, no. 1 (2019) 173–89.

Estes, Daniel J. *Hear, My Son: Teaching and Learning in Proverbs 1–9.* NSBT. Leicester, UK: Apollos, 1997.

Eswine, Zack. *Preaching to a Post-Everything World: Crafting Biblical Sermons that Connect with our Culture.* Grand Rapids: Baker, 2008.

Fee, Gordon D., and Stuart, Douglas. *How to Read the Bible for All its Worth.* London: Scripture Union, 1982.

Garrett, Duane A. "Preaching from the Psalms and Proverbs." In *Preaching the Old Testament*, edited by Scott M. Gibson, 101–14. Grand Rapids: Baker, 2006.

Goldsworthy, Graeme. *Preaching the Whole Bible as Christian Scripture.* Grand Rapids: Eerdmans, 2000.

Gowan, Donald E. *Reclaiming the Old Testament for the Christian Pulpit.* Edinburgh: T. & T. Clark, 1980.

Heim, Knut. *Like Grapes of Gold Set in Silver: An Interpretation of Proverbial Clusters in Proverbs 10:1—22:16.* Berlin: de Gruyter, 2001.

Hildebrandt, Ted A. "Proverb." In *Cracking Old Testament Codes*, edited by D. Brent Sandy and Ronald L. Giese, 233–54. Nashville: B&H Academic, 1995.

Kaiser, Walter C. *Preaching and Teaching from the Old Testament.* Grand Rapids: Baker, 2003.

———. *Towards an Exegetical Theology: Biblical Exegesis for Preaching and Teaching.* Grand Rapids: Baker, 1981.

Kidner, F. Derek. *Proverbs.* TOTC. Leicester, UK: IVP, 1964.

Long, Thomas G. *Preaching and the Literary Forms of the Bible.* Philadelphia: Fortress, 1989.

Longman, Tremper, III. "Preaching Wisdom." In *"He Began with Moses": Preaching the Old Testament Today*, edited by Grenville J. R. Kent, Paul J. Kissling, and Laurence A. Turner, 102–21. IVP, 2010.

McKenzie, Alyce M. *Preaching Proverbs: Wisdom for the Pulpit.* Louisville: Westminster John Knox, 1996.

Ryken, Leland. *How to Read the Bible as Literature.* Grand Rapids: Zondervan, 1984.

Waltke, Bruce K. "Fundamentals for Preaching the Book of Proverbs." *BSac* 165, nos. 3–12 (October–December 2008) 131–44, 259–67, 387–96.

Wilson, Lindsay. *Proverbs.* TOTC. Downers Grove, IL: IVP, 2017.

Wright, Christopher J. H. *Sweeter than Honey: Preaching the Old Testament.* Carlisle, UK: Langham Preaching Resources, 2015.

13

Honoring a Wise Tanzanian Woman
Ufoo Kassa George's Biblia Na Utajiri *(The Bible and Wealth)*

TAMIE DAVIS

THE YEAR WAS 2014 and I was sitting in a classroom in Dodoma, Tanzania with about twenty university students. It was an extracurricular seminar called "Binti Sayuni" (daughters of Zion) and a friend of mine, banker and Master of Business student Lizzy Msechu was teaching the assembled women. She wrote this equation on the board:

> Word of God + prayer + hard work = success

I waited to hear what she was going to say. The use of the equation was intriguing to me: was she suggesting a formula which guaranteed success? On what terms was this success available? Though the equation was written in English, her explanation was in Swahili.[1]

As she proceeded, the equation started to sound different to me. She took each part in turn, beginning by asking how you could expect success if you do not live in accordance with God's word, that is, to love God and to love others. Then she argued that prayer is necessary if you are to achieve success, because no one can succeed without God. However, to think that you would only need these two things would be foolishness. You must also

---

1. This kind of language switching is common among tertiary educated Tanzanians.

exert yourself. These points were peppered with examples from her own life. As I listened to her, I began to understand that she was providing the essential components that lead to success, that is, she was explaining how the world is set up. This was more descriptive than prescriptive.

Lizzy did not quote from Proverbs 21:21, but the parallels were striking to me:

> Whoever pursues righteousness and kindness
> will find life and honor.[2]

She was not exegeting Proverbs, but there were clear resonances with it both in content and methodology. It occurred to me that as I listened to Lizzy, I was listening to teaching like the Bible's wisdom tradition. Like Proverbs, Lizzy was drawing on day-to-day living to explain how to live well in God's world.

The Invitation of Proverbs to Wisdom Today

In terms of content, the book of Proverbs has been called "the classic expression of wisdom literature in the Old Testament,"[3] and is concerned with the general order of life. Unlike Ecclesiastes and Job, it does not interrogate "life situations that are unexpected, inexplicable or seemingly unconnected to human choice."[4] Lindsay Wilson summarizes the theological propositions of Proverbs 10–20 in this way:

1. That this is an orderly world, ruled by Yahweh, its wise Creator
2. That knowledge of this order is possible to the people who open themselves to wisdom
3. That the wise who thus align themselves with God's order will experience good things, while the fools will suffer their folly.[5]

He argues that "the whole of the book of Proverbs could be covered by the heading 'the good life.'"[6] This was precisely the goal of Lizzy's teaching too. Though "success" may not sound holistic to Western ears, the Swahili word was *mafanikio*, which does have holistic connotations.

---

2. English Bible references are from the NRSV.
3. Grillo, "Wisdom Literature," 185.
4. Hayes, *Proverbs*, 11.
5. Wilson, *Proverbs*, 18.
6. Wilson, *Proverbs*, 39.

In terms of methodology, it is well established that the book of Proverbs draws on source material from the world around and even other cultures.[7] Ernest C. Lucas identifies four sources of wisdom in Proverbs: observation and experience, instruction based upon tradition, learning from mistakes, and revelation.[8] Though the first three may go awry if not constrained by the fourth, they are nevertheless dignified by Proverbs as a fruitful source for understanding God's world. Thus, the instruction of Amenemope is not rejected by the sages of Proverbs, and otherwise secular proverbs are understood in the context of Yahwistic theology.[9] While in Christian theology the book of Proverbs comes to us as revelation, Hayes insists that reflection on one's own world is the invitation of that revelation:

> the sayings, instructions, and poems of Proverbs invite us to become students or disciples of wisdom, striving continually to comprehend what it means to be wise in our own time and place and as our circumstances change.[10]

Thus, in writing about the role of the various biblical genres for priestly formation, Andrew D. Mayes casually remarks, "the Wisdom literature invites us to make sense of today's confusions by pondering anew the meaning of a life well lived, with the providence of God."[11] Lizzy's own reflection on the world, her use of experience, reason, and common sense are not at odds with revelation any more than the book of Proverbs is.

Teaching about "the good life" and how to get it is a common feature of the Tanzanian Christian landscape, especially among the middle class and university educated.[12] Lizzy is not unusual, either in her teaching about the good life or the overlap with the Bible's wisdom tradition. I propose here to give a reading of the book *Biblia Na Utajiri* (The Bible and Wealth[13]) by Ufoo Kassa George as a way of interrogating and illustrating this argument. I will summarize the book's chapters and aims, then examine its wisdom sources, use of wisdom literature, and wisdom features.

---

7. Longman, "Proverbs," 545–47.
8. Lucas, *Proverbs*, 63.
9. Garret, "Proverbs," 566–78. See also Wilson, *Proverbs*, 17–18.
10. Hayes, *Proverbs*, 13.
11. Mayes, "Priestly Formation," 32.2013

12. Being middle class or university educated does not necessarily equate with wealth. Life is precarious even for this demographic and the temptation to despair is present. Teaching about the good life provides impetus to continue striving. Sharing of knowledge about the good life and how to attain it is an act of generosity.

13. All translations are mine.

Finally, I will anticipate a possible objection to viewing this book as a wisdom text and discuss its merits.

Content, Aims, and Audience of *Biblia Na Utajiri*

I first met Ufoo Kassa George in 2017 in Dar Es Salaam at a business forum for Associates of Tanzania Fellowship of Evangelical Students.[14] She was selling her book there and I purchased a copy. The contention of *Biblia Na Utajiri* is that "it is possible" (*inawezekana*) to produce wealth, and the central problem for people who experience poverty is a lack of knowledge. However, this book is not a survey of what the Bible says about wealth and how to get it, though it does include some content of this nature. Instead, the knowledge it supplies is about how the world is set up, and how the reader can operate well within it. There are four sections.[15] Chapter 1, "You have the ability to change your life," argues that actions are key in the production of wealth. Chapter 2, "What requires you to be wealthy?" asks what your motivation is and whether it is strong enough to sustain you through struggle. Chapter 3, "The opportunities to be wealthy are many," contends that it is untrue that there is not enough wealth to go around, because God created the world in abundance, and if you know him you will have access to this abundance. Finally, chapter 4, "Focus," is a reflection on the power of concentrating on one thing, either for good or ill.

Biblia Na Utajiri was written to combat several myths and malpractices around wealth. These include:

- That it is fine to pursue wealth at the expense of righteousness
- That you do not need to toil and should just wait for God to make you wealthy
- That it is impossible both to be wealthy and to care for those for whom you are responsible
- That getting rich happens by luck

---

14. Ufoo is pronounced oo-FOH. I will refer to her in the body of this essay by her first name Ufoo though I will follow convention for the footnotes and use George. Naming in Tanzania is more fluid than in many Western contexts. Surnames are not a common way to refer to women since women often have several which they interchange, including their husband's or father's first name. However, first names are a fairly standard way of identifying women, often with an honorific. For example, the late President John Pombe Magufuli was identified as President Magufuli while his successor, President Samia Suluhu Hassan, is most often President Samia.

15. Ufoo's argumentation style is more cyclical than linear, so the themes of the chapters are not as distinct as this outline.

- That only getting into heaven matters, and pursuing wealth is not a worthy Christian pursuit, and
- That the opportunities for wealth creation are few.[16]

Ufoo's audience is those who find themselves in situations that are intolerable (*mazingira magumu yasiyovumilika*) or which cause them to despair (*yanayokatisha tamaa*).[17] Implicit is the background of poverty in Tanzania and the widely held belief that wealth creation is good because it lifts people out of this situation.

Like the book of Proverbs, Ufoo acknowledges the dual nature of wealth: "For you and me to be wealthy is a dangerous thing from one perspective but it is good from another perspective."[18] Wilson says, "In Proverbs wealth is viewed positively, neutrally and negatively, and we must not simply 'cherry-pick' those sayings that suit us."[19] However, this does not mean that all proverbs about wealth are applicable to every situation. Indeed, elsewhere Wilson cautions that discernment is needed to know when to apply certain proverbs.[20] Tanzanian Lechion Peter Kimilike acknowledges that Proverbs' relativizing of wealth is healthy for the Christians in the West, but points out that this same message in Africa could have the effect of upholding the status quo, or implying that poverty is not inimical to human flourishing and in need of being addressed.[21] However, Proverbs' ambivalence to wealth is not extended to ambivalence towards poverty. South African womanist Madipoane Masenya argues that the Old Testament proverbs present poverty as "an affront to human dignity" because it makes the person vulnerable to theft, may result in them attracting hatred or losing friends, forces them to become dependent and shamed perhaps by begging, experience oppression and exploitation as their lot in life, and to hunger.[22] Thus, Kimilike's exhortation for all Christians to play their part in fighting poverty must be heeded.[23] This is a role that Ufoo is playing with her advice about wealth creation in the Tanzanian context. Though the emphasis on becoming wealthy may grate for Westerners who would prefer a more exhaustive treatment of the topic of wealth, it is appropriate for her

---

16. George, *Biblia Na Utajiri*, 23, 39, 41, 47, 48, 60.
17. George, *Biblia Na Utajiri*, iv.
18. George, *Biblia Na Utajiri*, 8.
19. Wilson, *Proverbs*, 26.
20. Wilson, *Proverbs*, 6.
21. Kimilike, *Poverty*, 9.
22. Masenya, "Eating the Louse," 452–59.
23. Kimilike, *Poverty*, 286.

context. Ufoo exhibits discernment in bringing the relevant message to her audience. Meanwhile, Westerners who fail to see the context into which she is teaching, and the need for wealth creation in the service of poverty alleviation would do well to remember Proverbs 21:13:

> If you close your ears to the cry of the poor
>
> You will cry out and not be heard.

Wisdom Sources of *Biblia Na Utajiri*

Nigerian David T. Adamo has noted with approval the move in recent scholarship towards bringing African proverbs into conversation with biblical proverbs in order to shed light on the social context of the latter.[24] In contrast to the earlier approach of scholars like Friedmann H. Golka who argued for a common source of African and biblical proverbs, these scholars argue for a similarity in culture that positions African proverbs and their modern-day users as interpreters of biblical proverbs.[25] However, Ufoo rejects drawing on traditional sources as following after the things of this world. It is repentance from these ways of thinking that are needed, she argues, because it is the Holy Spirit who teaches us and renews our minds.[26] Reflecting on Romans 12:2 she says:

> Many of us do not change our traditions, or we change them a little only and leave other parts. So some of our thoughts are following God but others are following the ways of the world.[27]

> This is dangerous because what is left over squeezes out God's wisdom:

> Other polluting thoughts are strong roots which fill up the spaces that would cause education of Christ or the word of God to miss their space in the traditions and hearts of humans.[28]

Ufoo positions herself not as a member of an African wisdom tradition, but as an inheritor and interpreter of the Bible's wisdom. Though African traditions are not Ufoo's authority, she nevertheless draws on some African proverbs and sayings in the course of her discussion. Several of these are

---

24. Adamo, "Ancient Israelite," 11.

25. Kimilike, "Friedemann W. Golka," 255–61. See, for example, Kimilike, "Poverty Context," 139. Also Masenya, "Eating the Louse," 452.

26. George, *Biblia Na Utajiri*, 14–15.

27. George, *Biblia Na Utajiri*, 19.

28. George, *Biblia Na Utajiri*, 20.

clumped together in the part where she is cautioning that her teachings are not a get rich quick scheme. They include Swahili's most famous proverb: *Haraka haraka haina baraka, polepole ndio mwendo!* (Haste brings no blessing; the best way is slowness.) There is also a Swahili translation of the English proverb, Rome was not built in a day. In this same section she also uses *Mwenda pole hajikwai, akijikwaa haanguki, akianguka haumii, kama akiumia itakuwa kidogo* (the one who goes slowly will not stumble, if they stumble, they will not fall, if they fall they will not be hurt, if they hurt it will be only a little) to reiterate the wisdom of a prudent approach.[29]

For Ufoo, the pursuit of wisdom is the obligation of all disciples (*wanafunzi*) with the Holy Spirit as teacher.[30] Following Jesus must mean reading, knowing, and using the words of the Bible.[31] Thus, she considers it appropriate to draw on the whole Bible in the pursuit of wisdom. This leads her to pull out lessons from Scripture which may be incidental to the narrative or argument in context but teach something about the world. For example, she notes that there is a relationship between bodily and spiritual wellbeing in 1 John 3:2, and that the source of something influences its product from the story of Elisha purifying Jericho's water in 2 Kings 2:19–22.[32] By far the biblical genre Ufoo utilizes most is the Gospels. Of fifty-seven Bible references in the book, eighteen of them come from the Gospels.[33] Drawing on the prologue to John's Gospel and John 8:31–32, she intuits that Jesus Christ is the one in whom knowledge and wisdom are found and this is reflected in her frequent references to Jesus's stories and conduct in the Gospels.[34] Though the wisdom literature is only the third most frequently cited source for Ufoo, passages from the book of Proverbs and the story of Solomon are given the most extensive treatment and appear at key moments in the argument and it is to examining them that I now turn.

Wisdom Literature in *Biblia Na Utajiri*

The first section of the first chapter of *Biblia Na Utajiri* ends with these words:

---

29. George, *Biblia Na Utajiri*, 22.
30. George, *Biblia Na Utajiri*, 13–14.
31. George, *Biblia Na Utajiri*, 21.
32. George, *Biblia Na Utajiri*, 10, 70.
33. The Pentateuch is second, with twelve references, and the wisdom literature and Psalms is third with seven references.
34. George, *Biblia Na Utajiri*, 17, 21.

I am full of the hope, faith and love of God for a new way, as I believe it will be for you too, if you are ready to be a person of understanding. As it says in the word of God in Proverbs 4:7b: Though it cost all you have, get wisdom.[35]

The conclusion to the second chapter is Solomon's dream from 1 Kings 3:14–15 in which he is invited to ask for anything and asks for wisdom. Everything between these two references circles around this theme of getting wisdom. Proverbs 1:24–33 is quoted in full as a warning to illustrate that merely waiting for God without seeking knowledge is despising God's wisdom,[36] and Ufoo renders Proverbs 3:13–18 into a striking first-person prayer as an example of how to claim wisdom and its benefits.

She prays, "Blessed am I who have wisdom and understanding," whose income is better than money, who has profit more than pure silver, who has a greater value than anything that can compare, who holds many days in her right hand and wealth and honor in her left, who has beautiful paths of peace, who is a tree of life for those who grasp her, etc.[37] While many English translations make a switch in subject between 3:13 and 3:14 to differentiate between the one who seeks wisdom and the personification of wisdom, in the most common Swahili Bible translation, the Swahili Union Version, the subjects are ambiguous. The most natural reading in the Swahili version is that the joyful one who finds wisdom in 3:13 is the same as the one who is described in the ensuing verses. While biblical scholars may cringe at a perceived inaccuracy of translation, the theology of Proverbs in which "the wise who align themselves with God's order will experience good things," ought to temper their criticism of Ufoo's interpretation.[38]

Having established the importance of seeking wisdom, Ufoo moves on to sharing wisdom in the following two chapters and it is in here that the final reference to Proverbs appears, Proverbs 16:1, "The plans of the heart are human, but the answer of the tongue comes from the Lord," as a warning to bring your plans into line with God's word.[39] This comes at the end of an extended section giving examples of people whose plans were not in line with God's, such as Adam and Eve disregarding God's instruction not to eat from the tree in the garden, Ananias and Sapphira, and the people of Israel who trusted their own assessment rather than going into the land of Canaan. Ufoo concludes by emphasizing the character of the

---

35. George, *Biblia Na Utajiri*, 4.
36. George, *Biblia Na Utajiri*, 39.
37. George, *Biblia Na Utajiri*, 4.
38. Wilson, *Proverbs*, 18.
39. George, *Biblia Na Utajiri*, 74.

wise person: "If you have no trickery, haste and evil desire, God is there close to you, ready to help you to understand and receive his word in your heart, in order to fulfil his will."[40]

Wisdom Features of *Biblia Na Utajiri*

I have argued that Ufoo positions herself as an inheritor of the Bible's wisdom tradition and that she uses its wisdom literature at key points in her argument. It is worth noting that the overarching theme of Proverbs, that of "God's active kingly rule in everyday life,"[41] is also present in *Biblia Na Utajiri*. As we have seen, Ufoo's audience are people who are struggling to live well in the everyday, and it is for them that she has written. She explicitly addresses the idea that everyday things are of little value:

> All my efforts were just to fix hunger, as the days went on. The thing which remained was to wait for wealth which I would find in heaven which the Lord Jesus had prepared for me. Surely my view was: let me not miss out on heaven. Life here on earth of barely satisfying hunger is enough. Entering heaven was everything for me. In my view, I was seeing life like this: eating the little you have is normal life, then you enter heaven.[42]

While she used to hold this view, she now rejects it on the grounds of God's active kingly rule. After all, God's will is to be done on earth as well as in heaven. One of Ufoo's favourite ways of referring to God is as the "God who created heaven and earth": he who is described by Jesus in many parables as kind, wealthy, and having many possessions is the same who has given his wisdom to his children to study that they might live well in his world.[43] She cautions against those who claim they can give or take what is God's, for example, those who specify large offerings (*masharti ya kutoa sadaka*).[44] God is not miserly (*choyo*), she insists, and the beginning of understanding wealth in his world is to fear the Lord (*wanaomcha Mungu*) and to know him.[45] In fact, it is because God is the Creator that opportunities to become wealthy exist. God is a God of abundance and so his world is created with opportunities for abundance for those who know him. To

---

40. George, *Biblia Na Utajiri*, 74.
41. Wilson, *Proverbs*, 23.
42. George, *Biblia Na Utajiri*, 48.
43. George, *Biblia Na Utajiri*, 3, 5, 13, 46.
44. George, *Biblia Na Utajiri*, 11.
45. George, *Biblia Na Utajiri*, 3.

illustrate this abundance Ufoo uses the image of how big the earth is, and how large the ocean, saying of Malachi 3:10:

> This is the measure of God, even for you and for me. Opportunities are there eternally, to overflowing.[46]

Accessing this abundance is twofold. First, there is acquiring knowledge about God's world. Second, there is tithing to God and claiming from him. While the first of these is very much in line with the theology of Proverbs, the second is more problematic, and so it is to this complication of viewing Ufoo's teaching as in line with the Bible's wisdom tradition that I now turn.

Claiming from God in *Biblia Na Utajiri*

In the third chapter, about the many opportunities to become wealthy, Ufoo argues that God has promised to pour out more blessings than you have space for if you bring the tithe, that is, 10 percent of your income.[47] She presents this as something of a formula: "God promised that if you do A, he will do B."[48] She argues that the person who brings their tithe has a right to claim this abundance from God, using causative forms of Swahili like *kulazimisha* (to force someone to do something).[49] The idea of forcing God to do something may at first seem to contradict the idea of God's active kingly rule: who are humans to make demands on God? However, in Tanzania's patronage context, it is not only those who are subordinate in a hierarchy who have obligations. On the contrary, having others claim from you is a sign of your higher status; a person makes no claim on those who do not have. When you make a claim on someone, it is a recognition of their abundance and jurisdiction. This is why it is pointless to try to claim from Satan: this is not his world. Ufoo asks, "How can it be that a person can provide wealth if they have none?"[50] In a Tanzanian context, claiming from God may in fact be a recognition of his kingship rather than a mockery of it.

Nevertheless, the issue of the formulaic nature of her claim remains. While in this section she does not quote any proverbs to argue for a guarantee of blessings from God, the strength with which she argues for assurance of wealth does contradict the theology of Proverbs which offers a picture of

---

46. George, *Biblia Na Utajiri*, 52.
47. George, *Biblia Na Utajiri*, 53–54.
48. George, *Biblia Na Utajiri*, 54.
49. George, *Biblia Na Utajiri*, 54.
50. George, *Biblia Na Utajiri*, 5.

an ordered world rather than a guarantee of wealth. Scholars of the Proverbs are at pains to emphasize that its wisdom is not formulaic and must not be read as such.[51] In the light of this, Ufoo's formula is problematic and may at first evoke concerns about "Name it and claim it" theology. However, four factors are crucial in order to understand the nature of her claim. They reveal her apparent formula to have a relational context.

First, only those who are in right relationship with God are able to claim from him. Wealth is available through other means such as deception, theft, corruption, etc., but this is ill-gotten wealth which is out of line with God's instructions and these people have no claim on God.[52] They, like the rich young ruler, will find that they cannot be wealthy and enter the kingdom of heaven "without the help of God himself to enable both things."[53] This is only possible for those in right relationship with God, that is, those who allow him to lead, teach, advise, and shape (*amchonge awe mdogo*) them.[54] Only those who continue to seek "a heart of wisdom and knowledge will be able to walk in his ways and care for his directions and commands."[55] While Ufoo views one of those commands as bringing the tithe, this is in the context of a life devoted to being a disciple of Christ and learning to live his way. Thus, while Ufoo brings a formula, its context encourages a righteous life rather than providing an alternative to it.

Second, the timing of the fulfillment of the formula remains undefined and so perseverance is essential. Living in God's way brings opposition from Satan: "He will try to use all his might to stop you from getting everything that has been promised."[56] This is a normal Christian experience, she confirms, "for since the book of Genesis in the Bible we read that various servants of God passed through difficult tests while doing the things they were commanded by God."[57] Therefore, there may be a considerable delay in the fulfillment of this promise. During this time, you have the chance to prove your fealty to God by continuing to grow in wisdom and seeing the world God's way. This way will be hard, she insists: "Let us not give up, even when things look opposite to our expectations . . . it will not be easy."[58] Such perseverance does not preclude continuing to claim vehemently from God.

---

51. Longman, *How to Read Proverbs*, 121; Wilson, *Proverbs*, 18.
52. George, *Biblia Na Utajiri*, 3, 21.
53. George, *Biblia Na Utajiri*, 9.
54. George, *Biblia Na Utajiri*, 9.
55. George, *Biblia Na Utajiri*, 46, 57.
56. George, *Biblia Na Utajiri*, 57.
57. George, *Biblia Na Utajiri*, 57.
58. George, *Biblia Na Utajiri*, 57.

On the contrary, the Christian must not be shy about doing so but must approach God with courage because this shows that they believe he will indeed fulfill his promise.[59] However, this must not tip over into complaining or implying that God's ways are imperfect.[60] While Ufoo affirms that God will indeed bring resolution, no promise is given regarding timing and the exhortation to trust God in the meantime and continue walking in his ways prevents this formula from becoming a shortcut to wealth, a pathway which Ufoo herself deplores.[61]

Third, the goal of the formula on view is providing for others. Ufoo gives extensive treatment to the concern that it is impossible both to be wealthy and to care for those for whom you are responsible. In Tanzanian culture, wealth does not insulate the possessor from having to worry about daily needs;[62] it brings greater obligation to care for others. There may be a temptation to eschew wealth in order to avoid these obligations, or to assume that teaching about pursuing wealth would default to minimizing these obligations. Ufoo is at pains to affirm that relational obligations need not be done away with in order to pursue wealth. On the contrary, these obligations are God-given and to reject or avoid them is to fail to play your part in bringing God's kingdom of earth.[63] Likewise, those who are overwhelmed by the many people relying on them and instead look for wealth and possessions by unrighteous paths have given in to Satan's temptations.[64] The right source to look to for the wealth to fulfill the obligation of providing for those who are dependent on you is God himself. The main example Ufoo gives is the prayer of Jabez from 1 Chronicles 4:9–10. In line with her cultural background, she reads the reference to Jabez being more honored than his relatives as an indication that his family expected him to provide for them. Therefore, his prayer for God to increase his territory is both an example of turning to the right person to fulfill these obligations and a fulfillment of the command of the Lord Jesus to love your neighbor as yourself.[65] The reason the Christian can be confident that God will indeed provide for these obligations is grounded in the character of God. After all, she says, if God is the one who causes the rain to fall on both good and evil people, you can know that he is together with you in wanting good things

---

59. George, *Biblia Na Utajiri*, 55.
60. George, *Biblia Na Utajiri*, 37, 59.
61. George, *Biblia Na Utajiri*, 22.
62. Wilson, *Proverbs*, 21.
63. George, *Biblia Na Utajiri*, 60.
64. George, *Biblia Na Utajiri*, 35.
65. George, *Biblia Na Utajiri*, 35–38.

for humankind.⁶⁶ Indeed, this concern to provide for others, especially the poor, is endorsed by Proverbs, like the rest of the Old Testament.⁶⁷

Finally, Ufoo's insistence that if you tithe God will provide for you in abundance must not be read in purely economic terms. *Biblia Na Utajiri* is the first of a series of three books which provide teaching about the three foundations of life: wealth, health, and relationships.⁶⁸ She uses the illustration of an African charcoal stove (*jiko*) which requires three legs in order to remain upright. All three of these things are required to be brought under the lordship of Christ, for if they are not, inner fulfillment (*utoshelevu wa ndani*) will be elusive and expected happiness blown away on the wind.⁶⁹

Ufoo consistently grounds her teaching about wealth—even the formula discussed here—in a holistic view of the world where there is a relational and ethical context to claiming from God. It ought to be little surprise then that in her teaching about this formula, she references the parable of the persistent widow in Luke 18:1–8, with its patronage connotations and encouragement of persistence and insistence on behalf of the supplicant because God is not insensitive to our pleas like the judge.⁷⁰ Even as she presents this formula, Ufoo maintains theology key to the book of Proverbs, that is, as Wilson puts it, of "treating God as God . . . the only true foundation for knowledge and living wisely . . . a necessary condition for living successfully in God's world."⁷¹

Conclusion

While there are points of disjuncture between *Biblia Na Utajiri* and Proverbs, such as Ufoo's theology of tithing, both call for people to seek God's wisdom that they may live well in his world. This call carries particular weight in Africa. In her paper about Woman Wisdom in Proverbs 9, South African Funlola Olejede says:

> [A] situation in which millions of African children go to bed hungry every night is indefensible. Mother Africa should arise and feed her own children. There is clearly a dearth of wisdom in an environment where poverty is king and wealth is

66. George, *Biblia Na Utajiri*, 42.

67. Wilson, *Proverbs*, 30.

68. The latter two are still forthcoming, but George refers frequently to the other two "legs" in *Biblia Na Utajiri*.

69. George, *Biblia Na Utajiri*, 6.

70. Malina, *Social-Science Commentary*, 298–99.

71. Wilson, *Proverbs*, 22.

concentrated in the hands of a few who are reluctant to share. Africa has enough resources to take care of her own and a holistic dialogue on wisdom must take into account Wisdom's ability to minister to the poor.[72]

She concludes, "Being wise and being female in Africa entails responding positively and urgently to Woman Wisdom's call!"[73] In *Biblia Na Utajiri* Ufoo also diagnoses the lack of wisdom about wealth and affirms that the resources to combat poverty are available. *Biblia Na Utajiri* is her contribution to addressing this, and it is in this sense that she can be seen as an inheritor of and teacher in line with the Bible's wisdom tradition. Like Woman Wisdom, she invites others to come and learn the wisdom that is grounded in the fear of the Lord that they too might experience the good of life lived his way. Some of her teaching may be uncomfortable for Western ears, but it must nevertheless not be mistaken for folly; indeed, she must be honored as wise!

Bibliography

Adamo, David T. "Ancient Israelite and African Proverbs as Advice, Reproach, Warning, Encouragement and Explanation." *HTS Teologiese Studies/Theological Studies* 71, no. 3 (November 16, 2015) 11.
Garret, D. "Proverbs 3: History of Interpretation." In *Dictionary of the Old Testament: Wisdom, Poetry and Writings*, edited by Tremper Longman III and Peter Enns, 566–78. Downers Grove, IL: IVP, 2008.
George, Ufoo Kassa. *Biblia Na Utajiri*. Dar Es Salaam: Self-published, 2016.
Grillo, Jennie. "The Wisdom Literature." In *The Hebrew Bible: A Critical Companion*, edited by John Barton, 182–205. Princeton, NJ: Princeton University Press, 2016.
Hayes, Katherine Murphey. *Proverbs*. Collegeville, MN: Liturgical, 2013.
Kimilike, Lechion Peter. "Friedemann W. Golka and African Proverbs on the Poor." *Zeitschrift Für Die Alttestamentliche Wissenschaft* 114, no. 2 (2002) 255–61.
———. "Poverty Context in Proverbs 31:1–9: A Bena Tanzanian Analysis for Transformational Leadership Training." *Old Testament Essays* 31, no. 1 (2018) 135–63.
———. *Poverty in the Book of Proverbs: An African Transformational Hermeneutic of Proverbs on Poverty*. New York: Peter Lang, 2008.
Longman, Tremper, III. *How to Read Proverbs*. Downers Grove, US: InterVarsity, 2002.
———. "Proverbs 1: Book Of." In *Dictionary of the Old Testament: Wisdom, Poetry and Writings*, edited by Tremper Longman III and Peter Enns, 539–51. Downers Grove, IL: IVP, 2008.
Lucas, Ernest C. *Proverbs*. Grand Rapids: Eerdmans, 2015.

---

72. Olojede, "Being Wise," 472–79.
73. Olojede, "Being Wise," 478.

Malina, Bruce J. *Social-Science Commentary on the Synoptic Gospels*. 2nd ed. Minneapolis: Fortress, 2002.

Masenya, Madipoane J. "Eating the Louse and Its Larva!: The Indignity of Poverty as Embedded within Selected African and Old Testament Proverbs." *Scriptura* 111 (2012) 452–59.

Mayes, Andrew D. "Priestly Formation." In *Developing Faithful Ministers: A Theological and Practical Handbook*, edited by Tim Ling and Lesley Bentley, 29–41. London: SCM, 2013.

Murphy, Roland E. *The Tree of Life: An Exploration of Biblical Wisdom Literature*. 3rd ed. Grand Rapids, MI: Eerdmans, 2002.

Olojede, Funlola. "Being Wise and Being Female in Old Testament and in Africa." *Scriptura* 111 (2012) 472–79.

Wilson, Lindsay. *Proverbs: An Introduction and Commentary*. Downers Grove, IL: IVP, 2017.

14

"I Hear and Forget, I See and Remember, I Do and Understand"

Helping People in Central Asia to Understand and Use the Old Testament

ROBIN PAYNE

MY ASSOCIATION WITH LINDSAY Wilson began with his arrival at Ridley, where we worked as colleagues for several years teaching Old Testament. We have had continued contact over the past thirty years. I have appreciated Lindsay's interest, advice, and generous sharing of resources for teaching in a vastly different context in an interdenominational theological college in Central Asia.

Christianity was brought to Central Asia in the first century and Nestorian missionaries had established a strong church by the end of the fifth century.[1] However, by the fourteenth century, due to various factors, it virtually disappeared.[2] During the period of Russian imperial dominance in the nineteenth century the Russian Orthodox Church was established to meet the needs of Russian immigrants. Evangelical Christianity was brought

---

1. Mambetaliev, След Христа includes a full bibliography of literary and archaeological sources.

2. Factors such as internal church conflicts and persecution by the descendants of the Mongol emperor Amir Temir. See Jenkins, *Lost History* and Mambetaliev, След Христа.

to the region by German Mennonites and Baptists in the late nineteenth century.[3] With the repression of all religion during the time of the Soviet Union the church continued underground in the face of persecution.[4] The fall of the Soviet Union at the end of 1991 created a spiritual and cultural vacuum which led to many people turning from state-imposed atheism to embrace the Christian faith or the traditional Islamic religion.

After the fall of the Soviet Union, thirty years ago, the young evangelical church that emerged after seventy years of atheism now faces the rapid growth of Islam.[5] The church grew rapidly in the early 1990s, though Christians are a still a small minority. The relatively new believers have a background in atheism or shamanism combined with folk Islam. This latter background leads to believers' fear of spirits and understanding of God as harsh and fault finding, leading to difficulty in fully embracing God's love and grace. Frequently young believers will say, in the face of ill-health or some difficulty, that God is punishing them for some reason or another.

The College and Its Students

The college, established in 1996 to provide theological education for church leaders, in a three-year full-time program, has seen over three hundred students graduate. Since 2010 the college has been locally run, with most of the teachers local and teaching part-time. Students comprise women and men, younger and older, with various levels of education and Christian understanding, some having experienced misunderstanding or persecution for their faith. Serving in various ways as leaders in church and society, they wish to understand more of their faith. In 2009 an extension program, with two weeks' face-to-face teaching four times a year over three years was initially developed to provide pastors with a government recognized diploma.[6] Evening classes began in 2014 to accommodate

---

3. See Vyssotskaia, "Central Asia," for a concise summary of the history of Christianity to the present day.

4. Vyssotskaia, "Central Asia."

5. The Russian Orthodox and the Russian (German) Baptist churches continued underground during the persecutions of the Soviet era and re-emerged in the 1990s. Since that time, many churches were formed with new believers from outside the Orthodox and Baptist churches including many from the national Central Asian culture. This chapter refers specifically to the relatively new believers from this background. For a short overview of the present situation in the former Soviet Union, in relation to the publication of the Slavic Bible Commentary see Penner, "Unity in Diversity," 67–80.

6. Because of the threat of extremism and instability in the region, a government recognized diploma is now required for all Muslim and Christian leaders in congregations.

people in full-time employment. Branches now operate in two regional towns. A present challenge is developing online courses. The diploma program is accredited through the Eurasian Association for Accreditation of Theological Education (E-AAA)[7] and the degree program has the status of candidate for accreditation.

Many of the present church leaders grew up in villages where the standard of education was poor. Consequently, reading literature is not a priority, though people gain information from social media and the internet, chiefly through mobile phones, which are universal, even in the poorest villages. Most church leaders have had little opportunity for serious theological and biblical study and acquaintance with helpful theological books. Though many believers know their Bibles well, they tend to read and teach it with little attention to the exegetical and hermeneutical skills used in Western countries. The teachers at the college are also relatively new believers who are eager to learn and develop in both understanding and teaching.[8] With few resources in their own language Christians are dependent on effective biblical teaching to help them to grow and to reach out with confidence to others.

Teaching in This Context

Helping people to learn has some different challenges to those faced in Australia. Central Asians[9] belong to a largely oral, storytelling culture where rote learning is dominant and critical thinking has not been part of their experience.[10] Learning in an Asian context tends to take place not in the abstract but through stories, parables, and songs.[11] People learn better with concrete rather than theoretical ideas. They also like to work together and help each other, being more social than individual in their learning.

Active learning, by including such things as stories, role play, dramatic presentations, drawing, reading in chorus, has proved to be helpful in encouraging a deeper understanding of the Bible and especially of the Old

---

7. See http://e-aaa.org/.

8. For almost sixteen years, until COVID-19, I had the privilege of working with several teachers to teach various subjects, providing material, team teaching, learning from them, and then handing over the subjects for them to teach independently.

9. See https://en.wikipedia.org/wiki/Central_Asia for further information and an extensive bibliography.

10. See Kinnally, "Oral Culture" for a detailed discussion of the way artistic and cultural practices, including songs, poetry, oral history, storytelling, and performance are ways to remember and pass on knowledge, ideas, and values across generations.

11. Gener, "Divine Revelation," 32 quotes Chan, "Evangelical Theology," 228.

Testament. The truth of the saying "I hear and forget, I see and remember, I do and understand" has been important in helping adults in Central Asia to understand, teach, and preach from the Old Testament. These are in fact important principles of adult learning and have been effective in working with students, teachers, and preachers in Central Asia.

Some Principles of Adult Learning[12]

Adult learning theory reminds us that adults learn best by experience. Learning is more effective when it is an active rather than a passive process. Adults learn through doing, so theoretical learning needs to be accompanied by practice. Acceptance of new ideas (head), attitudes (heart), and behaviors (hands) is a whole person process. Learners must believe that what they are learning has practical relevance to them. They must be confident that they are capable of doing certain things and must believe they are appropriate to their situation before they will engage in them.

Although information often creates interest in a subject, it takes more than information to change ideas, attitudes, and behavioral patterns. Real-life situations, accomplishing tasks, and solving real life problems encourage learning. Motivation flows from a belief that what we learn will benefit us personally. Without relevance, apathy follows. The connection between desire for growth and potential results must be clear, personal, and realistic.

The more supportive, accepting, and caring the social environment, the freer a person is to experiment with new behaviors, attitudes, and ideas. It is easier for a person to change ideas, attitudes, and behavioral patterns when he or she feels part of a group. Learning done in the group helps people to be committed and encouraged to change more than when learning alone. A strong "motivational climate" in a group is a powerful influence for learning, change, and action. A "demotivational climate" is a strong force for disinterest, apathy, and resistance to change.

In working with first generation believers from a culture where stories are the main method of learning from youth upwards, methods based on such principles have been effective in helping them to see the big picture of the Old Testament. We have found that active, participatory learning in a supportive social environment has been effective in helping people not only to learn but to change in their understanding and practical use of the Bible. As learners need to appreciate the relevance of a subject to them, it is important for them to see the big picture before they

---

12. These are based on the work of Kurt Lewin, Malcolm Knowles and others, including Knowles, *Informal Adult Education* and *Adult Learner*.

engage in more detailed study. So we have tried to help them see that the Bible as a whole is a coherent story.

The Bible's Big Story[13]

New believers know many of the stories in the Bible, but most of them do not understand the Bible's big picture. People need to see the big picture before they can begin to understand the details, including how the stories that they have heard fit together. Understanding the Bible as a single, unified story has helped people to see where its parts fit in. Symbols showing the story of the Bible as a drama in six acts help people to visualize the story.[14] We have developed a lecture with a PowerPoint presentation with pictures for students to identify which illustrate each of the acts of the drama in symbols as seen below.[15]

Act 1: Creation	Genesis 1–2
Act 2: Fall	Genesis 3–11
Act 3: Promise	Genesis 12–Malachi
Act 4: Gospel	Matthew, Mark, Luke, John
Act 5: Mission	Acts–Revelation
Act 6: New Creation	Revelation 21–22

By the end of this presentation students can draw the diagram and explain each of the acts including where these are found in the Bible. This helps them to see the importance of the Old Testament in the whole Bible story. It is dominated by God's promise to bless the world, spoiled by human rebellion, through the family of Abraham and Sarah. This promise is fulfilled in the life, death, resurrection, and exaltation of Jesus the Messiah. Through this presentation students also begin to understand that we too are part of that story, involved in God's mission, as we wait for its fulfillment in the new creation.

---

13. The idea of the Bible as a drama in several acts has been developed variously by Chris Wright, *Sweeter than Honey*, Bartholomew and Goheen, *Drama of Scripture*, N. T. Wright, *People of God*, and others.

14. Chris Wright, *Sweeter than Honey*, 17–20. This was translated into Russian in 2017 and a translation into the Central Asian language is in progress. Chris, speaking at the IFES World conference in 2019, has now extended the acts in the drama to seven to include final judgment before the new creation. See "Hope." See also *Old Testament*, 5–6.

15. Chris Wright, *Sweeter than Honey*, 18.

Other helpful material which presents the big picture not only of the Bible but of individual books of the Bible is found online at the Bible Project.[16] We are now able to use many of these excellent videos which are available in Russian.[17] We are hoping we might be able to see them in the Central Asian language and local colleagues are trying to work on this. The producers hope that through their videos on the Bible, "By the end of this series, you will be familiar with every part of the Bible and how it uses language to communicate who God is, who we are, and the big, redemptive story that we are all living."[18]

The Old Testament Story

Understanding the Bible as the single story of the fulfillment of God's promise to bless his creation, spoiled by human rebellion, helps people appreciate the importance of the Old Testament in this single story. Once this is understood, the Old Testament story is then filled out in more detail. One teacher has developed a series of cards with pictures representing events and people in the Old Testament story. The cards are given to students to work together to put into order and peg onto a line. Not only do students find this informative and enjoyable, but they also work together and help each other to learn.

Once the order of events in the Old Testament is understood, we follow up by presenting a simple time line showing the key events and people in the Old Testament, with a broken line for the intertestamental period before a line continuing into the New Testament period. Once students have put these events and people in order themselves, they are ready to appreciate seeing them in written diagrammatic form. Just presenting a theoretical chart is not helpful for our people. They need to put things in order in their own experience for the theoretical to make sense.

The same is true for understanding the historical and geographical context of the events of the Old Testament. We have found the best way to do this is using a world map, in which students can identify their country in Central Asia, then showing where the biblical events took place. This helps them to understand that these events actually took place in history, which contrasts to the teaching of the other books of faith known to them. A class set of a simple atlas allows students to see the biblical history for themselves as we show the map of the Middle East, Abraham's journey, the Exodus,

---

16. https://bibleproject.com/.
17. https://bibleproject.com/Russian/.
18. https://bibleproject.com/explore/how-to-read-the-bible/.

settlement in Canaan, the kingdom, the divided kingdom, then the empires of Babylon, Persia, Greece, and Rome.[19]

It is also helpful for students to know how to find their way around the Old Testament, so some time is spent helping students to learn the order of books of the Old Testament. After some rote learning in class, which they are good at, and practice at home, they can then repeat the books in order. They also work in pairs to fit together a puzzle of pieces of paper with the names of the books written them. Then they enjoy a quiz to find verses in their Bibles and read them out.

Some of these things may seem very basic to readers in a Western context but they have proved to be both engaging, enjoyable, and effective in helping people to appreciate the Old Testament, in quite a different context. The Old Testament story belongs to a particular historical and geographical context. The promised blessing has reached believers in Central Asia many centuries later.

We also include some understanding of how the Bible reached them in Central Asia. The gospel was brought to the Slavic peoples in 862 through the missionaries Cyril and Methodius, who developed a form of Cyrillic language, and some sections of the Bible were translated into Old Church Slavonic. Many years later after the founding of the Russian Bible Society in 1813, the Russian Slavic Bible was published in 1876.[20] Other Russian Bible translations have since been published, along with Bibles in the Central Asian languages.

Careful Study of Old Testament Texts

As well as helping students to appreciate the big picture of the Bible and the Old Testament, it is important to help them learn how to understand and interpret the Bible text itself. The emphasis on rote learning results in students being able to repeat many Bible passages. The cultural emphasis on storytelling enables them to rephrase a verse or passage and retell a narrative. However careful study of the text in order to explain its meaning and significance is a new skill for most students to learn.

---

19. Даули, Библейский Атлас.

20. The Russian Bible Society, founded in 1813, began working on a translation of the Bible in 1816. After the difficulties of the communist era the Bible Society was renewed in 1990–1991 and became a member of the United Bible Society in 1995. See https://biblia.ru/.

Understanding Context

Understanding the context is fundamental to this. Using the educational principle of moving from the known to the unknown we read a short passage from a book or poem and ask students if they can explain what it is all about. They soon discover that they can only fully understand this excerpt if they know where it fits in the whole writing. This exercise helps them to appreciate the importance of knowing the literary context to understand a Bible passage fully.

Quoting from an older classical writer helps students to appreciate the need to understand the historical, cultural, and geographical context. We ask such questions as: When or where might this have been written? What might have led to its being written? Who might it have been written for? Why might it have been written? Such questions are designed to help students think about writing in general and then about the biblical writings.

Understanding Genre

It is the same with genre. One teacher with whom I have worked has developed a quiz with excerpts from various kinds of writing such as a letter, a poem, a fairy tale, a history book, and a computer manual. Students quickly identify the kind of writing in each and so begin to understand that there are different types of writing in the Old Testament. This helps them to appreciate how genre affects interpretation and that, for example, metaphorical language is not meant to be taken literally.

Careful Reading

Then we look at a particular passage to read it carefully to understand it. Careful study of the text itself is new to many here. Because people are used to reading a passage and thinking they know it, it has been important to help them to read it slowly and carefully. As well as looking at context, literary genre, and historical and cultural background, we help them to pay attention to repetitions, patterns, meaning of words, connecting words, contrasts, and the like.

Because people like working together and they learn from each other, we do this together to begin with, then give time for students to work individually, and then share the results of their observation. In this way the teacher also learns from students and models the need for humility and continued learning. It is often gratifying to hear students remark that there is far more in the passage than they ever saw with a quick reading, that the passage is much deeper and more meaningful than they thought. This leads to their thinking about what it might mean for us today, which in turn is often more encouraging than they thought, and often leads to praise of God and encouragement in their Christian lives, worthy results of biblical study.[21]

Theory Follows Practical Experience

We then ask students to identify the steps that helped them to find such riches in the passage, which they identify. Once we have worked through these steps of biblical interpretation, we then introduce them to the words "exegesis" and "hermeneutics," terms which mean nothing to them unless they understand their meanings by going through the process. Theory is best appreciated following practical understanding.

The style of teaching is inductive rather than deductive, as the teacher allows students to discover the process for themselves. The teacher then helps students to articulate, and memorize, the steps they need to use when approaching any Bible passage.

As many of our students are church leaders who themselves have had little or no formal theological education, understanding these steps is particularly important for them in their role of teaching others. It is easy for people to interpret a text as being written directly to them today, sometimes resulting in strange interpretations. So it is important to help them distinguish what was meant "then and there" before they interpret what it might mean "here and now."[22] This is particularly important in preaching and we have benefitted greatly from the resources now published by Langham Preaching in the local languages. These are available to students from our preaching classes so they can consolidate and practice what they have learned together.[23] So study of the text is always related to the practical task of preaching and teaching.

---

21. Coming from a different faith background and often also because of childhood experience, many people, including teachers I work with, see God as always demanding and finding fault. It is often harder for them to appreciate God's compassion, love, and encouragement.

22. Fee and Stuart, *How to Read the Bible*.

23. From the Bible passage.

Some Approaches to Studying Old Testament Books

We have used various approaches, based on adult learning, to help students to understand and use the Old Testament. These approaches make use of students' own experience and cultural awareness, their love of storytelling, group recitation and reading, working together in various ways, including in dramatic performances. Providing resources in their own language has been of crucial importance.

Using the Senses, Cultural Awareness

In studying Genesis 1:1—2:3 we use various methods to help students discover important things for themselves, using all their senses as well. For example, noticing the verbal and structural patterns helps them to see it as a kind of song of praise. With the repetition "of every kind" in Genesis 1 we ask students to name as many plants and fruit as they can, savoring their sight, smell, and taste to appreciate the beauty and abundance of God's creation, which leads to praising God our Creator. As we talk about God making the "two great lights" and the "great sea monsters" we ask what people in Central Asia fear or think has power over them and show how this chapter encourages freedom from such fears. With these and other examples, as well as information about other ancient Near Eastern texts and a drawing of the ancient Near Eastern cosmology, we show how Genesis 1 is also a polemic against other worldviews. One year, at the end of the lecture, some students wrote and performed a song based on a deep understanding of the passage. This song is still used by one teacher.

Storytelling

In studying narrative writings, we often give each student a passage to study carefully and then prepare to speak to the class in the role of a particular character. Usually the teacher gives an example of how to do this, with careful reference to the text itself. While imagination is required, it is always constrained by the text itself with emphasis on the points indicated there. This has proved highly effective in an oral, storytelling culture. Students enjoy doing it, sometimes even using dress or props creatively. It is interesting and engaging for all and the text itself provides boundaries for their story. It also allows for both women and men to tell their story, for example, speaking as either Abraham or Hagar in Genesis 16. All that remains for the teacher is to focus on the key important points to consolidate the learning.

We have used this method for several narrative texts, including for the journeys in Exodus and the many characters in the books of Samuel.[24] Students are actively learning as they prepare and speak. They also have experience communicating what they have learned and so learn from each other. Many students have reported going home to tell their families or their home group what they have learned, an important principle in consolidating learning and making it one's own as well as passing it on.

Reading Aloud Together

People are used to reciting material together when at school, so reading together works well in this culture. Reading aloud together is also important for students to get the feel and mood of the text. For example, after studying Exodus 14, we read Exodus 15 together antiphonally. One speaker reads the first section of the verse and the whole class joins in the rest. This is very powerful and helps people to feel the difference poetry gives to the account. It also enables us to talk about the use of parallelism, repetition, and imagery, which is important in studying the psalms and other poetic literature.

Understanding Poetic Imagery and Genre

When studying the book of Psalms students work in pairs on selected psalms to practice identifying parallelism and imagery. Then they share their findings and explain how these contribute to the psalm's effectiveness. To show the difference between poetry and prose we usually hand out copies of Hebrew Bibles from the library so students can see for themselves the difference and the patterns and the use of acrostics in poetry. Most will never have the opportunity to study Hebrew, though one teacher now has a basic understanding of the language.

Before explaining the different genres of the psalms, a teacher usually reads out some verses from songs or poems from the local culture. Students quickly identify the type of poem and the situation where it might be used. We look at several psalms for students to identify what the psalm does for us or what we are doing as we recite them. This process leads to students giving a name to each type before we explain a standard classification of Psalm types.

---

24. Some helpful insights were provided for teachers in Goldingay, *Men Behaving Badly*.

Pairs of students are then given a few clearly identifiable psalms to read and identify what type of psalm it is and how it might be used in worship. Students also work together to identify the psalm types and then share some of their findings with the rest of the class. The same process is used for identifying imagery and parallelism in the psalms. Students writing their own psalm of a particular type and sharing it with the class has been a regular assignment.

Applying Biblical Principles

When studying Old Testament law in the book of Deuteronomy we try to help students understand the principles behind the laws given as a gift of grace to God's people, for their good and the good of society as a whole. After presenting some examples, pairs of students are given laws or groups of laws to think about, for example laws concerning workers, the courts, women, debt or slaves. We ask them to think about questions such as: How does a particular law show what God is like and what is important to God? How might the things God values be embodied in contemporary laws?[25] Selected students then share their findings with the class.

In addition, we ask students to think about such questions as: What was the aim of this law? What kind of situation was it trying to prevent or encourage? Who would have benefited from or been protected by this law? Whose power would have been restrained? What values or principles are behind this law? How are people encouraged to obey it? When some of their findings are shared, students begin to see the importance of the laws for a just and caring society. This leads to a discussion of how the principles contained in the laws could be applied practically today in personal, church, and social life.[26] I remember a particular experience which provided an example to discuss in relation to laws of ownership such as in Deuteronomy 22:1–3. Two students found a mobile phone that someone had lost. One rejoiced that God had given them a phone. The other waited for the owner to call on the phone and was pleased to be able to return it.

Active Learning

Study of the prophets provides an opportunity for students to be actively engaged. They memorably demonstrate the symbolic actions of Ezekiel. Years

---

25. See Chris Wright, *Sweeter than Honey*, 134.
26. Chris Wright, *Sweeter than Honey*, 156.

ago, a student at Ridley with artistic gifts drew a sketch of the chariot throne of Ezekiel 1, suitably hazy and indistinct. A copy of this has been enlightening to generations of Central Asian students, along with some pictures of Babylonian winged creatures. A group dramatic performance showing corruption in the marketplace, well-known in our markets, helps to show the relevance of the book of Amos. Such educational principles of active learning have been effective in this cultural context. Many of the images remain in my mind and hopefully in the minds of students.

Study of the wisdom literature has involved active shared learning. Recalling local proverbs helps students appreciate their universal nature. Students share with the class proverbs on particular topics, showing how they provide wisdom for everyday life. Recognizing students may be single, married, divorced or widowed, we ask them to write down their observations or experience of relationships between women and men and attitudes to each other. After some of these responses are shared, we study the text to discover how the man and the woman speak about and address each other. We find a relationship of equality, mutuality, respect, and love between the man and the woman in the Song of Songs.

Providing Resources

In helping people to understand the Bible it has been important to provide literature resources in their own language so that they can then read and discover things for themselves. Christian literature has mainly been published in Russian and mostly at a popular level. So, translation of suitable theological books into the Central Asian language has been an important task.[27] This has been complicated by the fact that this language is still in flux and new spelling rules are being put forward regularly. Being an oral culture, encouraging students to read books and to find the important points has been essential. When asked to do research, students have tended to just copy whole sections of a book rather than find or even summarize the main point. So, for example, when we have asked students to read Chris Wright's *Knowing Jesus through the Old Testament*, we have given questions to students on various sections. This has helped them to find what is significant to then present to the rest of the class.

27. With a team of translators, we have had Chris Wright's *Knowing Jesus* translated into both Russian and the Central Asian language and his *Old Testament in Seven Sentences* and *Sweeter than Honey* are in progress. The majority of N. T. Wright's, *New Testament for Everyone* series of commentaries, all of which had already been translated into Russian, have been published in the Central Asian language. The work continues at a distance.

In some of the ways described, we have sought to help relatively new believers in a Central Asian culture understand and use the Old Testament, and to know and love it, and most importantly, its author, the God of the Bible. Our aim has been to provide resources, equip teachers, teach in ways which adults learn best, and to be sensitive to societal and cultural issues, while showing another story, God's story, with its invitation to a new future and new way of life.

Bibliography

Bartholomew, Craig C., and Michael W. Goheen. *The Drama of Scripture*. London: SPCK 2006.

Bible Project. https://bibleproject.com/. https://bibleproject.com/Russian/. https://bibleproject.com/explore/how-to-read-the-bible/.

"Central Asia." Wikipedia. https://en.wikipedia.org/wiki/Central_Asia.

Chan, Simon. "Evangelical Theology in Asian Contexts." In *The Cambridge Companion to Evangelical Theology*, edited by Timothy Larsen and Daniel J. Treier, 225–40. Cambridge: Cambridge University Press, 2007.

Даули, Тим. Библейский Атлас. Москва: Российское Библейское Общество. мг.пер, 1995.

Eurasian Association for Accreditation of Theological Education. http://e-aaa.org/.

Fee, Gordon D., and Douglas K. Stuart. *How to Read the Bible for All It's Worth*. Grand Rapids: Zondervan, 1981.

Фи, Гордон Д., и Дуглас Стюарт, *Как Читать Библию и Видеть Всю Ее Ценность*. Логос, пер., 2002.

From Bible Passage to Biblical Sermon. A Resource Kit for Teaching and Practice. Carlisle: Langham Preaching Resources, 2015. Russian translation 2018, *От Библейского отрывка к библейской проповеди. Материалы для обучения и практики*.

Gener, Timoteo D. "Divine Revelation and the Practice of Asian Theology." In *Asian Christian Theology: Evangelical Perspectives*, edited by Timoteo D. Gener and Stephen T. Pardue, 13–37. Carlisle: Langham, 2019.

Goldingay, John. *Men Behaving Badly*. Carlisle: Paternoster, 2000.

Jenkins, Philip. *The Lost History of Christianity: The Thousand-Year Golden Age of the Church in the Middle East, Africa, and Asia—And How It Died*. New York: Harper One, 2010.

Kinnally, Cara Anne. "Oral Culture: Literacy, Religion, Performance." *Oxford Research Encyclopaedia*. Published online, January 25, 2019. https://oxfordre.com/literature/view/10.1093/acrefore/9780190201098.001.0001/acrefore-9780190201098-e-437.

Knowles, Malcolm S. *The Adult Learner: A Neglected Species*. Rev. ed. Houston: Gulf, 1990.

———. *Informal Adult Education: A Guide for Administrators, Leaders, and Teachers*. New York: Association, 1950.

Mambetaliev, Askar. След Христа на Шелковом Пути. История Христианства Кыргызских Племен [Footprints of Christ on the Silk Road: The History of Christianity among the Kyrgyz Tribes]. Bishkek: Self-published, 2018.

Penner, Peter. "Unity in Diversity: The Slavic Bible Commentary." In *Breath and Bone: Living out the Mission of God in the World*, edited by Riad Kassis, Pieter Kwant, and Paul Windsor, 67–80. Carlisle: Langham Global Library, 2017.
Russian Bible Society. https://biblia.ru/.
Wright, Christopher J. H. "Hope in the Bible's Grand Narrative." https://www.youtube.com/watch?v=tKuBzbcojeo.
———. *Knowing Jesus through the Old Testament*. Carlisle: Langham Preaching Resources, 2014.
———. *The Old Testament in Seven Sentences*. Downers Grove: IVP Academic, 2019.
———. *Sweeter than Honey. Preaching the Old Testament*. Carlisle: Langham Preaching Resources, 2015.
Wright, N. T. *The New Testament and the People of God*. London: SPCK, 1992.
———. *The New Testament for Everyone Series*. London: SPCK, 2004–2011.
Vyssotskaia, Anneta. "Central Asia: Christianity's Past and Present." Evangelical Alliance Foundation Religious Liberty Prayer Bulletin, RLPB 078, October 20, 2010. http://www.ea.org.au/ea-family/Religious-Liberty/CENTRAL-ASIA—CHRISTIANITY-S-PAST-AND-PRESENT———.

15

Worldly Wisdom in 1 Corinthians and Its Implications for Theological Education

Brian S. Rosner

Introduction

The words "wisdom" (*sophia*) and "wise" (*sophos*) appear more often in 1 Corinthians than any other book in the New Testament, some twenty-eight out of a total of seventy-seven times. Intriguingly, twenty-six of these occur in the opening three chapters of the letter.[1] Indeed, Paul's main argument against Corinthian factionalism in 1 Corinthians 1:17—3:23 revolves around the topic of wisdom. Apparently, members of the church of God in Corinth were judging Paul as deficient in a certain kind of wisdom and preferring other Christian leaders on the same score. Paul responds vigorously and at length.[2]

---

1. Only Colossians rivals 1 Corinthians for its interest in "wisdom," with seven occurrences of the terms. Relative to the length of each letter, wisdom words appear 2.88 per 1000 words in 1 Corinthians, and 3.38 per 1000 words in Colossians. In Colossians, too, the explanation may be that Paul seeks to counter a wrong view of wisdom; arguably, Paul opposes the claims of false teachers concerning "wisdom" (Col 1:9, 28; 2:3, 23; 3:16; 4:5), "insight" (1:9; 2:2), and "knowledge" (1:6, 9–10; 2:2–3; 3:10).

2. First Corinthians 1:10—4:21, Paul's full treatment of factions in the church in Corinth, is longer than Titus and 2 Thessalonians and roughly the same length as 1 Thessalonians and Colossians.

Two things stand out in Paul's treatment of the theme of wisdom in these chapters. First, Paul distinguishes between two sorts of wisdom, the wisdom of the world and the wisdom of God: "We do, however, speak a message of wisdom among the mature, but not the wisdom of this age or of the rulers of this age, who are coming to nothing. No, we declare God's wisdom" (1 Cor 2:6–7a).[3] Secondly, Paul grounds his condemnation of worldly wisdom with reference to no less than three Old Testament texts: Isaiah 29:14 in 1 Corinthians 1:19; and Job 5:13 and Psalm 94:11 in 1 Corinthians 3:19–20.

Given Paul's extended treatment of what he takes to be the Old Testament theme of worldly wisdom it is remarkable that some studies of Old Testament wisdom have given it such scant attention. For example, Bartholomew and O'Dowd's excellent introduction to Old Testament wisdom, which includes not just the wisdom books but also "wisdom theology, language and metaphors . . . [in] Deuteronomy, 1–2 Kings, many of the psalms, the Song of Songs, and prophets like Isaiah and Jeremiah,"[4] makes no mention of worldly wisdom. Likewise, the edited volume, *Where Shall Wisdom Be Found? Wisdom in the Bible, the Church and the Contemporary World*,[5] finds no reason to mention worldly wisdom that doesn't fear the Lord, despite having three chapters on wisdom in the Old Testament. Paul, it seems, is a better biblical theologian than many Old Testament scholars!

This chapter has four parts: (1) a brief consideration of the theme of "worldly wisdom" in the Old Testament; (2) a careful look at Paul's appropriation of the theme in 1 Corinthians 1–3; (3) a short summary of what we may learn about worldly wisdom from 1 Corinthians 1–3; and (4) some reflections on the implications of the dangers of worldly wisdom to the task of theological education. The subject of wisdom and theological education is an appropriate tribute to Lindsay Wilson, the godly and wise theological educator.

"Worldly Wisdom" in the Old Testament

This section seeks to answer two questions: How common is non-godly wisdom in the Old Testament? And how can wisdom be non-godly, anyway?

Along with the three texts that Paul quotes in 1 Corinthians, examples of non-godly wisdom include Proverbs 28:11 (where the rich are "wise" in their own eyes), the pagan wise in Daniel, and prophetic oracles denouncing the

3. All Bible quotations are from the NIV unless otherwise indicated.
4. Bartholomew and O'Dowd, *Wisdom Literature*, 22.
5. Barton, *Where Shall Wisdom Be Found?*

wisdom of opposing nations (e.g., Isa 19:11, 12; Obadiah 8). Some wisdom terminology can also be used both positively and negatively, such as the same word translated as "prudent" in Proverbs 1:3 and "crafty" in Genesis 3:1. And in Jeremiah 4:22 someone can be "skilled" in doing evil.

As it turns out, many wisdom words have a range of meaning, referring simply to skillfulness and success in achieving certain goals, without any value judgment; the end to which the particular wisdom is put determines whether or not the wisdom is godly. Instructions concerning wisdom in the Old Testament urge activity that is aligned with God's ordering of the world and carried out with due reverence to God.

Three Old Testament Worldly Wisdom Texts in 1 Corinthians 1–3

In developing the theme of worldly wisdom, what does Paul do with the three Old Testament texts in question? Before answering this question, some general remarks on wisdom in 1 Corinthians 1–3 are needed to set things in context.

The first reference to wisdom in the letter is in 1 Corinthians 1:17: "Christ did not send me to baptize, but to preach the gospel—not with wisdom and eloquence, lest the cross of Christ be emptied of its power." It introduces Paul's negative treatment of the wisdom of this world in 1:18—2:5, which he will then counterbalance with a positive treatment of the wisdom of the cross and the Spirit in 2:6—3:4. This material does not address divisions in the church directly, but rather "the values which lie behind them."[6] A mirror reading would suggest that Paul has been criticized, or unfavourably compared with leaders like Apollos, on the score that he does not speak with the impressive wisdom of sophisticated eloquence.

Wisdom words in these chapters have a wide semantic range. Barrett explains helpfully that Paul uses "wisdom" and "wise" in two bad senses and two good senses: (1) the skilled marshalling of human arguments with a view to convincing the hearer; (2) the measure of truth, both theological and ethical, by human standards and reasoning (which judges the cross to be foolishness); (3) God's plan of redeeming the world through a crucified messiah; and (4) the actual substance of salvation itself. The latter two positive uses find a parallel in "righteousness" as a description of the way in which God acts and the gift that he bestows upon us via those saving

---

6. Pogoloff, *Logos and Sophia*, 119.

actions.⁷ These four senses of "wisdom" develop roughly in this sequence moving through 1 Corinthians 1–3.

In order to grasp the full significance of Paul's appropriation of three Old Testament worldly wisdom texts we need to read them in their original contexts as well as their new contexts and consider any changes to them Paul may have made. It is also profitable to take a look at how non-canonical Jewish texts developed similar ideas.

The first Old Testament quotation is of Isaiah 29:14 in 1 Corinthians 1:19. Verses 18–20 give the context:

> For the message of the cross is foolishness to those who are perishing, but to us who are being saved it is the power of God. For it is written: "I will destroy the wisdom of the wise; the intelligence of the intelligent I will frustrate." Where is the wise person? Where is the teacher of the law? Where is the philosopher of this age? Has not God made foolish the wisdom of the world?

Paul shows that there is implacable opposition between human wisdom and the "word of the cross." The quotation of Isaiah helps establish that this observation is linked to the OT narrative of judgment and grace and shows that the paradox of the cross, foolishness to some but in reality power for salvation, is in accord with Scripture.

Several features of Isaiah 29:14 and surrounding verses suggest its attractiveness to Paul and its aptness in relation to his argument. Part of a woe oracle condemning various human practices (cf. 29:1, 3), the previous verse associates wisdom with "lip service," "people drawing near [to God, only] with their mouths."

The first part of v. 14 indicates that the judgment of the "wisdom of the wise" will occur when God will do "shocking and amazing" things. The threefold appearance of the Hebrew root "wonder" in this verse may imply messianic involvement. The first name of the messianic figure in Isaiah 9:6 is "wonderful" (cf. 25:1) and in 28:29 the Lord who announces the plan of salvation is said to be "wonderful in counsel." Furthermore, that the messiah should be associated with the judgment of human wisdom is suggested by Cyrus's involvement in the reversal of wisdom in 44:25, a type of the messiah.

A wide range of Jewish texts, which have affinities with Isaiah 29:14, treat the theme of the absence and judgment of wisdom:⁸ Baruch 3:9–14; 2 Baruch 48:31–37; 70:3–6; 4 Ezra 5:9–13; 13:29–32; 1 Enoch 39:8; 42; 1Q27

---

7. Barrett, *First Epistle*, 67–68.
8. Williams, *Wisdom of the Wise*, 61–73.

1 I, 1–9; 1QH III, 12–17; 3 Maccabees 6:19–29; Targum Isaiah 29:13–14. In these texts the absence of wisdom occurs in situations where strife and division are plaguing a community. Under such circumstances, God's people are enjoined to appreciate the future intervention of God in order to help sort out their present difficulties. In particular, a dearth of wisdom is seen as part of a great judgment or as a sign pointing to the final, universal judgment. The absence of wisdom and its ultimate judgment is associated with the work of the coming messiah.

Paul quotes Isaiah 29:14 verbatim except the final word has been changed from *krypsō*, "hide," in the LXX to *athetēsō*, "frustrate," in 1 Corinthians 1:19. As Stanley notes,[9] the latter term serves Paul's purposes better: "Paul's point in 1 Corinthians 1:18–29 is not that God has simply 'hidden' understanding from the 'wise,' but rather that he has done a work in the death of Jesus that defies all purely rational understanding. By substituting the stronger *athetēsō*, Paul creates a chiastic parallel with the preceding *apolō* [destroy] that serves to drive home his point to his readers."

The text seems to have exerted an influence on Paul's language and thought at various points in the surrounding verses in 1 Corinthians. "Those who are being destroyed" in v. 18 anticipates the "destruction" (*apolō*) in v. 19. A purely verbal show of piety, the very thing Paul faults the Corinthians for in chapters 1–4, recalls the superficial "lip service" of Isaiah 29:13. And the "wonderful" and yet "shocking" things (29:13–14) the prophet foretells, with messianic overtones, are what Paul declares have now transpired through Christ crucified.

Especially when read in the context of its early Jewish interpretation, Isaiah 29:14 is used by Paul to announce that God's eschatological judgment and salvation are taking place in the midst of the Corinthians. As Hays puts it,[10] "God has already put the wise to shame through the foolishness of the cross, the apocalyptic event that has shattered the old order of human wisdom." The Corinthians who still value "the wisdom of the wise" have failed to notice God's apocalyptic judgment on such wisdom through the crucified messiah. The fact that in 1:18 people are still in the process of being saved (or destroyed) indicates that the unfolding of the drama of salvation is not yet complete. Isaiah's words are for Paul not just a judgment on ancient Judean leaders, but also "an indictment of the rhetorical affectations of the Corinthians."[11]

---

9. Stanley, *Language of Scripture*, 186.
10. Hays, "Conversion," 403–4.
11. Hays, "Conversion," 404.

The second and third Old Testament texts that Paul cites are in 1 Corinthians 3:18–20:

> Do not deceive yourselves. If any of you think you are wise by the standards of this age, you should become "fools" so that you may become wise. For the wisdom of this world is foolishness in God's sight. As it is written: "He catches the wise in their craftiness"; and again, "The Lord knows that the thoughts of the wise are futile."

To demonstrate the futility of human wisdom, Paul appeals to two OT texts that offer a pithy summary of his argument in 1:18—3:21.[12] The first, Job 5:13, quoted in 3:19, declares God's ability to frustrate the goals of those claiming to be wise.

The unit in which the verse appears in Job, part of the first speech of Eliphaz, reinforces the idea of God's superiority over human wisdom and strength. In a passage depicting the God who does "great, unsearchable and marvellous things" (5:8–9), Job 5:8–16 sets up an opposition between "the wise" and "the poor." The passage in question develops the theme of God's deliverance of the latter (5:15–16: "he saves the needy from the sword of their mouth . . . so the poor have hope") and his frustration of the former (5:14: "the schemes of the wily are brought to a quick end").

A number of Jewish texts develop themes arising out of or overlapping with the sentiments of Job 5:13.[13] For example, Baruch 3:20–28 protests the futility of human striving to attain wisdom, which can only be granted by God's revelation (cf. 3:36—4:4). That God makes certain wise people ineffectual and thwarts their plans is seen in: Psalms of Solomon 8:20 (the wise Jewish leaders when the Romans captured Jerusalem); Wisdom 17:7–11 (the wise Egyptians at the time of the exodus); 3 Maccabees 1–2 (King Ptolemy planning to enter the holy of holies); Judith 2:2–3 (Holofernes and Nebuchadnezzar planning to lay waste to Judea).

The MT, LXX, and 1 Corinthians 3:19 carry an equivalent sense but differ in some details. Compared to the LXX, Paul has *katalambanō* rather than *drassomai* (both meaning "lay hold of") and *en tē panourgia autōn* ("in their craftiness") instead of *en tē phronēsei* ("in prudence/understanding"). Concerning the latter, the Hebrew is closer to Paul's rendition using a word which implies a sly and crafty form of wisdom. The differences may be explained either as Paul offering his own Hebraizing revision of the present

---

12. Koch, *Zeuge des Evangeliums*, 275.
13. Williams, *Wisdom of the Wise*, 307–15.

LXX, his own translation of the Hebrew, or that he is quoting a wholly independent translation of the Hebrew text of Job.[14]

Although in the book of Job as a whole Job's friends' advice is shown to be unhelpful, misapplied wisdom, as Hays puts it, "Paul cites Job 5:13 here as an authoritative disclosure of the truth about God's debunking of human wisdom."[15] The immediate context of the quotation resonates with the themes of reversal and the mystery of divine mercy that Paul has introduced earlier in the letter (1:18—2:16).

Paul quotes Psalm 94:11 in 1 Corinthians 3:20 to make a further, related point. If in 1:18–25 Paul says that what God does in wisdom seems foolish to the world, here we have the converse: what the world thinks is wise, God declares to be futile folly.[16]

Psalm 94 is a prayer for God to overthrow the wicked oppressors and vindicate the righteous. Thiselton's summary is accurate: "Psalm 94 stresses that in spite of manipulative and corrupt leadership by those in authority (Psalm 94:5–7, 16), the 'schemes' of these human persons fail because their best 'thinkers' are fallible (Psalm 94:11)."[17] The psalm also promises that blessing awaits those who depend on God; he will not abandon them, but teach them and aid them in their time of need (vv. 12–23).

The contrast between human thinking and God's thoughts is widespread in Jewish literature.[18] The *Targum of Job* contains numerous references to the futility of the human intellect without God's revelation. Likewise, Baruch 3:29–37 asserts the inaccessibility of God's wisdom. In 1 Maccabees 2:61–64 the plans (*dialogismos*) of sinners will perish. Other texts emphasize the benefits of cooperating with God's plans and call on people to turn to God asking for wisdom.

The MT, LXX, and 1 Corinthians 3:20 are equivalent except Paul renders the verse, "the thoughts of *the wise*" instead of "men" (*anthrōpōn*). No known OT manuscript has any other reading. A few lesser Pauline manuscripts agree with the MT and LXX and read *anthrōpōn* instead of *sophōn* in 1 Corinthians 3:20, but this is probably a deliberate conforming of Paul's wording to the Psalm. "There is little reason to doubt that the present modification goes back to Paul himself."[19] The futility of human wisdom is a central theme in 1 Corinthians 1:19–27a, 2:4–6, and 3:18–19. However, it is not that

---

14. Stanley, *Language of Scripture*, 188–94.
15. Hays, *First Corinthians*, 59.
16. Fee, *Corinthians*, 152.
17. Thiselton, *First Epistle*, 323.
18. Williams, *Wisdom of the Wise*, 315–25.
19. Stanley, *Language of Scripture*, 195.

Paul has altered the text in cavalier fashion simply to suit his argument. Paul's quotation of Psalm 94:14 in Romans 11:2 indicates that he knew the psalm well. What makes the form of his quotation in 1 Corinthians 3:20 explicable is the link Psalm 94 itself forges between "fools" and the "wise." Psalm 94:8 reads: "Understand, O dullest of the people! *Fools*, when will you be *wise*?" The "humans" spoken of in Psalm 94:11, whose thoughts the Lord knows to be futile, are the same group described as "fools" earlier in the psalm. That Paul feels free to label them, ironically, as "the wise" fits his rhetoric and does no violence to the larger context of Psalm 94.

Psalm 94 and early Jewish literature emphasize not only that God thwarts the plans of the wise, but also that there is great blessing for those who are part of and cooperate with God's plans. Thus, not only does the citation of v. 11 signal the futility of acting or thinking independently of God, but as 1 Corinthians 3:21–23 goes on to celebrate, there are great benefits to those who boast not in human leaders but in God.

Together the two Old Testament texts cited in 1 Corinthians 3:19–20, which testify to the futility of human thoughts apart from God's revelation and the consequent emptiness of human wisdom, support Paul's conclusion in 3:21a: "Let no one boast about human leaders" (NRSV).

Worldly Wisdom According to Paul

What, then, do we learn about worldly wisdom from Paul in connection with the three Old Testament texts?

A modest mirror reading of 1 Corinthians 1–3 would suggest that the Corinthians were saying that they belonged to their favourite leaders and boasted about their wisdom and power and Paul's deficiencies in these areas. As Judge notes, the sophisticated rhetoric to which the Corinthian Christians were attracted "enshrined the beautiful and the strong in a position of social power," standards which, as Paul goes on to show, the gospel of the cross of Christ by definition opposes.[20] To heal their divisions, Paul says three things about wisdom: (1) the message of the cross spells the end of human wisdom and power; (2) the cross redefines wisdom and folly, power, and weakness; and (3) instead of boasting in their leaders' wisdom and power they should boast in the wisdom and power of God in the gospel which gives them a favourable and secure status before God. As Carson observes, the Corinthians' "love of pomp, prestige, rhetoric, social approval, publicly lauded 'wisdom'

---

20. Judge, "Classical Education," 14.

... demonstrated that they had not reflected very deeply on the entailments of the gospel of the crucified messiah."[21]

The apostle Paul is not just distancing himself from a sophistic valuing of form over content, presentation over substance. Rather, Paul is arguing against the whole worldview of Roman Corinth in general, and sophists in particular, which he labels worldly wisdom. In 1 Corinthians 1–3 Paul insists that in order to nullify any human attempt at self-salvation, God "chose a means of revelation actually contradictory to [human] wisdom—the foolish proclamation of a crucified Savior (1:21b)."[22] Paul insists that the truth of the cross "cannot be achieved through the best of human intellect and strength but must be received as a gift in the humble submission of faith and trust."[23]

In short, from 1 Corinthians 1–3 we learn that worldly wisdom values human brilliance, power, and achievement, leads inevitably to pride, envy, and division, and is under the judgment of God through the cross of Christ.

Some Implications for Theological Education

What dangers does worldly wisdom, so defined, have for the task of theological education?

A theological college is many things: a Christian worker training centre, a place of worship, a community of believers in Christ, a setting for godly discernment, a venue for spiritual thought leadership, and so on. Two descriptions of most colleges overlap with things that are not distinctively Christian: a theological college is a government-accredited institution of tertiary education and a not-for-profit business. In both cases there are risks associated with worldly wisdom.

As an institution of higher education, a theological college is committed to high academic standards. This affects many dimensions of the educational enterprise, including the qualifications of the teachers, the stringent assessment of students, the standard of library facilities and resources, and the program of studies. There is a sound theological basis for taking such matters seriously: Jesus taught unequivocally that we are to love God with all our minds (Matt 22:37); and having a good reputation with society at large is essential for the progress of the gospel—Jesus himself "increased in wisdom and stature, and in favor with God and *with people*" (Luke 2:52, CSB).

---

21. Carson, *Cross and Christian Ministry*, 70.
22. Polhill, "Factionalism," 329.
23. Polhill, "Factionalism," 330.

On the other hand, the values of academia can easily lead down a path to worldly wisdom. The prizing of human achievement can leave the impression that what matters most is intellectual prowess. And rigorous student assessment and comparison can produce envy and pride, and poison community. Theological colleges must find ways to protect and promote Christian character and gospel-honoring culture in line with the wisdom of the cross, while at the same time maintaining educational standards. Along with celebrating the best students, we need to support and encourage those who struggle, remembering that not many of us are noteworthy, not many world class, not many highfliers. We must avoid giving the false impression that ministry training is all about high marks. And we must find ways for students and faculty to avoid the trap of self-focus and self-promotion and to serve one another in love.

As a not-for-profit business, a theological college is committed to efficient use of resources and the sustainability of the enterprise. Good management and corporate governance, at their best, aim to make the most of opportunities, protect the organization from foreseeable risks, and ensure accountability, fair treatment of staff, and attention to profitable professional development. Indeed, the wisdom of the book of Proverbs contains many calls to diligence and commends common sense that might be legitimately compared to the best organizational practice.

On the other hand, corporate wisdom can become an end in itself. It can conduce a tight focus on measurable key performance indicators which can lead to the unintended consequence of a neglect of intangible matters of culture. And ends can be pursued without due attention to the means of attaining them. Theological colleges need to remember that all performance appraisals are provisional. As Paul puts it in 1 Corinthians 4:3–4, "I care very little if I am judged by you or by any human court; indeed, I do not even judge myself . . . It is the Lord who judges me." And in the context of 1 Corinthians that judgment is conditioned on appreciating that many of the world's values have been turned upside down by the fact that God saved the world through the weakness and foolishness of a crucified messiah. In the end, a theological college cannot think of itself primarily as a university or a business.

Bibliography

Barrett, C. K. *First Epistle to the Corinthians*. London: Continuum, 1994.
Bartholomew, Craig G., and Ryan P. O'Dowd. *Old Testament Wisdom Literature: A Theological Introduction*. Downers Grove: InterVarsity, 2011.

Barton, Stephen C., ed. *Where Shall Wisdom Be Found? Wisdom in the Bible, the Church and the Contemporary World*. Edinburgh: T. & T. Clark, 1999.

Carson, Donald A. *The Cross and Christian Ministry: An Exposition of Passages from 1 Corinthians*. Grand Rapids: Baker, 1993.

Fee, G. D. *The First Epistle to the Corinthians*. NICNT. Grand Rapids: Eerdmans, 1987.

Hays, R. B. "The Conversion of the Imagination: Scripture and Eschatology in 1 Corinthians." *NTS* 45 (1999) 391–412.

———. *First Corinthians*. IBC. Louisville: John Knox, 1997.

Judge, Edwin A. "The Reaction against Classical Education in the New Testament." *JCE* 77 (1983) 7–14.

Koch, D. A. *Die Schrift als Zeuge des Evangeliums: Untersuchungen zur Verwendung und zum Verständnis der Schrift bei Paulus*. BHT 69. Tübingen: Mohr Siebeck, 1986.

Pogoloff, Stephen M. *Logos and Sophia: The Rhetorical Situation of 1 Corinthians*. Atlanta: Society of Biblical Literature, 1992.

Polhill, John B. "The Wisdom of God and Factionalism." *Review and Expositor* 80, no. 3 (1983) 325–29.

Stanley, C. D. *Paul and the Language of Scripture: Citation Technique in the Pauline Epistles and Contemporary Literature*. SNTSMS 69. Cambridge: Cambridge University Press, 1992.

Thiselton, A. C. *The First Epistle to the Corinthians*. NIGTC. Grand Rapids: Eerdmans, 2000.

Williams, H. H. D., III. *The Wisdom of the Wise: The Presence and Function of Scripture within 1 Cor. 1:18—3:23*. AGJU 49. Leiden: Brill, 2001.

Part V

Wisdom in Life

16

Where Shall Wisdom Be Found?

Peter Adam

It is a privilege and pleasure to contribute to this book. Lindsay not only teaches wisdom, but lives it! I know him as a wise person, a wise colleague, and a wise friend. And his wisdom is complemented and enhanced by Clarissa's wisdom: a wise woman indeed. He has contributed much wisdom in his ministry at Ridley College, not only in his teaching, but also in his wider ministry of administration and personal encouragement to students, faculty, and staff. In God's mercy Lindsay puts into practice his own observation:

> Our foundational stance [fearing the Lord] and our fundamental choice to embrace the way of wisdom are presented as the only pathway to life in the book of Proverbs.[1]

Where shall wisdom be found? Here are three keys to finding God's wisdom.

1. We find wisdom as a theological category in the Bible.
2. We find God's wisdom in Christ.
3. We find God's wisdom in Christ crucified.

---

1. Wilson, *Proverbs*, 62.

We need this wisdom of God, our church needs this wisdom, and so does our world.[2]

1. We Find Wisdom as a Theological Category in the Bible

One of the privileges and responsibilities of being human beings made in the image of God is our need for variegated wisdom. We need wisdom to know God. We need wisdom for daily tasks of life, wisdom in relating to other humans, wisdom in our work, wisdom in politics, economics, culture, interpreting our world, and caring for our world. We need wisdom to evaluate all the information that fills our world.

Sadly, we are deluged with fake news, fake information, fake promises, and fake wisdom. It is increasingly difficult to discern the truth in minor matters, let alone major issues. No wonder we are vulnerable to conspiracy theories, and seek to find a false security in belonging to our own familiar and trusted tribe. In addition to this contemporary social pressure, we remember that Satan is "the father of lies,"[3] and that we are prone to "wisdom" which is "earthly, unspiritual, demonic."[4] We desperately need God's wisdom!

Christians need extra wisdom, in knowing how to serve God in their particular culture and their time in human history. We need wisdom to know what to affirm in our world, and what to deny. We need wisdom to interpret and apply the ancient texts which comprise our Holy Bible. We need wisdom to be effectively "in the world," but not "of the world."[5] We need wisdom in belonging to God's people, and wisdom in evangelizing our world and loving our neighbor.

People in trained gospel ministry need even more wisdom! We can be asked at any time to interpret any part of the Bible, and also how to interpret any aspect of human life and the universe. We need wisdom in relating to individuals and to groups within our ministries, and to those who are not yet believers, or who oppose Christianity. We need wisdom to value the past, but not be trapped by it; as we need wisdom for contemporary life and ministry, without losing our theological moorings. We need wisdom in ordering our lives and our work, when the work is never-ending, and when it is hard to evaluate the quality of our ministries.

---

2. This chapter is a development of Adam, "Biblical Theology of Wisdom," 4–27, and includes some material from that source.

3. John 8:44. Bible quotations are from NIV11.

4. James 3:15.

5. John 17:16–18.

Where shall wisdom be found? A key is to search the Bible for wisdom as a *theological entity*, rather than a *literary entity*. This is because wisdom in the Bible is not confined to the books of the Bible we call "wisdom literature," such as Job, Psalms, Proverbs, Ecclesiastes, and the Song of Songs. The characteristic literary features of "wisdom literature" are of vital importance in understanding and expounding these styles of literature: but wisdom is found elsewhere as well.

Similarly, if we want to find the gospel, we should not confine our attention to Matthew, Mark, Luke, and John. We use the literary term "gospel" to describe those books (the titles are not original), but we need to read all of the Bible to know the fullness of the gospel!

We can learn much about wisdom from the narratives, prophecies, and letters of the Bible. We learn that Christ is God's wisdom, and we can learn to live wisely and do wise ministry as well. To find out what the Bible means by wisdom, we must read Old Testament books that are not "wisdom literature," and we need to read the Gospels, the Epistles, and Acts and Revelation as well![6]

Thinking of biblical wisdom only as a literary entity can lead us to what I have described as "a destructive dichotomy between wisdom literature and the rest of the Old Testament; and between wisdom, and the saving works and covenant words of God; and between wisdom, and the Law, history, and prophets."[7] We are wrong to identify wisdom with creation, and not with salvation. The weakness of dealing with biblical wisdom in solely literary terms is evident when we see that the book of Psalms, part of the so-called "wisdom literature" of the Bible, presents us with salvation history and covenant (e.g., Pss 89, 103, 104), and encourages us to meditate on God's law: "The law of the Lord is perfect, refreshing the soul. The statutes of the Lord are trustworthy, making wise the simple" (Ps 19:7, see also Pss 1 and 119). We find the themes of salvation, covenant and wisdom brought together clearly in these words of praise to God:

> He provided redemption for his people;
>   he ordained his covenant forever—
>   holy and awesome is his name.
> The fear of the Lord is the beginning of wisdom;
>   all who follow his precepts have good understanding.
>   To him belongs eternal praise. (Ps 111:9, 10)

---

6. For discussion of wisdom as literature or theology see Longman, *Fear*, 1–3, 275–82.

7. Adam, "Biblical Theology of Wisdom," 6, and also see Clements, *Wisdom*, 13–39.

We find wisdom in Bible narratives. Joshua, successor to Moses as leader of God's people, was a man of wisdom: "Now Joshua son of Nun was filled with the spirit of wisdom because Moses had laid his hands on him" (Deut 34:9).

Joseph in Egypt was endued with wisdom from God, as Lindsay Wilson has demonstrated.[8] As we read in Acts: "[God] gave Joseph wisdom and enabled him to gain the goodwill of Pharaoh king of Egypt. So Pharaoh made him ruler over Egypt and all his palace" (Acts 7:9, 10). As I have observed, "Joseph interpreted dreams, ruled wisely, taught wisdom to the elders of Egypt, cared for God's people, brought blessing to the Egyptians, and showed wisdom in dealing with his brothers."[9]

Solomon, king of Israel, was famed for his wisdom. His wisdom was expressed in proverbs and songs, and included study of plant life, animals, and birds (1 Kgs 4:29–34).[10] Solomon at his best, as portrayed in 1 Kings and 1 Chronicles, combines what we might separate: trust in God's promises (1 Kgs 8:12–26, 56); keeping God's covenant and obedience to God's commands (1 Kgs 8:57, 58); and receiving God's wisdom (1 Kgs 3:5–15). The extent of Solomon's wisdom and wealth shows that he is enjoying the blessings of covenant obedience, and the blessings of wisdom.

In my words, "Yet Solomon turned to folly, he turned his heart away after other gods, and engaged in idolatry, and so faced the judgment of God (1 Kings 11:1–9)."[11] In this he broke God's commandments and God's covenant (1 Kgs 11:9–11). Had Solomon been wise, he would have kept the commandments and covenant of God. True wisdom was inseparable from keeping covenant and commandments.

So too the prophet Daniel received and spoke God's wisdom.

> "Praise be to the name of God for ever and ever;
>   wisdom and power are his.
> He changes times and seasons;
>   he deposes kings and raises up others.
> He gives wisdom to the wise
>   and knowledge to the discerning.
> He reveals deep and hidden things;
>   he knows what lies in darkness,
>   and light dwells with him.

8. See Wilson, *Joseph, Wise and Otherwise*.
9. Adam, "Biblical Theology of Wisdom," 14.
10. See also 1 Kgs 5:12; 10:1–9, 23, 24; 11:41; and 2 Chr 9:3, 22, 23.
11. Adam, "Biblical Theology of Wisdom," 16.

> I thank and praise you, God of my ancestors:
> You have given me wisdom and power,
>> you have made known to me what we asked of you,
>> you have made known to us the dream of the king."
> (Dan 2:20–23)[12]

Humans are often so foolish as to trust their own wisdom, not God's. God's response to that is to destroy human wisdom, to show its innate foolishness and folly. As we read of God in Job,

> He thwarts the plans of the crafty,
>> so that their hands achieve no success.
> He catches the wise in their craftiness,
>> and the schemes of the wily are swept away. (Job 5:12, 13)

And God says through Obadiah, "'In that day,' declares the LORD, 'will I not destroy the wise men of Edom, those of understanding in the mountains of Esau?'" (Obad 1:8).[13] And Jeremiah says,

> Who should not fear you, King of the nations? This is your due. Among all the wise leaders of the nations and in all their kingdoms, there is no one like you. (Jer 10:7)

Furthermore, if God's people forsake the Scriptures, they will not understand what happens to them:

> Who is wise enough to understand this? Who has been instructed by the LORD and can explain it? Why has the land been ruined and laid waste like a desert that no one can cross?
>
> The LORD said, "It is because they have forsaken my law, which I set before them; they have not obeyed me or followed my law." (Jer 9:12, 13)

And, even more alarmingly, Bible interpreters and teachers who misread and misinterpret the Scriptures will also be brought low.

> Even the stork in the sky
>> knows her appointed seasons,
> and the dove, the swift and the thrush
>> observe the time of their migration.
> But my people do not know

---

12. See also Dan 1:20; 2:14; 5:11, 13.
13. See also Zech 9:1–4.

> the requirements of the Lord.
> How can you say, "We are wise,
>   for we have the law of the Lord,"
> when actually the lying pen of the scribes
>   has handled it falsely?
> The wise will be put to shame;
>   they will be dismayed and trapped.
> Since they have rejected the word of the Lord,
>   what kind of wisdom do they have? (Jer 8:7–9)

In addition, in studying wisdom in the Bible we have to go beyond a simple word study, because the notion of wisdom is also conveyed by synonyms. We need to include words such as "understanding," "insight," "skill," "counsel," "advice," "perception," "plan," "teaching," "knowledge," as well as the word "wisdom" itself.[14]

The wisdom of the Christ to come was promised in the Old Testament. We see the promise of a wise Davidic king in Isaiah, for David's descendant will be the "Wonderful Counselor, Mighty God, Everlasting Father, Prince of Peace" (Isa 9:6). As I have written,

> "Wonderful Counselor" means "a wonderfully wise leader, giving supernatural wisdom. This hope is followed by the . . . promise which includes the striking combination of a Davidic ruler, the Spirit of wisdom, and the fear of the Lord:

> A shoot will come up from the stump of Jesse;
>   from his roots a Branch will bear fruit.
> The Spirit of the Lord will rest on him—
>   the Spirit of wisdom and of understanding,
>   the Spirit of counsel and of might,
>   the Spirit of the knowledge and fear of the Lord—
>   and he will delight in the fear of the Lord . . . [Isa 11:1–3]."[15]

And again, "These are themes of messianic hope, and wisdom. Graeme Goldsworthy points out the remarkable similarities between the words of this prophecy, and the account of wisdom in Proverbs 8:12–15. 'I, wisdom . . . have counsel, sound wisdom, insight, and strength . . . the fear of the Lord is the hatred of evil . . . by me kings reign.'"[16]

---

14. Schnabel, "Wisdom," 843.
15. Adam, "Biblical Theology of Wisdom," 16.
16. Adam, "Biblical Theology of Wisdom," 16, quoting Goldsworthy, *Gospel*, 122.

We see the same promise in Jeremiah: "The days are coming," declares the LORD, "when I will raise up for David a righteous Branch, a King who will reign wisely and do what is just and right in the land" (Jer 23:5). The wisdom prophesied of the king of David's line is also prophesied of the servant of the LORD later in Isaiah.

> See, my servant will act wisely . . . by his knowledge my righteous servant will justify many, and he will bear their iniquities. (Isa 52:13; 53:11)

We have found wisdom as a theological entity throughout the Old Testament. This points us toward finding the fullness of God's wisdom in Christ.

2. We Find God's Wisdom in Christ

Calvin reminds us that we should expect to find God's wisdom in Christ: "For he has . . . always been the eternal Wisdom of God."[17] And again, "Will he not be wise who is God's eternal wisdom?"[18]

The boy Jesus grew in wisdom.

> And the child grew and became strong; he was filled with wisdom, and the grace of God was on him . . . And Jesus grew in wisdom and stature, and in favor with God and man. (Luke 2:40, 52)

Jesus was a teacher of wisdom. He was a travelling teacher, a rabbi, but his style of preaching and teaching was not a systematic exposition of the law of Moses, nor did he often speak like a prophet. He spoke more like a teacher of wisdom. Ben Witherington claims that 70 percent of his teaching is some sort of wisdom utterance such as aphorism, riddle, or parable.[19] Christ's teaching did not deal with timeless truths, rather his words created the new culture and lifestyle of the kingdom of God. His words required wisdom and insight to understand, and also the wisdom to know when and in what way to apply them.[20] Although their style was that of wisdom, in many ways their content was prophetic.[21] Like Joseph and Daniel in the Old Testament, Christ reveals God's secrets, the secrets of the kingdom and

---

17. Calvin, *Institutes*, 3.20.48, 916.
18. Calvin, *Institutes*, 1.13.24, 152.
19. Witherington, *Jesus*, 156.
20. Witherington, *Jesus*, 157, 164, 187.
21. Witherington, *Jesus*, 158, 183.

his own identity. Like the wisdom teachers of the Old Testament, he reveals these secrets to his disciples:

> He replied, "Because the knowledge of the secrets of the kingdom of heaven has been given to you, but not to them . . . This is why I speak to them in parables:
>
> "Though seeing, they do not see;
> though hearing, they do not hear or understand" . . .
>
> But blessed are your eyes because they see, and your ears because they hear. (Matt 13:11, 13, 16].

So too in Matthew 11 we find the same theme.

> At that time Jesus said, "I praise you, Father, Lord of heaven and earth, because you have hidden these things from the wise and learned, and revealed them to little children. Yes, Father, for this is what you were pleased to do." (Matt 11:25, 26)

On one occasion he referred to his own teaching ministry in these words: "Because of this, God in his wisdom said" (Luke 11:49). And, like the Old Testament teachers of wisdom, he spoke on his own authority.[22] People were amazed at Christ's wisdom: "Where did this man get this wisdom and these miraculous powers?" (Matt 13:54). As the people asked, "What's this wisdom that has been given him?" (Mark 6:2).

Jesus presented wisdom greater even than Solomon, and so to reject him and his words would be to invite greater condemnation.

> The Queen of the South will rise at the judgment with this generation and condemn it; for she came from the ends of the earth to listen to Solomon's wisdom, and now something greater than Solomon is here. (Matt 12:42)

The "something greater than Solomon" could be Jesus's teaching, but is more likely to be Jesus himself, the personification of wisdom. For look at the parallel claim in the previous verses in regard to Jonah.

> For as Jonah was three days and three nights in the belly of a huge fish, so the Son of Man will be three days and three nights in the heart of the earth . . . and now something greater than Jonah is here. (Matt 12:40, 41)

Something greater is Jesus himself, greater than Jonah because of his death and resurrection, and greater than Solomon because of his wisdom.

---

22. Witherington, *Jesus*, 157, 163–65.

In Witherington's words, Jesus's life teaching death and resurrection are an "embodied parable" of wisdom.[23] He models his life of wisdom.

> Instead, whoever wants to become great among you must be your servant, and whoever wants to be first must be slave of all. For even the Son of Man did not come to be served, but to serve, and to give his life as a ransom for many. (Mark 10:43–46)

Jesus warns us of the two ways in which we might live:

> Enter through the narrow gate. For wide is the gate and broad is the road that leads to destruction, and many enter through it. But small is the gate and narrow the road that leads to life, and only a few find it. (Matt 7:13–15)

In Jesus's teaching, the first expression of wisdom is to welcome him, hear his words, and do them. He reinforces the contrast between wisdom and folly in his parable of the two builders.

> Therefore everyone who hears these words of mine and puts them into practice is like a wise man who built his house on the rock. The rain came down, the streams rose, and the winds blew and beat against that house; yet it did not fall, because it had its foundation on the rock. But everyone who hears these words of mine and does not put them into practice is like a foolish man who built his house on sand. The rain came down, the streams rose, and the winds blew and beat against that house, and it fell with a great crash. (Matt 7:24–27)

Some people rejected John the Baptist for his austerity, and said that he had a demon, and then rejected Jesus as a glutton and drunkard, a friend of tax collectors and sinners (Matt 11:18, 19). "But wisdom is proved right by her deeds" (Matt 11:19): wise people welcomed God's wisdom in both John and Jesus. As when Jesus was a child, wise people sought him and worshipped him (Matt 2:1, 2).

In Colossians, Paul writes that "all the treasures of wisdom and knowledge" are hidden in Christ (Col 2:3). It is significant that these words follow the Christ hymn of 1:15–20. For there we read of Christ's role in creation:

> The Son is the image of the invisible God, the firstborn over all creation. For in him all things were created: things in heaven and on earth, visible and invisible, whether thrones or powers or rulers or authorities; all things have been created through him

---

23. Witherington, *Jesus*, 204.

and for him. He is before all things, and in him all things hold together. (Col 1:15–17)

And then of his role in reconciliation:

And he is the head of the body, the church; he is the beginning and the firstborn from among the dead, so that in everything he might have the supremacy. For God was pleased to have all his fullness dwell in him, and through him to reconcile to himself all things, whether things on earth or things in heaven, by making peace through his blood, shed on the cross. (Col 1:18–20)

Christ's wisdom is seen in creation as well as salvation. His work of salvation leads to the reconciliation of creation, of "all things" (Col 1:20). So "all the treasures of wisdom and knowledge" hidden in Christ (2:3), include creation and salvation.[24] Wisdom is about the reconciliation of the creation through Christ who rules it and restores it, through the blood of his cross. Wisdom includes creation and salvation history. It is to the theme of this salvation which we now turn our attention.

3. We Find God's Wisdom in Christ Crucified

As we have just seen, Christ reconciled all things to God, "making peace through his blood, shed on the cross" (Col 1:20).

Paul develops the theme of Christ's death and wisdom in 1 Corinthians. Here he explains that one reason why God decided on the cross of Christ was to show the poverty and futility of human wisdom.

For it is written:
"I will destroy the wisdom of the wise,
the intelligence of the intelligent I will frustrate" (1 Cor 1:19).

Here is God's subversive wisdom:

Where is the wise person? Where is the teacher of the law? Where is the philosopher of this age? Has not God made foolish the wisdom of the world? For since in the wisdom of God the world through its wisdom did not know him, God was pleased through the foolishness of what was preached to save those who believe. Jews demand signs and Greeks look for

---

24. We find a similar theme in Ephesians: "With all wisdom and understanding, he made known to us the mystery of his will according to his good pleasure, which he purposed in Christ, to be put into effect when the times reach their fulfillment—to bring unity to all things in heaven and on earth under Christ" (1:8–10).

> wisdom, but we preach Christ crucified: a stumbling block to Jews and foolishness to Gentiles, but to those whom God has called, both Jews and Greeks, Christ the power of God and the wisdom of God. (1 Cor 1:20–24)

Christ crucified is the most significant expression of God's wisdom and power, though in human eyes it looks like foolishness and weakness. This reality is reflected in the lack of wisdom in the church, and in its weakness.

> For the foolishness of God is wiser than human wisdom, and the weakness of God is stronger than human strength. Brothers and sisters, think of what you were when you were called. Not many of you were wise by human standards; not many were influential; not many were of noble birth. But God chose the foolish things of the world to shame the wise; God chose the weak things of the world to shame the strong. God chose the lowly things of this world and the despised things—and the things that are not—to nullify the things that are, so that no one may boast before him. (1 Cor 1:25–29)

Christ is God's wisdom, in whom alone we must boast.

> It is because of him that you are in Christ Jesus, who has become for us wisdom from God—that is, our righteousness, holiness and redemption. Therefore, as it is written: "Let the one who boasts boast in the Lord." (1 Cor 1:30, 31)

Similarly, Paul did not minister among them "with eloquence or human wisdom," but preached "Jesus Christ and him crucified" (1 Cor 2:1, 2).

God's wisdom in Christ crucified is revealed to the apostles by the Holy Spirit.

> We do, however, speak a message of wisdom among the mature, but not the wisdom of this age or of the rulers of this age, who are coming to nothing. No, we declare God's wisdom, a mystery that has been hidden and that God destined for our glory before time began. None of the rulers of this age understood it, for if they had, they would not have crucified the Lord of glory. However, as it is written: "What no eye has seen, what no ear has heard, and what no human mind has conceived"—the things God has prepared for those who love him—these are the things God has revealed to us by his Spirit (1 Cor 2:6–10).

In my words, "Through the Spirit, the apostles know the mind of God from the mouth of God in words taught by the Spirit, so they can in turn teach these words to others."[25]

> The Spirit searches all things, even the deep things of God . . . What we have received is not the spirit of the world, but the Spirit who is from God, so that we may understand what God has freely given us. This is what we speak, not in words taught us by human wisdom but in words taught by the Spirit, explaining spiritual realities with Spirit-taught words. (1 Cor 2:10, 12, 13)[26]

This theme of God's wisdom and human foolishness continues in both 1 and 2 Corinthians, for example in 1 Corinthians 3:18–23, 4:8–13, and 2 Corinthians 11 and 12. This theme of wisdom is also echoed elsewhere: "the Holy Scriptures, which are able to make you wise for salvation through faith in Christ Jesus" (2 Tim 3:15).

It is so striking that in Paul's great doxology in Romans 11 he does not praise God's grace, or his love, but God's wisdom and knowledge. After his proclamation of the gospel in terms of wrath, sinfulness, atonement, justification, faith, peace with God, conformity to Christ's death and resurrection, adoption as God's children, the indwelling Spirit, the restoration of the world, and God's plan for his gospel word to flourish among Jews and Gentiles, he exclaims,

> Oh, the depth of the riches of the wisdom and knowledge of God! How unsearchable his judgments, and his paths beyond tracing out! "Who has known the mind of the Lord? Or who has been his counselor?" "Who has ever given to God, that God should repay them?" For from him and through him and for him are all things. To him be the glory forever! Amen. (Rom 11:33–36).[27]

---

25. Adam, "Biblical Theology of Wisdom," 24.

26. As Ciampa and Rosner point out, this theme of the death of Christ on the cross, as revealed to the apostles and prophets by the Spirit of God, lies within the theological structure of most of 1 Corinthians. The cross of Christ shapes chapters 1–4, the sacrifice of Christ the Passover lamb shapes chapter 5, righteous suffering like Christ shapes chapter 6, redemption through Christ shapes chapter 7, and the death of Christ shapes chapters 8–11. Ciampa and Rosner, *Corinthians*, 123. They write, "For Paul, *Christ crucified* is more than just the means of forgiveness and salvation; rather, it informs his total vision of the Christian life and ministry." Ciampa and Rosner, *Corinthians*, 114.

27. Note that the quotations in 1:34, 35 are a mixture of Isaiah 40:13; Job 15:8; 36:22, 23; 35:7; and 41:11. It is striking that Paul uses "wisdom literature" about God the Creator to help us marvel at God the Savior! We should not separate what God has joined together.

God's glory is found in his saving wisdom.

Then again in the concluding doxology of Romans, Paul links "my gospel," "the message I proclaim about Jesus Christ," and "the revelation of the mystery hidden for long ages past, but now revealed," and attributes them to "the only wise God":

> Now to him who is able to establish you in accordance with my gospel, the message I proclaim about Jesus Christ, in keeping with the revelation of the mystery hidden for long ages past, but now revealed and made known through the prophetic writings by the command of the eternal God, so that all the Gentiles might come to the obedience that comes from faith—to the only wise God be glory forever through Jesus Christ! Amen. (Rom 16: 25–27)

According to Paul, the life of the believer and of the church is an ever-deepening discovery of the riches of God's wisdom in Christ.

> I keep asking that the God of our Lord Jesus Christ, the glorious Father, may give you the Spirit of wisdom and revelation, so that you may know him better. I pray that the eyes of your heart may be enlightened in order that you may know the hope to which he has called you, the riches of his glorious inheritance in his holy people, and his incomparably great power for us who believe. (Eph 1:17–19)

This life-long learning is productive of lives worthy of the Lord Jesus, pleasing him, doing good works, growing in our knowledge of God, power to endure, and joyful thanksgiving:

> We continually ask God to fill you with the knowledge of his will through all the wisdom and understanding that the Spirit gives, so that you may live a life worthy of the Lord and please him in every way: bearing fruit in every good work, growing in the knowledge of God, being strengthened with all power according to his glorious might so that you may have great endurance and patience, and giving joyful thanks to the Father, who has qualified you to share in the inheritance of his holy people in the kingdom of light. For he has rescued us from the dominion of darkness and brought us into the kingdom of the Son he loves, in whom we have redemption, the forgiveness of sins. (Col 1:9–14)

So, to conclude: We do not know God's wisdom unless we find it as a theological category in the Bible. We do not know God's wisdom unless we know Christ. We do not know God's wisdom unless we know Christ crucified. So then, let us search diligently for the breadth and depth of God's wisdom throughout the Bible. Then we will praise Christ the slaughtered and risen Lamb, and our great and holy God, in these heavenly words:

> "Worthy is the Lamb, who was slain, to receive power and wealth and wisdom and strength and honor and glory and praise!" . . . "Praise and glory and wisdom and thanks and honor and power and strength be to our God for ever and ever." (Rev 5:12; 7:12)

Bibliography

Adam, Peter. "A Biblical Theology of Wisdom: The Only Wise God." *Vox Reformata* 79 (2014) 4–27.

Calvin, John. *Institutes of the Christian Religion*. Edited by John T. McNeill. Translated by Ford Lewis Battles. LCC. Philadelphia: Westminster, 1960.

Ciampa, Roy E., and Brian S. Rosner. *The First Letter to the Corinthians*. PNTC. Grand Rapids: Eerdmans, 2010.

Clements, R. E. *Wisdom in Theology*. Carlisle: Paternoster, 1992.

Goldsworthy, Graeme. *Gospel and Wisdom: Israel's Wisdom Literature in the Christian Life*. Homebush West: Lancer, 1987.

Longman, Tremper, III. *The Fear of the Lord is Wisdom: A Theological Introduction to Wisdom in Israel*. Grand Rapids: Baker, 2017.

Schnabel, E. J. "Wisdom." In *New Dictionary of Biblical Theology*, edited by T. D. Alexander and Brian S. Rosner, 843–48. Leicester: IVP, 2000.

Wilson, Lindsay. *Joseph, Wise and Otherwise: The Intersection of Wisdom and Covenant in Genesis 37–50*. Carlisle: Paternoster, 2004.

———. *Proverbs*. TOTC. Downers Grove: InterVarsity, 2017.

Witherington, Ben, III. *Jesus the Sage: The Pilgrimage of Wisdom*. Minneapolis: Fortress, 2009.

17

Old Testament Calls to Thankfulness

ANDREW S. MALONE

WE CAN ENHANCE OUR personal and corporate worship by growing in appreciation for the whole Bible's consistent emphasis on thanksgiving. Thankfulness in our prayers and our church services is sometimes lacking, perhaps more absent in affluent suburbs and nations.[1] So adding the Old Testament's expectations to the New Testament's frequent commands for gratitude can aid our development. Yet we may be unsure how the Old Testament joins the New in casting thankfulness as an essential element of worship, especially when scholars themselves complain how little attention is given to the Old Testament's contributions to this topic.[2]

This chapter encourages those who would live wisely and minister wisely to amplify biblical enthusiasm for thanksgiving. It modestly aims to signpost some of the more obvious and less obvious avenues for exploring this element of thankfulness, especially corporate gratitude to God. After brief surveys of the New Testament's weighty emphases and the Old Testament's direct calls to thankfulness, we inspect some of the more subtle ways in which the Old Testament—three-quarters of the Bible—further

---

1. Some of the psychological and sociological challenges to thankfulness are identified by the likes of Butler Bass, *Grateful*.

2. Block, *For the Glory of God*, 3–6; Webber's foreword to Hill, *Enter His Courts with Praise!*, xv. Works progressively filling this lacuna include Longman, *Immanuel in Our Place*; Pierce, *Enthroned on Our Praise*; Thompson, *Greatly to be Praised*.

drives readers to recognize the importance of gratitude to God and to respond accordingly.

The Value of the Quest

The New Testament transparently offers direct commands to thankfulness and gratitude, often in the context of corporate gatherings, prayer, and worship. Alongside Pauline calls to intercession or peace or praise, thankfulness is forcefully expected (esp. Eph 5:18–20; Phil 4:4–7; Col 3:15–17; 1 Thess 5:16–18). Jesus makes pointed calls "to rejoice" (e.g., Matt 5:12; parabolically Luke 15:6, 9, 32). The climactic instruction in Hebrews 12:28 is to "be thankful," likely summarizing the whole homily and controlling its remaining ethical injunctions.[3] That verse also declares thankfulness a core element of "acceptable worship."

Direct commands are matched by indirect modelling. Throughout Paul's letters, not least in their introductions, "prayers of gratitude or thanks were a major part of his prayer."[4] There are consequently several significant studies of Pauline thankfulness.[5] Luke's narratives promote examples of praise and joy as positive models (e.g., Luke 24:52; Acts 2:47; 5:41; 13:52). Thankfulness to God is one of Paul's ministry goals (2 Cor 4:15; 9:11–12) and such thanks is depicted in Revelation's images of heavenly worship (Rev 4:9; 7:12; 11:17). Conversely, thanklessness typifies unbelievers (Rom 1:21; 2 Tim 3:2; cf. Eph 5:3–5).

We might excuse all this as some new-covenant excess or a cultural phenomenon shaped by Greco-Roman patronage. But there are many Old Testament precursors encouraging us to detect a whole-canon biblical theology of thankfulness. As with some of their New Testament counterparts, some of these Old Testament precursors are more obvious and others are easily overlooked.[6]

A canonical study of thankfulness is all the more important when scholars prematurely protest the scarcity of relevant material. One biblical-theological dictionary opens its study pessimistically: "Early in the Old Testament both the language and the concept of thanksgiving are conspicuous by their absence. The Old Testament lacks an independent vocabulary

---

3. Koester, *Hebrews*, 554–56; DeSilva, *Perseverance in Gratitude*, 473–79.

4. Witherington, *Thessalonians*, 154.

5. For example, O'Brien, *Introductory Thanksgivings*; Pao, *Thanksgiving*. Pao's opening chapter (esp. 21–33) surveys relevant OT and NT terminology.

6. I acknowledge here my debt to Lindsay Wilson, who first introduced me to the language and practice of biblical theology.

of thanksgiving or gratitude."[7] The prominent *Anchor Bible Dictionary* acknowledges the thanksgiving genre within the Psalter, but its dedicated article on "Thanksgiving" concerns only New Testament phenomena.[8] As with similar topics, the clarity and popularity of the New Testament threaten to drown out the Old Testament's contributions.

Direct Calls to Thankfulness

Certainly, the Old Testament offers overt commands for thankfulness. Psalms 105, 106, 107, 118, and 136 each opens with the same directive: "Give thanks to the Lord." The same notion also concludes the latter two psalms, and the third-person equivalent constitutes the structuring refrain of Psalm 107. We cannot read and appropriate such psalms without hearing this call.

The call's prominence, however, is easily muddied by the overlapping of related terms and ideas, and this overlapping occurs along several axes. (1) Hebrew distinctions are not always clear to English readers. The Hebrew word group (verb *ydh*) is variously translated "to give thanks" or "to praise" or "to confess," even though "praise" also renders another lexical family (*hll*). (2) These two lexical families already overlap, and they also overlap with the idea of "bless(ing)" (*brk*).[9] (3) Traditional studies, especially in the psalms, have appropriated these terms as genre labels, sometimes attempting to distinguish too rigidly between "thanksgiving" (largely individuals' declarative songs of God's specific actions) and "praise" (largely corporate descriptive hymns of God's character and attributes). It is valuable to acknowledge the disadvantages of such overlap—but also the advantageous doors that this overlap can open.[10]

Thus, even though we might start with narrow "thank(fulness)" language, the concept is readily glimpsed in the wider overlapping terms. Between them we easily find many commands to thank (and praise and bless) Yahweh. Just as we must be wary of multiple word groups, we must also be alert to the varied grammatical forms through which thankfulness is encouraged. A few examples from the Psalter must suffice. Readers are

---

7. Doriani, "Thankfulness, Thanksgiving," 769.

8. Wolff, "Thanksgiving."

9. Other terms are also relevant. So Ps 34:3: "*Glorify* the Lord with me, and let us *exalt* his name together." The three verbs already identified are regularly deemed primary. (All translations are my own.)

10. See the recognition of substantial overlap in Miller, *They Cried to the Lord*, 402–4, and in the primary and secondary sources in Pao, *Thanksgiving*, 25–27.

encouraged that "It is good to give thanks to Yahweh ... to praise musically ... to declare ..." (Ps 92:1–2 [2–3]). Psalm 95 opens with the invitation: "Come, let us sing to Yahweh, let us shout joyfully ... Let us come before his presence with thanksgiving, with songs ..." (95:1–2; cf. 147:7). Variations in terminology and grammar are neatly showcased in the one psalm inscribed "A Psalm for Thanksgiving": "Enter his gates with thanksgiving, his courts with praise. Give thanks to him; bless his name" (100:4).

Indirect Calls in Independent Poems

We are starting to observe that unmistakable *calls* to thankfulness are not always cast as direct *commands* to be thankful. Psalm 33:2 insists, "Give thanks to Yahweh," but the preceding colon is equally instructive in affirming, "Praise befits the upright." We turn to consider these more indirect calls, looking first at another independent poem within the Psalter before turning to poetry recorded within narratives. These less direct calls to thankfulness are more subtle, so we grant them more attention.

The one psalm overtly titled "Praise" exhibits these more subtle elements. Even if scholars are not agreed on every element, several likely hints cumulatively endorse Psalm 145 as another call to thankfulness.

- Key verbs of thanks and praise are found in the opening, middle, and closing verses (145:1–3, 10, 21). Competing structural options each acknowledge these verses as significant.[11]

- This psalm depicts one Israelite at worship. Yet this worshipper describes how God's people (along with his works) should join in such recounting of Yahweh's magnificence (e.g., 145:4–7, 10–12). There is even overt identification of all humanity and every living thing doing so, beyond the covenant people (145:12, 16, 21). It is little surprise then that several translations interpret the final colon more prescriptively: "All flesh *must* bless his holy name forever and ever" (cf. NIV, ESV, CSB).

- Westermann thus counts this among the "Imperative Psalms"—even though it appears to lack much in the way of direct commands.[12] Prinsloo builds on this to identify Psalm 145 as "a persuasive text."[13] Indeed,

---

11. So Lindars, "Psalm CXLV"; Kimelman, "Psalm 145," esp. 40–41, 48, 57; Goldingay, *Psalms 90–150*, 696, 704; all confirmed by DeClaissé-Walford, "Psalm 145." The verses remain influential, e.g., Tucker and Grant, *Psalms 2*, 988, 994; Estes, *Psalms 73–150*, 604; Rahn, "Aspects," 207.

12. Westermann, e.g., *Praise and Lament*, 130–32.

13. Prinsloo, "Psalm 145," 468–69 ("'n oorredende teks").

Allen names *many* of its verbs "indirect calls to praise" and translates them in the same prescriptive way that many render the final verse.[14]

- Some suggest this psalm formed the original conclusion to Book V, which itself begins with the call to thanksgiving in Psalm 107.[15]
- This possibility further highlights the prominence of the closing *Hallel* collection (Pss 146–150), with its direct calls to praise, and of the title assigned to the whole Psalter: "the term *praises* (*tᵉhillîm*) does accurately caption the *telos* toward which both individual songs and the collection as a whole move—toward praise of the Lord."[16]

We must thus be alert to various indirect ways in which thankfulness is promoted in such poems. It may influence a psalm's framing and themes (e.g., Pss 117, 118), its internal structure and refrains (e.g., Pss 107, 136), and perhaps even its placement within the collection (e.g., Ps 145).

Indirect Calls in Embedded Poetry

It is widely known that biblical narratives can incorporate poetic elements, including elements found also in the Psalter. Whether we call them "embedded psalms" or "inset hymns,"[17] such labels imply *intentional* incorporation. Careful inspection of these texts demonstrates that a narrator's intention can be to solicit thankfulness from readers. We see this in examples from the earliest and latest Old Testament narratives.

Early Victory Hymns

The song(s) of Moses and Miriam (Exod 15) and the song of Deborah (Judg 5) are considered among the earliest source materials in the Old Testament. Inclusion in their respective narratives seeks to evoke thankfulness as much as to report it.

Exodus 15 is heavily studied by scholars but easily overlooked in contemporary church settings. Moses and Miriam lead the people in musical praise that theologically interprets and celebrates what Yahweh has done

---

14. Allen, *Psalms 101–150*, 366–67 (translation), 368 (quote).

15. Wilson's influence (*Editing of the Hebrew Psalter*) is still seen in the likes of Grogan (*Prayer, Praise and Prophecy*, 246–47) and Boda (e.g., *Severe Mercy*, 448–50).

16. DeClaissé-Walford et al., *Psalms*, 3; cf. McCann, *Theological Introduction*, 53–54.

17. Respectively, e.g., Pierce, *Enthroned on Our Praise*, 4; the subtitle of Watts, *Psalm and Story*.

for his people in the dramatic narrative of prior chapters. Caught up with myriad textual and historical matters, commentators can fail to address the rhetorical purpose for the inclusion of this lyrical reflection. Many lay readers naively assume that this is simply "what happened next" and can fail to ask the same question. Potentially worse, narrative-focused ministry may simply skip ahead to the next action scene.

Enns refreshingly asks, "So why select this [song]?" Whether we are convinced by his every rationale, we should agree that "Built into Scripture is the notion that the song should be repeated."[18] The same conclusion is reached by Watts's studies of poetry integrated into narratives—sometimes at a narrative's climax: "hymnic poetry in this position invites readers to join in the celebration, an effect which is especially strong in the victory songs of Exodus 15, Judges 5, and Judith 16."[19] Later readers are caught up with the Israelite women, and probably also with the Israelite men, when Miriam commands them, "Sing to the LORD" (15:21). The notion is further reinforced if Janzen is correct that Miriam's song and command are primary, and that the longer record of Moses and the Israelites in 15:1–18 already serves as one example.[20]

In short, while Miriam's prescriptive command is clearly addressed to freshly rescued Israelites, and while that command may be overshadowed by Moses's descriptive example, both the command and its exemplar are intended to tutor later readers in thankfulness. The Song at the Sea functions for future generations as an indirect call to thanks and praise.

We have just observed the parallels that Watts sees between the placement of the hymns of Exodus 15 and Judges 5. Other parallels between the hymns are commonly adduced.[21] Like Miriam's song, Deborah's takes shape calling the Israelites (and perhaps pagan leaders) to "bless the LORD" (Judg 5:2). Several analysts see the first poetic section (5:2–8) repeated in the second (5:9–13): both sections open with this same command and furnish bases for doing so.[22] Indeed, Block is confident that Deborah's calls to "bless Yahweh" in musical format "set the tone for the entire song" and

---

18. Enns, *Exodus*, 306–7; cf. 314; Alexander, *Exodus*, 307; Fretheim, *Exodus*, 161–63.

19. Watts, "Song," 139; cf. Watts, *Psalm and Story*, e.g., 60–62.

20. Janzen, "Song," 212–16, followed by such as Hamilton, *Exodus*, 235; Alexander, *Exodus*, 286, 305–6.

21. Scholars remain particularly reliant on Hauser, "Two Songs."

22. Younger, *Judges, Ruth*, 148–49; Webb, *Judges*, 199–203; cf. O'Connell, *Rhetoric of Judges*, 113–14.

"also announce the theme."[23] Just as Exodus 15 has subsequent generations of readers in mind, so too does Judges 5.

> The placement of the victory hymn *after* the prose account of the battle intentionally mirrors the celebration of victors *after* the historical event . . . and inspires the reader to rejoice with them. The poem was deemed useful to the author of the book because it draws the reader into the ancient celebrants' praise to God.[24]

Thus we come to appreciate that such hymns are typically not mere descriptions to inform us of an individual's praise. Just as the form and content of inset hymns is consistent with free-standing psalms,[25] so too can be their function. We should be confident that some first-person "descriptive" accounts are designed to be "prescriptive" for wider participants. There are more calls to thankfulness than a surface reading may disclose.

Later Liturgical Narratives

The early victory hymns can have prescriptive intent, even when recorded as first-person descriptions. The liturgical elements that pervade the postexilic narratives carry equally prescriptive undertones for later readers, even if cast as second-person commands or third-person narratives concerning earlier generations. We find the same indirect calls to thankfulness in these late writings that conclude the Hebrew canon.

Our entrée into Chronicles is provided by the liturgical formula that opens Psalms 106, 107, 118, and 136: "Give thanks to the LORD, for he is good, for his faithfulness endures forever."[26]

This formula dominates the embedded song in 1 Chronicles 16. The hymns of Exodus and Judges are placed after the narrative events they celebrate. But the Chronicler infuses this composite psalm into the center of the narrative it enhances. This "interruption" sparks several fruitful observations and questions. Japhet argues attractively that the Chronicler has taken a source such as 2 Samuel 6:17–20, has (compiled and) inserted the composite psalm therein, and has further wrapped the new poetic

23. Block, *Judges, Ruth*, 221.
24. Block, *Judges, Ruth*, 184.
25. Childs, *Exodus*, 249–50.
26. Miller's detailed study of prayers of doxology and trust (*They Cried to the Lord*, ch. 6) persistently labels this formula "the model prayer of thanks" (e.g., 205) and argues that it is paradigmatic of OT thankfulness—akin to the NT's Lord's Prayer (e.g., 194–95, 407 n. 29). While alert to the OT's use of "praise" and "bless" language, Miller favors "thanks(giving)" as the foundational concept.

composition in additional paired layers of introduction and conclusion.[27] What do the extra framing narratives and the poem contribute to the installation of the ark in Jerusalem? Nielsen insightfully observes that any contribution could have been cast purely as a narrative, even just a short report. Why then craft such a lengthy and poetic version?[28]

Why are these verses here, and why in this form? Commentators are commonly distracted by the synoptic parallels with Samuel or with the three psalms from which the new song is derived, or by the linguistic and theological links with nearby chapters. Their questions primarily concern *how* these verses are here. The *why* questions are largely unaddressed, and the impression can be given that this singing is simply "what happened" on this occasion. But if "[t]he Chronicler skillfully uses the Song of Asaph to achieve a desired effect,"[29] we should investigate his intentions.

It is generally agreed that the song recorded in 16:8–36 was assembled by the Chronicler and was not previously in independent circulation. These were thus unlikely the exact lyrics sung in David's day. Rather, the current record offers "an example of the kind of expressions David had in mind."[30] Such textual updating suggests that the Chronicler had particular application in mind for his own later readers.

One important hint is commonly noted: such a song was not sung merely on the day of the ark's installation. The additional narrative introduction and conclusion both assure us that the liturgists' behavior before the ark occurred "perpetually" (16:6, 37; cf. 40; the later verses add further temporal markers). Indeed, both introduction and conclusion define the leaders' tasks: Asaph and his Levitical peers are appointed "for ministering before the ark" (16:4, 37). The prior chapter has already used similar language to confirm that Yahweh had designated the Levites "to minister to/before him forever" (15:2). The flavor of the scene suggests that it represents not merely a single occasion but exemplifies "the typical work of the Levitical singers."[31]

In turn, we hear that such typical ministry is intended "to invoke and to thank and to praise the LORD God of Israel" (16:4). As is regularly demonstrated, this is precisely what the poetic element illustrates. With a fresh reminder that David appoints Asaph and company "to give thanks to

---

27. Japhet, *Chronicles*, 311–12; cf. Klein, *1 Chronicles*, 351; Selman, *1 Chronicles*, 166.

28. Nielsen, "Whose Song of Praise?," esp. 329, 331–33.

29. Doan and Giles, "Song of Asaph," 29.

30. Boda, *Chronicles*, 148. An example extended or rendered in later wording need not deny the historicity of David's appointed liturgists or their singing. On textual updating to benefit later readers, see Malone, "Acceptable Anachronism."

31. Watts, *Psalm and Story*, 155–56.

Yahweh" (16:7), readers witness the celebrants leading in thanksgiving and prayer in a song drawn from Psalms 105, 96, and 106. The song opens with the command, "Give thanks to the LORD" (16:8; cf. Ps 105:1). Subsequent cola rattle off various synonyms and attendant actions, including "sing . . . praise musically . . . boast [another form of *hll*] . . ." Each new incorporation of an existing psalm marks a fresh section, and each section continues in this vein. The liturgical leaders thus again command the congregation (along with all creation) to "Sing to Yahweh" (16:23; cf. Ps 96:1). The final section in the medley picks out the start and end of Psalm 106, which is heavy on thanksgiving language:

> Give thanks to the LORD, for he is good,
>
> > for his faithfulness endures forever . . .
>
> Save us, LORD our God,
>
> > and gather us from the nations,
>
> so that we may give thanks to your holy name
>
> > and may glory in your praise.
>
> Blessed be the LORD God of Israel,
>
> > from everlasting to everlasting.
>
> (Ps 106:1, 47–48; cf. 1 Chr 16:34–36)

Hill even argues that the imperatives throughout the song ("give thanks," "sing") sit behind the Chronicler's choice and arrangement of the original psalm extracts.[32] The overall focus on thanksgiving sits prominently both on the surface of the text and behind its arrangement, in both the new poetic composition and the new narrative that frames it. (Even though the camera then pans to the tabernacle at Gibeon, 16:41 portrays the musicians there likewise giving thanks to Yahweh accompanied by the paradigmatic liturgy.)

In turn, this liturgical celebration is cast to speak to the Chronicler's own readers. The Levitical singers speak in second-person plural language. Even if this might appear incidental, the reimaged composition adds an additional imperative. The worship leaders cry out "Give thanks" in 16:34, but the next verse is now prefaced "And say . . ."; this offers 16:35 as a prayer for salvation that hearers themselves should pray. Narratively those hearers are Jerusalemites in David's day, but we gain the impression the narrator is extending this invitation to *his* readers.[33]

---

32. Hill, "Patchwork Poetry," 99–100.

33. Thus Williamson (*Chronicles*, 128) warns against dismissing the composition as a random example: "it would be surprising if it did not reflect some of his major

This sensation is reinforced when we discover similar language in similar contexts as Chronicles progresses. Much the same happens, on grander scale, when Solomon installs the ark into the newly constructed temple. Like his father before him, Solomon organizes the Levitical procession with the elders and "all Israel" to establish the ark in its new dwelling (2 Chr 5; cf. 1 Chr 15). The musical Levites—again headed by Asaph—then assemble "to praise and to give thanks to Yahweh," and the ensuing words ("For he is good, for his faithfulness endures forever") are regularly interpreted as the content of their song (2 Chr 5:13). Throughout the Psalter, this is the obedient rejoinder to calls to "Give thanks to the Lord!" Chronicles then gives an extended report on Solomon's dedicatory prayers. In response to Solomon's invitation, Yahweh's glory fills the temple, at which point the people's response (and the Chronicler's choice of inclusion and prominence) is salutary: "all the Israelites . . . bowed facedown and gave thanks to the Lord [saying], 'For he is good, for his faithfulness endures forever'" (7:3). David is soon posthumously remembered as crafting instruments for thanksgiving, accompanied by this same refrain (7:6).

These two major incidents are not chosen randomly, either in our study or by the Chronicler. When the ark is first brought to Jerusalem by David, the scene is depicted with an extended example of thanksgiving which is itself wrapped in overt narrative reinforcing this effect. We have seen that the chapter likely functions as a call to thanksgiving for the Chronicler's own readers. Then when the Jerusalem temple is dedicated by David's chosen son, it is similarly wrapped in examples of liturgical thanksgiving. Whether or not we press as far as seeing a chiastic presentation of the entire Solomon account, certainly these thanksgivings function as "a framing device enclosing Solomon's prayer."[34] The Chronicler may not be calling his readers to thanksgiving in the same way that he does in 1 Chronicles 16, but this significant human response before Yahweh cannot be overlooked.

Such modelling of thanksgiving pervades the book. The Chronicler recounts God's positive and negative responses to successive monarchs. God's verdict is often tied closely to a king's treatment of Yahwistic worship, itself epitomized by the monarch's treatment of the temple and its cultic system. And we find that the role of thanksgiving is commonly a part of this treatment.

---

concerns." Note also the arm's-length, third-person ideas recast as immediate second-person notions; this recasting "allows the Chronicler to turn audiences into active participants" (Doan and Giles, "Song of Asaph," 35–39, quote 38).

34. Thompson, *Chronicles*, 234. For chiastic arrangement of 2 Chr 1–9, see Dillard, *2 Chronicles*, 5–6, 55–56.

- When David organizes the temple personnel in anticipation, we hear again that some of the Levites have a "perpetual" service "to give thanks to and to praise Yahweh" (1 Chr 23:30–31). Japhet identifies this role as earning the most detail and thus being the most important of the Levites' attendant responsibilities.[35]

- As David hands over the throne and temple-building responsibility to Solomon, readers are shown examples and summaries and public instructions of his "blessing" Yahweh (1 Chr 29:10–20). The extended example itself is captured in its final verse, where David describes his blessing with this result: "Now therefore, our God, we are giving thanks to you and praising your glorious name" (29:13).[36] The emphasis on thanksgiving is even more pronounced if this prayer intentionally parallels the thanksgiving song in 1 Chronicles 16 such that the two chapters frame David's temple preparations.[37]

- Before an international battle, Jehoshaphat leads his people in worship and praise. A stirring speech to trust God's promised victory is accompanied by the appointment of some to sing to Yahweh and some to praise. Their central lyric is recorded: the liturgical refrain familiar from the days of the united monarchy, "Give thanks . . ." The Chronicler is also at pains to record their musical gratitude after victory, after which gratitude a local landmark is renamed (2 Chr 20:18–28). Such expressions of worship "are so numerous in this pericope as practically to dominate the story."[38] The emphasis on thanksgiving and praise is all the more pertinent if this occasion is the "showpiece" of the Chronicler's presentation of the divided monarchy.[39]

- When Hezekiah purifies the temple generations later, the musical Levites are again expressly identified (29:13–14). The reforming king and his entourage not only enjoy musical accompaniment to their sacrifices, but musical worship overtly climaxes the rededication (29:25–30). Although the language here favors "praise" terminology over "thanksgiving," we might observe that (1) the lyrics are expressly named as "the words of David and Asaph the seer," suggesting an

---

35. Japhet, *Chronicles*, 420. This example and the next are identified by Hoglund, "Priest of Praise," 187.

36. The concluding force of the idiomatic term opening 29:13 is promoted by *DCH* 6, s.v. "עַתָּה"; Japhet, *Chronicles*, 510. Some structure 29:13 as starting a longer applied thanksgiving (e.g., Braun, *1 Chronicles*, 282–83; Hill, *Chronicles*, 348–50).

37. Williamson, *Chronicles*, 185–86.

38. Japhet, *Chronicles*, 782.

39. Selman, *2 Chronicles*, 420–21.

allusion to the extended thanksgiving at the installation of the ark in 1 Chronicles 16;[40] and (2) the reopened temple is immediately pronounced ready for sacrifices and thank-offerings, the latter term (*tôdôt*) indistinguishable from the noun for thanksgiving (2 Chr 29:31). Thankfulness is not the obvious focus of the chapter, yet "Chronicles also implies that atonement is not to be seen as an end in itself but as a preparation for praise and thanksgiving."[41]

- Asaphite musicians are also mentioned when Chronicles records an extended account of Josiah's reforms. As the Passover is instituted more permanently, and perhaps with a symbolic reenactment of the ark's installation (35:3), we hear both of Asaphite lineage and of conformity to the prescriptions of David, Asaph, and other musical leaders (35:15).

The connection between Chronicles and Ezra-Nehemiah is readily acknowledged, even if the details of that connection remain debated. To the extent that the reader of Chronicles was familiar with the text or events of Ezra-Nehemiah, we see the same connections further fortified. The foundation of the Second Temple is celebrated by Asaphite musicians, according to David's design, described as "giving praise and thanks to Yahweh," and again quoting the liturgical refrain (Ezra 3:10–11). The ancient models of David and Asaph in thanksgiving are repeatedly observed (Neh 11:17; 12:24, 45–47), giving every intimation that such thanksgivings (and other forms of worship) were thoroughly resumed in the postexilic community. The idea is so prevalent that the term for thanksgiving (*tôdâ*) comes to mean "a thanksgiving choir" (Neh 12:31, 38, 40).[42]

Scholars of the postexilic corpus remind us that these images intentionally highlight continuity with preexilic ideals.[43] They sometimes draw attention to this very expectation in the optimistic chapters of Jeremiah. The prophet had foreseen a time when celebrations would return to Jerusalem, including "those saying, 'Thank the LORD of hosts, for the LORD is good, for his faithfulness endures forever,' while bringing a thank-offering

---

40. Japhet, *Chronicles*, 929: "Hezekiah's acts are here presented as a full revival of David's institutions." Other elements of David's collusion with Asaph may be in mind, and those too include overt mention of music employed "in thanksgiving and praise to Yahweh" (1 Chr 25:3).

41. Selman, *2 Chronicles*, 491.

42. Allen, "ידה," 407. Williamson (*Ezra, Nehemiah*, 367–68) finds this usage also in 12:27.

43. So Kidner (*Ezra and Nehemiah*, 47), speaking of "conscious echoes of Solomon's celebrations."

[to] the house of the Lord" (Jer 33:11). We have not previously noted that verbal thanksgiving accompanies such thank-offerings, though the two are aligned elsewhere (e.g., Ps 107:21–22).[44]

A Pervasive Expectation

Expectations concerning thankfulness flow throughout the temporal and canonical sweep of the Old Testament, including calls to thankfulness that are less obvious. The songs preserved in Exodus 15 and Judges 5 are not simply lyrical interpretation of historical events. We have noted the prevalence of thanksgiving from the earliest highlights of the Davidic dynasty, reprised at subsequent key moments through the divided monarchy and after the return from exile. It is entirely relevant that Chronicles' retelling of monarchical history and Israelite worship joins Ezra-Nehemiah in completing the Hebrew canon. Nor are these merely convenient bookends; the themes emphasized in the postexilic narratives intentionally highlight important continuities, reinforcing "new beginnings that recreated old ideals."[45]

Between the earliest and latest of the Old Testament texts, there are many further points that reinforce these expectations of thanksgiving. Among the earlier books, we might note the institution of thank-offerings (esp. Lev 7:12–15). It is even argued that the thanksgiving variant is the most elaborate of the fellowship offerings, "perhaps suggesting that it was the most sacred of the three."[46] Hamilton similarly argues that the first three broader categories of offerings in Leviticus, including the fellowship offerings, focus on praise and thanksgiving; it is only the subsequent categories that facilitate restoration when worship is interrupted by transgression.[47] Among the later writings, we sometimes overlook that Daniel's thrice-daily prayers in exile—those for which he is sentenced to death—are typified as involving thanksgiving (Dan 6:10). For contemporary churches keen to emphasize God's provision of Old Testament sacrifices and liturgies for atonement, we do well to enhance our appreciation also of Old Testament sacrifices and liturgies for thankfulness.

There is much more to be done to investigate thanksgiving in the Old Testament. There remain other inset poems and fleeting reports of

---

44. Allen, *Jeremiah*, 376. The pairing of thanksgiving in song and sacrifice is often noted in the two halves of Ps 116; e.g., Creach, "Cult, Worship: Psalms," 73.

45. Allen, "For He Is Good," 34.

46. Sklar, *Leviticus*, 134; cf. 135.

47. Hamilton, *Handbook on the Pentateuch*, 233–37.

thankfulness.[48] And there are yet further rhetorical ways to craft exhortations.[49] There is every motivation to continue such study. And there is every indication that much of the Old Testament canon from beginning to end models and invites—and instructs—thanksgiving to God.

Bibliography

Alexander, T. Desmond. *Exodus*. ApOTC 2. London: Apollos, 2017.
Allen, Leslie C. "'For He Is Good . . .': Worship in Ezra–Nehemiah." In *Worship and the Hebrew Bible: Essays in Honour of John T. Willis*, edited by M. Patrick Graham, et al., 15–34. JSOTSup 284. Sheffield: Sheffield Academic, 1999.
———. *Jeremiah: A Commentary*. OTL. Louisville: Westminster John Knox, 2008.
———. *Psalms 101–150*. Rev. ed. WBC 21. Nashville: Thomas Nelson, 2002.
———. "ידה." In *NIDOTTE* 2:405–8.
Block, Daniel I. *For the Glory of God: Recovering a Biblical Theology of Worship*. Grand Rapids: Baker Academic, 2014.
———. *Judges, Ruth*. NAC 6. Nashville: Broadman & Holman, 1999.
Boda, Mark J. *1–2 Chronicles*. Cornerstone Biblical Commentary 5A. Carol Stream: Tyndale House, 2010.
———. *A Severe Mercy: Sin and Its Remedy in the Old Testament*. Siphrut 1. Winona Lake: Eisenbrauns, 2009.
Braun, Roddy L. *1 Chronicles*. WBC 14. Waco: Word, 1986.
Butler Bass, Diana. *Grateful: The Transformative Power of Giving Thanks*. San Francisco: HarperOne, 2018.
Childs, Brevard S. *The Book of Exodus: A Critical, Theological Commentary*. OTL. Philadelphia: Westminster, 1974.
Creach, Jerome F. D. "Cult, Worship: Psalms." In *DOTWPW* 71–78.
DeClaissé-Walford, Nancy L. "Psalm 145: All Flesh Will Bless God's Holy Name." *Catholic Biblical Quarterly* 74 (2012) 55–66.
DeClaissé-Walford, Nancy L., et al. *The Book of Psalms*. NICOT. Grand Rapids: Eerdmans, 2014.
DeSilva, David A. *Perseverance in Gratitude: A Socio-Rhetorical Commentary on the Epistle "to the Hebrews."* Grand Rapids: Eerdmans, 2000.
Dillard, Raymond B. *2 Chronicles*. WBC 15. Waco: Word, 1987.
Doan, William, and Terry Giles. "The Song of Asaph: A Performance-Critical Analysis of 1 Chronicles 16:8–36." *Catholic Biblical Quarterly* 70 (2008) 29–43.
Doriani, Daniel. "Thankfulness, Thanksgiving." In *Evangelical Dictionary of Biblical Theology*, edited by Walter A. Elwell, 769–70. Grand Rapids: Baker, 1996.
Enns, Peter. *Exodus*. NIVAC. Grand Rapids: Zondervan, 2000.
Estes, Daniel J. *Psalms 73–150*. NAC 13. Nashville: B&H, 2019.
Fretheim, Terence E. *Exodus*. IBC. Louisville: John Knox, 1991.
Garland, David E. "Blessing and Woe." In *Dictionary of Jesus and the Gospels*, edited by Joel B. Green and Scot McKnight, 77–81. Leicester: Inter-Varsity Press, 1992.

---

48. For example, Gen 29:35; 1 Kgs 8:33, 35; 2 Chr 30:22; Isa 12:1, 4; 25:1; 51:3; Jer 30:19; Jonah 2:9.

49. Garland, "Blessing and Woe," 78.

Goldingay, John E. *Psalms, vol. 3: Psalms 90–150.* BCOTWP. Grand Rapids: Baker Academic, 2008.
Grogan, Geoffrey W. *Prayer, Praise and Prophecy: A Theology of the Psalms.* Fearn: Mentor, 2001.
Hamilton, Victor P. *Exodus: An Exegetical Commentary.* Grand Rapids: Baker Academic, 2011.
———. *Handbook on the Pentateuch.* 2nd ed. Grand Rapids: Baker Academic, 2005.
Hauser, Alan J. "Two Songs of Victory: A Comparison of Exodus 15 and Judges 5." In *Directions in Biblical Hebrew Poetry*, edited by Elaine R. Follis, 265–84. JSOTSup 40. Sheffield: JSOT, 1987.
Hill, Andrew E. *1 & 2 Chronicles.* NIVAC. Grand Rapids: Zondervan, 2003.
———. *Enter His Courts with Praise! Old Testament Worship for the New Testament Church.* Grand Rapids: Baker, 1993.
———. "Patchwork Poetry or Reasoned Verse? Connective Structure in 1 Chronicles XVI." *Vetus Testamentum* 33 (1983) 97–101.
Hoglund, Kenneth G. "The Priest of Praise: The Chronicler's David." *Review & Expositor* 99 (2002) 185–91.
Janzen, J. Gerald. "Song of Moses, Song of Miriam: Who Is Seconding Whom?" *Catholic Biblical Quarterly* 54 (1992) 211–20.
Japhet, Sara. *I & II Chronicles: A Commentary.* OTL. London: SCM, 1993.
Kidner, Derek. *Ezra and Nehemiah: An Introduction and Commentary.* TOTC 11. Leicester: IVP, 1979.
Kimelman, Reuven. "Psalm 145: Theme, Structure, and Impact." *Journal of Biblical Literature* 113 (1994) 37–58.
Klein, Ralph W. *1 Chronicles: A Commentary.* Hermeneia. Minneapolis: Fortress, 2006.
Koester, Craig R. *Hebrews: A New Translation with Introduction and Commentary.* AB 36. New York: Doubleday, 2001.
Lindars, Barnabas. "The Structure of Psalm CXLV." *Vetus Testamentum* 39 (1989) 23–30.
Longman, Tremper, III. *Immanuel in Our Place: Seeing Christ in Israel's Worship.* Phillipsburg: P&R, 2001.
Malone, Andrew S. "Acceptable Anachronism in Biblical Studies." *Bible Translator* 67 (2016) 351–64.
McCann, J. Clinton, Jr. *A Theological Introduction to the Book of Psalms: The Psalms as Torah.* Nashville: Abingdon, 1993.
Miller, Patrick D. *They Cried to the Lord: The Form and Theology of Biblical Prayer.* Minneapolis: Fortress, 1994.
Nielsen, Kirsten. "Whose Song of Praise? Reflections on the Purpose of the Psalm in 1 Chronicles 16." In *The Chronicler as Author: Studies in Text and Texture*, edited by M. Patrick Graham and Steven L. McKenzie, 327–36. JSOTSup 263. Sheffield: Sheffield Academic, 1999.
O'Brien, Peter T. *Introductory Thanksgivings in the Letters of Paul.* NovTSup 49. Leiden: Brill, 1977.
O'Connell, Robert H. *The Rhetoric of the Book of Judges.* VTSup 63. Leiden: Brill, 1996.
Pao, David W. *Thanksgiving: An Investigation of a Pauline Theme.* NSBT 13. Leicester: Apollos, 2002.
Pierce, Timothy M. *Enthroned on Our Praise: An Old Testament Theology of Worship.* NACSBT 4. Nashville: B&H Academic, 2008.

Prinsloo, Willem S. "Psalm 145: Loof Jahwe van A tot Z." *In die Skriflig* 25 (1991) 457–70.

Rahn, Nancy. "Aspects of Dynamic Remembering and Constructing in Psalm 145: A Contribution to the Study of Prayer in Persian and Hellenistic Times." In *Prayers and the Construction of Israelite Identity*, edited by Susanne Gillmayr-Bucher and Maria Häusl, 203–27. AIL 35. Atlanta: SBL, 2019.

Selman, Martin J. *1 Chronicles: An Introduction and Commentary*. TOTC 10A. Leicester: IVP, 1994.

———. *2 Chronicles: A Commentary*. TOTC 10B. Leicester: IVP, 1994.

Sklar, Jay. *Leviticus: An Introduction and Commentary*. TOTC 3. Nottingham: IVP, 2013.

Thompson, J. A. *1, 2 Chronicles*. NAC 9. Nashville: Broadman & Holman, 1994.

Thompson, Michael E. W. *Greatly to be Praised: The Old Testament and Worship*. Eugene: Pickwick, 2016.

Tucker, W. Dennis, Jr., and Jamie A. Grant. *Psalms, Volume 2*. NIVAC. Grand Rapids: Zondervan, 2018.

Watts, James W. *Psalm and Story: Inset Hymns in Hebrew Narrative*. JSOTSup 139. Sheffield: JSOT, 1992.

———. "Song and the Ancient Reader." *Perspectives in Religious Studies* 22 (1995) 135–47.

Webb, Barry G. *The Book of Judges*. NICOT. Grand Rapids: Eerdmans, 2012.

Westermann, Claus. *Praise and Lament in the Psalms*. Translated by Keith R. Crim and Richard N. Soulen. Atlanta: John Knox, 1981.

Williamson, H. G. M. *1 and 2 Chronicles*. NCB. London: Marshall, Morgan & Scott, 1982.

———. *Ezra, Nehemiah*. WBC 16. Waco: Word, 1985.

Wilson, Gerald H. *The Editing of the Hebrew Psalter*. SBLDS 76. Chico: Scholars, 1985.

Witherington, Ben, III. *1 and 2 Thessalonians: A Socio-Rhetorical Commentary*. Grand Rapids: Eerdmans, 2006.

Wolff, Christian. "Thanksgiving." In *ABD* 6:435–38.

Younger, K. Lawson, Jr. *Judges, Ruth*. NIVAC. Grand Rapids: Zondervan, 2002.

18

Waiting with Wisdom

Michelle Brennan

Throughout the Bible, believers are called upon to "wait." For what do we wait? We wait for God's promises to be fulfilled and for our prayers to be answered. The manner of our waiting determines whether or not we have faith and wisdom. Because faith is needed when promises are far off or delayed, and when answers to prayer are not immediate. In biblical terms, "waiting" is not passive, but active—waiting with hope and expectancy. To be wise in waiting requires patience and fortitude, having faith in both the promises of God and his character. The desire for wisdom is commended by God (1 Kgs 3:9–12), thus waiting with wisdom should be the aim of every Christian, not only for the fulfillment of God's promises for the future, but also for the day-to-day path through this earthly life. Those believers who follow Scripture's instructions and the biblical examples on how to wait in accordance with God's will, are indeed wise. Let us explore what the Old and New Testaments say about waiting with wisdom, and how it can instruct and help us today.

Wisdom While Waiting in the Old Testament

A key Old Testament example of waiting with faith is Abraham. God promised that he would be the father of many nations, and through him all the families on earth would be blessed (Gen 12:3; 13:4). As a first step to the realization of these promises, Abraham would father a son (Gen 15:4). Yet months and months, then years and years of waiting, did not see the promise of a son realized. When Isaac was finally born, and spared through God's intervention, Abraham's faith, through waiting and through testing, was now firmly anchored. He learnt through experience that God keeps his promises, and God can be trusted. The fulfillment of promises is thus rooted in God's character and his word. What he has said *will* come to pass, because of who God is.

The narratives of the Old Testament, particularly the deliverance of God's people from slavery in Egypt, give concrete proof that God keeps his promises. He can be trusted, and is sovereign over all things, and this includes our own personal journey through life. Our contemplation of the attributes of God should leave us awestruck. In biblical terms, this response is the "fear of the Lord"—total wonder, reverence, and awe.[1] Scripture confirms that the "fear of the Lord is the beginning of wisdom" (Ps 111:10). When we are experiencing difficulties in life, we can count on God's promises in Scripture, because of who God is. Even though God may not answer our prayers in the way we expect, or in *our* ideal timing, we should be waiting with total trust in a loving God who is all-powerful and all-good.

This is what Job ultimately learnt, after going through terrible hardships that he could not understand: "I cry to you and you do not answer me" (Job 30:20a). In response to Job's bewilderment, God pointed out to him that he, as a mere mortal, cannot possibly fathom the ways and purposes of the Almighty (Job 38–41). God gives a similar message through the prophet Isaiah, explaining that the ways of God are so much higher than ours (Isa 55:8, 9).

True wisdom must acknowledge that we are the created and God is the Creator, and yet, as God's commendation of Job shows, the wisdom of "fearing the Lord" embraces our honest feelings before the One who created us (Job 42:7). Faith is not negated by expressing emotions such as pain, despair, and anger. The very fact that we are expressing such feelings to God shows that we believe God is able to hear us. "[Job's] way of complaint, confrontation, and confusion is then a paradoxical way of expressing faith. Job is at the very least being genuine and honest before God."[2] This honesty before God is later commended by Jesus himself, who spoke vehemently against the pious hypocrisy of the Pharisees. Both Abraham and Job are commended in

---

1. The "fear of the Lord" is a constant thread throughout the Old Testament, from Genesis 20:11 through to Malachi 3:16. It also forms the framework of the book of Proverbs (1:7; 31:30), the content of which gives general wisdom in everyday living. Bible quotations are from the NRSV unless otherwise noted.

2. Wilson, *Job*, 257.

the New Testament for their patient endurance.[3] They present us, then, with further insight into how we should wait. It should be with faith, honesty, and patient perseverance through any adversity.

The Psalms bring a very personal dimension to "waiting." David often cries out to the Lord for immediate help—for immediate relief from fear, depression, and sickness. He knows that God will answer prayer because he knows God's character. Many Psalms start with this agonising plea for help, and end on a note of comfort or even triumph, as the Psalmist is reassured that God will answer his prayer, even though he may have to wait for the answer.[4] This involves waiting for God to act to relieve distress (37:7), to vindicate (25:3), or to protect in times of danger (33:20). In all cases the answers to prayer, for which the psalmist waits, are for this *present life*. In Psalm 130 the psalmist first calls on himself to wait, and then extends it to all God's people:

> I wait for the LORD, my soul waits,[5]
>
> and in his word I hope;
>
> my soul waits for the Lord
>
> more than those who watch for the morning,
>
> more than those who watch for the morning.
>
> O Israel, hope in the LORD!
>
> For with the LORD there is steadfast love. (Ps 130:6, 7a)

The waiting, which is entwined with hope, is thus grounded in God's word and his steadfast love. Knowing God's character in that he can do all things by his sovereign power, believers can wait with courage and confidence (Ps 27:14).

Isaiah also encourages the people of God to gain strength from the Lord by waiting upon him, and adds a further dimension—this strengthening through waiting will lead to action:

> But those who wait for the LORD shall renew their strength,[6]
>
> they shall mount up with wings like eagles,

---

3. Heb 6:15; Jas 5:11. See also Rom 4:1–3; Heb 11:8–19; and Jas 2:21–23 for references to Abraham.

4. For example, Psalm 13.

5. The Hebrew root for "wait" in this line is קָוָה which means waiting with eager expectation. "It means enduring patiently in confident hope that God will decisively act for the salvation of his people." Hartley, "קָוָה," 791.

6. Because of the intertwining of "wait" with "hope" in this context, the NIV translates the start of this verse (one word in the Hebrew—וְקֹוֵי) as, "But those who hope."

> they shall run and not be weary,
>
> they shall walk and not faint." (Isa 40:31)

At the start of his prophetic ministry, Isaiah had been given a vision of the holiness of God (6:1–8) and this certainly instilled the fear of the Lord into the prophet. For as God's holiness, as well as his divine sovereignty and power are acknowledged, the response of the wise can only be total awe. Isaiah looks forward to the day when God will redeem his people, "swallow up death forever," and "will wipe away the tears from all faces" (25:7, 8). These prophecies are clearly in the future, and will be reiterated by the apostle John in his visions many centuries later (Rev 21:4). How should the people of God respond?

> It will be said on that day,
>
> "Lo, this is our God; we have waited for him,
> so that he might save us,[7]
>
> This is the LORD for whom we have waited;
>
> let us be glad and rejoice in his salvation." (Isa 25:9)

The message of the prophets is for the people to repent and return to the Lord in obedience, and to await God's decisive action, whenever that might be. The Old Testament prophets were waiting for two wonderful future events: the coming of the Messiah, and the tremendous day of the Lord. They knew that both these events were outside their control; it would be God himself who would bring these events about. Hardships could be endured with the divine promise of these two happenings. The Messiah would bring deliverance to Israel, and the day of the Lord would bring judgment and the final defeat of Israel's enemies. In this regard, the waiting for these events was a corporate one; "the wise" in Israel waited patiently for the future intervention of an awesome God on his people's behalf. Thus the prophet Habakkuk relays the Lord's instructions:

> For there is still a vision for the appointed time;
>
> it speaks of the end, and does not lie.
>
> If it seems to tarry, wait for it;[8]
>
> it will surely come, it will not delay. (Hab 2:3)

Again, the root is קָוָה. It does strongly embrace the concept of "hope"; in fact, the Hebrew noun for "hope" תִּקְוָה is derived from it.

7. The NIV translates "waited" as "trusted." The Hebrew root for this word and Isaiah 40:31 cited above, is again קָוָה. It does imply waiting with both trust and hope.

8. The Hebrew word for "wait" here is חָכָה which does not occur as frequently as

As Armerding comments: "man never sees the entire pattern of salvation, so that events may seem delayed and disappointing from his perspective. For this reason man may lay hold of the future that God has revealed, waiting for it with an eager faith and hope that surpass the apparent obstacles to its realisation."[9]

In the book of Daniel, apocalyptic pictures of future events are given. Daniel is told to wait for certain events to take place, and that those who "persevere" during these days will be blessed (12:12).[10] Daniel is told by the divine messenger that "those who are wise shall shine like the brightness of the sky and those who lead many to righteousness, like the stars forever and ever" (12:3). Thus, those who reach out to save souls will be blessed. This will be reiterated in the New Testament, as Christ instructs his disciples on how they should wait for his second coming. The divine messenger announces to Daniel that some of those who have died shall awake "to everlasting life, and some to shame and everlasting contempt" (12:2). This prophecy anticipates things to come. However, it is only with the advent of the incarnate Christ, his teachings and his atoning death, resurrection, and ascension, that a "living hope" is realized (1 Pet 1:3).

Wisdom While Waiting in the New Testament

Now waiting takes on a new dimension. Whereas in Isaiah's prophetic vision (Isa 25:9, cited above) the joy is future, now, with the New Testament Scripture promises, the believer can wait *with joy* in the present. Yes, there will be hardships, but now there is "a sure and steadfast anchor of the soul" (Heb 6:19). We wait with eager expectation because we have Christ's own words, the words of his apostles, and the indwelling Holy Spirit to give reality to the promises. And in the person and mission of Jesus Christ, the reality of God's love is made manifest.

While Old Testament believers waited patiently for the coming Messiah and the day of the Lord, believers of today know that the Messiah has already come in the person of Jesus Christ and we wait for his promised return—his parousia (appearing) or second coming. While this will bring in the final judgment, for believers it will be a day of unparalleled joy as the

---

קָוָה. However, in the prophetic writings, it also carries with it the concept of waiting, or tarrying, with "an attitude of earnest expectation and confident hope." Yamauchi, "חָכָה," 282.

9. Armerding, *Habakkuk*, 512.

10. The NRSV translates חָכָה here as "persevere" rather than its usual meaning of "wait."

Lord Jesus takes us to himself, to be with him forever. The New Testament, including Jesus's own words, give us the promise of the parousia, and also tell us how we should wait for this tremendous event.

When asked by messengers from John the Baptist whether he was indeed the promised one, Jesus recounted the miracles he was performing (Matt 11:4-6) which fulfilled the prophecy of Isaiah. However, when asked under oath by the high priest whether or not he was the Son of God, Jesus, in his affirmative reply, did not refer to his miracles in the here and now, but referred to the *future*: "you will see the Son of Man seated at the right hand of the Power, and 'coming with the clouds of heaven'" (Mark 14:62). In these words, Jesus gives us a profound promise, echoing the words spoken to his disciples (Mark 13:26; Luke 17:24; 21:27), and promising the fulfillment of the vision of Daniel (Dan 7:13).

Jesus gives five parables to illustrate how he wants us to wait for his return. We must be alert and prayerful. Again, this is not passive waiting; the parables stress the need for preparation and readiness.[11] Jesus himself links this attitude with being wise. The ten virgins who have their lamps lit in readiness for the coming of the bridegroom (Matt 25:1-13) are described as wise—φρονιμοι, which can be translated as wise, sensible, or thoughtful; it implies having insight. Jesus uses this word four times in this parable. Similarly, the servant who is prepared for his master's return (Matt 24:45-51) is also described as wise—φρονιμος. "The wise hearer will stay ready, even though we cannot know the precise day and hour."[12]

There are two strands to our hope as individuals. One is that we will pass through death into eternal life, and the other is that Christ will return before we die. The apostle Paul speaks of both, and uses ἀπεκδεχομαι—to wait with eager expectation, for both. We eagerly await the culmination of our redemption (Rom 8:23, 25) and we eagerly await the coming of our Lord (1 Cor 1:7). In his letter to Titus, Paul calls this the "blessed hope" that believers have, "the manifestation of the glory of our great God and Saviour Jesus Christ" (Titus 2:13).

Jesus has promised to prepare a place for us (John 14:2), a place where there is no more sin and no more suffering (Rev 21:4). It is for this, our eternal home, that we wait. It is not wishful thinking, but a solid hope grounded in the character of God and his promises in Scripture. Our destiny is assured. It is seeing the glory of God in heaven, sharing in that glory

---

11. As Boice summarizes: "In each of these stories the Lord challenged his hearers to see life in terms of eternity and plan accordingly." Boice, *Parables*, 97.

12. MacArthur, *Second Coming*, 142. Jesus told his disciples that the exact day and hour of his return were known only to God the Father (Mark 13:32).

in our resurrected bodies, seeing Jesus face-to-face, and worshipping the triune God for all eternity.

James also gives clear instruction on how to wait with godly wisdom—the wisdom that comes "from above." This wisdom is "first pure, then peaceable, gentle, willing to yield, full of mercy and good fruits, without a trace of partiality or hypocrisy" (Jas 3:17). James instructs us to wait patiently, with steadfast hearts, "for the coming of the Lord is near" (5:8).

Both Paul and James present us with another aspect of Christian endurance in the midst of suffering—an aspect which is perhaps incomprehensible to unbelievers—and that is the characteristic of joy. "Rejoice in hope, be patient in suffering, persevere in prayer" (Rom 12:12). James states that believers have reason to rejoice even while suffering: "whenever you face trials of any kind, consider it nothing but joy, because you know that the testing of your faith produces endurance" (Jas 1:2, 3). This joy was promised by Jesus (John 16:24); it is different from "happiness," which is largely dependent upon circumstances or disposition—it is a fruit of the Holy Spirit (Gal 5:22).

James also tells us that if anyone lacks wisdom, he or she should ask God for it in prayer (Jas 1:5). One can conclude, therefore, that wisdom, and joy in trials, plus steadfastness in faith, are all God-given attributes (1:17), which will grow through prayer. Those who persevere in their Christian walk will be given "the crown of life that the Lord has promised to those who love him" (1:12). Our patient enduring thus shows our love for Christ.

The writer to the Hebrews confirms that Christ "will appear a second time . . . to save those who are eagerly waiting for him" (Heb 9:28).[13] So our waiting, in order to be wise, is to be expectant and eager, yet patient and steadfast. It is also to be fruitful; thus it is not passive waiting, but active waiting.

Christ intimated that there would be a large time span before his return: "this good news of the kingdom will be proclaimed throughout the world as a testimony to all the nations; and then the end will come" (Matt 24:14). Peter, also, indicates that the return of Christ might well be far into the future (2 Pet 3:8, 9), because of the Lord's desire to save many souls. Peter urges his fellow believers to stand firm during their time of waiting, as "scoffers" will try to undermine their faith (2 Pet 3:3, 4). Is this not a picture of today's society?

Then Peter adds another surprising development. As we continue "waiting for" the parousia, preparing for it by leading holy and godly lives, we can actually be "hastening" the Lord's return (2 Pet 3:12)! Some translate

---

13. Again the compound ἀπεκδεχομενοις is used here.

this as "earnestly desiring,"[14] but, as Kistemaker convincingly argues from its other occurrences in the New Testament, the verb σπευδω, always means "haste."[15] How can we hasten the Lord's return? The answer is from the Lord himself—by proclaiming the gospel so that souls are saved (Matt 24:14, cited above). "Accordingly, if we wish to speed the coming of God's day, we should evangelize the world."[16] This was the impetus behind the missionary zeal of two centuries ago, and it is still the inspiration of missionaries today. Now, with our Western society becoming increasingly secular, our mission field could well be our own neighbourhood.

There may be another important aspect of "hastening" our Lord's return. And that aspect is fervent, persistent prayer. God responds to such prayers (Luke 18:7, 8). Isaiah prayed for God to "tear open the heavens and come down" (Isa 64:1). Surely, we should be doing the same as we wait for that final day. We need to pray for the strengthening of our churches, that they would remain faithful to Christ's teaching, and be active in proclaiming the gospel. This is the mission of every Christian. "While we patiently wait for Christ's return and maintain our readiness for his coming, Christians must labour with zeal in the cause of the gospel and the building of the church."[17]

Both Paul and Peter urge us to lead holy lives in readiness for the Lord's return (1 Thess 3:13; 2 Pet 3:14, 15). Peter further remarks that Paul's exhortations are indeed "wisdom given him" (2 Pet 3:15). Jesus taught about his return as a vitally important future fact, and we are encouraged to preach it, talk about it, and ponder it. Paul tells the Thessalonians that they can "encourage one another" by reminding each other of the Lord's return (1 Thess 4:18; 5:11).[18] Our lives now, are a preparation for our future.

Wisdom While Waiting Today

However, while we wait in preparation for Christ's return at the end of history, believers are also required to wait, in the here and now, for answers to

---

14. The translation "earnestly desiring" is a margin note in the NIV and a footnote in the RSV. This translation is inadequate.

15. Kistemaker, *Peter*, 339. See Luke 2:16; 19:5, 6; Acts 20:16; 22:18.

16. Kistemaker, *Peter*, 339.

17. Phillips, *Thessalonians*, 324.

18. The verb used in both these verses, is παρακαλειτε, literally "calling alongside." It implies comfort as well as encouragement, hence the RSV translation of "comfort" in 4:18 and "encourage" in 5:11. Hence the Holy Spirit is referred to as "the Paraclete" (John 14:26).

prayer and for the Holy Spirit's leading. Again, our waiting is not passive but active. However, this does not mean frenetic activity for its own sake; active waiting embraces worship, prayer, and contemplation as well as fruitful service in the kingdom, building up Christ's church.

Before his ascension, Jesus told his disciples to "stay" in Jerusalem until the Holy Spirit came and "you have been clothed with power from on high" (Luke 24:49).[19] Only then could the fledgling church begin its mission. And that mission continues to this day. Through the Holy Spirit's guidance and giftings, we will know what tasks are required of us. Paul, in his Letter to the Colossians, prays that the Holy Spirit will guide the believers into "spiritual wisdom and understanding" so that their work will "bear fruit" (Col 1:9, 10).

Our present life will include trials and hardships; waiting with endurance will be required. Again, the knowledge of God's character is of vital importance here. Believers know that God is good, and that he will choose the best path for their ultimate good (Rom 8:28). Thus, believers who fear the Lord can endure hardships without their faith being eroded, even though it may be severely tested. The apostle Peter gives sound advice and comfort to those who are experiencing such hardships (1 Pet 1:6–8). Persevering, waiting with patience and fortitude, and fully trusting in God, will never be pointless. God will reward such faith.

This is especially applicable to those Christians who suffer from a disability, a chronic illness, or increased frailty. Active waiting is not the same as "activity"; people who are confined to a wheelchair, a hospital bed, or an aged care facility can still wait actively with eager expectation by remaining vigilant in prayer and steadfast in faith.

Amy Carmichael was a missionary in India from 1895 until her death in 1951. She devoted herself to rescuing girls destined to a life of temple prostitution. However, after an accident, she became bedridden, and was in constant pain for the last decade of her life. During that time, she was "active" in writing letters of encouragement to fellow Christians all over the world. "Which is harder, to do or to endure? I think to endure is much the harder, and our Father loves us too much to let us pass through life without learning to endure."[20]

Perhaps the greatest challenge to waiting with steadfast faith, and enduring with joy, is persecution. Being imprisoned for one's faith, undergoing torture, and even martyrdom, is a situation facing many Christians in today's

---

19. The word translated as "stay" here is καθισατε which literally means "sit." It suggests that active work could not commence until the empowering of the Holy Spirit.

20. Carmichael, *Candles*, 81.

world. Yet Christianity often grows under persecution, and it is purified (1 Pet 1:7). Our Lord Jesus predicted such persecution (Matt 24:9) and this gives believers reassurance that their suffering is not in vain. How do those suffering persecution show wisdom in waiting—waiting in cold prison cells, waiting for the next beating, waiting for an executioner's blade?

Richard Wurmbrand (1909–2001) spent fourteen years imprisoned by the Communist regime in Romania, three years of which were in solitary confinement in an underground cell, thirty feet underground, in total darkness.[21] He remarks that the Christians who survived best in prison, through months and months of deprivation and even torture, were those who were able to show the love of Christ to their fellow prisoners and even to their guards,[22] as the following true account reveals.

Liuba Ganevskaya was imprisoned for her faith in the Soviet Union. She was kept in a solitary cell, starved and repeatedly beaten by one prison guard, in particular. One day Liuba observed that the guard was as tired as she was. Her attitude, guided by the Holy Spirit, changed. Richard Wurmbrand, to whom she told the incident, relates what happened next:

> Liuba looked up at the one who had already lifted the whip to beat her and smiled. Stunned, he asked her, "Why do you smile?" She replied, "I don't see you as a mirror would reflect you right now. I see you as you surely once were, a beautiful, innocent child. We are the same age. We could have been playmates."[23]

Liuba then went on to tell the guard about Saul of Tarsus, who was a man like him, who then became Paul, a messenger of the Lord Jesus Christ. The guard put down his whip, and his life was touched by the love of Christ pouring out through this bruised and battered woman: "he became a changed man."[24]

Over the centuries, Christians facing martyrdom have shown extraordinary courage and a peace which passes all human understanding. Elizabeth Atwater, missionary to China, was martyred by decapitation in the Boxer Rebellion of 1900. Her final letters reflect her state of mind as she awaited execution. In her last letter to her co-workers, she wrote: "No one talked at meals. We seemed to be waiting for the end, and I, for my part, longed that it might come speedily . . . there will be a joyful welcome for us all above . . . Heaven seems very near, these last hours, and I feel

---

21. Wurmbrand, *Sermons*, 7.
22. Wurmbrand, *Tortured*, 53–94.
23. Wurmbrand, *Face of Surrender*, 67.
24. Wurmbrand, *Face of Surrender*, 67.

quite calm . . . I am fixing my thoughts more and more on the glorious hereafter, and it gives me a wonderful peace."[25] Her letters reflect a courageous yet serene waiting; it seems that ones who are sure of their heavenly destiny can face such terrors.

In the past twenty years Christians have been victims of shocking violence in various countries around the globe. When we hear of terrible persecutions and sufferings inflicted on our fellow believers, we echo the Psalmist's cry, "How long, O God?" (Ps 74:10). We need to learn from the example of the persecuted church, on how to be "overcomers"—those who have steadfast faith and who persevere even under the most difficult circumstances.

Those Christians who have, through the grace of God, persevered through trials and persecution, are given special recognition in heaven (Rev 12:11; 21:7). While it must be remembered that the apostle John paints his visions with broad brushstrokes, he does use words we can understand. The souls of martyrs are depicted as being "under the altar" (Rev 6:10), signifying sacrifice. In response to their cry—a cry repeated often in the Bible—of "how long?" before their suffering and death are vindicated, they are told to "rest a little longer" (6:11).[26] While this involves waiting, the verb "rest" indicates that these souls are at peace. They know God's character; they call him "sovereign" and "holy and true" (6:10). Therefore, they know he *will* act.

Then follows a further indication as to when the last day will occur. It is when the God-ordained total number of martyrs is reached (6:11). This glimpse into the heavenly realm, albeit in symbolic apocalyptic language, engenders hope and courage for those facing suffering even to the point of martyrdom, and also deep consolation for the families of those who have died for their faith.

Daily we need to remind ourselves of the character of our God and hold onto his promises, the "blessed hope" that trusts in the midst of turmoil, that remains steadfast and strong in the midst of our circumstances. Jesus's words, as recorded in the Gospels, assure us that he *will* return to this earth, and that our eternal heavenly home *is* real.

We need to raise our eyes and hearts heavenward when distressed by the evil and apathy around us, showing Christ's love and sharing the gospel to those who do not yet know the Savior. Finally, we need to wait wisely, remembering that in this life we are "in transit," rejoicing in knowing that our eternal destination is assured. Amen, come Lord Jesus.

25. Wong, *In Remembrance*, 2.

26. The verb used for "rest" is ἀναπαυσονται. It carries with it the concept of "respite" (Rev 4:8). Thus, the NIV translation "wait" is not wholly adequate.

Bibliography

Armerding, Carl E. "Habakkuk." In *The Expositor's Bible Commentary*, edited by Frank E. Gaebelen, 7:491–534. Grand Rapids: Zondervan, 1985.

Boice, James Montgomery. *The Parables of Jesus*. Chicago: Moody, 1983.

Carmichael, Amy. *Candles in the Dark*. Fort Washington: CLC, 1981.

Hartley, John E. "קָוָה." In *Theological Wordbook of the Old Testament*, edited by R. Laird Harris, Gleason L. Archer, and Bruce K. Waltke, 2:791. Chicago: Moody, 1980.

Kistemaker, Simon J. *Peter and Jude*. New Testament Commentary. Grand Rapids: Baker, 1987.

MacArthur, John. *The Second Coming*. Wheaton: Crossway, 1999.

Phillips, Richard D. *1 & 2 Thessalonians*. Reformed Expository Commentary. Phillipsburg: P&R, 2015.

Wanamaker, Charles A. *The Epistles to the Thessalonians*. NIGTC. Grand Rapids: Eerdmans, 1990.

Wilson, Lindsay. *Job*. THOTC. Grand Rapids: Eerdmans, 2015.

Wong, Sik Pui. *In Remembrance of Martyrs a Century Ago: Last Words and Letters from the Missionary Martyrs of the 1900 Boxer Incident*. Petaluma, CA: CCM, 2009.

Wurmbrand, Richard. *In the Face of Surrender*. North Brunswick, NJ: Bridge-Logos, 1998.

———. *Sermons in Solitary Confinement*. London: Hodder and Stoughton, 1969.

———. *Tortured for Christ*. Penrith, NSW: Stephanus, 1998.

Yamauchi, Edwin. "חָכָה." In *Theological Wordbook of the Old Testament*, edited by R. Laird Harris, Gleason L. Archer, and Bruce K. Waltke, 1:282. Chicago: Moody, 1980.

19

Lindsay Wilson: A "Living Treasure"

Edited and Compiled by Ruth Weatherlake

Past and present Ridley principals, Ridley colleagues, colleagues beyond Ridley, and Ridley students were invited to write a tribute to Lindsay.

Ridley Principals

Lindsay Wilson is the equivalent of a national treasure for Ridley College, the embodiment of the best of our heritage and identity. If Ridley is a boat, he has steadied the ship on numerous occasions. During my time as principal, he has proven to be the ideal senior colleague: patient and straight-talking, supportive and encouraging, wise and fair, with a deep knowledge of our history and context. It is no accident that he has been drawn to study the wisdom literature of the Old Testament. Lindsay's deep Christian faith and evident godliness is an ongoing encouragement to me personally and makes me glad I'm a Christian.

Brian Rosner
Principal, Ridley College, 2012–present

I greatly enjoyed working with Lindsay as a colleague at Ridley. As I reflect on his life and ministry in the college, the Bible verse that comes to mind is from Philippians 2:4, "not looking to your own interests but to the interests of others." Lindsay was constantly attentive to the needs and welfare of students, staff, and faculty. He is an example to us all. I say this not to praise Lindsay, but to praise God, who worked this constant quality into Lindsay's life. Praise God!

Peter Adam
Vicar Emeritus St Jude's Anglican Church Carlton
Principal, Ridley College, 2002–2012

I first met Lindsay at Moore College, and what an able student he proved to be. We then reconnected in Melbourne when I assumed the principal's role at Ridley. His scholarship is first rate. He became my vice-principal: competent, trustworthy, and so wise. I am grateful for the time we served together.

Graham A. Cole
Dean and Senior Vice President of Education and Professor of Biblical and Systematic Theology, Trinity Evangelical Divinity School
Principal, Ridley College, 1992–2001

Current Ridley Colleagues

What a joy to be able to honor my dear friend Lindsay Wilson on the occasion of this Festschrift! My relationship with Lindsay has been varied: his student, his mentee, his employer while I served on the Ridley Council, and now a valued colleague in academic ministry. In all these areas Lindsay has shown himself to be a man of balance, always ready to offer an alternative viewpoint and never to get locked into a position without nuance. Perhaps this comes from devoting your energy to the study of the wisdom literature of the Old Testament, though I have it on good authority that he owns some New Testament commentaries as well! He has taught me Hebrew, the value of lament, how to model the calm poise of a non-anxious presence, and the importance of perseverance. I am confident that his ministry in Melbourne will bear long-range fruit and am so thankful for him.

Rhys Bezzant
Senior Lecturer, Ridley College

Lindsay is a man respected by many people and has known many titles, among them Reverend, Doctor, Academic, Lecturer, and Author. But the title that I am honored to associate with Lindsay is "friend." Over the twenty-two years that I have known Lindsay he has been my colleague, supervisor, champion, supporter, mentor, and, at times, my pastor. He has stood by me during some of the happiest and saddest moments of my life. He has been unfailingly kind and supportive, quietly letting me know that he was there, offering wise words of advice, a typically dry joke, sympathy, or congratulations. His gracious, pastoral, patient, wise, and fair approach to academic administration and his ability to cut to the heart of an issue are skills I continue to aspire to! He has modelled the very meaning of "admin-istry" and, during periods when Lindsay was on leave, I have often joked that before proceeding, I would need to take a moment to ponder, "What would Lindsay do?" I have given thanks many times for Lindsay when listening to friends discuss issues they were encountering with their bosses when childcare or family issues arose. He has been a consistent advocate of a family-friendly work environment and has joyfully welcomed my children at meetings and in the office. Thank you doesn't seem to be a big enough word, but I will be forever grateful for Lindsay, and to God who placed him in my path!

Katrine Bramley
Registrar, Ridley College

Lindsay became my Hebrew teacher in 2002. He shared his love of Hebrew by walking us through slabs of text in the language class and in later exegetical units. Lindsay's dry humor was a feature of his classes, and some of his Old Testament exegesis lectures were death defying! With a straight face, he would respectfully lead us through a wide range of views, while we held our breath, our minds teeming with rebuttals. Then at the end, he would help us to land with a measured and thoughtful conclusion. I enjoyed a small class on biblical wisdom where left-handers (including Lindsay and I) outnumbered right-handers, but we were careful not to oppress them!

Lindsay invited me to present seminars in Old Testament in 2004, and opened the door to Hebrew lecturing in 2012, and he was of great encouragement to me when I was appointed to faculty. He was also my PhD supervisor (2010–2016), giving me great freedom as I sought to clarify my argument, always saying, "You are now the expert on your topic." One funny moment was when I turned up at a supervision session with a diagram instead of a page of text, and Lindsay requested words. Now, as a supervisor of others, I appreciate his wisdom in this.

Jill Firth
Lecturer in Hebrew and Old Testament, Ridley College

In faculty discussions, Lindsay is rarely quick off the mark in expressing an opinion, but I have found that it is always worth considering what he has to say. He will have carefully weighed the issues and holds the interests of students and the quality of the college's endeavours with considerable care.

In my role as Lecturer in Bible and Theology (Non-English Speaking Background Students), I particularly appreciated the support Lindsay gave to students from diverse backgrounds. He has been an advocate for refugee background students where my main teaching efforts at Ridley have been directed. When I faced a particular challenge with how to progress a course for those whose first language was not English, Lindsay quickly comprehended the issues and always had helpful suggestions for how we could proceed. Lindsay often assisted my thinking about possible assessment methods and with suggestions for suitable Old Testament resources.

Another quality I value is his mission heart and his willingness to give generously of his time and expertise to support overseas students who come to Ridley for postgraduate studies. He places a high value on travelling to places, especially in South Asia, where his teaching assists in raising the level of theological education.

Len Firth
Lecturer, Ridley College

I am so very grateful that when I started teaching Old Testament I had Lindsay to guide and encourage me. Not only did he give me hours of advice, and drop a memory stick with a lifetime's supply of lifesaving emergency lecture notes in my pigeonhole, but he was also so thoughtful, encouraging, and kind. When we taught our first class together, he insisted on taking the undergraduate seminar and leaving me to take the graduate seminar—he didn't want to give the students the impression that I wasn't up to the task of taking the higher level. I hadn't even thought about that!

Andrew Judd
Associate Lecturer in Old Testament, Ridley College

In the mid-1990s, one might have been surprised to spot Lindsay's athleticism. Along with others hailing from Australia's more northern states, he was a regular participant in the weekly bonding of students and staff over a game of touch football. To new students, accustomed to Lindsay's careful classroom demeanour, it was intriguing to observe him as the second fastest sprinter down the field (second only to the residential college's dean of students!).

Andrew Malone
Online Dean, Ridley College

Lindsay Wilson has many fine qualities and attributes, not the least being that he shares the same birthday and birth year as me. What an auspicious day that proved to be in 1955! Each March we share a cake at college and the title "Ridley twins." More seriously, it has been a great privilege to work alongside Lindsay for the past fifteen years. His contribution to Ridley has been immense—not only in his teaching but also his work as Academic Dean, chapel preacher, and "wise sage" in faculty meetings. A trustworthy colleague indeed!

Richard Trist
Senior Lecturer, Ridley College

I was already working at Ridley when Lindsay was appointed as an Old Testament lecturer, so have had the great privilege of working with him for around thirty years. I remember the day he and his family arrived at Ridley, because his young children were enjoying the freedom of playing exuberantly in the Ridley courtyard after the long drive from Sydney! Lindsay is a wonderful colleague, and for many years was also my manager who supported me both professionally in my role as College Librarian and personally. He is encouraging, insightful, quietly humorous, and caring, and gives me confidence by showing confidence in me. The only time he fails to be sympathetic is when I complain about it being hot, and this has become a running joke between us. I value enormously his collegiality and friendship, and he and I both delight in being part of a small band of left-handed staff at Ridley.

Ruth Weatherlake
College Librarian, Ridley College

Former Ridley Colleagues

When I arrived at Ridley, Lindsay was a tremendous colleague. Although he had decades of experience, he made me, a new lecturer who was still finishing my PhD, feel like a tremendous addition to the faculty. He shared his lecture notes with me to give me a boost in my preparations for teaching new subjects. All new lecturers are insecure, wondering if they belong, so Lindsay's encouragement and collegiality made a huge difference in my life. I will be forever grateful for the three plus years we had together on faculty at Ridley, and for the friendship we have maintained since then at conferences.

One can only dream of a legacy like the one Lindsay has had at Ridley. He has prepared many lay people and ministers to read and teach the Old Testament by integrating exegesis and biblical theology. Yet, most significantly, he has modelled what he espouses in his gracious ways with students and colleagues alike. אשרי־איש ירא את־יהוה ("Happy is the person who fears the LORD," Psalm 112:1).

Andy Abernethy
Associate Professor of Old Testament and Degree Coordinator for MA in Biblical Exegesis, Wheaton College

I met Lindsay when he first came to Ridley to teach in 1991 and I was a visiting lecturer also in Old Testament. Friendship was consolidated in co-leading tours to Israel, Jordan, Egypt, and later, Greece and Turkey, starting from 1994. There were several years of teaching at Ridley, with me as an adjunct lecturer and Lindsay on faculty, sometimes sharing courses. In addition, Lindsay and I have taught together and separately at several of the same institutions in Asia. Lindsay's godly and generous character, his concern for people in need, his willingness to serve in tough places, his carefulness in teaching the Bible and yet doing so effectively across cultures, and his stability and resilience are great strengths. His hard work ethic, his commitment and time for people, his humor, and his wide interests demonstrate a balanced life where head and heart combine in the service of God and for the sake of his glory.

Paul Barker
Assistant Bishop, Jumbunna Episcopate, Anglican Diocese of Melbourne

For a Ridley graduation ceremony some twenty years ago, I had been asked to give a short testimony about the benefit of my studies at Ridley. At that time I was teaching CRE at the local primary school in Horsham and had taught my Grade 3 class a few basic Hebrew words. At the graduation, with the Ridley staff seated behind me on the platform, I related how, on one particular morning as I walked across the school playground, a little Grade 3 girl had come bounding towards me, calling out, "Shalom,

Mrs Brennan!" Spontaneously, from behind me on the platform, came a shout, "Yay!" It was Lindsay!

Michelle Brennan
Visiting lecturer in Hebrew, and tutor in New Testament Greek and Old Testament, 2000–2001

I spent seven happy years at Ridley in an adjoining office to Lindsay Wilson. He was always available for a chat, some advice, or a theological discussion. I would come in late in the day, and he would be studiously working behind a wall of books around his desk, but always willing to give his time to me. Always even, always generous, always supportive, always wise, Lindsay is the epitome of a scholar and a person who lives what he teaches.

I have a special affection for Lindsay because when St Jude's Carlton was vacant, he told me, "You should be the next Vicar of St Jude's," and I was. Then fourteen years later when Tasmania was looking for a bishop, Lindsay said to me, "You should be the next Bishop of Tasmania," and I was. I will see if he is ready to tell me when I should retire!

Richard Condie
Bishop of Tasmania

Lindsay Wilson has been a constant pillar of my experience at Ridley College. As the Senior Lecturer in Old Testament, he taught most of the Old Testament units I studied. As a lecturer, Lindsay models clear evangelical commitments to Scripture, open and even-handed engagement with scholarship, wise judgment about what will serve people preparing for ministry of the word, and a responsive approachability towards students. His units on wisdom literature and the Psalms were standout experiences in those early years at Ridley.

As the supervisor of my postgraduate research on the Psalms, Lindsay was an astute academic advocate in opening a door to postgraduate study, a wise counsellor in molding my grand ideas into something achievable, and a meticulous reader of my evolving thesis.

When, after ten years' missionary work in Mexico, I returned to Ridley as a faculty member in 2011, Lindsay graciously agreed to be my mentor, and he was very generous with his time both as a guide to a junior colleague and as a friend and anchor while I navigated the rough waters of a challenging reentry period. As a colleague, I also grew to appreciate Lindsay's enormous behind-the-scenes contribution to the college as

Academic Dean, and his passion for encouraging emerging Old Testament scholars from the majority world.

Charlie Fletcher
Vicar, All Saints Anglican Church, Clayton

I greatly appreciated Lindsay's friendship when he and I were colleagues at Ridley in the 1990s, and I have continued to do so over the years since. His competence as an Old Testament scholar is well known, and I would simply like to say that, shortly after his commentary on Proverbs was published, I worked through it chapter by chapter in my morning devotions. I found it to be both illuminating and helpful, and I'm sure many others have also. Thanks Lindsay!

Colin Kruse
Emeritus Scholar, Melbourne School of Theology

Lindsay and I started at Ridley College simultaneously in February 1991. He was lecturing in Old Testament and I in Ministry Skills and Church History. His commitment to the Scriptures as God's word was exemplary. As an Old Testament specialist, Lindsay's understanding of the Old Testament, notably of Joseph, Job, and the Psalms, has brought me great delight. His commitment to the Bible as the foundation for all means that he is deeply committed to mission and evangelism, and to preaching and teaching the word of God. He was so helpful to me as we worked collegially in the teaching of evangelism, preaching, and pastoral care, and more generally in the formation of Christian leaders.

Furthermore, the wisdom of the texts Lindsay teaches so imbues his own life that I often processed difficult issues with him. His welcome, listening ear, and biblical perspective were always beneficial beyond words.

Adrian Lane
Victorian Regional Officer, Bush Church Aid

I worked as a colleague on the Ridley faculty with Lindsay Wilson between 2007 to 2020. He is one of a trio of Ridley faculty in my time (along with former lecturers Adrian Lane and Doug McComiskey) known for their ability to carry off wearing argyle diamond patterned vests and jumpers!

Lindsay was always extremely encouraging of my presence on campus, and my contribution to the college in mentoring, preaching, and training others. I know other women students and faculty experienced this too. Lindsay's humor was a great blessing at Ridley faculty meetings, as was his ability to "cut to the chase"—after long debates and discussions, Lindsay would often make an insightful comment that simplified or solved an issue. His long history at Ridley was also a bonus in bringing wisdom to planning.

Lindsay is well known for his love of travel and regular teaching for the church in Asia. A highlight of my time at Ridley was leading an Israel-Jordan study tour with him in November 2013. Lindsay was knowledgeable, competent, and easy-going, even in the face of several dramas we encountered along the way. While on tour I witnessed Lindsay's ability to sleep on the bus at the drop of a hat—surely a gift which has enabled him to manage the rigors of travel.

My appreciation of Lindsay as a Bible teacher came into its own when I was a Master of Theology student. I took a unit on the Joseph Narratives. It was my favourite unit, and I loved his book *Joseph: Wise and Otherwise*. His lectures and writing really helped me to understand and love Genesis 37–50, and to see the contemporary challenges and applications in preaching them.

Anthea McCall
Lecturer in New Testament and Greek, Ridley College, 2007–2020

It was my privilege to work with Lindsay for thirteen years. Not only is he that rare person who combines impressive administrative ability with a high standard of scholarship, but he does so with humility and a strong sense of service to God. As a lecturer, he is well loved by his students, deeply concerned for their preparation for service to the Lord, and is a godly model to them. In my time at Ridley, Lindsay was Vice-Principal. He led the faculty with clarity and confidence, and with warmth and care for each faculty member. He also has a great love for the majority world church and has always sought to serve these people both through training their leaders at Ridley College and through travel to other countries to teach. I am delighted to have had Lindsay as a colleague and to have him as a friend.

Douglas McComiskey
Former Head of the New Testament Department and Chair of Postgraduate Studies, Ridley College

Having come to St Andrew's Hall in 1983, I was asked by John Wilson to do some part-time Old Testament teaching. He was the only permanent Old Testament lecturer at a time of very large numbers of students. When my visa to India was refused and John Wilson left Ridley to serve as a bishop I was asked to continue teaching at Ridley. A couple of other Old Testament lecturers were appointed but only stayed for a short time, so it was wonderful to have Lindsay come for a long period outstaying me by many years!

I enjoyed time with Lindsay and Clarissa and their young children when they arrived in Melbourne. I always appreciated Lindsay's clear thinking and wisdom in faculty meetings. I was delighted that he was at my ordination, and I've been glad to have his support and interest as I moved into other ministries. It was Lindsay who suggested that I might be interested in teaching at the Bible College of Queensland (now Brisbane School of Theology) which led to the then principal inviting me to consider this. Lindsay was generous in providing me with his lecture notes to guide me as I prepared for a course I hadn't taught before. More recently I consulted Lindsay a number of times during the years I spent in Central Asia and appreciated his help, advice, and prayer as he continued to be interested in the work there.

Robin Payne
Lecturer in Old Testament and Hebrew, 1984–1998

Lindsay Wilson arrived at Ridley a year or two before me in the early 1990s. He has always been very collegial, both during our time together at Ridley and after I left. As Academic Dean he embodied proverbial patience with my regular questions and inability to navigate the *Australian College of Theology Handbook*. The wisdom theme was no mere literary preference for Lindsay. His PhD in that area and several commentaries show not only painstaking labour, but a longing for scriptural wisdom which became a lifestyle. His background in law and its professional wisdom was also an important gift to the Centre for Applied Christian Ethics that I directed. Reuniting at the same church is a recent pleasure and reminder of good chats over morning coffee at Ridley.

Gordon Preece
Honorary Director, Religion and Social Policy Network,
University of Divinity

Lindsay is often mentioned in the Reid household, not only because he has been the doctoral supervisor of both Heather and me, but more because of our deepest respect and affection for him. Our respect is for him as a careful, joyful, and insightful scholar with a deep commitment to quietly but skillfully examining, understanding, and applying Scripture wherever that leads, and a willingness to help anyone else wanting to do the same. Our affection for him is as a godly, prayerful, and dependable friend whose door has always been open not only to us, but to many others.

Andrew Reid
Principal, Evangelical Theological College of Asia

Two words come immediately to mind when I think of Lindsay Wilson and his influence on my life and ministry—"wisdom" and "covenant." I count it one of God's kindnesses to me that my first year as a full-time theological student was also the year Lindsay began teaching at Ridley College. I was a student in his first two classes in Old Testament exegesis on—no surprise here—Job and Ecclesiastes. It was in Lindsay's classes that the big picture of the whole Bible began to really take shape for me. I cannot imagine that I could have succeeded in my doctoral studies without the foundation in biblical theology which Lindsay laid in his teaching.

Lindsay was a wise senior colleague who could always be relied upon for sound advice, and a generous friend who often lifted the weight of wrestling with theology with lighthearted moments. One treasured memory comes from my first year as a Ridley lecturer. Very late one evening I was struggling to finish preparations for a Greek class I was teaching the next morning. I decided to take a short walk around the Ridley garden to clear my head, only to run into Lindsay doing the same thing in preparation for his Hebrew class! As Lindsay always appeared to be the model of an organized person it came as some comfort to me that he was also still preparing. I cannot recall his exact words but do remember very clearly the gist of what he said. He reminded me that even theology teaching takes place in the context of real life and that while careful preparation is important, life does not always allow us to follow an ideal schedule. Needless to say, I was greatly reassured and much better placed to focus on preparing not only my lecture for the following day but all those that followed—usually further in advance.

Anyone who lived at Ridley in the 1990s and early 2000s knew the importance of our twice-weekly games of touch football! Lindsay, who was a master of "try assists" preferred to run no more than ten to twenty meters. I'm sure I owed more of the tries I scored to Lindsay's assistance than any other player. I suspect there is a metaphor there for Lindsay's ministry in which he has helped many others get started on a clear path to effective gospel ministry.

Bill Stewart
Rector, Parish of New Town and Lenah Valley

Colleagues Beyond Ridley

Lindsay and I became good friends at Moore College and enjoyed many fruitful discussions about theology and ministry through the time of our studies. He outperformed me in academics, but perhaps more importantly, and sadly for me, he usually won on the tennis court too. Lindsay's academic ability was balanced by an unassuming competence and a pastoral concern for people, not least his fellow students. This was expressed practically when he was made Senior Student in 1987 and looked out for the interests of the student body.

Over the years it has been good to renew the friendship at different stages of ministry. Most recently Lindsay has done volunteer work for Overseas Council Australia, lecturing in Pakistan and elsewhere. He has been keen to contribute to scholarship internationally and this has shown itself not just in forwarding his own career in a Western context, but more importantly in building up biblical scholarship in Asia. He has a keen sense of cross-cultural interpretation which demonstrates insights into God's world and a cultural humility from which he has ministered well as a lecturer and mentor to lecturers.

Stuart Brooking
Executive Director, Overseas Council Australia

I first met Lindsay while attending the Tyndale Fellowship meeting in Cambridge. So began a friendship that has developed, even though we work at different ends of the world, only meeting up from time to time at international conferences, or on one occasion when I had the privilege of visiting Ridley. I have worked with Lindsay as an editor of his work (both his essay in *Interpreting Isaiah* and as series editor for his Tyndale Commentary on *Proverbs*), and then as we shared the editorial work for *Exploring Old Testament Wisdom*. Through the years, I have come to regard Lindsay as both a good friend and as someone whose work on Old Testament wisdom literature has encouraged the church to read these texts and see their abiding significance for us. Throughout, it has been a delight to share with him.

David Firth
Tutor in Old Testament and Academic Dean, Trinity College Bristol

The wisdom of Lindsay Wilson is on display in his commentaries on Proverbs and the book of Job, and in his other significant contributions to the study of the biblical books with wisdom themes. Is Lindsay wise because he has spent a lifetime studying wisdom literature, or is it because he was wise that he chose such a program of study? Perhaps we will never know, but I suspect that the answer to both questions is "Yes." All his writings give evidence of mature thought and scholarly effort, and the church and the academy are greatly in his debt. More than that, in daily speech and when making a comment at an academic committee meeting, his words are always measured, pertinent, insightful, and gracious. I praise God for the godly wisdom of Lindsay Wilson.

Greg Goswell
Academic Dean, Lecturer in Old Testament, and Postgraduate Coordinator, Christ College, NSW

I got to know Lindsay through the Tyndale Fellowship, a fellowship of evangelical scholars from around the world, and, in particular, through the summer conferences usually held in Cambridge, England. I'm always struck by Lindsay's calm, kind, gentle manner and his faithful and thoughtful scholarship. I've been glad to keep in touch with him and to maintain a friendship over thousands of miles.

James Robson
Ministry Director, Keswick Ministries

Ridley Students

Lindsay's most profound impact on me is his gentle joviality and his kindness and concern for others that he lives with every step. One of my favorite repeated moments was on the mornings when I arrived in Parkville at the same time as Lindsay was making his joyful walk across Royal Park to Ridley. Sometimes I would intentionally say hello, and on other occasions I would just smile as I walked behind him (in his steps?). Every time I could sense the Father's love for him, and communion with him. For me, it is in such habitual moments of life that the thankful and joyful beauty of a soul is evident. With regard to Lindsay, this is something that was deepened by my classes with him on the book of Ruth.

I'm deeply thankful for Lindsay's character shaped by wisdom and uncomplaining patience. He always strikes me as someone with whom I can not only process my thoughts about suffering and Job, but who has a profound quality of friendship and care that he freely shares with those who ask.

Maddy Bialecki
Bi-Vocational Barista and Garden-Variety Apologist

As a former Ridley student and now pastor with deep ties to Malaysia, I thank God for Lindsay's commitment to train gospel workers for the Malaysian church. Lindsay has always encouraged his students to serve where the needs are greatest and to make plans as big as God's active kingly rule over the nations. Praise God for his wise, patient, and faithful training of pastors and preachers in Melbourne, Malaysia, and beyond.

Adam Ch'ng
Pastor, Cross & Crown Melbourne

Lindsay was very persistent in encouraging me to pursue postgraduate studies. Towards the end of my MDiv at Ridley he suggested that I consider writing up some work for publication and then when I moved overseas, he would email me every year to reiterate that he thought it was something I should consider. I wondered if he had even marked in his diary an annual reminder to email me about doing a PhD! When the opportunity to do a PhD presented itself earlier than I had anticipated, Lindsay's dogged encouragement over the years gave me the confidence to do it.

The phrases "God's active kingly rule" and "it's a puzzle" were on high rotation in Lindsay's wisdom literature classes. They were delivered with warmth and also a wry smile as if Lindsay knew that he was saying it for the umpteenth time and could see the humor in that. Lindsay enjoyed a subtle joke, often inserting one with a completely straight face at the most humdrum point of a lecture, then moving swiftly on, but I think secretly satisfied by guffaws from students who were tuned in.

Before the "Amen," our family's grace at mealtimes always ends with "Please make us your thankful and grateful people," a phrase Arthur and I picked up from Lindsay's graces at Ridley mealtimes. Typical of Lindsay, it is a simple, pithy phrase that is loaded with depth and meaning. We love how it puts thankfulness and gratitude to God in the context of discipleship and belonging to him.

Tamie Davis
PhD Candidate, SMBC, Associate Researcher, Angelina Noble Centre

I'm extremely grateful for Lindsay's careful scholarship and pastoral heart. Over my years of pastoral ministry since leaving Ridley I have constantly drawn on Lindsay's teaching from my Old Testament classes. For example, earlier this year I taught a series from the Psalms called "In the Valley" focusing on the dark and difficult times. Lindsay's teaching about the importance of lament and crying out to God in the midst of pain featured prominently in this series. Lindsay always thought through how to teach and apply the Old Testament books to different pastoral situations, both one-on-one and in larger groups. I regularly go back to my notes from his classes, and my congregations have benefited greatly from his scholarship, wisdom, and pastoral heart as mediated through me, his student.

Tim Johnson
Senior Minister, St John's Anglican Church, Diamond Creek

Lindsay's obvious love and regard for the Scriptures, his careful and thorough evangelical scholarship, his innate sense of the Bible's pastoral function, and his passion to train able pastors and teachers of God's word all combine so that his contribution to the church, typically quiet and humbly undertaken in the background of showier things, has been simply outstanding. It would be quite a challenge to count up the vast number of his past students whose understanding and handling of the Old Testament is a direct result of Lindsay's teaching and example.

I also thank God for Lindsay's faithfulness in serving on innumerable committees at Ridley, in the Australian College of Theology, and beyond. His legal training and commitment to good process and administration has made possible a great deal of good ministry, and has no doubt put to death bad ones! The wheels in the machinery of administration sometimes move invisibly and slowly, but they have moved carefully and deliberately under Lindsay's wise guidance.

Over the years, I've been constantly humbled by Lindsay and Clarissa's lively and committed faith. They have been stalwarts of their local church and enthusiastic, committed members of the Church Missionary Society. I'm so thankful to be part of the particular circle of God's people that includes Lindsay and Clarissa Wilson. Long may their ministry of leading, teaching, care, and encouragement continue.

Wei-Han Kuan
State Director, CMS Victoria

I see two kinds of people in leadership: those who lead from the front and those from the rear. Lindsay belongs to the latter group, which fits well for a person like me, a shy and introverted rural Asian, to do serious study in a Western setting. I first met Lindsay on an Israel study tour in 2007, where he and Bishop Paul Barker co-led the expedition. Lindsay's strong Aussie accent was initially a struggle for me. But his quiet and welcoming conversations and pastoral attitude were charming.

Huge credit goes to Lindsay for the success of my academic career in theological education. He helped facilitate my student visa and scholarships at Ridley and even met me when I first arrived at the airport in Melbourne. It is well known that Lindsay is a world-class Old Testament (Wisdom) scholar, so it is no wonder that I received first-class academic supervision from him. His meticulous educational guidance and thought-provoking questions were the foundations which formed my thinking for my PhD work (2010–2013). What amazed me more was his attitude toward me. Lindsay treated me as a friend, co-worker, and even as a scholar. He listens to different people, cultures, traditions, and perspectives. To be honest, I struggle to emulate his ways of leadership and service in my circles.

Lindsay's help did not end at Ridley. He facilitated and organized funding for me for study leave in England at Cambridge, joining the Tyndale Study Group conference in June 2018. He wants me to be a writer and scholar like him. I wish and pray that I can reach the level he wants me to achieve one day.

The impact of Lindsay's service to me and my family will live on. It so happens that my wife, Mary, gave a name which included "Lindsay" to her nephew, meaning the memory of Lindsay is here to stay in Myanmar. There have been a few key mentors in my life who will not be forgotten, and Lindsay is one of these. He is my teacher, my pastor, and my friend. He helped shape my life into the way I am today. Praise be to God for Lindsay.

Ronald Laldinsuah
Academic Dean, Myanmar Evangelical Graduate School of Theology,
Yangon, Myanmar

Lindsay is a man who is wise and filled with humility. My encounters with Lindsay bear a resemblance to Proverbs 3:11–12. First, Lindsay makes regular references to the prevalence of the character of God in biblical texts such that this has shaped my own outlook on the Bible. And second, he has never given easy answers to the research problems I presented to him. Instead, he has maintained relationship such that I might seek them out as I walked with the LORD. In this manner, I have encountered a human expression of the "fatherly" love of God, as a son in whom he delights.

David Ray
Diocesan Business Manager/Registrar, Anglican Diocese
of the Northern Territory

On my first day at Ridley College as an international student who was going to write my MTh thesis under his supervision, Lindsay gave me a tour of Ridley College. He showed me around and introduced me to the people whom I should know. The tour finished in fifteen minutes because the Ridley campus is not that big. I've never forgotten what he said after the tour: "Our college campus is small, but we have all that we need." I found out later this was indeed true.

He has a strong sense of humor. Once I told him I had a question, but then I suddenly and nervously forgot my question. He replied to me with a smile on his face saying, "If you've forgotten your question, I've forgotten my answer too." I could not stop laughing.

Lindsay is a good listener and values others' opinions and knowledge. I am very grateful for his wisdom and academic guidance coupled with his thoughtful pastoral care. He gave me confidence to write, to think critically, to ask questions, and to challenge myself when necessary during the course of my study and beyond. His meticulous guidance and supervision of my thesis—passage by passage, word by word, letter by letter—helped me to complete my MTh thesis. My thesis is his thesis too.

Lwin Thida Samuels
Former Old Testament Lecturer, Holy Cross Theological College, Myanmar

Major Publications by Lindsay Wilson

Compiled by Ruth Weatherlake

Books

Joseph, Wise and Otherwise: The Intersection of Wisdom and Covenant in Genesis 37-50. Paternoster Biblical Monographs. Carlisle: Paternoster, 2004.
Job. The Two Horizons Old Testament Commentary. Grand Rapids: Eerdmans, 2015.
Proverbs: An Introduction and Commentary. Tyndale Old Testament Commentaries 17. Downers Grove: InterVarsity, 2017.
Doing Good, Living Wisely. Grand Rapids: Baker Academic, forthcoming.
Firth, David G., and Lindsay Wilson, eds. *Exploring Old Testament Wisdom: Literature and Themes.* London: Apollos, 2016.

Essays

"Artful Ambiguity in Ecclesiastes 1, 1-11: A Wisdom Technique?" In *Qohelet in the Context of Wisdom*, edited by Antoon Schoors, 357-65. BETL 136. Leuven: Uitgeverij Peeters, 1998.
"Human Beings: Species or Special?" In *Rethinking Peter Singer: A Christian Critique*, edited by Gordon Preece, 106-21. Downers Grove: InterVarsity, 2002.
"Wisdom in Isaiah." In *Interpreting Isaiah: Issues and Approaches*, edited by David G. Firth and H. G. M. Williamson, 145-67. Downers Grove: IVP Academic, 2009.
"On Psalms 103-106 as a Closure to Book IV of the Psalter." In *The Composition of the Book of Psalms*, edited by Erich Zenger, 755-66. BETL 238. Leuven: Uitgeverij Peeters, 2010.

"Spirit of Wisdom or Spirit of God in Proverbs 1:23?" In *Presence, Power and Promise: The Role of the Spirit of God in the Old Testament*, edited by David G. Firth and Paul D. Wegner, 147–58. Nottingham: Apollos, 2011.

"Let Sodom Be Sodom! Another Look at Genesis 19." In *Sexegesis: An Evangelical Response to Five Uneasy Pieces on Homosexuality*, edited by Michael Bird and Gordon Preece, 48–64. Sydney South: Anglican Press Australia, 2012.

"Unity Matters: A Study of Joshua 22:1–34." In *Mending a Fractured Church: How to Seek Unity with Integrity*, edited by Michael Bird and Brian Rosner, 37–55. Bellingham, WA: Lexham, 2015.

"Job as a Problematic Book." In *Exploring Old Testament Wisdom: Literature and Themes*, edited by David G. Firth and Lindsay Wilson, 60–80. London: Apollos, 2016.

"Lament as a Prayer of Faith." In *A Time for Sorrow: Recovering the Practice of Lament in the Life of the Church*, edited by Scott Harrower and Sean M. McDonough, 5–22. Peabody, MA: Hendrickson, 2019.

Articles

"The Place of Wisdom in Old Testament Theology." *Reformed Theological Review* 49 (1990) 60–69.

"The Book of Job and the Fear of God." *Tyndale Bulletin* 46 (1995) 59–79.

"Human Beings: Species or Special? A Critique of Peter Singer on Animals." *Centre of Applied Christian Ethics Newsletter* 1 (1996) 4–5.

"Realistic Hope or Imaginative Exploration: The Identity of Job's Arbiter." *Pacifica* 9 (1996) 243–52.

"The Role of the Elihu Speeches in the Book of Job." *Reformed Theological Review* 55 (1996) 81–94.

"Job 38–39 and Biblical Theology." *Reformed Theological Review* 62 (2003) 121–38.

Dictionary Articles

"Job, Book of." In *Dictionary for Theological Interpretation of the Bible*, edited by Kevin J. Vanhoozer, 384–89. Grand Rapids: Baker Academic, 2005.

"Job." In *Theological Interpretation of the Old Testament: A Book-by-Book Survey*, edited by Kevin J. Vanhoozer, 148–56. Grand Rapids: Baker Academic, 2008.

Dissertations

"Protest and Faith in the Book of Job: An Holistic Reading." MTh diss., Australian College of Theology, 1991.

"The Intersection of Wisdom and Covenant in the Joseph Narrative." PhD diss., University of Melbourne, 1999.

Published Lecture

"Job and Suffering." Mathew Hale Public Library Lecture 2015. Brisbane: Mathew Hale Public Library, 2016.

www.ingramcontent.com/pod-product-compliance
Lightning Source LLC
Chambersburg PA
CBHW071233230426
43668CB00011B/1418